Vatican Council II:

Reforming Liturgy

Edited by

Carmel Pilcher

David Orr

Elizabeth Harrington

ATF Theology
Adelaide

2013

Vatican Council II: Reforming Liturgy

Edited by

Carmel Pilcher

David Orr

Elizabeth Harrington

Vatican II Series

Vatican II Series

1. *Openings to Renewal: Letters to the Church,* Peter Cullinane, 2011.

2. *My Journal of the Council*, Yves Congar OP, translated by Mary John Ronayne OP and Mary Cecily Boulding OP. English translation Editor, Denis Minns OP, 2012

National Library of Australia Cataloguing-in-Publication entry

Title: Vatican Council II : reforming liturgy / edited by Carmel Pilcher, David Orr and Elizabeth Harrington.

ISBN: 9781922391327 (paperback)
Series: Vatican II ; v. 2.
Notes: Includes index.
Subjects: Catholic Church--Liturgy.
Vatican Council (2nd : 1962-1965)

Other Authors/Contributors:
Pilcher, Carmel, editor.
Orr, David, 1948- editor.
Harrington, Elizabeth, editor.

Dewey Number: 262.5

First Printed in 2013
Second Printing in 2013

Cover design by Tom Elich and Astrid Sengkey
Layout/Artwork by Anna Dimasi
Photograph of the congregation on the front cover is from *Liturgy News*, Brisbane, March 2004. The photograph is by Hamilton Lund. The proclaimer is Caroline Ryan RSM from the reopening of St Patrick's Cathedral, Parramatta, New South Wales, on 29 November 2003. Used with permission from Hamilton Lund and Caroline Ryan RSM.

Text Minion Pro Size 11

Published by:

ATF THEOLOGY

An imprint of the ATF Ltd.
PO Box 504
Hindmarsh, SA 5007
ABN 90 116 359 963
www.atfpress.com

Dedication

MICHAEL ERNEST PUTNEY STD, AM

Bishop of Townsville

Born 20 June 1946
Ordained Priest 28 June 1969
Ordained Bishop 27 July 1995
Bishop of Townsville 24 January 2001

This dedication honours
a wise pastor and teacher
who has helped explain and promote
the work of the Second Vatican Council,
and whose prophetic voice
has shaped ecumenical dialogue
in Australia and throughout the world.

It is all God's work.
It was God who reconciled us to himself through Christ
and gave us the work of handing on this reconciliation.

2 Corinthians 5:18

Mind the Gap: The Church in Australia Forty Years After the Second Vatican Council[1]

Michael Putney

The Great Grace of the Council

In *Tertio Millennio Adveniente*, calling for the celebration of the Great Jubilee in 2000, Pope John Paul II asked that the Church should examine itself on the reception it had given to the Second Vatican Council. Then in the almost concluding paragraph of *Novo Millennio Ineunte*, reflecting on the new millennium, he said of the Second Vatican Council:

> With the passing of the years, *the Council documents have lost nothing of their value or brilliance.* They need to be read correctly, to be widely known and taken to heart as important and normative texts of the Magisterium, within the Church's Tradition. Now that the Jubilee has ended, I feel more than ever in duty bound to point to the Council as *the great grace bestowed on the Church in the twentieth century:* there we find a sure compass by which to take our bearings in the century now beginning.[2]

1. The following paper is an abridged version of the book *Mind the Gap: The Church in Australia 40 years after the Second Vatican Council* (Strathfield: Catholic Institute of Sydney, 2006) which comprises two lectures given by Michael Putney at the 2004 Triennial Gathering of the Manly Union: 'The Great Grace of the Council' and 'Receiving the Council'. It has been included in this series to honour Bishop Michael Putney and his great contribution to the Church as scholar, ecumenist and pastor and because the issues raised by the author continue to be relevant.
2. #57. See reference at <http://www.vatican.va/holy_father/john_paul_ii/apost_letters/documents/hf_jp-ii_apl_20010106_novo-millennio-ineunte_en.html>. Accessed 20 June 2013.

It is far too early to locate the documents of the Second Vatican Council in some repository for ancient texts. We are not yet ready for a Third Vatican Council because we haven't yet received the Second Vatican Council in any way near adequately. Furthermore, there is a new vision in the documents of the Council which cannot be understood simply as a repetition of the past. Again, much of this new vision is still to be received. This is important as we try to discern how we ought to move forward as the Church at this point of history in our Australian context.

The 'big pictures' which follow are only one person's contribution to a reflection in which we can all engage, and in which we need to engage, if we are to find the best way forward. What we are really doing is trying to discern the way in which the Holy Spirit is leading us.

Finding the Way Forward

The Church cannot find the correct way forward unless it is faithful to the Word of God found in written form in the scriptures. We also know as Catholics that we need to be faithful to the great living tradition of the Church which continues to interpret the Word of God even today by many means,[3] including 'the great grace' of our age, the Second Vatican Council.

Like all powerful insights, this one can be turned into something constricting rather than liberating. Unfortunately, there are some who are so enamoured of the past and its beauty, that instead of moving forward with their direction shaped by the great tradition they have seen in the past, they actually move backwards towards a particular moment in that tradition. Perhaps they do this with some hope of re-establishing it or continuing it exactly in the present without any recognition of the new situation of the Church today.

There is another way of thinking which also deserves our attention and can inspire our imagination. One of the themes of the Council itself was that we are called to read 'the signs of the time'. This phrase is used theologically in different ways, but it can legitimately be used in some cases to mean signs of the presence and activity of God in

3. Pope John Paul II spoke of 'the relationship between Sacred Scripture, as the highest authority in matters of faith, and Sacred Tradition, as indispensable to the interpretation of the Word of God'. (*Ut Unum Sint* #79).

the world.[4] To see these signs we must be looking at the society and culture which surround us, and in a sense looking ahead of ourselves. If the Church is to carry out its mission in the world, it must engage with its culture and the society in which it lives. In some ways it can be led forward by 'the signs of the times' that it sees around it and ahead of it, and so our attention should be focused there.

Unfortunately again, there are some who are so dazzled by some signs of the times which they see around them, which they too quickly and easily interpret as signs of the Holy Spirit, that they run after them, following them wherever they lead and, in the process, let go of their connection with the past from which they have come. Because what they followed were not really or unambiguously signs of the presence of God, or they did not stay connected to their past, they end up surrendering to the culture and take their lead entirely from it.

Neither of the extremes of these approaches to finding our way forward can give any hope for the Church. To be so enchanted by the past that one goes backward, or so dazzled by the future that one is lost in the surrounding culture, is to take a very destructive path for the life and mission of the Church.

We cannot respond authentically to the 'signs of the times' which are of God unless we are faithful to the tradition which lies behind us. We can't be faithful to that living tradition which is always seeking new expression, in each time and place, unless we actually move forward and respond to the 'signs of the times' which we see around us. Because both the tradition and the 'signs of the times' are works of the Spirit, they cannot contradict each other. In fact, it is only when we read one in the light of the other that we will interpret them in the most authentic way for our time and place.

Pope John Paul II offered us a very important insight when he said of the Second Vatican Council that 'there we find a sure compass by which to take our bearings in the century now beginning'[5].

---

4. See Rino Fisichella, 'Signs of the Times' in *Dictionary of Fundamental Theology* edited by René Latourelle and Rino Fisichella, (New York: Crossroad, 1994): 995-1001.
5. *Novo Millenio Ineunte* #57 <http://www.vatican.va/holy_father/john_paul_ii/apost_letters/documents/hf_jp-ii_apl_20010106_novo-millennio-ineunte_en.html>. Accessed 24 June 2013.

A compass indicates the direction one needs to take, but does not describe the point of arrival. It does enable one to find one's way. Any 'signs of the times' which are genuinely signs of God's activity will be like beacons drawing us in the same direction as this compass provided by the Second Vatican Council. Any which take us in a direction contrary to that established by the compass are false lights which could lead us into the wilderness.

Sadly, our journey forward as the Church in Australia has not been as sure-footed and enthusiastic as it might have been. Too many people have become lost along the way, and others have headed off very determinedly in one direction only, rejecting the compass or ignoring the beacons, and have tried to pressure everyone else to go with them. We need to resist these pressures, to come together, and to move with enthusiasm into God's future, not our own. To do this, we will move most securely if we use the compass and take note of the beacons.

Minding the Gap

Another reflection to assist our new imagining arises when we endeavour to look with eyes fully open at the members of our Church communities in Australia today. We notice the ageing of our congregations and are alerted to the danger that in some places we will become a 'retirement village' Church. Everyone notices the numbers, but not everyone seems aware of the difference between those in 'the retirement village' and the many fewer who are younger. This difference is a crucial factor if we are to be able to do anything about the numbers.

There is a gap in the Church at the moment between my generation and those which have come after. Anyone who has ever caught the underground railway in London would know that as one alights from the train, a voice is heard over the loud-speaker alerting everyone to 'mind the gap'. The reference is to the gap between the train and the platform. I think those of us who are now in roles of pastoral leadership in the Church need to 'mind the gap' that exists between the ecclesiastical priorities and issues which shaped our thinking and claimed our energies after the Second Vatican Council and continue to shape the religious imagination of many of us, and the ecclesiastical culture of the present younger generation.

We make a serious error if we continue to act as if the issues of the Conciliar and immediate post-Conciliar generation are any longer the most important priorities for the Church. The growing awareness of this throughout the Church in the Western world may be able to be called a 'sign of the times'. It is certainly a large flashing light or beacon calling us to adjust our pastoral priorities.

We are all struggling to keep moving with the Holy Spirit, who alone knows fully where we are going, or ought to be going. We have no clear roadmap. We only have the compass and the beacons referred to before.

It is therefore essential that we have some very clear, imaginative frameworks and goals governing our activity at this time of the Church's history. One of these may be to recognise that we are at a stage where we need to, as it were, 'refound' the Church, and to 'refound' the priesthood and religious life for that matter. This is not used in the sense of the ecclesiogenesis of people like Leonardo Boff. Rather, it is a reference to the founding again of the same Church, the same priesthood, the same religious life, because of the 'gap' referred to before.

We need to find a way of enabling a younger generation to discover Jesus Christ, to discover the Triune God, to discover the Gospels, to discover the eucharist, to discover the Word of God, to discover the Church, to discover Mary and the saints, to discover the priesthood and the religious life, just as we did. We need somehow to cross the gap that divides us in age and culture in order to inspire them and support them as they do it again and build it again for the future.

It is essential at this time that we plan for the pastoral care of people, given the diminished number of priests to serve them, but what we must avoid is planning for not having any priests at all. If we decide that is our inevitable future, then it will be our future. Some presume that because there are too few candidates for priestly ministry in the Church of Australia that this is God's will, and that the priesthood as we know it is meant to die out and something different to be born. One cannot really say this with any certainty because no-one really knows the mind of God.

If we were able to 'cross the gap' and reconnect on a large scale with young people, might we not see an increase in candidates? It is only if priests believe in the priesthood themselves and endeavour to live it in its fullest form that they can offer something even to those fewer young men who are participating in the life of the Church and are open to something more. This is a gap they have to bridge if they are, as it were, to refound the priesthood in the Church in Australia.

The only way we will help young people to rediscover all of these things which have remained precious to us through the years, despite the fact that they have lost their hold on so many of our colleagues and our contemporaries, is if we turn to the deepest resources we have as a Church and offer them to the generations which follow.

Perhaps what they long for is an experience of God, not simply talking about God. What they long for may be an experience of Christ in the eucharist, not simply discussion of liturgical change. What they deserve is to hear the Word of God, not just discussion about the historical nature of our texts. What they deserve is the mystical, sacramental, marian, christic and trinitarian tradition of our Church, with all its saints and heroes and its incredible sacrificial commitment to the poor, the marginalised and the suffering throughout history. Perhaps what they long for is for us to share with them our personal relationship with Jesus Christ more than anything else.

They may not need at all to hear about all the issues of change and power which have so engaged the minds and hearts of so many for so long. They barely know there was a Council. What they deserve from us is God, not our views about what the Church ought to be like, no matter how wise these may be. What they want to find in us, maybe, is our holiness.

Age or cultural difference need not be a barrier to the communication of these deep sources of life, because they come from God and they need very little participation on our part to be communicated. The more attentive we ourselves are to the sources, the more chance they are of being tapped by others.

This does not mean that we don't need good contemporary scholarship and the wisdom of the theological community, or that we don't have to talk about and engage in practicalities and strategies and liturgical change and means of communication, hermeneutics and social analysis, etc. But these are secondary tools for 'refounding' or rebuilding the Church. They are only ways of assisting our response to that larger call to be the Church, to be the children of God, to be the disciples and the apostles of Christ, to be the priests of Jesus Christ. That alone will enable us to move convincingly across the gap and so 'to refound' or rebuild the Church for the future.

The Gospel Itself is our Agenda

Even if we are prepared to do this, it will not always be easy. It would be naïve not to acknowledge that there are real tensions in the Church between the two groups already described as heading in different directions, which we have to deal with. This cannot be denied. But the pastoral priority in the Church is not to fight on either side, or just to take on one or other of the protagonists. Those struggles, no matter how engrossing they may appear, are not the most important ones. No matter how necessary they may appear at times in order to defend either the gains that one attributes to the Second Vatican Council or to defend the tradition of the Church, which appears in some way to be compromised by the actions or attitudes of others, such struggles are still not the most important ones.

There is a spectrum between each extreme and it is not easy to locate people upon it, even ourselves. We can only see the whole spectrum from where we are standing, and most of us think we are located in the centre. Any group which has as its major agenda criticism of other people in the Church could not be seen as anywhere near the centre. We ought not give our support to any group which focuses above all on what is wrong with other people in the Church. In *Evangelii Nuntiandi*, Pope Paul VI wrote of the Church evangelising 'when she seeks to convert solely through the divine power of the message she proclaims, both the personal and collective consciences of people'[6]. This is the methodology for all communication within the Church. If we are supporters of any cause within the Church, we promote it best when we seek to share it with others as something positive, a blessing for the rest of the Church, not by showing how wrong and even unfaithful everyone is who does not accept what it is we have to offer.

We have a deep and incredibly significant responsibility, which is to realise in our communities and in our own lives, the death and resurrection of Jesus which we remember in the eucharist. This is our task and it is this deep call, this deep responsibility, upon which we need to focus.

We must not let polarised groups determine how we or anyone else perceives or experiences the Church. They must not be allowed

6. #18. Go to <http://www.vatican.va/holy_father/paul_vi/apost_exhortations/documents/hf_p-vi_exh_19751208_evangelii-nuntiandi_en.html>. Accessed 20 June 2013.

to set everyone's agenda. We cannot, nonetheless, avoid dealing with them. But we will only deal creatively with the tensions of the moment if we believe in something bigger than the issues, and the people who demand so much attention in our pastoral situations. We will only find this 'something bigger' if we ourselves rediscover the excitement, the beauty and the unimaginable depth of the Catholic tradition which offers us access to the unfathomable mystery of Jesus Christ and the Triune God whom he reveals. We have to hold on to this and it is because so many do that the Church continues to be so life-giving for so many.

The Church is very good at dialoguing with other Christian communities. It is becoming better at dialoguing with the world religions. It has a long way to go in learning how to dialogue with contemporary culture in the world around it, and it has barely started to learn how to become a community of dialogue within itself.

We have to find a way of lowering the barriers that have been put up between us, of softening the positions that we have felt the need to hold onto so firmly, and of looking with gentler eyes upon the opposition whom we have seen ourselves needing to resist. Too often we are dealing with people who love the Church and accept the teaching of the Second Vatican Council. They just see it differently. They belong to different schools of thought, with different priorities, and different values. If we were all to recognise this, we would be able to learn from each other, marginalising somewhat those who are on the extremes of either school of thought.

Still Receiving the Council

If one locates the Second Vatican Council in the great tradition of the Church, then one can understand why Pope John Paul II would so evocatively say of it that it is 'the great grace bestowed on the Church in the twentieth century'[7]. When one recognises just how long Councils take to be 'received' by the Church one can see how important it is that we plumb its riches for the sake of the next generation and our task of 'refounding' the Church. The Council has not yet been 'received' in its deepest levels by the Church.

In order to carry out this long overdue task, it is appropriate to remember the opening sentence of the Constitution on the Sacred Lit-

7. *Novo Millennio Ineunte* #57.

urgy, which was the first document passed by the bishops at the Second Vatican Council, and which names the four goals of that Council. These were: 'To impart an ever-increasing vigour to the Christian life of the faithful; to adapt more closely to the needs of our age those institutions which are subject to change; to foster whatever can promote union among all who believe in Christ; to strengthen whatever can help to call all people into the Church's fold.'

Adapting Institutions

Here in Australia and in many other parts of the world, we concentrated much of our energy on the goal of adapting our institutions to the needs of our age and of our culture. This was urgent and necessary, exciting and liberating. Perhaps it drew most of our attention because it was also practical and concrete and its results were able to be measured. This work is always unfinished and so it is still a cause of considerable tension within the Church.

The question which arises immediately for those engaged in this task is, how much and what kind of adaptation can take place in response to the needs of an age or a culture, or to the 'signs of the times', while still remaining faithful to the Catholic tradition, and the direction established by 'the compass' of the Second Vatican Council?

The Church as a gift of God bears the full mystery of Christ to us in many ways: in the Gospel which we receive through the Church's scriptures and its living tradition, in the liturgy of the Church, and in the larger communion of the Church which has carried the mystery of Christ to us through the ages. This gift of God asks of us only that we participate in the great life-giving mystery it offers us. It enables us to enter into the very heart of the Triune God, through the death and resurrection of Jesus.

But this great mystery can only be received by real men and women within their social relationships and structures, so it is that we human beings make a very real, concrete contribution to the realisation of the Church. It is our task to receive this gift by inculturating it, by making it real in our daily lives, by expressing it in forms of prayer and worship, by structuring the great communion of the Church in ways that enhance our appropriation of the mystery. Anyone engaged in pastoral planning in their parish or diocese needs to know that they have a task unlike that of any other planning group. Every other element in the Church is secondary to this encounter with the mystery.

As Pope John Paul II said of pastoral planning in *Novo Millennio Ineunte*:

> We are certainly not seduced by the naive expectation that, faced with the great challenges of our time, we shall find some magic formula. No, we shall not be saved by a formula but by a Person, and the assurance which he gives us: *I am with you!* It is not therefore a matter of inventing a 'new programme' (29).

He then went on to name more specific elements of this pastoral plan. His first was holiness:

> First of all, I have no hesitation in saying that all pastoral initiatives must be set in relation to holiness. It is necessary therefore to rediscover the full practical significance of Chapter 5 of the Dogmatic Constitution on the Church *Lumen Gentium*, dedicated to the 'universal call to holiness' (30).

At the same time, the Church is a human community and therefore it is not inappropriate to draw upon the social sciences to assist in any renewal of the Church. One of the dangers as we try to work out the best way forward for the Church of today in Australia, is that dialogue might occur only between bishops or pastors and experts or professionals in the Church, and that the needs and wishes of ordinary Catholics, which are sometimes quite different to those of their leaders and of Church professionals, will not be heard.

Through its living tradition, its scriptures, its sacraments, and its fellowship or communion, the Church bears to us, every person, and every age, the possibility of entering into the very life of the Triune God through Jesus' death and resurrection, and to do so with one's brothers and sisters. Any adaptation serves this and is only for the sake of this. In fact, the goal of the Council—'to adapt more suitably to the needs of our own times those institutions which are subject to change'[8]—was a practical goal which was always for the sake of the much more important first goal of the Council: to impart an ever-

8. *Sacrosanctum Concilium* #1.

increasing vigour to the Christian life of the faithful, and for the sake of the third ecumenical goal and the fourth missionary goal. It is only in their context that we can understand this more practical goal.

Imparting a New Vigour

Because it has not always been linked to these other goals in our thinking, our adaptation has sometimes been unfinished or even at times a little inadequate. Sometimes we may have failed in our adaptation to move beyond deconstruction, as it is called, to genuine reconstruction. When one fails to do that, deconstruction can actually become a form of destruction. There will have been a deconstruction of a previous account or experience of the mystery, which will not have resulted in a better way of sharing the mystery with others.

To take one very simple example, there is no good news, in itself, in showing people that some of the events in scripture are not to be interpreted as accurate scientific history. This is only the stage of deconstruction. What is needed is life-giving, enlivening, inspiring reconstruction that conveys the message of faith which is contained in the scriptural accounts.

Priests, preachers and teachers, parents and witnesses of any kind, are bearers of the mystery of a relationship with God available through Jesus Christ. No matter how much adaptation they engage in, it has to be for the sake of making that mystery more accessible. Its ultimate aim, therefore, is that first goal of the Second Vatican Council: 'to impart an ever increasing vigor to the Christian life of the faithful'.[9]

Maybe we sometimes have fallen into the trap of believing that our adaptation is complete because we have adapted the rules, the structures, or the formulation of our teaching or prayers. This was ever only the first stage of the process of adaptation. It is incomplete if it remains unrelated to that other goal of the Council, its first and primary goal, which is to convert human hearts, to assist people to become holy, as Pope John Paul pointed out in *Novo Millennio Ineunte,* or to become committed disciples of Jesus Christ, and to assist them to experience life in Christ more fully. If people do not love God and their neighbour more, pray more profoundly, live more dedicated lives, and make an impact on the world for the better, because of our

9. *Sacrosanctum Concilium* #1.

adaptation, then one has to question whether or not the adaptation has been authentic, or is still unfinished.

The Example of Lent

A little example of how we can fail to keep these two goals of the Council together is that of Lent. When I was a child, Lent was a very demanding period which made very clear and concrete claims upon the daily life of the individual Catholic and the communal life of parishes. Much of that has disappeared, and some of it rightly so. As we saw with many pious practices at the time of the Council, they could easily lose their connection with the true spirit which was meant to inspire them.

While Project Compassion has developed throughout this time as a great contemporary example of genuine Lenten self-denial for the sake of others, the larger claim of Lent upon our personal and ecclesial lives is not always as obvious any more. Parishes celebrate the season liturgically but sometimes not too much else changes in any obvious way. As a Church we do not seem to keep Lent in an observable way anymore.

We adapted Lent with good intentions but may have lost something of its capacity to increase the vigour of the Christian life of the faithful. Perhaps what is needed is a reconstruction of some of the Lenten practices of the past, through new ways of fasting and penance and new public devotional practices, along with the great Project Compassion, to enable the liturgical season to claim more of our lives.

This example also illustrates another difficulty in enhancing the vigour of the Christian life of the faithful through a time of change. Sometimes we were not able to assist people sufficiently to have the spiritual maturity and commitment they would need to make the choices they now needed to make in a Church of greater freedom.

We need to admit that not everything that has happened since the Council has been for the best. We didn't always get it right or, at least, completely right. We lost some things along the way. To want to recover them is not to go back, or to indulge in restorationism, but to reclaim the wholeness of our tradition. Any reclaiming will involve a revisioning, a relocating, rather than a restoring. We cannot just replant the practices and ideas of the 1950s into our post-Conciliar context without their being re-expressed because of that new context.

It is not a kind of restoration which is needed, but a reclaiming of all our riches. There are many examples of elements which might need to be reclaimed in some places or to some extent.

It is a question of balance, but also wholeness. The Catholic tradition has been greatly enriched by the new balance in our Christian life inaugurated by the Council, but unless we are faithful to the whole vision of the Council, what we have might not be balance but another partial version.

The major pastoral task in any parish is to help people to become holy, which means to become people who love God and their neighbour more and more, which in turn means people who can pray and can serve and even suffer for the cause of the Kingdom which always involves a commitment to justice and peace. We will only 'impart a new vigour' to the Christian life of God's people if they have a chance to be claimed by the whole Christian mystery in all its beauty. Only then, as well, will we have a chance of bridging the gap to the next generations and overcoming the tensions in our Church.

Promoting Christian Unity

The third goal of the Second Vatican Council was that of 'promoting unity among all who believe in Christ'[10]. We have achieved an enormous amount in this regard and the commitment of the Church in Australia is as good as anywhere in the world. This is one of the best signs of the Church in Australia genuinely receiving the teaching of the Second Vatican Council.

At the same time we ought not confuse an easy Australian tolerance and respect for different beliefs with the more profound engagement of divided communities in the search for a restored unity in Christ. This latter can build on the former but it can also settle for the former and hence fall far short of the Council's goal,[11] which is itself the goal of Christ's prayer: 'That they may be one' (John 17:22).

There is something humbling about the acknowledgement of the Second Vatican Council that one of the means it determined for the renewal of the Catholic Church was to foster whatever can promote union among all who believe in Christ, and vice versa. We too easily

10. *Sacrosanctum Concilium* #1.
11. For a fuller treatment of this see: Michael Putney, 'Ecumenism in Australia Today', in *Australasian Catholic Record*, 76/2 (1966): 208–216.

forget that our own struggles as a Church are part of a larger divine plan to draw the whole of humanity into communion with God and with each other, and indeed with the whole created order.

This mission for which Jesus was sent and died and for which the Spirit was sent means that our efforts to live a spirituality of communion and our efforts to restore communion with other Christians are intimately related because they are part of the one divine plan with which the Trinity is so intensely engaged and for which the second person of the Trinity died. All elements of the one divine program belong together.

Unity can never be achieved by compromise, but only by the two qualities of faithfulness and openness. This is true within the Church as much as it is true between the Churches. We need both truth and love. Without faithfulness, an adherence to the truth as we see it, love can easily lead us to settle for compromise. Without love, truth or faithfulness, insurmountable barriers can easily be created. What we need is loving truth and truthful love, within the Church and between the Churches.

Evangelisation

The final goal of the Second Vatican Council was 'to strengthen whatever can help to call the whole of mankind into the household of the Church'[12]. This goal has not yet fired the communal imagination of the Catholic Church in Australia. We need to remind ourselves that it is God in whom we are called to believe and it is the world and its needs about which we are called to be concerned.

We are called to transform the world by working to build communion between people, with our environment, and with God. This involves work for justice, peace and the integrity of creation, but it also involves offering to every person the possibility of knowing what is offered to them in the life and teaching, death and resurrection of Jesus Christ.

One rather urgent aspect of the Church's mission is the diminishing number of Catholics who wish to participate in a tangible way in the visible communion of the Church. We can't continue as we are for much longer and still claim that we are a viable sacrament of God's engagement with Australian humanity, serving that engagement, cre-

12. *Sacrosanctum Concilium* #1.

ating communion with God and among themselves for the whole of Australia. We will become an empty shell, a museum of a once-vital Australian Catholic Church.

The re-evangelisation or the new evangelisation of our baptised but disengaged Catholics, and the new evangelisation of secular Australians who are often seeking for authentic spirituality everywhere but in the Church, is one of the most urgent and exciting challenges confronting the Church today. We need to bridge the gap, for the sake of our mission. We need to rebuild or 'refound' the communion if we are to serve our mission of extending that communion to everyone and everything everywhere.

New Evangelisation of the Baptised

The new evangelisation of baptised Catholics who no longer participate in any significant way in the life of the Church is an extraordinary challenge, but also one rich with possibilities. One of these is our Catholic school system. The second is parish-based sacramental programs, or any sacramental programs, for that matter.

The fact that parents send their children to Catholic schools, or bring their children for the sacraments of initiations, is usually an indication that they have some desire to be connected to the Church, or hope that their child will find some connection with the Church. This is an opening for evangelisation that is rich with possibilities. Many parishes and schools make great efforts to reach the parents of the children whom they have in their care, either in the school or in a sacramental program. The Church in Australia could do well to draw upon the best practice of such parishes as a resource for all. Much more could happen if all were to have a quite clear pastoral plan for reaching the parents of these children.

Another major focus for new evangelisation in Australia is the group referred to above which is sometimes called Generation Y, and Generation X which preceded them. We need to become experts on making contact with them to bridge 'the gap', so that they have the possibility of accessing what we have to offer. We have to find doorways through which we can both move so that this kind of communication is possible. Their spiritual quest may be one of these and this would be congruent with the very deep spiritual resources we have to offer them. Another may be their openness to issues of justice and ecology. This too is now a very rich part of our Catholic tradition in which we can invite them to participate. They may also be seeking meaning for their lives and something larger to which to belong. We can offer both, but we can't do it if we are not reaching out to them in a welcoming kind of way, and are able to articulate the meaning and share the belonging.

The Way of the Future

Whatever the future may hold, it seems clear that the Church in Australia has still a way to go in receiving fully the teaching of the Second Vatican Council.

The way of the future is neither to go backwards into the tradition nor deeper into the culture. It is rather to go deeper into the tradition for the sake of our mission in the surrounding culture.

The resources are within us because the Church is a creation of the Holy Spirit. These resources are the deep streams of life of our Catholic tradition. We can draw upon the richness of the past in order to deal with, to confront, to embrace, to dialogue with, to accept and at times reject the culture that surrounds us; and 'minding the gap', to reach out in a creative way to share what we love with those who are across the gap and so to refound the Church of the future with them.

We have to continue to believe that we can inspire a new generation of young people to fall in love with the same Christ, the same Triune God, the same eucharist and the same troubled but beautiful Church which we know so well and sometimes forget how much we love.

As we do this, we can affirm again on its 40th anniversary, that the Second Vatican Council is 'the great grace bestowed on the Church in the twentieth century: there we will find a sure compass by which to take our bearings in the century now beginning.'[13]

13. *Novo Millennio Ineunte* #57.

CONTENTS

Dedication v

Mind the Gap: The Church in Australia Forty Years After the Second Vatican Council vii
Michael Putney

Contents xxiii

Introduction xxv

1. The Liturgical Reform: Most Visible Fruit of the Second Vatican Council 1
Piero Marini

2. Evolving Understandings of Church as Sacrament 11
Rhodora E Beaton

3. Full, Conscious and Active Participation 25
Tom Elich

4. Liturgical Intelligibility in *Sacrosanctum Concilium* 43
Clare V Johnson

5. Toward Inculturation: An Australian Indigenous Contribution 61
John Francis Fitz-Herbert & Carmel Pilcher

6. Towards Inculturation: Traditional Seasonal Rites in Indonesia 81
Bernardus Boli Ujan

7. Renegotiating Liturgical Leadership in Diverse Assemblies 95
Anthony Kain

8. Eucharist: The Assembly Offers Sacrifice 109
Carmel Pilcher

9. Eucharist: Scripture in Prayer and Song, Action and Sign 129
Gerard Moore

10. Eucharist: Inclusive of all Women and Men 145
Carol Hogan

11. Confirmation: Ordered to Sacrifice 161
David Orr

12. Reconciliation: Ever Evolving Sacrament 173
Julia Upton

13. The Divine Office in the Contemporary Church 189
Catherine Vincie

14. Liturgical Time: Celebration and Interpretation 203
Guy Hartcher

15. Postconciliar Church Music: Dissonance and Development 217
William A Jordan

16. Postconciliar Church Design: Continuity and Contradiction 233
Stephen Hackett

17. The Impact of *Sacrosanctum Concilium* on Protestant Traditions 253
Stephen Burns

18. Issues for a Twenty-First Century *Sacrosanctum Concilium* 269
Frank O'Loughlin

19. Afterword 287
Robert Gribben

20. Biographies of Contributors 293

21. Index 301

Introduction

Whenever a major reform occurs it takes many years for the dust to settle. Fifty years have now passed since one of the greatest Church Councils, Vatican II, promulgated *Sacrosanctum Concilium (SC)*, on 4 December 1963. This book commemorates that event. It has been created, designed and written by a group of liturgists who have been at the forefront of implementing the reform and have weathered the storm of change over the decades. Most have served in the Australian Church, one in the neighbouring island of Flores in Indonesia, while others have worked in the United States of America. Our most distinguished contributor—Archbishop Piero Marini—has served the Church's liturgical life at its heart in the Vatican: as secretary to the great liturgical reformer, Archbishop Annibale Bugnini CM, for many years as Papal Master of Ceremonies, modelling the reform in papal celebrations in various diverse cultural environments, as a teacher at Sant' Anselmo in Rome, and currently as the President for the Pontifical Committee on Eucharistic Congresses.

The purpose of this collection of essays is to focus on the situation of the liturgical life of the Church since the Council and to indicate challenges that still need to be addressed if the great vision of *Sacrosanctum Concilium* is to be fulfilled. We did not set out to dwell on the past but rather to look to the future. The chapters of the book closely follow the order of *Sacrosanctum Concilium.*

The book begins with a reflection by Piero Marini. We remember him from January 1995 in Sydney, Australia, where, as Papal Master of Ceremonies for the beatification of Mary MacKillop, he stretched the imagination of the local liturgists so that the celebration might became a kaleidoscope reflecting the diverse cultures of the Australian Church, including local languages, music, dance, and ritual elements of our first peoples.

A number of authors take principles from the reform and engage us with them in the contemporary Church. Rhodora Beaton focuses on the Church as sacrament. She gives a careful analysis of the changing understandings and the prevailing christological emphasis on the Church's visibility as the place of encounter with God and the sign of God's presence in the world.

Tom Elich returns to the goal of the reform and discusses full, conscious and active participation—words that have been repeated countless times, but his insights invite us to consider anew how this might be achieved in worshipping assemblies.

Clare Johnson addresses liturgical intelligibility and identifies issues in performance and meaning that need to be addressed if liturgy is to inspire the change of heart necessary to practise charity in the Christian life.

At a time when inculturation in the liturgy appears to have been compromised, John Fitz-Herbert, Carmel Pilcher and Bernardus Boli Ujan explore this significant principle of the Council. John Fitz-Herbert and Carmel Pilcher look specifically at inculturating elements of indigenous ritual into liturgy in the Australian context. Bernardus invites the bishops of Flores, Indonesia, to seek ways of incorporating Catholic liturgy into traditional rituals for various cycles of life.

Anthony Kain explores the issue of leading liturgy in the context of a diverse assembly and how to enable full engagement in worship. He uses the gospel of Mark as a model for the various ministerial skills that are required for this to be achieved.

The reform changed all aspects of the Church's liturgical life and its celebration of the sacraments. The next three writers take up a discussion on the area of the reform that has arguably most affected the assembly, the celebration of the Eucharist. Carmel Pilcher develops eucharistic sacrifice in light of current scholarship and concludes that full participation will be realised only when the assembly consciously exercises its significant role in offering sacrifice that flows into daily life. Gerard Moore highlights the significant connection between scripture and the prayer texts of the Mass. He establishes the relationship between the scripture and the prayer of the community, in particular the collect, the Eucharistic Prayer and ritual action. Carol Hogan speaks from her experience of the liturgical reform and its impact upon participation as a woman. She discusses ways that would support and enable women to engage consciously in the liturgy.

At a time when the ordering of the sacraments of initiation is contentious, David Orr speaks of the significance of confirmation as the passage to full participation by the priestly people at the table of the Eucharist. Julia Upton explores the history of the Sacrament of Penance, the theology and ritual practice of which has evolved over time. She offers ways for this sacrament to become again pastorally effective.

Prior to the Council the Divine Office was primarily used only by priests and religious. Catherine Vincie evaluates the response to the invitation by the Council to restore the Divine Office as the prayer of the entire Church.

Although *Sacrosanctum Concilium* (*SC*) dedicated a chapter to the liturgical year, its writers could not have envisaged the subsequent changes in our understanding of time. Guy Hartcher explores the impact of modern technology and changes in lifestyle—amongst other issues—on the liturgical cycle.

William Jordan reviews the multiple responses to the Council's call to restore music to its integral place in the celebration of liturgy. He explores the current challenges that liturgical musicians face when incorporating appropriate music into the liturgy and makes recommendations for ongoing implementation of the Council's vision. Sadly, Wililiam (Bill) died after a short illness before this book wwent to print. It is fitting that this essay be his 'last word' becaue he has made one of the most significant contributions to the promotion and development of liturgical music in Australia after the Council.

Stephen Hackett reviews the response by diverse communities to provide an appropriate home for the People of God engaged in liturgy. Stephen evaluates a number of church designs in light of the principles enunciated by the Council and concludes that more could be learned by returning to the directives and tradition of postconciliar church design.

Frank O'Loughlin takes us in a new direction. His contribution is to ask: What might *Sacrosanctum Concilium* look like if it was to be written today? He offers an interesting insight into the Church of the early twenty-first century and its liturgical issues.

Stephen Burns and Robert Gribben make a unique contribution to the collection. These colleagues, writing from an Anglican and Uniting Church perspective, reflect upon the impact the work of the Council has had on liturgical reform in Protestant Churches. Stephen, whose work has straddled three continents—the United

Kingdom, Australia and currently the United States—leaves us with a lament that the great bonds of ecumenism brought about by the Council are in danger of fragmenting. In the Afterword, Robert offers a valuable summary of the themes raised in this book and leaves us with a message of hope.

A project of this size is never possible without the contributions not only of the authors but of many behind the scenes.

The editors wish to thank our colleagues Kathleen Hughes RSCJ, Paul Turner, Robert Daly SJ, Paul Philibert OP, Bruce Morrill SJ, Orm Rush, John Frauenfelder, and Frances Gray who peer reviewed the papers.

We thank Paul Mason, Robert Schreiter CPPS and Joan Hendriks who provided research material, Mary Labruna SJBP who translated Piero Marini's paper and to our publisher, ATF Press. We are also extremely grateful to Hilary Regan, and his team, whose dedication and commitment to ATF Press goes way beyond that of a usual publisher. We cannot thank Hilary enough for his enthusiasm, encouragement, support and willingness to go the extra mile to do all he could to meet our requests.

Special thanks to Paul Taylor, secretary of the Australian Bishops' Commission for Liturgy, and to Patricia Malone RSJ, Professor Emeritus at Australian Catholic University, who offered expert advice and assisted greatly with the editorial process of the papers.

We also pay tribute to our colleagues and friends from every part of the world who have served the Church in the implementation and ongoing reform of the liturgy over the decades since the Council, often at great personal cost, but always with great energy and passion to enable God's people to live the liturgy.

Finally we dedicate this book to Bishop Michael Putney in recognition of his scholarly and ecumenical contribution to the work of implementing the conciliar reform. This book begins with an essay he wrote commemorating the fortieth anniversary of the Council. His message that 'those of us who are in roles of pastoral leadership in the Church need to mind the gap between our priorities and issues and the ecclesiastical culture of the present younger generation' continues to be relevant today.

Carmel Pilcher RSJ, David Orr OSB, Elizabeth Harrington

Liturgical Reform: Most Visible Fruit of the Second Vatican Council

Piero Marini

The Second Vatican Council was an important Council for the liturgy, so much so that the Church could state that 'the liturgical renewal is the most visible fruit of the whole conciliar effort'.[1] John Paul II affirmed this statement when he recalled that 'for many people the message of the Second Vatican Council has been experienced principally through the liturgical reform'.[2] It is not by chance that the first act willed by the Council was *Sacrosanctum Concilium* (*SC*).[3]

The importance of the liturgy for the Council is evident when we consider that in the entire history of the Church, it is the only Council that dedicated a specific document to the liturgy. Vatican II had available to it an overview of centuries of the evolution of liturgical practice in the West and in the East, a vision that four centuries before, at the time of the Council of Trent, was not possible due to a lack of adequate tools. Consider, for example, the great advantage that the invention of printing brought only after the Council of Trent to the dissemination of the Bible, of liturgical books and texts of the Fathers.

For the first time in the history of the Church, with Vatican II it was possible to delineate, partly as a result of the studies promoted by the liturgical movement, both the fundamental principles of the

1. Extraordinary Synod of Bishops 1985, Final report, II, B, b. 1, in *Enchiridion Vaticanum* 9 (Bologna: Dehonian Editions, 1987), # 1798.
2. John Paul II, Apostolic Letter *Vicesimus quintus annus*, 1988. #12. <http://www.vatican.va/holy_father/john_paul_ii/apost_letters/1988/documents/hf_jp-ii_apl_19881204_vicesimus-quintus-annus_en.html >. Accessed 6 May 2013.
3. The translation is from the text on the official Vatican website <http://www.vatican.va/archive/hist_councils/ii_vatican_council/documents/vat-ii_const_19631204_sacrosanctum-concilium_en.html>. Accessed 19 January 2013. All subsequent quotations from the Sacred Constitution are from this site.

liturgy and the essential elements of the liturgical celebration, bearing in mind also the experience of the liturgies of the Eastern Churches. In the fifty years or so since the liturgical reform sought by the Council begun on 7 March 1965,[4] a reform has been accomplished that exceeds in breadth and depth all other major reforms of the past, including the one attributed to St Gregory the Great and the reform of the sixteenth century.

Reforming the Liturgy to Reform the Church

The directives outlined by John XXIII in the Allocution *Gaudet Mater Ecclesia* at the end of opening rites of the Council on 11 October 1962 find their synthesis in the preface of *SC*:

> This sacred Council has several aims in view: it desires to impart an ever increasing vigour to the Christian life of the faithful; to adapt more suitably to the needs of our own times those institutions which are subject to change; to foster whatever can promote union among all who believe in Christ; to strengthen whatever can help to call the whole of mankind (sic) into the household of the Church. The Council therefore sees particularly cogent reasons for undertaking the reform and promotion of the liturgy.[5]

There were four objectives for the Council: the growth of the Christian life; the renewal of Church institutions according to the needs of our time; the unity of all believers in Christ, that is, ecumenism; and the call of all members of the Church to mission. To achieve these four objectives, the Council 'sees particularly cogent reasons for undertaking the reform and promotion of the liturgy'. For the Council the renewal of the Church, ecumenism and missionary activity are closely linked and depend on the way in which the Church celebrates and lives the liturgy.

The Council Fathers teach us, therefore, to consider liturgical celebrations in relation to the life of the Church. In fact, 'liturgy is the

4. Date of implementation of Instruction *Inter Oecumenici*, #26.
5. *SC* #1.

summit toward which the activity of the Church is directed; at the same time it is the font from which all her power flows'.[6]

Beyond Centralisation and Rediscovering the Local Church in the Liturgy

The type of centralised Church that had characterised the period before the Council was changed by Vatican II through the rediscovery of the relationship between Church and liturgy. This discovery led to the re-evaluation of the local Church. The first and fundamental direction given by *SC* focused upon the celebration of the liturgy: particularly the celebration of the Eucharist with the full, active participation of all God's holy people, presided over by the bishop surrounded by his priests and ministers in his cathedral church, in fact is to be considered as the main manifestation of Church.[7]

The Council Fathers then delineated the image of the Church starting not from a theological speculation, but precisely from the concrete celebration of the Eucharist.

The Foundations of the Liturgical Reform

As well as indicating some goals that they had proposed in undertaking the reform of the texts and rites, the Council Fathers established the basic criteria upon which to set the whole reform and renewal of the liturgy according to the tradition and the needs of our time. In *SC* we can identify a twofold series of principles: guiding principles and operational ones.

Guiding principles:

- Liturgy as an exercise of the priesthood of Christ (*SC* 7)
- Liturgy as source and summit of the Church's life (*SC* 10)
- Full, conscious, active participation (*SC* 8)
- Liturgy as the manifestation of the Church (*SC* 26)
- Substantial unity, not rigid uniformity (*SC* 38)
- Sound tradition and legitimate progress (*SC* 23)

6. *SC* #10.
7. See *SC* #41.

Operational principles:

- Language
- Scripture
- Catechesis
- Singing
- Reform of texts and rites

These principles, which are inextricably linked together, form the foundation of the liturgical reform and have already been extensively discussed and deepened.[8] I would like to dwell briefly on just two underlying principles that are, in my opinion, foundational to all the others: the return to the sources—*resourcement*—and a single priesthood for worship. The sources indicated by *SC* are essentially two: sacred scripture and the writings of the Fathers.

Sacred Scripture

The liturgy implements what is written in scripture. That is, scripture testifies a lived story of God and people, a story of salvation that continues in the liturgy through prayers and symbolic acts: *per ritus et preces*. Furthermore, scripture stresses the importance of God's people: the journey of salvation on which God leads his people is achieved not just by an individual but by all the people. Scripture helps us therefore to understand the importance of the assembly and the public nature of the liturgy.

For this reason sacred scripture is the norm, and the means to understand the liturgy and to reform its practice. 'To achieve the restoration, progress, and adaptation of the sacred liturgy, it is essential to promote that warm and living love for scripture.'[9] Thus, there is an intimate link between scripture and liturgical reform. Even the ancient mystagogical texts attest that knowledge of the liturgy is nothing more than knowledge of scripture. The relationship between scripture and liturgy is clearly expressed in *SC*: 'it is from the scriptures that actions and signs derive their meaning.'[10]

8. See Annibale Bugnini, *The Reform of the Liturgy 1948–1975* (Collegeville, MN: Liturgical Press, 1990), 39–48.
9. *SC* #24.
10. *SC* #24.

The Church of the Holy Fathers

If scripture is the source from which to draw the renewal of the liturgy, the early liturgical practice of the Patristic Church, 'the vigour which they had in the days of the holy Fathers' (see *SC* 50) is to be considered the norm and rule inspiring the reform. To understand the significance of the Church's conciliar principle of 'returning to the norm of the Fathers' it is of great help to refer to the address that Paul VI delivered on the occasion of the inauguration of the Patristic Institute of the *Augustinianum*.[11] The text opens with a general statement about the absolute necessity of returning to the sources. Without 'returning to the origins of Christianity it would not be possible to implement the biblical renewal, liturgical reform and the new theological research called for by the Second Vatican Council.'

Three reasons are brought to the defense of this claim:

a) The Fathers are witnesses to the faith of the early centuries vitally inserted in the tradition that comes from the apostles. They attest to 'the life-giving presence of this Tradition, showing how its riches are poured out in the practice and life of the Church that believes and prays.'
b) The Fathers, furthermore, are the protagonists of a second process: they gave systematic form to the apostolic preaching, hence they have been for the development of the Church that which the apostles had been for its birth. They, also as theologians, testify once again to the continuity of the Church with the tradition of the apostles.
c) The Fathers, finally, are witnesses of the process of adaptation that they have achieved by adapting the Gospel message to the mentality of their contemporaries. In fact, they were able to join catechesis, theology, sacred scripture, liturgy, spiritual and pastoral life in a vital unity that made their works speak not only to the intellect but to the whole person engaging thought, will and feeling.

11. See Paul VI, Inaugural address at the Patristic Institute of the Augustinianum, 4 May 1970. <http://www.vatican.va/holy_father/paul_vi/speeches/1970/documents/hf_p-vi_spe_19700504_inaugurazione-augustinianum_it.html>. Accessed 5 May 2013.

All this is seen in the holiness of the Fathers that is drawn not from rational argument but from concrete participation in the holy mysteries. For this reason the liturgical practice of the patristic Churches has become the original form of Christian liturgy against which the liturgical life of the Church in every age is called to measure and to test itself. Therefore, both the reform intended by the Council of Trent and the reform sought by Vatican II had as their guiding principle the return to the practice of the Fathers.[12] That is why some key features of the patristic period were assumed by Vatican II as guide and foundation of the reform. For example, the call for simplicity: 'the rites should be distinguished by a noble simplicity; they should be short, clear, and unencumbered by useless repetitions',[13] and again

> the rites are to be simplified, due care being taken to preserve their substance; elements which, with the passage of time, came to be duplicated, or were added with but little advantage, are now to be discarded; other elements which have suffered injury through accidents of history are now to be restored to the vigour which they had in the days of the holy Fathers.[14]

A Single Priesthood for Worship

> Rightly, then, the liturgy is considered as an exercise of the priestly office of Jesus Christ. In the liturgy the sanctification of the man (sic) is signified by signs perceptible to the senses, and is effected in a way which corresponds with each of these signs; in the liturgy the whole public worship is performed by the Mystical Body of Jesus Christ, that is, by the Head and His members. From this it follows that every liturgical celebration, because it is an action of Christ the priest and of His Body which is the Church, is a sacred action surpassing

12. See Paul VI, Apostolic Constitution *Missale Romanum*, 1969. Cf <http://www.vatican.va/holy_father/paul_vi/apost_constitutions/documents/hf_p-vi_apc_19690403_missale-romanum_en.html>. Accessed 5 May 2013.
13. *SC* #34.
14. *SC* #50.

> all others; no other action of the Church can equal its efficacy by the same title and to the same degree.[15]

Public worship is the liturgy celebrated by the Mystical Body of Christ, that is, Head and members. The liturgy has as its centre Christ, in particular his Paschal Mystery. Focus is then on the assembled congregation, body and members, to be the memorial of the Lord Jesus.

The 1962 Missal has the *Ordo Missae* open with the following text: 'Having vested, the priest moves to the Altar, and after due reverence he signs himself with his right hand from forehead to breast with the sign of the cross saying in an intelligible voice: In the name of the Father . . .'[16]

The Missal of Paul VI begins the celebration of the typical form of the Mass with the following words: 'After the people have assembled, the priest and the ministers go to the altar while the entrance song is being sung'.[17]

In the text of the 1962 Missal, the emphasis is on the figure of the priest who celebrates, whereas in the Missal of Paul VI what is emphasised foremost is the presence of the gathered assembly, then the priest and the ministers.

The priesthood of the faithful is a participation in the priesthood of Christ, and on this basis all baptised persons have the ability and the right to give acceptable worship to God. 'Like living stones, let yourselves be built into a spiritual house, to be a holy priesthood, to offer spiritual sacrifices acceptable to God through Jesus Christ' (1 Pt 2:5). The priesthood of the faithful, therefore, empowers the baptised to exercise liturgical worship.

Through the sacrament of ordination the ministerial priest configures to Christ specifically as head and shepherd of his people. The ministerial priesthood is understood, therefore, only in relation to the universal priesthood. The sacrament of baptism is foundational and thereby makes possible the sacrament of holy orders within, and

---

15. *SC* #7.
16. 'Ordo Missae' in *Missale Romanum* 1962 (Fort Collins: Roman Catholic Books, 1966), 216.
17. 'The Order of the Mass with a Congregation', in *The Roman Missal* (Sydney: EJ Dwyer, 1974), #1.

at the service of, the assembly. Ordained priesthood is at the service of the common priesthood of the faithful.[18] In this sense, one should never forget the twofold perspective that grounds the ministerial priesthood: the priest sacramentally represents Christ-shepherd, 'one mediator between God and humankind' (1 Tim 2:5), the Christ who gathers and leads his people, but he also represents the Church, in whose service he fulfills his action.

Liturgy as a Source of Renewal of the Church

Almost fifty years after *SC* we can, however, point to a change of perspective in liturgical practice: from an attention to 'reform' the liturgy to an understanding of the liturgy as the 'form' for the renewal of the life of the Church. One could say that it is almost a return to the intention of the Council to reform the Church through the liturgy (see *SC* 1).

In the first phase after the Council, all attention was centred on the liturgy as an 'object to be reformed': an object to attribute meaning, an object to beautify, to purify, from which to remove the 'incrustations' to render it more beautiful, but nevertheless still an object. The liturgical reform was understood as 'liturgy to be reformed' according to the indication of *SC* 34: 'The rites should be distinguished by a noble simplicity; they should be short, clear, and unencumbered by useless repetitions; they should be within the people's powers of comprehension, and normally should not require much explanation.'

Now that the reform of the liturgy has been complete, it is not enough to know the meaning of what has been done; rather what matters is the act of doing it and doing it with style. Healthy liturgical creativity at the beginning of the reform was primarily seen as the possibility of choosing texts or ritual sequences; today it consists especially in the manner of celebrating. 'The *ars celebrandi* is the best way to ensure their *actuosa participatio*.'[19] Placing liturgy at the centre of the life and activity of the Church is one of the first and most sig-

18. *The General Instruction of the Roman Missal*. (Strathfield: St. Pauls, 2012), #93.
19. Benedict XVI, Post-Synodal Apostolic Exhortation, 2007 *Sacramentum caritatis*, #38. <http://www.vatican.va/holy_father/benedict_xvi/apost_exhortations/documents/hf_ben-xvi_exh_20070222_sacramentum-caritatis_en.html>. Accessed 5 May 2013.

nificant fruits of the Council. Today we willingly return to the liturgy to start afresh, because the believer experiences the liturgy as a new beginning.

The focus today seems geared towards the liturgy as 'source' of renewal for the life of the Church. That is, the liturgy itself becomes the 'subject of renewal' and not the object. *SC* is a *magna carta* able to inspire the renewal of the Church before being a manual for reforming the rite. This awareness is well expressed in the words spoken by Paul VI at the promulgation of the Constitution on the Liturgy on 4 December 1963:

> May our hearts rejoice at this result. We pay homage to its values and duties: God in first place, our first obligation is prayer, the liturgy is the first source of life communicated to us, the first school of our spiritual life, the first gift that we can give to Christian people by our believing and praying, and the first invitation to the world, because it dissolves the tongue-tied into blessed and true prayer and engages the ineffable, regenerative power of our singing the divine praises and human hopes, through Christ the Lord and in the Spirit.[20]

The Church must let herself be formed by the liturgy. Today we have to learn to allow ourselves to be formed by the liturgy.

20. Enrico Cattaneo, *Il Culto Cristiano in Occidente: Note Storiche* (Roma: CLV, 1992), 532.

Evolving Understandings of Church as Sacrament

Rhodora E Beaton

The timing of the Second Vatican Council affects the imagery used in the first document, *Sacrosanctum Concilium* (*SC*). It is situated after the beginnings of the liturgical movement, the ecumenical movement, and the move to a historical-critical approach to biblical scholarship and reflects in its imagery many of the affirmations of these movements. It predates the rise of secularism in the West, globalisation, the sexual abuse crisis which shook the Roman Catholic world beginning in the second half of the twentieth century, and which found negative overtones in some of these images of Church. At the heart of this event is the liturgical and ecclesiological image of Church as sacrament, which appeared for the first time at the Council in *SC* 5 and which would be referenced several times more throughout later documents. This image, taken from the liturgical homilies of Augustine, is a rich metaphor which suits the incarnational theology dominant before the Council and which points the way towards a more trinitarian sacramental theology which would develop in the late twentieth century. It reflects the idea of the Church triumphant, 'a sign lifted up among the nations' (*SC* 2), which echoes the First Vatican Council,[1] and yet also fits a more tentative liturgical ecclesiology, such as that of Louis-Marie Chauvet, which emerges in the late twentieth century. It retains meaning even now at the beginning of the twenty-first century, an era which has forced the Church to ask itself what it means to be a sacrament—a visible sign of an invisible reality which causes grace—when the visible image of the Church is

1. See also '*Dei Filius*', in *Decrees of the Ecumenical Councils*, edited by Norman P Tanner (Washington, DC: Sheed and Ward, 1990).

commonly associated with clerical sexual abuse. This essay will trace *SC*'s claim that 'it was from the side of Christ as He slept the sleep of death upon the cross that there came forth "the wondrous sacrament of the whole Church"' (*SC* 5), beginning with the incarnational Christology which shaped the ecclesiology of the pre-Vatican II Church, to the innovative work of the Council, through the work of sacramental theologian Louis-Marie Chauvet in the late twentieth century. It will conclude with a brief discussion of the ongoing potential of the term 'sacrament' used to describe a Church whose visible reality at times fails to signify the presence of Christ within.

Glimpses of Sacramental Ecclesiology: The Early Twentieth Century

In the years prior to the Second Vatican Council, theologians and ministers were shaped by the deeply incarnational Christology and institutional ecclesiology which were the fruits of the First Vatican Council. This theological framework informed the theology of the seminary manuals which were popular prior to Vatican II, and which in turn formed the foundational theologies of priests who taught and studied theology.[2] Institutional ecclesiology and incarnational Christology are thus building blocks for the sacramental ecclesiology which emerged in *SC*. For a sense of the christological and ecclesiological climate prior to the Council, we turn briefly to one of the popular seminary manuals which informed the pastoral practice of the day, and then to the more constructive theology of Edward Schillebeeckx, in whose thought incarnation and institution converge to suggest a theological understanding of Church as sacrament.

The incarnational Christology of the seminary manuals is directly connected to their institutional ecclesiology. As Avery Dulles points out, the institutional model of the Church emphasises both visibility and the authority of the magisterium.[3] The pastoral applica-

2. As Jared Wicks points out, these seminary manuals are fundamentally pastoral texts. Although their popularity would decrease after the Council, 'the manuals kept theology in close touch with the life of the Church of its own day.' See Jared Wicks, 'Theologies: Manualistic Theology.' In *Dictionary of Fundamental Theology*, edited by Rene Latourelle and Rino Fisichella (New York: Herder and Herder, 1994), 1105.
3. Avery Dulles, *Models of the Church* (New York: Doubleday, 2002), 27.

tion of this model is clear in the seminary manuals of the day. Here the beginnings of the Church are discussed in terms of the actions of Jesus and the resulting authority of apostolic succession. As the popular Tanquery *Manual of Dogmatic Theology* describes it, 'Christ *chose* twelve Apostles . . . ; He *trained* them . . . ; He *sent* them forth to preach the kingdom of God . . . Very explicitly He made known His mind by *promising* them the power of teaching, or ruling, and of sanctifying the faithful in His Kingdom.'[4] The text emphasises Christ's actions and choices before his ascension in selecting the apostles and approving the visible hierarchical structure of the Church as it would develop.[5] The Church as institution is clearly portrayed and is directly linked with the actions of Jesus.

Coming in the wake of the documents of the First Vatican Council, particularly *Pastor Aeternus*, which dealt explicitly with papal infallibility, the *Manual's* christological focus on the magisterium is to be expected. In the scant four pages (out of two volumes) devoted to the 'members of the Church', Tanquerey, in addition to dealing with the membership status of infidels, heretics, schismatics, apostates, sinners, and the excommunicated, speaks of baptism as the mark of membership in the Church.[6] Here the focus is on the visible requirements for membership, emphasising that for an adult Catholic to maintain full membership 'he must be subject exteriorly to the rule of legitimate Pastors and, in a particular way, to the rule of the Roman Pontiff, who has been constituted the Head of the Body of the Church.'[7] As Richard McBrien observes, in the prevailing pre-conciliar ecclesiology, 'one "belongs" to the Church',[8] in the Council's later understanding, 'one participates in the life of the Church and, with all its other members, constitutes the very reality of the Church.'[9] Although the verbs 'belonging' and 'participating' convey very different

4. A Tanquerey, *A Manual of Dogmatic Theology*, 2 volumes (New York: Desclee, 1959) 1:107.
5. See also Francis Schüssler Fiorenza, 'Systematic Theology: Task and Methods', in *Systematic Theology: Roman Catholic Perspectives*, edited by Francis Schüssler Fiorenza and John PGalvin (Minneapolis: Fortress, 2011), 20–26.
6. Tanquerey, *Manual of Dogmatic Theology*, 1:158–61.
7. Tanquerey, *Manual of Dogmatic Theology*, 1:159.
8. Richard P McBrien, *The Church: The Evolution of Catholicism* (SanFrancisco: HarperOne, 2008), 165.
9. McBrien, *The Church*, 165; See also 42–45.

things, both emphasise visible association and are thus compatible with the idea of Church as institution and as sacrament.

While the pastoral seminary manuals developed an institutional ecclesiology grounded in an incarnational understanding of the relationship between Christ, the apostles and the current magisterium, the more academic Christology of the pre-conciliar era developed a somewhat more nuanced understanding of the relationship between the role of God incarnate in the person of Jesus and the Church as it functions in history. Central to these developments was the argument, advanced in 1960 by Edward Schillebeeckx, that Christ is the sacrament of the encounter with God,[10] and indeed that the Church, laity and hierarchy, is the sacrament of the Risen Christ.[11] Building on the institutional framework of the Church as a visible sign, Schillebeeckx suggests an incarnational Christology which emphasises the presence of God in the world. This presence is both signified and effected in the person of Christ. Shifting the emphasis from the institution of the Church by Christ to the ongoing presence of Christ abiding in the Church and in the sacraments, Schillebeeckx's personalist philosophy of encounter paved the way for a broader use of the term 'sacrament.' In applying the term to Church, Schillebeeckx maintained a link to the model of Church as institution, but also opened the door to the liturgical ecclesiologies which would develop during and after the Council.

Prior to the Council, the visible unity of the Church both as it was presented theologically and as it was experienced in the pastoral practice of the day established the importance of the Church as sign of God's presence in the world. Although the focus was on the visible role of the hierarchy understood in direct relationship to an incarnational Christology which emphasised Jesus' divine intentions manifest in human form, members of the Catholic Church were aware of belonging to something which was both greater than themselves and distinct from the surrounding culture. This background sets the stage for Schillebeeckx's work and for the Council's retrieval of the ancient image of Church as sacrament.

---

10. Edward Schillebeeckx, *Christ the Sacrament of the Encounter with God* (Franklin, WI: Sheed and Ward, 1999).
11. Schillebeeckx, *Christ the Sacrament of the Encounter with God*, 48–49.

SC 5—Retrieval and Renewal

Emerging out of the confluence of the pastoral theology of the manuals and the contributions made by theologians such as Schillebeeckx to the converging fields of Christology, ecclesiology, and sacramental theology, the Council adopted the image of Church as sacrament early in its proceedings. Although *SC* was not intended to be one of the explicitly ecclesiological documents of the Council, this image, and indeed the entire document, has since been recognised as laden with ecclesiological implications. We turn now to these implications and to the corresponding theological shift, exemplified in *SC* 5, from a dominantly incarnational Christology to a broader and more trinitarian theological perspective.

In recent years, ecclesiologists have increasingly argued that the *Constitution on the Sacred Liturgy* should be counted among the ecclesiological resources produced by the Council. Richard Gaillardetz, in suggesting that *SC* contains 'the beginnings of a liturgical ecclesiology,'[12] has argued that the document's most enduring contributions will lie not in the context of liturgy itself, but rather 'in what it says about the Church.'[13] Massimo Faggioli argues that *SC*'s chronological position in the first session of the Council made it possible for a nascent conciliar ecclesiology to develop in the liturgy constitution 'before the fight about the continuity with Vatican I began in the second session, in the fall of 1963.'[14] Although the discussion was ostensibly about liturgical practices and principles, the ancient adage of *lex orandi, lex credendi* holds true here as well. As Faggioli observes, 'changing worship sets off a rethinking of ecclesiology in a more profound and long-lasting way than the definition of the Church in *Lumen Gentium*.'[15] This foundational document of the Council can thus

12. Richard R Gaillardetz, 'Vatican II's Liturgy Constitution: Beginnings of a Liturgical Ecclesiology', in *Origins*, 33/21 (2003): 347.
13. Gaillardetz, 'Vatican II's Liturgy Constitution: Beginnings of a Liturgical Ecclesiology'.
14. Massimo Faggioli, *True Reform: Liturgy and Ecclesiology in SC* (Collegeville, MN: Liturgical Press, 2012), 72. Faggioli goes on to note that '*SC* did not suffer the wounds of the war waged by the conciliar minority against episcopal collegiality as it was worded in chapter 3 of *Lumen Gentium* and subsequently 'reinterpreted' in the '*Nota Explicativa Praevia*' to *Lumen Gentium*.'
15. Faggioli, *True Reform: Liturgy and Ecclesiology in SC*, 17.

offer important insights into the theological currents which provided the groundwork for subsequent documents.

Maintaining an emphasis on the visible nature of the Church, the theology of *SC* remains christological. It shifts, however, from an exclusively incarnational Christology towards attention to the Paschal Mystery. This adjustment could itself be the result of the liturgical reform of the Triduum which began in 1955.[16] As Jungmann points out, with this first document of the Council, the ecclesiological emphasis evolves from juridical to sacramental.[17] In *SC* 5, which speaks of the birth of the Church as sacrament from the side of the crucified Christ, we find a metaphor which shifts from the incarnational perspective of Jesus actively selecting and dispatching the apostolic leaders, to a more tragic image. The focus is on the wounded side of the crucified and not yet risen Christ. This image of Church as sacrament here points to the broken body of Christ, and to the strength in weakness which is the Paschal Mystery. In the absence of the apostles who symbolise the organisational hierarchy of the Church, the image of the crucified body of Christ opens the door for reflection on the many broken bodies of the faithful throughout history who themselves make up the Church as body of Christ.

In this image of birth from a place of suffering and loss, the Church emerges as a sacrament of the love of God in the midst of horror and desolation. If, as John O'Malley has recently suggested, 'in so far as it is possible, we should shift the focus from *what* the Council said to *how* it said it',[18] the implications for this image of Church as sacrament are significant. While the document does not reject the idea of the divine institution of the Church during Christ's earthly ministry as emphasised by Tanquerey, it presents an ancient alternative and

16. Ferdinand Antonelli, 'The Apostolate: The Reform of Holy Week', in *Worship*, 31/3 (1957), 144–161. See also *Maxima Redemptionis Nostrae Mysteria*, available at: <http://www.vatican.va/roman_curia/congregations/ccdds/documents/rc_con_ccdds_doc_19551116_maxima-redemptoris_lt.html>. Accessed 28 March 2013.

17. As Josef Jungmann observes in a relatively early commentary on Vatican II, *SC* portrays the Church not as a juridical structure, but 'in its sacramental character.' Josef Andreas Jungmann, 'Constitution on the Sacred Liturgy', in *Commentary on the Documents of Vatican II*, edited by Herbert Vorgrimler (New York: Herder and Herder, 1967), 9.

18. John O'Malley, 'Vatican II: Did Anything Happen?', in *Theological Studies*, 67/1 (2006): 17.

symbolic image of the birth of the Church. The tone of this image differs greatly from the manuals' image of the healthy, active and charismatic leader who deliberately chose his successors. Instead it focuses on God's work of bringing new life out of sin and death.

In shifting the focus from an exclusively incarnational Christology to a focus on the Paschal Mystery, *SC* 5 invites a more trinitarian perspective on the birth of the Church. With the body of Christ broken and pierced, it becomes the work of the Father, and the Spirit active in history, to raise Christ from the dead. The beginnings of the Church are thus more closely linked with a trinitarian understanding of God and with the gifts of the Spirit given at Pentecost and referenced in *SC* 6. Although it cannot be argued that *SC* is fundamental pneumatological or even robustly trinitarian, the connection between the Paschal Mystery and the birth of the Church sets the stage for post-conciliar liturgical ecclesiologies which will become more explicitly trinitiarian. The work of Louis-Marie Chauvet offers one such example.

Church as Sacrament: Insights from Louis-Marie Chauvet

The theology of Louis-Marie Chauvet offers one example of the ways in which contemporary theologians have built on the foundations of the Council. Chauvet develops a liturgical ecclesiology which is both rooted in the tradition and which seeks to meet the evolving needs of the modern world. He takes the image of the Church as sacrament for granted, yet offers a caution. Within the ecclesial context Chauvet's focus is primarily on the Christian identity of all of the faithful as they live out their responsibilities. Finally, Chauvet's ecclesiology is robustly pneumatological; that which was deliberate yet somewhat underdeveloped in *SC* flows naturally in Chauvet's work.

Formed as a theologian in the wake of the Council, and active as the pastor of a parish in France, Chauvet does not hesitate to employ the language of sacrament for the Church. Although the Church is clearly a sacrament, Chauvet is not uncritical. He emphasises that it is 'only' a sacrament, and is *not* the actual, unmediated presence of Christ: 'the Church is not Christ, but his symbolic witness, which means that its original and constant *raison d'être* is to direct everything back to him.'[19] Chauvet stresses the significance of the Church's sign value, while also observing that it is made up of error-prone human beings; this fact only serves to remind us of its relative inadequacy. Chauvet writes:

> Such a representation [the visible sign of the Church as all too human and flawed] is also the radical mark of [Christ's] absence. It is not at all self-evident that it is he, the living Lord, who presides over the assembly; that the assembly is the 'holy Church' even while it is made up of sinners, the 'body' of Christ even while its members are divided among themselves, or the 'temple of the Holy Spirit' who makes all things new even while its members are imprisoned in the chains of their habits.[20]

For Chauvet, the limitations of the Church must be acknowledged and yet also embraced. This perspective builds on the idea of Church as sacrament, yet also emphasises the importance of a visible institution as described by Tanquerey.[21] Chauvet points out that Christians today tend towards two different, false understandings of the Church. Some believers 'too comfortably ensconced in the institution, forget that it is *only* a sacrament and overlook the distance between it and Christ . . . [Others] because of their critical suspicions toward the institution [fail to see] that it is indeed a sacrament.'[22] From Chauvet's vantage point in the 1990s, the idea of Church as sacrament has been ingrained and must be critically analysed.

Building on the diverse ecclesiologies of the twentieth century, Chauvet suggests that the idea of Church as sacrament is, in fact, closely related to the idea of Church as institution. As a sacrament, or an efficacious sign in the world, Chauvet emphasises that the Church is at its best as a sacrament when it is acting in ways which are distinctly, even institutionally, Christian.[23] These include pilgrimages,

19. Louis-Marie Chauvet, *The Sacraments: The Word of God at the Mercy of the Body* (Collegeville MN: Liturgical Press, 2001), 28.
20. Chauvet, *Symbol and Sacrament: A Sacramental Reinterpretation of Christian Existence* (Collegeville MN: Liturgical Press, 1995), 187.
21. Dulles, *Models of the Church*, 33.
22. Chauvet, *Symbol and Sacrament*, 186.
23. Chauvet, *Symbol and Sacrament*, 181-82.

traditions, gathering in the liturgy to hear the word and celebrate the sacraments, and as a result, acting in an ethical manner in the world. This institutional understanding, however, does not focus exclusively on the magisterium. For Chauvet, the Church is most truly a sacrament of the presence (and absence) of God when all the faithful are gathered together as the liturgical assembly, participating in liturgical actions which are distinctly Christian. As Chauvet describes it, 'it is insufficient to think that the community celebrates only by uniting itself to what the priest does . . . [the community] acts *as a* body, as a constituted body, as the body of Christ, even though the roles and functions . . . are distributed within it in different ways.'[24] This body of humanity, gathered on the basis of faith and baptism, is the sacrament of the body of Christ in the world.

In keeping with the hopes of *SC* paragraph 1, the lives of the faithful as well as the lives of those who encounter the faithful are invigorated by encounter with this sacrament of the body of Christ. Chauvet emphasises that Christians must accept that we can only seek God through one another. 'The true scandal is ultimately this, the path to our relation with God passes through our relation with human beings and most especially through our relation with those whom the judgment of the mighty has reduced to "less than nothing"'.[25] The laity, human beings, even the ones who seem most insignificant, have become the 'visible sign' of the reality of God's presence.

Finally, we turn to the trinitarian aspects of Chauvet's theology. While the pre-Conciliar manuals focused on Christology, and *SC* gestures towards a more trinitarian understanding of the birth of the Church, Chauvet's understanding of the Church flows more organically from his understanding of the Paschal Mystery which has been nurtured by the post-conciliar liturgy. In *Symbol and Sacrament*, Chauvet observes that the proclamation of the Paschal Mystery, 'He . . . has risen', is the 'word from which the Church is born and which structures it according to its threefold manifestation in Scripture, sacrament and ethics.'[26] This statement, which echoes *SC* 5, gets to the heart of Chauvet's own project. While the Church occupies the place

24. Chauvet, *The Sacraments*, 33.
25. Chauvet, *Symbol and Sacrament*, 187.
26. Chauvet, *Symbol and Sacrament*, 173.

of the risen Christ who 'has departed',[27] it does so as an efficacious symbol by maintaining the *difference* between Christ and itself.

To adequately respect this difference, Chauvet argues that 'the christological dimension of sacramental theology is not theologically acceptable unless it is balanced by a second, pneumatological dimension'.[28] Patrick Prétot observes that this claim is in continuity with the revised liturgical rites themselves, specifically baptism and the eucharistic prayers, which bear a trinitarian structure.[29] Suggesting that a strictly christological approach implies that the sacraments are simply futile attempts to 'prolong' the incarnation,[30] Chauvet argues that instead of looking backwards to the past, physical, presence of Christ, a sacrament should be understood as a 'living memorial',[31] which profoundly affects the present. This living memorial is made possible through the action of the Spirit, 'the personal name traditionally given to what, *of God*, gives present and future vigour to such a memorial of the past.'[32] It is thus the work of the Spirit to continue to be the place of the encounter between God and humanity. As Chauvet puts it, 'the Spirit's proper function is to invest humanity and the universe with the resurrectional power of Christ . . . through the effusion of the Spirit, humanity is made a participant in the Pasch of the Lord, and is thereby journeying with him, toward the Father.'[33] In Chauvet's work, Paschal Mystery and a deep awareness of the Spirit as active in history and in humanity are foundational.

Chauvet's theology builds almost seamlessly on the work of *SC*, yet also pushes beyond it. As a priest and theologian formed in the wake of the post-conciliar liturgical reforms, Chauvet is comfortable with the idea of the Church as sacrament—so comfortable in fact that he warns against a too-ready acceptance of this model. His image of Church begins with the Christian identity of the liturgical assembly, baptised human bodies as the body of Christ. He accepts the laity as

27. Chauvet, *Symbol and Sacrament, 173*.
28. Chauvet, *Symbol and Sacrament*, 509.
29. Patrick Prétot, 'The Sacraments as 'Celebrations of the Church': Liturgy's Impact on Sacramental Theology,' in *Sacraments: Revelation of the Humanity of God: Engaging the Fundamental Theology of Louis-Marie Chauvet*, edited by Philippe Bordeyne and Bruce T Morrill (Collegeville MN: Liturgical Press, 2008), 32.
30. Chauvet, *The Sacraments*, 160.
31. Chauvet, *Symbol and Sacrament*, 510.
32. Chauvet, *Symbol and Sacrament*, 511.
33. Chauvet, *Symbol and Sacrament*, 520.

active and potentially vibrant participants. Rather than simply striving to be aware of the presence of the Spirit, Chauvet, it seems, cannot imagine a Church which does not relate to God in both word and spirit. His ecclesiology is infused with the presence of the Spirit, acting as the 'difference' between the Risen Christ and humanity.

Recontextualising Church as Sacrament

In the years since the Second Vatican Council, the context for understanding the Church as sign and sacrament of God's presence in the world has changed. In the wake of Vatican II, the Catholic Church entered into dialogue with the modern world, projecting an aura of openness and welcome. At the close of the twentieth century, Roman Catholics found themselves reeling in the face of reports of predator priests and of bishops who sought to avoid the appearance of a scandal which could taint the image of the Church as sacrament. As we enter the second decade of the twenty-first century, the signifying power of the Church as body of Christ has been diminished. No longer clearly a triumphant sign of God's sustaining presence or symbol of encounter with God, in the minds of many people the Catholic Church now symbolises a community which prizes outward appearances over the safety of children. The effort to avoid public scandal has instead brought greater scandal. In this new context, I would suggest that *SC*'s image of the Church as sacrament continues to offer a way forward. This path can be found not in the early twentieth century understanding of the institutional Church as a sign lifted up among the nations, but rather in the late twentieth century understanding of the Church as 'only a sacrament,' and in the early Church's understanding of the difficulties of Christian life and practice.

Among Chauvet's many late twentieth century insights is his argument that while the Church is called to mediate the presence of Christ to the world, in the recognition that mediation is required, we find the acknowledgment that the Church is not in fact the same as Christ, and that the Risen Christ is both present in and absent from the world. This recognition of absence could help to validate the pain of those who have suffered abuse at the hands of Church officials and who have experienced the horror of the absence of God in the symbol of the Church. Called to be the sacrament of Christ's presence in the world, the Church does not always function well as a sacrament.

Augustine, who was one of the first to apply the terminology of sacrament to the Church, offers insights into the very real difficulties of becoming the body of Christ. In one famous Easter homily, Augustine speaks to the newly baptised, telling them that they have become part of the sacramental Church. Explaining what has happened to them at their first communion, he points to the altar and says, 'The bread and wine on the altar become the body and blood of the Word, which he made us into as well.'[34] Augustine does not, as an early twentieth century homilist might have, tell the newly baptised that they have automatically become members of a perfect institution which is 'a sign lifted up among the nations'.[35] He instead reflects with them on their long journey towards becoming the body of Christ which they have celebrated. He reminds them that just as the grain was ground for the bread, so have they been 'threshed by the labor of oxen, that is of the preachers of the gospel'.[36] Just as water was added and the dough pressed into 'one lump'[37] so, 'with the application of the heat of the Holy Spirit [they] were baked and made into the Lord's loaf of bread'.[38] The images of grinding and baking reflect the formation which is the ongoing task of Christians who continually receive the body of Christ in order to be shaped more fully into the body of Christ. As the newly baptised know, it is not an easy process to become the body of Christ.

The twenty-first century has much to learn from Augustine's vivid description of what it takes to become a member of the Church. Intended as an explanation to individuals, this description can also be applied to the Church's process of becoming what it receives. As the Church seeks to become more adequately the body of Christ in the world, Catholic Christians must recognise the ongoing need for the self-discipline, scrutinies and self-sacrifice which are a necessary part

34. Augustine, 'Sermon 229 "On Holy Easter Sunday about the Sacraments of the Faithful"', in *Sermons (184–229Z) on the Liturgical Seasons,* Part III, volume 6 *The Works of Saint Augustine: A Translation for the 21st Century,* edited by John E Rotelle, translated by Edmund Hill (New York: New City Press, 1996).
35. 'Dei Filius,' in *Decrees of the Ecumenical Councils*, edited by Norman P Tanner. (Washington, DC: Sheed and Ward, 1990). See also *SC* #2.
36. Augustine, 'Sermon 229 "On Holy Easter Sunday about the Sacraments of the Faithful."'
37. Augustine, 'Sermon 229'.
38. Augustine, 'Sermon 229'.

of initial formation. This ongoing formation is not contrary to the image of sacrament, but very much compatible with it. Rather than a perfect institution, here we find an image of the Church always becoming sacrament. This more modest image includes room for scrutiny, correction and repentance. It yields a loaf of lumpy bread which nonetheless has divine potential.

Conclusion

In the early years of the twentieth century, the seven sacraments were neatly compartmentalised into an institutional ecclesiology which understood the Church as a perfect society established by Christ and a visible sign of God's presence in the world. Building on the work of theologians such as Schillebeeckx and on the pastoral experience of bishops and pastors, *SC* synthesised the prevailing Christological emphasis on the Church's visibility and suggested an understanding of Church as sacrament which relied on the liturgical theme of Paschal Mystery. The humble image of the birth of the Church from the side of the crucified Christ, drawn from the homilies of Augustine, opened the door for late twentieth century liturgical theologies which explored the concept of the Church as sacrament. Increasingly, trinitarian and cautious theologians such as Louis-Marie Chauvet further revised the understanding of Church as sacrament to reflect Vatican II's universal call to holiness and the realities of the Church's limitations as compared to Christ. In the late twentieth and early twenty-first century, the actions of some Church leaders precipitated a worldwide scandal which has diminished the Catholic Church's ability to describe itself in unqualified terms as the place of encounter with God and the sign of God's presence in the world. A careful look at the history of sacramental ecclesiology indicates, however, that the symbol can still function. The birth of the Church as sacrament from the side of the crucified and wounded Christ points the way towards the Church's vocation of solidarity with all the victims of history. Augustine's image of the Church as a lumpy loaf of bread, ground by the word of God and baked by the Holy Spirit, speak to the challenges of becoming a visible sign in history and to the unfinished work of becoming the sacrament of the absent body of Christ.

Full, Conscious and Active Participation

Tom Elich

Strong language is used about 'full, conscious and active participation'.[1] It is demanded by the very nature of the liturgy. It is the aim to be considered before all else in the restoration and promotion of the liturgy. It is the right and duty of Christian people by reason of their baptism. It is the primary and indispensable source from which they are to derive the true Christian spirit. It is to be zealously promoted by pastors in their pastoral work (*SC* 14).

How is the phrase to be understood? Some interpretations seem to spiritualise the notion of participation, making it refer primarily to people's interior dispositions at worship. Others place more emphasis on external activity in ministry, word and gesture. I argue that both sides come together if 'full, conscious and active participation' is understood to mean that the baptised are the subject of the liturgical action, that is, that they are present at liturgical celebrations as agents or doers of the liturgy. *Actuosus* is a doing word; *conscius* indicates that one knows what one is doing.

'Active Participation': A Key Concept

An analysis of the vocabulary of participation demonstrates that it is a key concept in *SC*.[2] The verb *participare* occurs thirteen

1. The English translation of *SC* 14 from www.vatican.va is incorrect (*fully conscious, and active participation*). The letter 'y' has mistakenly replaced a comma. The Latin has three adjectives: *plenam, consciam, actuosam*. All subsequent quotations of *Sacrosanctum Concilium* are from the text on the official Vatican website <http://www.vatican.va/archive/hist_councils/ii_vatican_council/documents/vat-ii_const_19631204_sacrosanctum-concilium_en.html>. Accessed 19 January 2013.
2. A good analysis of the vocabulary of *SC* is found in Armando Cuva, 'La participation des fidèles à la liturgie selon la constitution *Sacrosanctum*

times[3] and the noun *participatio* occurs fifteen times[4]. The adjective/adverb *actuosus/actuose* occurs sixteen times[5], twelve times paired with the noun and four times with the verb.

The subject of the verb *participare* is always the liturgical assembly, generally called Christ's faithful, but sometimes the (Christian) people, or once 'the children of God by faith and baptism'. Likewise, when the noun *participatio* is used, it is commonly the participation of 'all the faithful' or 'all the people'.

What does the assembly participate in? The short answer is 'the liturgy'. In *SC*, participation envisages a concrete role for the assembly in liturgical celebrations[6] with their texts, rites and singing (*SC* 30). However, while it certainly includes external actions, it is clearly more than simply external participation: 'in the earthly liturgy we take part in a foretaste of [the] heavenly liturgy . . . where Christ is sitting at the right hand of God . . .' (*SC* 8). 'Both texts and rites should be drawn up so that they express more clearly the holy things which they signify' (*SC* 21) so that in participating in the former, the Christian people also participate in the latter. Twice, participants in the liturgy are exhorted to attune their minds to their voices (*SC* 11, *SC* 90). In short, the active participation of the faithful is both 'internal and external',[7], both devout and active (*pia et actuosa*, *SC* 50).

In a sense this is obvious. Full, conscious and active participation is demanded by the very nature of the liturgy and the liturgy–like the human body itself–has both internal and external dimensions. It is not just human words and gestures but God's action. The work of our redemption is accomplished through the liturgy, and the mystery of Christ and the real nature of the true Church are expressed:

Concilium', in *La Maison-Dieu*, 241 (2005): 137–149.

3. *SC* #8, 10, 11, 17, 21, 33, 48, 53, 56, 85, 90, 106, 113.
4. *SC* #12, 14 (thrice), 19, 26, 27, 30, 41, 50, 55, 79, 114, 121, 124.
5. *SC* #11, 14 (thrice), 19, 21, 27, 30, 41, 48, 50, 79, 113, 114, 121, 124.
6. '*Celebratio*' in Latin contains within it the idea of a great assembly, a concourse, a congregation. The etymology of '*liturgia*' of course combines the Greek words *laos-people* and *ergon-work*.
7. '. . . actuosam fidelium participationem, internam et externam . . .' (*SC* #19). See also *SC* #99: 'All . . . should fulfil the task entrusted to them as fully as possible: this refers not only to the internal devotion of their minds but also to their external manner of celebration.'

> It is of the essence of the Church that she be both human and divine, visible and yet invisibly equipped, eager to act and yet intent on contemplation, present in this world and yet not at home in it; and she is all these things in such wise that in her the human is directed and subordinated to the divine, the visible likewise to the invisible, action to contemplation, and this present world to that city yet to come, which we seek (*SC* 2).

To accomplish his saving work, 'Christ is always present in his Church, especially in her liturgical celebrations' (*SC* 7). Every liturgical celebration is a sacred action surpassing all others because it is an action of Christ the priest and of his Body which is the Church (*SC* 7). There is more to liturgy than meets the eye.

Finally, we need to ask what words the Council uses to describe liturgical participation? A key word is *actuosus*. One should not be tempted to translate this as 'actual participation' (in fact, the phrase *actualis participationis* occurs in *SC* 26). Nor should we expect to find in the Latin *participatio activa* for this adjective means 'practical' as opposed to speculative or contemplative. *Actuosus* means 'full of activity', 'very active or lively', 'with zealous energy'. So it would be a mistake to suppose that the Council Fathers intended something different from committed physical 'active participation'. They contrast such active participants with strangers and silent spectators (*SC* 48).

Other words amplify this description. Participation is also to be full and complete (*plenus* and *plenarius*). People are to participate consciously, knowingly, intelligently, fully aware (*conscius* and *scienter*). Liturgical participation is devout and conscientious (*pius*), fruitful and enriching (*fructuose*), and communal (*comunitatis propria*).[8]

---

8. *SC* #11 scienter, actuose, fructuose
   SC #14 plenam, consciam, actuosam / plena, actuosa
   SC #17 toto animo
   SC #21 plena, actuosa, communitatis propria
   SC #41 plenaria, actuosa
   SC #48 conscie, pie, actuose
   SC #50 pia, actuosa
   SC #79 conscia, actuosa, facili

'Active Participation' in the Twentieth Century

Introducing the liturgy schema to the Council, secretary of the new conciliar liturgical commission, Fernando Antonelli, nominated 'leading the faithful into an ever more active participation in the liturgy' as one of five key criteria that had guided the Preparatory Commission in preparing the text.[9] However the Council Fathers' debate on the liturgy document focussed on the vernacular, concelebration, communion under both species, liturgical adaptation and the role of bishops, and the reform of the liturgical books.[10] The promotion of active participation was largely accepted and taken for granted, though it was joyfully recognised as a significant dimension of the document.[11] Cardinal Spellman of New York supported the need for the active participation of the laity in the Mass, though Cardinal McIntyre of Los Angeles was a dissenting voice when, late in the debate, he commented that 'Active participation of the faithful in the Mass is nothing but a distraction'.[12] In an interview after the vote on *SC*, Austrian Bishop Zauner of Linz, a member of the Preparatory Commission, recognised as the first of *SC*'s aims and principles 'that divine worship must be a community action, that is, the priest should do everything with the active participation of the people and never alone'.[13]

That 'active participation' was *not* the subject of extensive debate is due to the fact that, by the time of the Council, it had already had a long history in the liturgical movement and had been regularly employed in papal documents.[14] The history of the term usually begins

9. John W O'Malley, *What Happened at Vatican II* (Cambridge: Harvard University Press, 2008), 130–131.
10. *History of Vatican II*, volume II edited by Guiseppe Alberigo and Joseph Komonchak (Louvain: Peeters, 2000), 112.
11. Alberigo and Komonchak, *History of Vatican II*, volume II, 113, n. 35; 127, n. 134–135.
12. Xavier Rynne, *Vatican Council II* (New York: Farrar, Straus and Giroux, 1968), 66 (Spellman) and 72 (McIntyre).
13. Ralph Wiltgen, *The Rhine Flows Into the Tiber: The Unknown Council* (New York: Hawthorn Books, 1967), 137.
14. For good accounts of the history of 'active participation', see: Paul De Clerck, 'La Participation Active: Perspectives Historico-Liturgiques, de Pie X à Vatican II', in *The Active Participation Revisited: La Participation Active 100 ans après Pie X et 40 ans après Vatican II*, Textes et Etudes Liturgiques, Studies in Liturgy XIX (Louvain: Peeters, 2004), 13–31; and Josef Lamberts, 'L'évolution de la notion de 'participation active' dans le mouvement liturgique du vingtième siècle', in *La*

with Pius X who mentioned it in his 1903 document, *Motu Proprio*, on the restoration of church music: he spoke of his ardent desire to restore the true Christian spirit which the faithful will acquire *from its foremost and indispensable fount, which is the active participation in the holy mysteries and in the public and solemn prayer of the Church.*[15]

It was the Benedictine, Lambert Beauduin, however, who took up the concept and made it the catchcry of the liturgical movement. His address, 'The True Prayer of the Church', at the national congress at Malines in September 1909 began by citing Pius X: 'The first and indispensable source of the true Christian spirit is found in the active participation of the faithful in the liturgy of the Church.' The phrase recurs in his 1914 book, *La Piété de l'Église: Principes et Faits:*

> Let us change the routine and monotonous assistance at acts of worship into an active and intelligent participation; let us teach the faithful to pray and confess these truths in a body: and the liturgy thus practised will insensibly arouse a slumbering faith and give new efficacy, both in prayer and action, to the latent energies of the baptised souls . . . [16]

We need to keep these historical notes brief. We might say that the emphasis in the first forty years (1903–1943) focussed on liturgical *renewal,* while in the second period (1943–1963) the focus was on liturgical *reform.* At first, the effort was directed towards adapting people to the liturgy; later there was a growing desire to adapt the liturgy to the people. In the first period, the instrument was the people's missal and the project was the dialogue Mass.[17] In the second, under the impetus of Pius XII's *Mediator Dei* (1947), considerable reform of

---

Maison-Dieu, 241 (2005), 77–120 or in English, J Lamberts, 'Active Participation as the Gateway towards an Ecclesial Liturgy', in *Omnes Circumadstantes: Contributions Towards a History of the Role of the People in the Liturgy,* edited by Charles Caspers & Marc Schneiders (Kampen: Uiteversmaatschappij, 1990), 234–261.

15. *Tra le Sollecitudini* (1903) preamble in Kevin Seasoltz, *The New Liturgy: A Documentation 1903–1965* (New York: Herder and Herder, 1966), 4.
16. Published in 1926 as *Liturgy: The Life of the Church* (Farnborough: Saint Michael's Abbey Press, 2002), 21.
17. This neat phrase is drawn from Paul De Clerck, 'La Participation Active', 16–17.

the liturgy was achieved: the use of the vernacular in the ritual, the restoration of the Easter Vigil and Holy Week, revision of the rubrics of the Mass, rules about the fast and evening Masses, and new norms for sacred music.[18]

In the early years, the idea of active participation by the laity was not received without controversy. Paul De Clerck cites a 1921 article written by a certain G Lefebvre:

> Ah, you tell me! Do we always need to make noise when we pray? If we ourselves experience the need to meditate during the Mass and to let ourselves be drawn more towards an interior devotion, why impose on us the tyranny of all this 'exteriorisation' which upsets us in our recollection. Making us dialogue the Mass is to distract us.[19]

Perhaps Cardinal McIntyre had read the article before his intervention at the Council!

Still, by the 1950s this battle had been won. Pope Pius XII, in his Allocution for the first International Congress of Pastoral Liturgy held at Assisi-Rome in September 1956, offered a resounding endorsement of the liturgical movement and the idea of active participation.

> The liturgical movement is shown forth as a sign of the providential dispositions of God for the present time, of the movement of the Holy Spirit in the Church, to draw people more closely to the mysteries of the faith and the riches of grace which flow from the active participation of the faithful in the liturgical life.[20]

This phrase would be quoted in *SC* 43: 'Zeal for the promotion and restoration of the liturgy is rightly held to be a sign of the providential dispositions of God in our time, as a movement of the Holy Spirit in his Church.'

---

18. See Seasoltz, *The New Liturgy*, for a comprehensive collection of documents.
19. Paul De Clerck, 'La Participation Active',19.
20. Seasoltz, *The New Liturgy*, 234.

Interpreting 'Active Participation'

Just weeks after the vote on *SC*, liturgical changes began to roll out: at first, interim measures and provisional translations. Towards the end of the 1960s, revised liturgical books began to appear and for a decade the new rites came thick and fast. Initial translations were approved at once for interim use until feedback allowed definitive versions to be produced. The new texts presumed new attitudes to liturgical symbols (whether baptism by immersion or communion under both kinds). The rites promoted a wide range of lay liturgical ministers who needed to be selected and formed. Liturgy committees were established to help prepare the parish liturgy for different feasts and seasons. A huge effort on the part of diocesan and national liturgy commissions and educational institutes was directed to helping people understand the new rites, their structure and theological foundations. Soon there were second editions of liturgical books and, in English, revised translations of liturgical books that had been adapted and expanded for easier pastoral use. Now, on the fiftieth anniversary of *SC*, after two decades of controversy and wrangling over liturgical translations, an entirely new approach to arranging and translating the liturgical books is making its appearance, a process which will not be completed for another decade at least. Over this half century, liturgists have devoted their energy to promoting and explaining the liturgical reform. It is inevitable that in such a period of tumultuous and extensive change, a vast amount of attention and effort is given to the external aspects of the liturgy. It is not surprising that active participation has often been seen through the lens of outward activity.[21]

Indeed *SC* itself encourages an emphasis on exterior participation: 'To promote active participation, the people should be encouraged to take part by means of acclamations, responses, psalmody, antiphons,

---

21. For a documentation of the first decade or so after the Council, see Annibale Bugnini, *The Reform of the Liturgy 1948–1975* (Collegeville: Liturgical Press, 1990); International Commission on English in the Liturgy, *Documents on the Liturgy 1963–1979: Conciliar, Papal, and Curial Texts* (Collegeville: Liturgical Press, 1982); *History of Vatican II*, volume III (Louvain: Peeters, 2000), 234-256. For an account of the implementation in Australia, see Clare V Johnson, 'A Deep and Vast Renewal of the Church's Inmost Life' in *Vatican II: Reception and Implementation in the Australian Church* (Mulgrave, VIC: Garratt Publishing, 2012), 35–46.

and songs, as well as by actions, gestures, and bodily attitudes' (*SC* 30). However, lest this be misunderstood to exclude a certain interiority, the bishops in Council added in the final text: 'and at the proper times all should observe a reverent silence'. Notice that these actions are not in themselves 'active participation'; they serve to *promote* 'active participation'.

When she proposes the notion of 'contemplative participation', Benedictine Mary Collins recognises the influence so much reforming activity has had on our understanding of active participation and argues for a new, more balanced phase of liturgical renewal. Contemplatives, she says, are attentive to presence.

> Sometimes in all this activity we have come dangerously close to wearying ourselves with ritual busyness. Yet subtly the ritual engagement—now become more familiar—is drawing the laity into mystery at levels beyond what we initially intended or understood to be possible. We are moving from self-conscious activity to contemplative participation, rooted in the mystery of grace. Having internalised much of the new ritual behaviours required of the laity in the *editio typica* of the Roman liturgical books, we are assuming our identity as the reformed and renewed Church of Jesus Christ.[22]

Thomas Potts, charged specifically with exploring the interior dimensions of active participation, suggests that it belongs to the order of *being* rather than *doing*. He compares liturgical participation to taking a bath. One lets oneself be taken, invaded by the warmth of the water and the perfumes which penetrate the body. This 'permission', at first sight highly passive, is also truly active, not only in the decision to deliver oneself to the bath, but also in taking charge of the

22. Mary Collins, *Contemplative Participation: Sacrosanctum Concilium Twenty-five Year Later* (Collegeville: Liturgical Press, 1990), 83. Ormond Rush takes a similar position suggesting that 'perhaps we have been good at the formation for more active, external participation but neglectful of formation for full, conscious and active *internal participation*.', in 'Full, Conscious and Active Participation: Liturgy—A Sacred Action Surpassing all Others, A Symposium', in *Liturgy News*, 33/4 (2003), 3. Italics in the original.

effects it has on the body. The experience is conscious without being rational. In short, he asks how one is present at the liturgy.[23]

On the other hand, Rita Ferrone notes that there does exist a kind of minimalism which exaggerates internal participation at the expense of the external: 'When the people don't utter the responses or the choir director wants the choir alone to sing settings of the people's parts of the Mass, well, who is to say the assembly is not participating spiritually? Yet the role of the assembly is easily compromised by such excuses or inappropriate decisions.'[24] Laurence Paul Hemming demonstrates such a minimalist approach:

> We have been strongly schooled by the implementation of liturgical reform to interpret *actuosa participatio* as intense, conscious, agent, participation in the rites—the right and ability to say and perform the actions of the liturgy for ourselves. In reality this is about the one thing that *actuosa participatio* cannot mean . . . *Actuosa participatio* is not a description of what we must be 'doing', but a synonym for our life in the Spirit, by means of which we are drawn (and so 'done to'), and so we are placed 'into' the life of the Divine Trinity.[25]

How do we hold together the internal and external in a balanced approach to active participation? We need to understand how the two are related. On the one hand external participation is not an end in itself, nor does it constitute the entirety of people's participation. It is a means to an end, but that does not imply that it is peripheral or that it can be discarded for a 'higher' or 'purer' spiritual purpose. The

23. Thomas Potts, 'Une réflexion spirituelle et mystagogique renouvelée sur la participation active', in *The Active Participation Revisited,* 78–80. Patrick Prétot proposes active participation as a *mise en présence* (a becoming present) intentionally in the liturgical act: 'Retrouver la « participation active »: une tâche pour aujourd'hui', in *La Maison-Dieu,* 241 (2005): 158.
24. Rita Ferrone, *Liturgy, Sacrosanctum Concilium,* Rediscovering Vatican II (New York: Paulist Press, 2007), 98.
25. Laurence Paul Hemming, *Worship as a Revelation: the Past, Present and Future of Catholic Liturgy* (London: Burns and Oates, 2008), 31–32. Patrick Prétot argues the case against those whose writings present active participation as the source of all evils: in *La Maison-Dieu,* 241 (2005): 151–177.

external is integral to achieving the internal. This takes us to the heart of a Catholic sacramental imagination. A sacrament is an effective sign. Scholastic theology emphasised the minimum requirements for making a valid sacrament which was then said to work *ex opere operato.* Contemporary sacramental theology shifts the emphasis to the making of a fruitful sacrament. The dicton 'sacraments effect what they signify' is flipped back on itself, and we ask, 'do they also signify what they effect?' A sacrament works by signifying. It is the sacramental sign which takes the participant into the mysterious reality which is the source of spiritual life. That is why it is worthwhile to focus on how we make our sacramental signs (immersing in baptismal water, receiving communion under both kinds, and so on): it invites us into a more fruitful participation. Immersion in baptism 'is more suitable as a symbol of participation in the death and resurrection of Christ'.[26] 'Holy Communion has a fuller form as a sign when it takes place under both kinds.'[27]

> Pastors of souls must therefore realise that, when the liturgy is celebrated, something more is required than the mere observation of laws governing valid and licet celebration; it is their duty to ensure that the faithful take part (*participent*) fully aware of what they are doing *(scienter)*, actively engaged in the rite *(actuose)*, and enriched by its effects *(fructuose)* (*SC* 11).

Mark Searle neatly makes this point using the traditional scholastic structure of a sacrament.[28] This offers not the twofold structure of signifier/signified or external/internal, but three dimensions of the sacramental sign.

1. The *sacramentum tantum* is the signifier taken on its own. It is the whole visible, human, ritual performance: plunging into water, taking and breaking and eating, or pouring and drinking, and so forth.

2. The *res et sacramentum* is what is immediately signified by the rite, but which also in turn signifies something more than itself. A

26. General Introduction to Christian Initiation, #22.
27. General Instruction of the Roman Missal, #281.
28. Mark Searle, *Called to Participate: Theological, Ritual, and Social Perspectives* (Collegeville: Liturgical Press, 2006), 17ff.

man and a woman become husband and wife, a person is now a baptised member of the Church, bread and wine are changed into the body and blood of Christ. A new reality is both signified and created.

3. The *res tantum* is what the sacrament ultimately means, what all the signs point to, namely, our union with God called grace, the gift of the Spirit, sharing the divine life.

Each level of the sacrament involves a corresponding level of participation, which we might call external, sacramental and internal. At the first level, Searle discusses participation in ritual behaviour, which is collective, formal, performance (and performative), and formative. At the second level, Searle speaks of participation in the liturgy of the Church as the work of Christ. This is participation 'in Christ' as part of the Body of Christ, the Church. It calls faith into play. Searle gives an example:

> The difference between singing the *Gloria* in practice or in a concert, for example, and singing it in the liturgy is that in the liturgy it becomes prayer, that is, the outward and audible form of that deeply inward and utterly inaudible prayer of the Spirit which is the prayer of Christ himself to God whom he called, and taught us to call, 'Father'.[29]

Notice that, at this second level which I have called 'sacramental', participation is both external and internal. At the third level, Searle meditates on grace, a participation in the life of God, the ultimate purpose of the liturgy. The transition from the second to the third level is expressed in Eucharistic Prayer II: 'Humbly we pray that, partaking of the Body and Blood of Christ, we may be gathered into one by the Holy Spirit'. We are led by our full, conscious and active participation to a mystery beyond telling: as we participate in the *rite*, we participate in the *priestly work of Christ*, and are led to participate in the *divine life of the Trinity*.

The Ecclesiology of 'Active Participation'

We participate in a symphony concert by listening in silence. It can transport us to another world or move us to tears. We do indeed par-

29. Mark Searle, *Called to Participate*, 28.

ticipate in the music, but is this the active participation demanded by the liturgy? I would say not. Because, while we are engaged personally in *receiving* the music, we are not sharing in *making* the music. Likewise, people have been known to become most actively involved in an exciting football match, even leaping to their feet and shouting out. Is this the active participation demanded by the liturgy? No, because they remain spectators; they are not actually playing football. I argue that full, conscious and active participation in liturgical celebrations means that people are present as doers of the liturgical action.

Perhaps the problem lies with the very word 'participation'. It can give the impression that one joins oneself to a larger enterprise that is actually performed by others. So in the liturgy, we imagine that we associate ourselves with what the priest is doing but we cannot get beyond the feeling that our share in the action is rather extraneous. The adjective *actuosus* should take us the extra step, placing us at the liturgy as agents, not individually but as part of the corporate action of the Church. 'Such participation by the Christian people as "a chosen race, a royal priesthood, a holy nation, a redeemed people" is their right and duty by reason of their baptism' (*SC* 14). This is more than a mental and spiritual concentration on what someone else is doing. It is being part of the doing.

Pius XII set out the principle in *Mediator Dei*:

> The sacred liturgy is . . . the public worship which our Redeemer as Head of the Church renders to the Father, as well as the worship which the community of the faithful renders to its Founder, and through him to the heavenly Father. It is, in short, the worship rendered by the mystical body of Christ in the entirety of its Head and members.[30]

Half a century later, the Catechism of the Catholic Church would ask: 'Who celebrates the liturgy?' Liturgy, it answers, is an 'action' of the whole Christ *(Christus totus)* . . . it is the whole community, the Body of Christ united with its Head, that celebrates.' (CCC 1136, 1140) Writing in his Vatican Council journal on 24 October 1962, Yves Congar had lamented the pragmatic level of the bishops' interventions on the vernacular, adding the note:

30. *Mediator Dei* #20, in Seasoltz, *New Liturgy*, 112.

> In general, the liturgical movements have not provided themselves with the ECCLESIOLOGICAL basis that they ought to have. In this case, the fundamental theological question which has not been asked, is: who or what is the subject of the liturgical action?! It is the mystical, organic Body, to which the *plebs sancta* [holy people] belongs.[31]

Just four years later, in an important article only recently published in English, Congar elaborated on the idea of the liturgical celebration as an act of the *ecclesia*. 'The fundamental question is the nature of the liturgy . . . the question is fundamentally ecclesiological.'[32] Congar shows how the theology of the liturgy in Pius XII's *Mediator Dei* is based on the Christology of the Mystical Body but without the ecclesiology of the people of God. He demonstrates the significant development in the Second Vatican Council, seen first in *SC* and then elaborated in *Lumen Gentium*.

In any event, *SC* does make this point clear.

> Christ is always present in his Church, especially in her liturgical celebrations . . . Christ indeed always associates the Church with himself in this great work wherein God is perfectly glorified and people are sanctified . . . Rightly then the liturgy is considered as an exercise of the priestly office of Jesus Christ . . . in the liturgy, the whole public worship is performed by the Mystical Body of Jesus Christ, that is, by the Head and his members. From this it follows that every liturgical celebration, because it is an action of Christ the priest and of his Body which is the Church, is a sacred action surpassing all others . . . (*SC* 7).

31. Yves Congar, *My Journal of the Council* (Adelaide, SA: ATF Press, 2012), 117.
32. Yves Congar, 'The *Ecclesia* or Christian Community as a Whole Celebrates the Liturgy', in *At the Heart of Christian Worship: Liturgical Essays of Yves Congar*, edited by Paul Philibert (Collegeville: Liturgical Press, 2010), 49. See also Massimo Faggioli, *True Reform: Liturgy and Ecclesiology in* 'Sacrosanctum Concilium' (Collegeville: Liturgical Press, 2012), 74ff.

The consequences for the liturgy are also clarified. It is not just that the liturgy is the action of the Church, but it must be evidently so.

> Liturgical services are not private functions, but are celebrations of the Church, which is the 'sacrament of unity', namely, the holy people united and ordered under their bishops.
>
> Therefore liturgical services pertain to the whole body of the Church; they manifest it and have effects upon it; but they concern the individual members of the Church in different ways, according to their differing rank, office, and actual participation.
>
> It is to be stressed that whenever rites, according to their specific nature, make provision for communal celebration involving the presence and active participation of the faithful, this way of celebrating them is to be preferred, so far as possible, to a celebration that is individual and quasi-private (*SC* 26–27).

Now the Church is not an undifferentiated, homogeneous group of people, but a hierarchically structured organism. This is mirrored within the liturgical assembly by the different roles and offices exercised by individuals. The role of the priest, in particular, is essential in order that the gathering of the baptised be adequately constituted as the Body of Christ, but it does not annul the action of the faithful in the liturgy. As *Lumen Gentium* (*LG*) explained:

> Though they differ from one another in essence and not only in degree, the common priesthood of the faithful and the ministerial or hierarchical priesthood are nonetheless interrelated: each of them in its own special way is a participation in the one priesthood of Christ. The ministerial priest . . . acting in the person of Christ, makes present the eucharistic sacrifice, and offers it to God in the name of all the people. But the faithful, in virtue of their royal priesthood, join in the offering of the Eucharist (*LG* 10).

Therefore while the role of the ordained person in the liturgical assembly is unique and indispensable, everyone has received a share in the priesthood and an active role in offering the sacrifice of Christ by their baptism. This is why the bishops in Council added the phrase 'by reason of their baptism' to the key statement, that the faithful have a right and duty to full, conscious and active participation (in *SC* 14).[33]

The various ministerial roles are signs of a common baptismal participation in a corporate or communal action. They are ministries of service within the action of the Church. Congar uses the patristic image of a choir in which there are many voices, parts and harmonies but where the choral music produced is a collective work, greater than the sum of its parts. The liturgy is the shared activity of a single body, often displaying the character of a dialogue between the priest and the assembly.[34]

Much of this understanding of the liturgy draws from the notion of the liturgical assembly explored in the early 1950s by Aimé-Georges Martimort.[35] The assembly is a manifestation or sign of the Church which celebrates the liturgy. In the community of the altar, 'though frequently small and poor, or living in the Diaspora, Christ is present, and in virtue of his presence there is brought together one, holy, catholic and apostolic Church' (*LG* 26). The pre-eminent manifestation of the Church consists in the full, active participation of all God's holy people in liturgical celebrations, especially in the same Eucharist, in a single prayer, at one altar, where the bishop presides surrounded by the presbyterium (*SC* 41). Because the bishop cannot always and everywhere preside, parishes represent the visible Church constituted throughout the world (*SC* 42). The liturgical assembly is a concrete

---

33. A full account is found in Lamberts, 'Active Participation', 253–254. Also *History of Vatican II*, volume II, 161. The vote on this amendment had 2096 in favour, with only 10 against and 7 invalid.
34. Congar, '*The* Ecclesia', 59–60.
35. Four articles in *La Maison-Dieu*, 20 (1949): 153–175; 40 (1954): 5–29; 57 (1959): 55–84; 60 (1959): 7–34. Also Yves Congar, 'Réflexions et recherches actuelles sur l'assemblée liturgique', in *La Maison-Dieu*, 115 (1973): 7–29. For a convenient summary, see André Haquin, 'Le concept d'*Assemblée* chez A-G Martimort' in *The Active Participation Revisited*, 98–110. Haquin points out that Martimort himself made little explicit connection to baptism or to active participation. See also A-G Martimort, *The Church at Prayer: volume 1, Principles of the Liturgy* (Collegeville: Liturgical Press, 1987) II, chapter I, 'The Assembly', 89–111.

and specific body of the faithful which nevertheless makes present the whole Church as the Body of Christ.[36]

This approach to *SC* has recently been strongly affirmed by Massimo Faggioli who credits the reform process which he calls *ressourcement* with the rediscovery of a eucharistic ecclesiology. This provides the grounds for renewal process he calls *rapprochement.* Here we see a reconciliation or bringing together of local and universal ecclesiologies, individual and corporate prayer, and an expression of the Church in relationship to the world in which we live.

> 'Rapprochement' requires and fosters 'active participation'... One of the consequences of the liturgical reform in the direction of 'rapprochement' is the essential feature of the rediscovery of the role of the liturgical assembly as an 'integral player of the liturgical act'. The Church is no longer primarily an idea; it is a real gathering... In fact, one of the most important implications of the liturgical reform for 'rapprochement' in the Church is the notion that 'participation' must be extended to other fields in the life of the Church: *leitourgia, diakonia, martyria*, Church governance, teaching.[37]

Full, active and conscious participation in the liturgy, because it is profoundly a self-defining action of the Church, demands a parallel ecclesial participation in the workings of the Church and its mission. Liturgical participation implies for the baptised full, prophetic and ecclesial participation in the life of the Church, of which the liturgy is summit and source.[38] Which neatly takes us back to the beginning of the liturgical movement when Lambert Beauduin saw in the restoration of the sacred liturgy an opportunity for the social restoration of

36. Francis Mannion wrongly assesses this as congregationalism. He begins by asking the wrong questions: Who celebrates the Eucharist: the priest or the Christian assembly? What does it mean to say that the role of the priest is to preside at Mass? In what sense is the liturgy a celebration of communal faith? See M Francis Mannion, *Masterworks of God: Essays in Liturgical Theory and Practice* (Chicago: Hillenbrand Books, 2004), 65.
37. Faggioli, *True Reform,* 104–106.
38. Edward Foley, 'Passing the Torch: Full, Prophetic and Ecclesial Participation', in *Worship,* 86/5 (2012): 386–402.

humanity. 'Let us spread the "liturgical life" ... We shall then have put a leaven into the populace and into the higher social spheres, which will sooner or later give rise to good works and completely transform the social sense.'[39] No doubt this will be a challenge in today's world, in anonymous and impersonal cities where people so often experience social fragmentation and compartmentalisation.[40]

Conclusion

The liturgy does not exist in the abstract or on the pages of a book. The liturgy is an event, an action, of real people at a particular time and place. It is a representation of something broad and beautiful. The liturgical assembly is convoked by God to be the Body of Christ and to make the Church's offering with Christ on the cross. In the liturgical celebration people do not just participate in what the priest is doing; rather priest and people participate as one in what Christ is doing when 'his arms were outstretched between heaven and earth to become the lasting sign of [God's] covenant.'[41]

By our liturgical participation, we are transformed, saved, reconciled by God. Something deeply personal happens to us in the liturgy, but it is not at the level of individual devotion as much as it is a sharing in a corporate act. Our words, actions and gestures are not distractions from personal prayerfulness, but a reminder that we are part of communal prayer. The liturgy is my prayer in so far as I throw my lot in with the Church at prayer. We participate 'fully, actively, and as befits a community—*plena, actuosa, et communitatis propria*' (*SC* 21).

Full, conscious and active participation is a mindset. It is not doing things. It is the mindset of being present as doers, a mindset of doing together a corporate ecclesial action.

The proclamation of the word is not the performance of the reader before an auditorium: it is the activation of God's saving word in an auditory event which moves from heart to heart, from faith to faith, engaging the entire liturgical assembly in receiving God's word as 'something alive and active' (Heb 4:12). The liturgy of the word is

39. Beauduin, *Liturgy*, 46.
40. Richard Gaillardetz, Catherine Clifford, *Keys to the Council: Unlocking the Teaching of Vatican II* (Collegeville: Liturgical Press, 2012), 27.
41. Eucharistic Prayer for Reconciliation I, *Roman Missal*, 791.

ministered by a reader or cantor but is a divine event for and within the whole assembly.[42]

Liturgical silence is not a retreat into private mediation: it is a moment for the gathered faithful to hold sacred God's action in the midst of the assembly, sharply aware of each and all in the corporate action of the Church.

The Eucharistic Prayer is given voice by the priest but it is the whole gathering of the baptised which offers in thanksgiving the holy and living sacrifice. The 'doing' of the liturgy does not demand that each individual does every part of the liturgy, but it certainly means that each individual is fully conscious that they are involved in making a communal action.

Achieving the mindset of active participation at the liturgy is partly about education and formation but has to be more than mere intellectual explanation. It is also about drawing people into the experience of doing, an experience which has both internal and external dimensions. Since achieving this mindset is the aim to be considered before all else in the restoration and promotion of the sacred liturgy, we must be constantly asking the questions: What architectural arrangement will place people at the ambo, altar and font as doers of the liturgical action?[43] What liturgical music will give people the sense that, when they sing, the Church gives praise? What words, movement, gestures and actions will yank them from their comfortable distance as spectators in pews and thrust them into the event itself where God may reconcile them, fill them with the Holy Spirit, so they 'may become one body, one spirit in Christ'? (EP III).

---

42. Partick Prétot takes the liturgy of the word as an example of active participation, lamenting that its didactic dimension is often privileged over the dimensions of epiphany and contemplation. *La Maison-Dieu,* 241 (2005): 171.

43. This is the only sentence in *SC* on building churches: 'And when churches are to be built, let great care be taken that they be suitable for the celebration of liturgical services and for the active participation of the faithful' (*SC* #124).

Liturgical Intelligibility in *Sacrosanctum Concilium*

Clare V Johnson

One of the central principles guiding the restoration and reform of the liturgy called for by the Second Vatican Council was the principle of 'liturgical intelligibility'. *Sacrosanctum Concilium* (hereafter *SC*) states in paragraph 21:

> Holy Mother Church desires to undertake with great care a general restoration of the liturgy itself . . . In this restoration, both the texts and rites should be drawn up so that they express more clearly the holy things which they signify; the Christian people, so far as possible, should be enabled to understand them with ease and to take part in them fully, actively and as befits a community.[1]

The Council characterised the type of liturgy to be produced by the reform as having 'a noble simplicity.' The prayers of the liturgy 'should be short, clear, and unencumbered by useless repetitions; they should be *within the people's powers of comprehension, and normally should not require much explanation*'.[2] The principle of liturgical intelligi-

1. Second Vatican Council, '*Sacrosanctum Concilium*,' Constitution on the Sacred Liturgy (4 December 1963), source: <http://www.vatican.va/archive/hist_councils/ii_vatican_council/documents/vat-ii_const_19631204_sacrosanctum-concilium_en.html>. Accessed 14 April 2013. All references to *SC* are taken from this source.
2. *SC* #34, italics mine. Kathleen Hughes explains that *SC* intended simplification and hence intelligibility of the liturgy to be achieved via 'suppression (dropping useless repetitions), addition (adding options where pastorally appropriate),' restoration (recovery of forms lost over the course of time), adaptation

bility itself is articulated in *SC* 79 in relation to sacramentals: 'The sacramentals are to undergo a revision which takes into account the *primary principle of enabling the faithful to participate intelligently*, actively and easily . . .'[3] According to *SC* 79 liturgical intelligibility enables 'that full, conscious and active participation in liturgical celebrations which is demanded by the very nature of the liturgy' and is 'the aim to be considered before all else' (*SC* 14) in the reform of the liturgy. An intelligible liturgy would promote *understanding* of the sacred rites among clerics in seminaries and houses of formation (*SC* 17); priests, both secular and religious who are already working in the Lord's vineyard (*SC* 18); and among Christ's faithful (*SC* 48).

SC also specifies the means via which an intelligible liturgy is to be facilitated, which includes the promotion of direct understanding through liturgical instruction of the faithful by pastors of souls (*SC*19) and the promotion of indirect understanding through 'active participation in the liturgy both internally and externally' (*SC* 19). The promotion of indirect understanding through active participation in the liturgy is reiterated more specifically in *SC* 33 which notes that the liturgy itself

> . . . contains much instruction for the faithful . . .Thus not only when things are read 'which were written for our instruction' (Rom 15:4), but also when the Church prays or sings or acts, the faith of those taking part is nourished and *their minds are raised to God*, so that they may offer Him their *rational service* and more abundantly receive his grace.[4]

According to *SC* 52, liturgical intelligibility is to be promoted through the liturgical homily which is to enunciate 'the guiding principles of the Christian life . . . expounded from the sacred text during the course of the liturgical year'.[5] *SC* 118 calls for the 'intelligent fostering'

(admission of cultural elements into the liturgy), and 'development (organic growth from forms already existing).' 'Overview of the Constitution on the Sacred Liturgy,' in *The Liturgy Documents: A Parish Resource* edited by Elizabeth Hoffman, (Chicago: Liturgy Training Publications, 1991), 3.

3. *SC* #79. Italics mine.
4. Italics mine.
5. *The General Instruction of the Roman Missal* (Strathfield: St Paul's Publication,

of religious singing as a means of encouraging active participation in the liturgy which in turn promotes liturgical intelligibility. *SC* 59 makes reference to the promotion of understanding through the use of signs and symbols in sacramental liturgies, stating:

> The purpose of the sacraments is to sanctify men (sic), to build up the body of Christ, and, finally, to give worship to God; because they are signs, they also instruct. They not only presuppose faith, but by words and objects they also nourish, strengthen and express it.

Understanding liturgical symbols and symbolic ritual actions entails an appreciation that their meaning has been acquired over time and through repetition of words joined to actions which, when performed within the ritual context, convey quite specific meanings while remaining open to further levels of interpretation.

The most notable means by which *SC* intended to promote liturgical intelligibility is found in paragraph 36.2 which calls for extended 'use of the mother tongue, whether in the Mass, the administration of the sacraments, or other parts of the liturgy' as this 'frequently may be of great advantage to the people . . .' It was left to 'the competent territorial ecclesiastical authority . . . to decide whether, and to what extent, the vernacular language is to be used',[6] and within a few short years following the Council, at the request of the various competent territorial ecclesiastical authorities, full vernacular translations of the liturgy began to appear.[7] Council peritus and American leader of the liturgical movement, Fr Godfrey Diekmann OSB, called use of the vernacular '*the* burning issue within the liturgical renewal; it was the very heart of the liturgical movement and the symbol of what "full

2013), #65.

6. *SC* #36.3.
7. In offering an explanation of the meaning of *SC* #54 which states that 'In Masses which are celebrated with the people, a suitable place may be allotted to their mother tongue . . .', Annibale Bugnini wrote: 'We have formulated the article in this manner so that those who wish to celebrate the entire Mass in Latin may not be able to force their viewpoint on others, while those who wish to use the vernacular in some parts of the Mass may not be able to compel others to do the same . . . The door is not closed to anyone.' *The Reform of the Liturgy 1948–1975* (Collegeville MN: Liturgical Press, 1990), 111.

and active liturgical participation" meant'.[8] The consequences of taking seriously and implementing fully the principle of liturgical intelligibility via vernacular translation are momentous. Rather than a form of liturgy in which the presider as ritual expert performed the rite in the foreign Latin language in front of and on behalf of the passive, observing assembly, the point of liturgical intelligibility was to enable the whole assembly to perform the rite intelligibly, each according to their appropriate role, fully, consciously, actively, dialogically.

When all of the references to liturgical intelligibility found in *SC* are aligned, it is apparent that there is an implicit rationale at work which accents the crucial importance of the principle: vernacular translation (*SC* 36.2) enables full, conscious and active participation in the liturgy (*SC* 14), for priests (*SC* 17, 18) and the faithful (*SC* 48), both internally and externally (*SC* 19), which makes it possible for the faithful to derive the true Christian spirit (*SC* 14) within the liturgy; engage in worship 'as befits a community' (*SC* 21); 'offer Him their rational service and more abundantly receive His grace' (*SC* 33) 'conscious of what they are doing, with devotion and full collaboration,' (*SC* 48) so that, 'enriched by its effects' (*SC* 11), they may be disposed to receive God's gift of 'grace in a fruitful manner, to worship God duly, and to practise charity' (*SC* 59). While this rationale is not stated in this manner in *SC* itself, by placing the various references to intelligibility/understanding/rationality/consciousness and the desired outcomes of a liturgy that promotes all of these cognitive characteristics next to one another, the ultimate purpose of promoting the principle of liturgical intelligibility becomes clear, namely, to enable the faithful to understand what they are saying/hearing/singing/doing in the liturgy in order to express and nourish their faith, practise charity and receive God's grace more abundantly.

The principle of liturgical intelligibility provides a way for the Christian community to 'negotiate (or renegotiate)—regularly, repeatedly, ritually—the connections between creation and grace'[9], and to generate, reinforce and clarify meaning within and beyond the liturgy. *SC* assumes worshiping subjects who have the capacity for intelligent thought and rational action, and the principle of liturgi-

8. Keith Pecklers, *Dynamic Equivalence: The Living Language of Christian Worship* (Collegeville, MN: Liturgical Press, 2003), 172.
9. Nathan D Mitchell, 'The Amen Corner', in *Worship*, 85/1 (2011): 80.

cal intelligibility is supposed to assist those worshiping subjects to pray correctly (doxology = correct praise) in order that they might believe correctly (orthodoxy = correct belief) so that they might live out those beliefs every day (orthopraxy = correct action/practice). Liturgical intelligibility thus constitutes the start of a logic chain which encompasses and directs the whole of the Christian life.

Noting the presence of the principle of liturgical intelligibility, highlighting its various iterations within *SC* and pointing out the Council's hoped-for outcomes of restoring and reforming the liturgy so that it is intelligible is but a first step in the process of unpacking this principle and comprehending its importance for the celebration of meaningful liturgy as source and summit[10] of the Church's activity within the Christian life as a whole.

What is Liturgical Intelligibility?

Determining whether and to what extent the liturgy is intelligible to the faithful is a somewhat difficult task. Comprehending how people come to a position of 'understanding' requires knowledge of the cognitive functions involved in learning, recalling, applying knowledge and apprehending one's own mental processes in order to discern whether or not something has been understood/made intelligible.

Learning involves movement through various phases of awareness: the cognitive, the associative and the autonomous.[11] The cognitive phase of awareness equates with the acquisition of declarative knowledge (one's memory for concepts, facts or episodes)[12] while the associative phase has to do with relating prior knowledge to a new situation in an attempt to comprehend 'the new' relative to 'the already known'. The autonomous phase of awareness equates with the operation of procedural knowledge that is automatically accessed and requires little conscious attention[13] (for example, automatically mak-

10. See *SC* #7.
11. See Parviz and Amir Hossein Rahimi, 'The Effect of Metacognitive Strategy Instruction on the Listening Performance of EFL Students', in *International Journal of Linguistics*, 4/2 (2012): 498.
12. See Danielle S McNamara and Tenaha O'Reilly 'Knowledge Acquisition, Representation and Organization' in *Encyclopedia of Education*, volume 4, edited by James W Guthrie (New York: Macmillan, 2002), 1431.
13. McNamara and O'Reilly, 'Knowledge Acquisition', 1432.

ing the sign of the cross while speaking the words 'In the name of the Father and of the Son and of the Holy Spirit').

When one does not understand the meaning of a word, a phrase, a symbol or a symbolic ritual action within the liturgy, one tends to become aware of oneself and one's lack of understanding at a metacognitive level. John H Flavell explains that:

> . . . metacognitive experiences are any conscious cognitive or affective experiences that accompany and pertain to any intellectual enterprise. An example would be the sudden feeling that you do not understand something another person just said.[14]

The operation of metacognition within the liturgy draws one's attention away from the content of the liturgy/prayer (that is, the meaning behind the words or actions or symbols) and focuses it onto one's own level of comprehension (or lack thereof) of what is occurring in the liturgy. If metacognition occurs one's attention can become engaged in a conscious attempt to acquire declarative or explicit knowledge of what a word/phrase/symbol/symbolic ritual action means. In contrast, operating with implicit or procedural knowledge (which occurs when what has engaged one's attention is intelligible) allows one to focus on performing the ritual somewhat automatically (that is, being able to operate by unconsciously retrieving surface-level meanings[15]) and hence provides mental space for the possibility of accessing a deeper level of meaning inherent in the liturgy.

It is probable that implicit/procedural knowledge, declarative/acquisitive knowledge, associative knowledge and metacognition will all be in operation to varying degrees at different times for each individual within the liturgy, depending on their established levels of implicit/procedural knowledge and their capacity to integrate new

14. John H Flavell, 'Metacognition and cognitive monitoring: A new area of cognitive-developmental inquiry', in *American Psychologist*, 34 (1979): 908. Birjandi and Rahimi expand on this by noting that 'metacognitive awareness consists of three parts: thinking of what one knows (metacognitive knowledge), thinking of what one is currently doing (metacognitive skill) and thinking of what one's current cognitive or affective state is (metacognitive experience).' Birjandi and Rahimi, 'The Effect of Metacognitive Strategy Instruction', 496.
15. See Henry L Roediger III and Lisa Geraci, 'Implicit Memory,' in *Encyclopedia of Education*, volume 5, 1597, 1599.

knowledge. No one liturgical celebration is exactly the same as another, even when performed by the same presider and assembly, because the propers and other variable parts of the liturgy (music, homily, universal prayers, etc) change while some elements are repeated, and so there will always be the acquisition and integration of new pieces of knowledge as a regular part of liturgical celebration.

When the words or actions of the liturgy are changed significantly through a liturgical revolution such as occurred as a result of Vatican II or through the introduction of subsequent editions of rites or new ritual translations (as was seen in the implementation of the English translation of the third edition of the Roman Missal [2010]), the members of the assembly are moved from operating with implicit/procedural ritual knowledge into a state of metacognition where their attention focuses on the acquisition of new declarative knowledge or on relearning or repatterning what had been implicit knowledge previously. The move from declarative knowledge to procedural knowledge can take some time, as one must move from consciously remembering facts to acquiring 'habitual behavioural routines that can be performed without conscious control'.[16] Within this process, the frequency with which new words/phrases/constructions appear in liturgical prayer and their phonemic similarity to words/phrases/constructions already in a person's vocabulary or memory aid in the process of meaning extraction and eventual embedding of those new words/phrases/constructions as implicit knowledge. However, this process will not be as smooth (or will take far longer than is necessary) if one is not aided in comprehending the meaning of those new words/phrases/constructions relative to prior implicit/procedural knowledge, through explicit definition and explanation of how they relate to the context in which they are used. For example, words such as 'consubstantial' or 'oblation', phrases such as 'profit our conversion' or 'the sacrifice of conciliation' or awkward and stilted constructions such as 'Be pleased, O God, to bless, we pray', which are found in the English translation of the third edition of the Roman Missal, can become stumbling blocks to liturgical intelligibility being realised in the celebration of the Eucharist. Usually, however, the liturgy is not something Christians attend only once; it is repeated, thus providing

16. Howard Eichenbaum, 'Neurological Foundation,' in *Encyclopedia of Education*, volume 4, 1436.

opportunities for growing congregational familiarity with the texts of the liturgy which can promote intelligibility via repetition.

The Generation of 'Meaning' via Liturgical Intelligibility

Ideally, the principle of liturgical intelligibility provides access to meaning for the majority of worshippers the majority of the time. Through its prayers, readings, music and symbolic ritual actions, liturgy communicates the truths of the faith to Christian believers and is therefore experienced as meaningful to those who participate in it with understanding.[17] The meaning that is generated is shared, inherited, taught, enacted, culturally determined and affected by those who constructed the rite initially (historically and proximally), those who enact the rite in each instance (presider, faithful, God), and those who are the full, conscious and active recipients of the words/signs/symbols/symbolic ritual actions of the liturgy, because, as Nathan Mitchell explains, liturgical rites are 'the church's public, repeated rehearsal of its deepest identity, unity, values, convictions, and *meanings*'.[18]

In attempting to specify what is understood by the construction of 'meaning' within liturgy, Graham Hughes delineates three criteria for, or dimensions of, meaning:

> . . . the event has to *make sense* to some degree or another (that is, some level of rationality is demanded); the meanings have to be *multisensory*, transmitted and apprehended as much along nonverbal as verbal channels of signification; and they have to be *theologically competent* (make sense in terms of a theistic reading of the world).[19]

While it is unlikely that Hughes' criteria for meaning in the liturgy (or others like them) were applied scientifically as an intelligibility litmus

17. See Steffen Lösel, 'What Sacred Symbols Say about Strangers and Strawberries: Gordon W. Lathrop's Liturgical Theology in Review', in *The Journal of Religion* (2005): 636.
18. Nathan D Mitchell, *Meeting Mystery: Liturgy, Worship, Sacraments* (Maryknoll NY: Orbis, 2006), 59. Italics in original.
19. Graham Hughes, *Worship as Meaning: A Liturgical Theology for Late Modernity* (Cambridge: Cambridge University Press, 2003), 31.

test when the English translation of the third edition of the Roman Missal was being completed, they do constitute a useful framework to employ in analysing the translation after the fact, to determine whether the principle of liturgical intelligibility has been upheld or impeded within the most recent revision of the eucharistic liturgy.

As a Constitution produced by an ecumenical council, *SC* epitomises the highest level of Catholic Church teaching on the liturgy of the last fifty years; its practical implementation, however, has been channelled in particular directions by subsequent instructions from the Congregation for Divine Worship and the Discipline of the Sacraments, designed to guide and shape the liturgy in practice throughout the world. The English translation of the third edition of the Roman Missal was produced in accordance with the rules laid down in *Liturgiam Authenticam* (LA), the Fifth Instruction for the Right Application of the Conciliar Constitution on the Liturgy, on the use of Vernacular Languages in the Publication of the Books of the Roman Liturgy,[20] in concert with the *Ratio Translationis for the English Language.*[21] Whether abiding by the prescriptions of LA and the *Ratio* in the production of the latest translation of the Mass has resulted in the promotion of *SC*'s principle of liturgical intelligibility or has obscured this principle in favour of emphasising other agendas is a question for further consideration.

The framers of SC believed that simplifying the rites, 'omitting duplications and less satisfactory accretions', 'restoring more venerable forms'[22] of liturgy (SC 34) and laying bare the words of the liturgy in the vernacular (SC 36) would enable the faithful to move beyond the surface level of liturgical text to encounter the deeper meaning of the liturgy conveyed by the text. Comprehending the meaning of

20. Congregation for Divine Worship and the Discipline of the Sacraments, *Liturgiam Authenticam*, (25 April 2001), <http://www.vatican.va/roman_curia/congregations/ccdds/documents/rc_con_ccdds_doc_20010507_liturgiam-authenticam_en.html>. Accessed 16 April 2013. The other four instructions on *SC* are: *Inter oecumenici* (26 September 1964), *Tres abhinc annos* (4 May 4 1967), *Liturgicae instaurationes* (5 September 1970) and *Varietates legitimae* (29 March 1994).
21. Congregation for Divine Worship and the Discipline of the Sacraments, *Ratio Translationis* for the English Language (Vatican City: Vatican Polyglot Press, 2007).
22. Frederick R McManus, *Sacramental Liturgy* (New York: Herder and Herder, 1967), 69.

the words is not the ultimate goal of translating the liturgy into the vernacular; rather, the ultimate goal is conversion (change of heart) so that the Christian faith can be lived out beyond the liturgy in acts of charity (SC 59). The text of the liturgy should not be a distraction to the faithful; its proclamation should not be a *raison d'être*, rather, it should serve as a vehicle for conveying the faith so meaningfully that lives are changed. If the attention of the faithful is overly focused on determining the meaning of liturgy's words rather than simply praying them, then the ultimate goal of vernacular translation is at risk.

The translators of the final English version of the third edition of the Roman Missal appear to have sacrificed the principle of liturgical intelligibility in service of another principle: fidelity to rendering the translation of the Latin into the vernacular as precisely and literally as possible utilising the translation principle of formal equivalence. This has resulted in a degree of opacity in the prayers produced. While poetic language can certainly be evocative when it provides *entrée* to levels of meaning accessible only when the religious imagination is engaged, translation by formal equivalence rarely results in poetic constructions in the receptor language.

The process of translating the liturgy into the vernacular is unlikely to reach a point of permanent completion, as the history of liturgical translations subsequent to Vatican II has shown. All of the post-conciliar translations so far have been attempts to render the liturgy more intelligible for those who pray it in their native languages; whether this goal has yet been achieved is a point of ongoing debate, and hence further translations are likely in the future.

Extra-Textual Forms of Liturgical Intelligibility

In addition to having knowledge about the cognitive functions involved in the process of understanding/making intelligible, an explication of the principle of liturgical intelligibility must also take into account other ways of knowing/making intelligible that are operative in the liturgy besides understanding promoted through comprehension of its verbal components. There is a great difference between liturgical intelligibility understood only in terms of linguistic intelligibility, and an understanding of liturgical intelligibility that recognises and incorporates the full potential of linguistic intelligibility alongside semiotic, kinaesthetic, artistic, musical, proxemic, hierarchic, communicative, emotional, mimetic, anamnetic, temporal, theological and cultural forms of intelligibility also. Peter Jeffrey argues that the Consilium responsible for reforming the liturgy according to the precepts of SC was focused squarely on reform of the liturgical texts, 'privileging verbal understanding over any other kind'. He asserts that 'the massive effort required to convert everything into vernacular only seemed to confirm the impression that liturgy is essentially text.'[23] He explains that a consequence of 'equating worship with word is that, when problems develop, textual remedies seem to be the only ones available.'[24]

As liturgical worship is an embodied (not just spiritual or mental) activity, focusing on the liturgy only in terms of the intelligibility of its verbal components (the oral/aural aspects of worship) risks overlooking the potential sources of liturgical intelligibility located in the visual, kinetic, gustatory and olfactory realms as well as what can become intelligible through the far less easily accessible realm of the human spirit and the apophatic realm ('the way of knowing by way of unknowing'[25]).

There are limitations to the principle of liturgical intelligibility which centre on the fact that at the heart of the liturgy is God, the pure Mystery whose presence, grace and action is encountered and experienced within liturgical celebration both through and beyond the texts, symbols and actions of the ritual. Michael Downey advises that:

> . . . no matter how appropriate a word or symbol may be to express the holy . . . no one symbol or constellation of symbols is capable of fully expressing the ineffable, the Being beyond being, that mystery which overspills any and all attempts to speak it. The presence of the holy both *is* and *is not* expressed in word and sacrament, due to the surplus of meaning that is not communicated in any presencing through word and sacrament.[26]

---

23. Peter Jeffrey, *Translating Tradition: A Chant Historian Reads*, Liturgiam Authenticam (Collegeville, MN: Liturgical Press, 2005), 112.
24. Jeffrey, Translating Tradition, 113.
25. Michael Downey, 'Lex Orandi, Lex Credendi: Taking it Seriously in Systematic Theology,' in *A Promise of Presence*, edited by Michael Downey and Richard Fragomeni (Washington DC: The Pastoral Press, 1992), 18.
26. Downey, 'Lex Orandi,' 15.

While acknowledging that the principle of liturgical intelligibility is not without its limitations, the rationale for an intelligible liturgy expressed in SC has distinct aims and hoped-for outcomes, one of which is the generation of enacted liturgical theology.

Enacted Liturgical Theology

The methodology of liturgical theology emerged during the years following Vatican II as scholars reflected[27] on a phrase attributed to Prosper of Aquitaine[28]: *ut legem credendi lex statuat supplicandi* (the law of prayer grounds the law of belief), often shortened to: *lex orandi, lex credendi*. Alexander Schmemann saw the task of liturgical theology as elucidating the theological meaning of worship, and he proposed that liturgical theology occurs in two main phases: *theologia prima*, theology conveyed within liturgical celebration itself or the act of praying viewed as an expression of primary theology, and *theologia secunda*, theological reflection which occurs subsequent to liturgical celebration on the basis of what has been conveyed theologically within the liturgy. Later, Kevin Irwin proposed a third phase of liturgical theology, which he termed '*lex vivendi*': the enactment or living out of the theological meaning inherent in liturgy and pondered subsequent to liturgy.[29]

In explaining *theologia prima*, Aidan Kavanagh writes:

> A liturgical act *is* a theological act of the most all-encompassing, integral, and foundational kind. It is both precipitator and result of that adjustment to the change wrought in the worshiping assembly by its regular encounter in faith with its divine Source.[30]

---

27. The chief architects of this approach to studying the theological meaning of liturgy were Alexander Schmemann, *Introduction to Liturgical Theology* (Portland MD: American Orthodox Press, 1966) and Aidan Kavanagh, *On Liturgical Theology* (Collegeville, MN: Liturgical Press, 1984/1992).
28. Kevin Irwin explains that this phrase is 'generally ascribed to Prosper of Aquitaine's indiculus as written between 435–442.' *Context and Text: Method in Liturgical Theology* (Collegeville, MN: Liturgical Press, 1994), 32.
29. Irwin, *Context and Text*, 311.
30. Kavanagh, *On Liturgical Theology*, 89.

It is clear that if *theologia prima* is to occur within worship then the liturgy, as the assembly's primary expression of faith, must be intelligible. If the liturgy is not intelligible to the performing assembly, then its capacity to serve in its enactment as an encompassing, integral and foundational theological act which affects profound change in the hearts of the assembly is severely compromised. Kavanagh explains:

> What results from a liturgical act is not only 'meaning,' but an ecclesial transaction with reality . . . The act both changes and outstrips the assembly in which it occurs. The assembly adjusts to that change, becoming different from what it was before the act happened.[31]

According to SC 59, it is of 'the highest importance that the faithful should easily understand the sacramental signs' because understanding the sacraments they celebrate 'most effectively disposes the faithful to receive' sacramental 'grace in a fruitful manner, to worship God duly and to practice charity'. Comprehending the liturgy is but the first step toward the ultimate goal of liturgical celebration: intra-liturgically, the worship of God and extra-liturgically, living the Christian life in acts of charity.

Writing just prior to Vatican II, Yves Congar explained that

> . . . every 'sacrament' exists for the sake of its *res*, which is the spiritual reality *in the believer*. Therefore, liturgy, rituals, and the church, which is itself the Great Sacrament, have to find their fulfilment and their verification *in the persons who live out their meaning*.[32]

Liturgical intelligibility is crucial if the faithful are to understand the meaning of sacraments and consequently live out 'the ethical imperative that flows from the Christian's encounter with God'[33] in the liturgy. This living out can be facilitated far more determinedly by an

31. Kavanagh, *On Liturgical Theology*, 88.
32. Yves Congar, '"Real" Liturgy, "Real" Preaching', in *At the Heart of Christian Worship: Liturgical Essays of Yves Congar*, edited by Paul Philibert (Collegeville, MN: Liturgical Press, 2010), 5.
33. Mitchell, *Meeting Mystery*, 39.

intelligible liturgy in which the symbols are comprehensible. However, this entails the 'awakening and sustaining of social capacity to respond to symbols' as Don Saliers notes, and 'perhaps the greatest task ahead is to restore a sense of history and transcendence to the symbols embedded in the liturgical actions' in a way that is 'evocative, imaginative, and experiential'.[34]

The intelligibility of the words, symbols and symbolic ritual actions of the liturgy is affected greatly by the manner in which it is performed. While the text is now in the vernacular, and while better communication and dialogue is facilitated by the priest facing the assembly to preside, the comprehensibility of worship is still dependent upon the rites being *performed* intelligibly.

Performed Intelligibility: The Ongoing Challenge

In his Apostolic Exhortation *Sacramentum Caritatis*, Benedict XVI highlighted the need for further attention to be paid to the *ars celebrandi* of liturgy which he defines as the 'art of proper celebration, and the full, active and fruitful participation of all the faithful'. Benedict XVI stressed the need for 'faithful adherence to the liturgical norms in all their richness' because 'for two thousand years this way of celebrating has sustained the faith life of all believers'.[35] Benedict XVI directly links celebrating the liturgy well with full, conscious and active participation by the faithful in the liturgy and sustenance of the faith life of the believer. 'The art of proper celebration of the liturgy' includes focusing on how liturgical intelligibility can be enhanced through good performance practice, which can be achieved in a number of ways.

'Proper celebration of the liturgy' requires intelligible performance of the liturgical texts prayed aloud. Graham Hughes notes that

34. Don E. Saliers, *Worship as Theology: Foretaste of Glory Divine* (Nashville: Abingdon, 1994), 146.

35. Pope Benedict XVI, '*Sacramentum Caritatis*', Post-Synodal Apostolic Exhortation on the Eucharist as the Source and Summit of the Church's Life and Mission, (22 February 2007), #38. <http://www.vatican.va/holy_father/benedict_xvi/apost_exhortations/documents/hf_ben-xvi_exh_20070222_sacramentum-caritatis_en.html#Ars_celebrandi>. Accessed 6 April 2013.

> . . . the *sound of the voice* becomes directly a dimension of the meaning which such language is to carry . . . the *tone and quality of its enunciation* (its physicality) have as much to do with the meanings transmitted as the *semantic values* (its cognitive content) wherein it consists.[36]

The manner in which the words of the liturgy are proclaimed can affect the extent to which those listening to them comprehend their meaning. The pace, volume, enunciation, rhythm, accent, pitch and intent of the presider praying the texts, combined with their own personal level of understanding of what they are proclaiming, can enhance or impede an assembly's ability to comprehend the text and go beyond the surface level to engage with the content it conveys. George Shannon explains that 'as texts move from transactional to expressive to poetic, the sounds of words and the rhythm of their linking become as expressive as their definitions and what they describe.'[37] Under normal communication circumstances, visual speech cues combine with auditory speech cues to enable listeners to extract meaning from speech.[38] Liturgical intelligibility can be fostered through the use of visual aids to support the auditory information being conveyed in worship. Clarity of proclamation of liturgical texts is crucial for helping an assembly to move from unintelligibility to intelligibility and many performance related issues can be addressed by teaching presiders to be consciously aware of the need for 'performance for comprehension', so that the intelligibility of the liturgy is enhanced.

'Proper celebration of the liturgy' entails the incorporation and intelligible use of carefully chosen, rich and appropriate symbols within

---

36. Hughes, *Worship as Meaning*, 37.
37. George Shannon, 'Writing the Empty Cup: Rhythm and Sound as Content', in *Children's Literature*, 19 (1991):138–147.
38. See Karen Iler Kirk, Lindsay Prusick, Brian French, Chad Gotch, Laurie S Eisenberg and Nancy Young. 'Assessing Spoken Word Recognition in Children Who are Deaf or Hard of Hearing: A Translational Approach', in *Journal of the American Academy of Audiology*, 23 (2012): 467. Kirk explains further: 'It has been hypothesised that visual cues enhance speech understanding because they provide segmental and suprasegmental information that is complementary (that is, place of articulation) to the acoustic speech cues and because they reduce the attentional demands placed on the auditory signal.' Kirk *et al*, 468.

the liturgy which both create meaning and express/reinforce corporate beliefs. The symbols utilised in liturgy have acquired meaning over time and the more exposure believers have to the Christian community's 'shared symbolic code'[39] the more deeply they may understand the many facets of symbolic meaning inherent within liturgical celebration.

Sacramentum Caritatis 38 states that 'The primary way to foster the participation of the People of God in the sacred rite is the proper celebration of the rite itself. The *ars celebrandi* is the best way to ensure their *actuosa participatio*.' Understanding the meaning of 'full, conscious and active participation in liturgy' means taking seriously the role played by the assembly in constructing the liturgy via its participation. The assembly's responses, proclamations and activity constitute a vital part of the liturgy itself, and without the assembly taking its part, the ideal of liturgy as envisaged in *SC* is not realised in practice.[40] Liturgical celebration is at once a somatic process, a cerebral process and a spiritual process because our mental and spiritual existence is dependent upon our physicality.[41] Our physical/kinetic participation in liturgy encompasses a complex of unspoken understandings which are enacted meaningfully within liturgical celebration.[42] Such embodied knowing must be learned through imitation, repetition, direct instruction and via engagement in secondary theology which reflects on the meaning of the rites outside of liturgical celebration.

'Proper celebration of the liturgy' is enhanced by intra-liturgical and extra-liturgical catechesis which encourages greater understanding of the liturgy. Meaning creation within the liturgical context relies on allowing the rites to teach us how to pray and act in the very doing of them. We can learn how to relate to God by encountering God in liturgy and our liturgical participation can lead us to knowledge of God. Intra-liturgical catechesis can occur when the liturgy is performed in an intelligible manner; extra-liturgical catechesis can

39. David N Power, '*SC* to GIRM, and Beyond: The *Ars Celebrandi*', in *Liturgical Ministry*, 20 (2011): 4.
40. See *SC* #26 and 27 which express the public nature of the liturgy and evidence a clear preference for communal celebration wherever possible.
41. See Hughes, *Worship as Meaning*, 24–25.
42. See Saliers, *Worship as Theology*, 153.

unpack the meaning of the liturgy and its specific symbolic ritual actions through education which occurs outside the liturgy via bulletin inserts, parish information sessions, religious education classes, *et cetera.*

'Proper celebration of the liturgy' entails the expenditure of some effort on the part of the faithful to foster a proper disposition both for receiving and living out the liturgy's gift of grace individually and communally. Realising the principle of liturgical intelligibility in practice is impacted by the problem of its reception by the liturgical assembly. The composition of any given liturgical assembly is not static; hence it is unlikely that its liturgical intelligence quotient ('liturgical IQ') will be consistent, which means that the theoretical intelligibility of liturgy may not always achieve practical realisation. New members join and are born into the body of worshippers; older members die and the body is changed. In any given liturgy, different members of the body (including the presider) are present or absent depending on circumstances, and capacity for and levels of attention being deliberately focused on the liturgy by the members of the body can differ, which means that reception issues will affect the consistency with which liturgical intelligibility can be guaranteed in practice. Understanding the symbols, symbolic ritual actions and metaphors of the liturgy requires 'an investment of interpretation and cooperation on the part of believers'.[43] The liturgy cannot be expected to be so self-explanatory that there is no need for any effort on the part of believers to learn its meaning; conversely, it cannot be so opaque as to baffle and alienate the faithful intellectually to the point where detachment or introversion result.

Conclusion

It is clear that the principle of liturgical intelligibility was of central importance in the reform of the liturgy envisaged by the Council Fathers in *SC*. The achievement of its practical realisation remains an ongoing challenge for the Church as we continue to determine the best ways to foster intelligibility and generate meaning through appropriate liturgical texts, symbols, symbolic ritual actions, mind-

43. Yves Congar, 'Where Does the "Sacred" Fit into a Christian Worldview?', *At the Heart of Christian Worship*, 109.

ful performance practice, embodied participation, intra- and extra-liturgical catechesis, and efforts at fostering conscious reception of liturgical meaning throughout each assembly of the faithful. If the rationale for intelligible worship enunciated by *SC* is to be realised, the importance of liturgical intelligibility cannot be overstated. It is via liturgical intelligibility that the alignment of our doxology, orthodoxy and orthopraxy is facilitated, in order that our worship not only glorifies God, expresses and nourishes faith and enables the reception of God's grace, but also inspires the change of heart necessary to practise charity in the Christian life beyond worship.

Towards Inculturation: An Australian Indigenous Contribution

John Francis Fitz-Herbert and Carmel Pilcher

At Blatherskite Park in Alice Springs, Northern Territory in 1986, John Paul II spoke the following words to the indigenous people of Australia—Aboriginal and Torres Strait Islanders:

> The gospel of Our Lord Jesus Christ speaks all languages. It esteems and embraces all cultures. It supports them in everything human and, when necessary, it purifies them. Always and everywhere the Gospel uplifts and enriches cultures with the revealed message of a loving and merciful God.
>
> That Gospel now invites you to become, through and through, Aboriginal Christians. It meets your deepest desires. You do not have to be a people divided into two parts, as though an Aboriginal had to borrow the faith and life of Christianity, like a hat or a pair of shoes, from someone else who owns them. Jesus calls you to accept his words and values into your own culture. To develop in this way will make you more than ever truly Aboriginal. The old ways can draw new life and strength from the Gospel. The message of Jesus Christ can lift up your lives to new heights, reinforce all your positive values and add many others, which only the gospel in its originality proposes. Take this gospel into your own language and way of speaking; let its spirit penetrate your communities and determine your behaviour towards each other, let it bring new strength to your stories and ceremonies. Let the gospel come into your hearts and renew your

> personal lives. The Church invites you to express the living word of Jesus that speak to your Aboriginal minds and hearts.
>
> All over the world people worship God and read his word in their own language, and colour the great signs and symbols of religion with touches of their own traditions. Why should you be different from them in this regard, why should you not be allowed the happiness of being with God and each other in Aboriginal fashion?
>
> . . . seek out the best things of your traditional ways. If you do, you will come to realise more and more your great human and Christian dignity . . . Your Christian faith calls you to become the best kind of Aboriginal people you can be . . . Only then will you make your best contribution to all your brothers and sisters in this great nation. You are part of Australia and Australia is part of you. And the Church herself in Australia will not be fully the Church that Jesus wants her to be until you have made your contribution to her life and until that contribution has been joyfully received by others.[1]

In the decades since those prophetic words were first uttered in this ancient land, they have been understood, interpreted and celebrated by the First Peoples of Australia and other Australian Christians as a call to the Catholic Church in Australia to engage in the process of true and genuine inculturation. In light of John Paul's empowering message that finds its foundation in *Sacrosanctum Concilium*[2] (*SC*), how has the official Church in Australia engaged with its indigenous peoples to inculturate aspects of traditional aboriginal ceremony into Australian Catholic worship? This paper will draw on two very different responses to such an engagement and suggest some ways forward.

1. The text of the address can be found in *Reconciling our Differences*, edited by Frank Brennan, (Melbourne: David Lovell Publishing, 1992), 93–101.
2. The translation is from the text on the official Vatican website <http://www.vatican.va/archive/hist_councils/ii_vatican_council/documents/vat-ii_const_19631204_sacrosanctum-concilium_en.html>. Accessed 19 January 2013. All subsequent quotations from the Sacred Constitution are from this site.

Liturgical Inculturation

SC set a path forward for inculturation in the liturgy by providing 'Norms for adapting the liturgy to the culture and traditions of peoples' (37–40)[3]. *SC* 37 states that 'even in the liturgy, the Church has no wish to impose a rigid uniformity in matters which do not implicate the faith or the good of the whole community; rather does she respect and foster the genius and talents of the various races and peoples.' The Church envisages the possibility of welcoming elements from 'these peoples' way of life . . . into the liturgy itself, as long as they harmonise with its true and authentic spirit.' John Paul II's words in Alice Springs (hereafter Address) further acknowledge that 'the gospel speaks all languages' and his invitation to 'take this gospel into your own language and way of speaking' seems to echo the intention of the Council Fathers to engage the Roman rite with the richness and diversity of all peoples.

Australian Aborigines and Torres Strait Islanders (ATSI) are the First Peoples and Nations of Australia—'the oldest continuing cultures in human history'.[4] Just how long ATSI have inhabited Australia is not known. There is scientific evidence to suggest that humans have lived on this large southern landmass for at least 40,000 years, but they could have migrated here as long as 60,000 years ago.[5] While many tribes no longer exist and others have become displaced from their 'country' of origin—the area of their birth, some aboriginal communities have remained relatively traditional, especially in the remote northern and central parts of the continent. From the two hundred

---

3. 'Certain principles expressed in general terms in those articles are explained more precisely, the directives are set out in a more appropriate way and the order to be followed is clearly set out, so that in future this will be considered the only correct procedure.' With the *Fourth Instruction for the Right Application of the Conciliar Constitution on the Liturgy* (Ns. 37–40) the Congregation for Divine Worship and the Discipline of the Sacraments on 29 March 1994, N. 3, continued to apply these principles.
4. Kevin Rudd, 'Apology to Australia's Indigenous Peoples, 13th of February 2008', <http://www.aph.gov.au/house/Rudd_Speech.pdf>. Accessed 20 February 2013.
5. Human origins and antiquity in 'Australia: an historical perspective'. An edited and shortened version of this article was published in Peter Brown, 'Australian Palaeoanthropology', in *History of Physical Anthropology: An Encyclopedia*, 2 volumes edited by Frank Spencer. (New York: Garland Publishing, 1997) 138–145. Available at <http://www-personal.une.edu.au/~pbrown3/AusOrigins.html>. Accessed 20 May 2013.

and fifty original languages that were thought to have been spoken about half are still in existence. Given the rich traditions of this ancient culture compared to the relatively short period of Christianity, it is not surprising that John Paul II could implore: 'Why should you not be allowed the happiness of being with God and each other in Aboriginal fashion?'

John Paul II invited indigenous Christians to make their contribution to the life of and within the Church in Australia. He also invited a corresponding response from the local Church to 'joyfully receive' the contributions of indigenous Christians, especially within the liturgy. Anscar Chupungco (1939–2013)—considered by many to have made the greatest contribution in developing an understanding of liturgy and culture in post-conciliar times—describes inculturation as a necessary and indispensable process by which the gospel of Jesus Christ and the local culture (in which the Church lives) enjoy a mutual and life-giving relationship.[6] He identified three foundational elements within the process of inculturation: a dialogue between Christianity and culture, 'the integration of pertinent cultural elements' and 'the dynamic of transculturation, whereby the parties involved retain their identity in the process of interaction and integration'.[7]

The unexpected proposal of John Paul II in his Address can be seen to be an example of 'the dynamic of transculturation' which is further explained by Chupungco:

> inculturation fosters mutual enrichment. Culture is evangelised when it comes in contact with the gospel message that the church proclaims during worship . . . In turn, however, Christian worship is enriched by the culture it embraces, as the liturgies of the Eastern and Western Churches attest.[8]

6. Anscar Chupungco suggests 'inculturation' is a theological term that has had a relatively short life span within contemporary theological discourse appearing as recently as the early 1960s cf Anscar Chupungco, 'Liturgy and Inculturation', in Fundamental Liturgy, volume 2 of *Handbook for Liturgical Studies,* edited by Anscar Chupungco (Collegeville, MN: Liturgical Press, 1998), 337ff.
7. Chupungco, 'Fundamental Liturgy', 339.
8. Anscar Chupungco, 'Mission and Inculturation: East Asia and the Pacific', in *The Oxford History of Christian Worship*, edited by Geoffrey Wainwright and Karen Westerfield Tucker (New York: Oxford University Press, 2006), 661.

John Paul II clearly goes beyond the provisions of *SC* when he invites ATSI Christians to 'seek out the best things of your traditional ways . . . (and) make your best contribution to all your brothers and sisters in this great nation. You are part of Australia and Australia is part of you'. While *SC* proposes a vision whereby the liturgy is adapted to the local culture and is celebrated by a local assembly, John Paul II proposes that an inculturated liturgy flow over into regular celebration of liturgy in Australian parishes and this is to be 'joyfully received' by non-indigenous Australian Christians. The very process proposes the renewal and transformation of the Church itself as it celebrates the liturgy— this is integral to the process of inculturation.

The Smoking Ceremony

One example of a liturgy that attempted to engage local culture was the Mass to beatify Mary MacKillop presided over by John Paul II in Sydney, Australia, in 1995. The committee charged with preparing the liturgy determined a set of principles to govern all decision making concerning the Mass. Hospitality has long been cherished in the Christian tradition, so they identified that 'the ceremony be inclusive of all Australians' and that it 'particularly highlight the poor and the marginalised'.[9] Since European settlement a shameful history of abuse and the disempowerment of many indigenous Australian has resulted in their being counted among the poor and marginalised. The methodology of the liturgy committee was clear: dialogue with a group of aboriginal people to determine what would be an appropriate cultural inclusion for such a national celebration, and allow aboriginal people to have the 'first' and 'last word'.[10]

After many, many hours of dialogue between liturgists and the aboriginal elders it was decided that a smoking ceremony would be integrated into the Roman rite. As the introduction to the 'Missal' that was prepared for the occasion by the Vatican stated:

> The smoking ceremony replaces the incensation at the beginning of Mass. This is used widely among the Ab-

9. Principles for the Beatification Rite of Mary MacKillop, (Sydney Australia January 1995). (Unpublished paper).
10. An aboriginal elder welcomed John Paul II to Australia at the beginning of the Mass, and an aboriginal deacon pronounced the final dismissal.

> origines around Australia as a rite of purification and wholeness; it has been included in Christian ritual and is well-received by the most devout Catholic Aboriginals. Green gum leaves are placed on the fire and participants walk through the smoke, washing the 'smoke' over their faces with their hands.[11]

The rubrics printed in the 'Missal' leave no doubt that this ritual was considered part of the opening rites and replaced the incensation.

> While the Holy Father and ministers proceed to the altar, the entrance hymn is sung.
>
> Aboriginal elders prepare the smoke through which the procession passes. The Holy Father, after passing by the smoke, moves to reverence the altar and then moves to the chair. The altar is then reverenced with smoke.[12]

As the ministers, including John Paul II, were 'smoked', more than sixty aboriginal people moved amongst the many tens of thousands of members of the assembly. No thurible or other form of incensing was used during this solemn celebration.

Since that time a smoking ceremony usually accompanies major celebrations in Australia, but rarely if ever is part of a liturgical celebration for various reasons.[13] One exception was the opening of St John the Baptist church in Woy Woy, New South Wales. The rite of blessing of the church began at the outdoor entrance on a special section of ground that had been left bare for a smoking ceremony to be performed by local aboriginal people. This space continues to be set aside as a place for smoking on significant occasions, and also for the annual new fire at the celebration of the Easter Triduum.

---

11. *Liturgical Celebrations Presided over by His Holiness Pope John Paul II* (Vatican City: Typis Vaticano, 1995), 11.
12. *Liturgical Celebrations*, 131.
13. These reasons might include the fact that for a smoking ceremony to be included an aboriginal person must perform the rite. Liturgy teams do not always take the time to recognised the need to include ATSI peoples in the liturgy.

Water Ritual

SC 40 acknowledges that for some regions and peoples it will be necessary for the bishops' conferences to propose 'an even more radical adaptation of the liturgy'.

One such radical adaptation has been the experimental use of the *Missa Kimberley* in remote communities of Aboriginal peoples. While this has never been formally approved and is rarely used except among particular aboriginal Catholic communities, it is important to include it in this discussion. The *Missa Kimberley* follows the structure of the Roman Rite but is sung in local language with a melody that is familiar to the local communities.[14] One element of the Opening Rite is the water ritual. The blessed water, held in a coolamon,[15] is liberally sprinkled on each member of the assembly with a branch from a local tree. This ritual takes some time, but as each is blessed with the sign of the cross it offers a strong sense of belonging and of hospitality. A hymn of praise accompanies the ritual. But the deep significance of this water ritual and its origin has a much longer history.

For thousands of years it was customary in desert communities for the women to leave their community and journey through the parched land of their country in search of water for their families. Before setting out they always sang to the spirits of the past inhabitants to help them find the living water. Other indicators helped as well: flocks of birds or other animals indicated where water might be found. When at last they were successful in finding the precious life source, the women first sprinkled the water on their bodies while singing in gratitude to the spirits and then collected the water in their coolamons to share with their community. The *asperges*—an element of our Roman Rite—is not dissimilar to the water ritual of the aboriginal desert women.

14. Father Kevin McKelson, known as Japulu to his friends and congregation, ministered for fifty-two years in the west Kimberley community. He learnt five indigenous languages around Bidyandanga and translated religious texts, including the Missa Kimberley.

15. A coolamon is an Indigenous Australian carrying vessel. It is a multi-purpose shallow vessel, or dish with curved sides, ranging in length from 30–70 cm, and similar in shape to a canoe. Coolamons were traditionally used by Aboriginal women to carry water, fruits, nuts, as well as to cradle babies.

SC 37–40 recognised that the liturgy needed to be adapted to the cultural genius and include the gifts of the Christian people who were celebrating the Paschal Mystery. Earlier in *SC*, the competent authorities with responsibility for the liturgy were urged to play their part: the local bishop, the conference of bishops and the Apostolic See (*SC* 22). We may ask: how have the provisions of *SC* 37–39 and of *SC* 40—where a radical adaptation of the liturgy is needed for ATSI peoples—been implemented by the Australian Catholic Bishops Conference (ACBC)? How have the provisions for the adaptation of the liturgy in the many other articles of *SC*, and in liturgical books, been explored by the local bishops to honour John Paul II's challenge for the Church to joyfully receive the contributions of indigenous Australians?

Celebrating National Aboriginal and Torres Strait Islander Sunday in the Australian Catholic Church

Ten years after the 1986 visit of John Paul II the ACBC designated the first Sunday in July as 'National Aboriginal and Torres Strait Islander Sunday' and added it to the Australian liturgical calendar.[16] This commemoration was proposed by the National Aboriginal and Torres Strait Islander Catholic Council (NATSICC) in November 1995.[17] While this is an important Sunday for the Catholic Church in Australia it is especially so for ATSI Catholics.

As an official commemoration in the liturgical calendar NATSI Sunday is to be celebrated in all parishes within local dioceses throughout Australia. But is this so? Informal conversations with a small and random selection of Catholics and Catholic pastors around the nation suggest wide variances in this annual commemoration. Some parishes prepare well for this Sunday liturgy. Many parishes may mention it in their newsletter, and/or in the words of introduction to the liturgy spoken by a welcomer or the presiding minister, and/or in a petition within the General Intercessions. Some parishes, it seems, ignore this commemoration altogether.

16. Australian Catholic Bishops Conference, The Celebration of Eucharist and the Liturgy of the Hours for the Dioceses of Australia and New Zealand following the *General Roman Calendar: Ordo 2013* (Brisbane: LiturgyBrisbane, 2012), 133.
17. Elizabeth Delaney, Australian Catholic Bishops Conference, email message to author, 16 February 2010.

One barrier to this as a national celebration might be the chosen date because the first Sunday of July falls during the mid-year school holidays. Informal conversations with Aboriginal elders about the best approach to the timing of this celebration may be summarised as follows: 'It may make sense to wait until the school community has returned. Any Sunday in July is appropriate. Then your parish celebration of Aboriginal and Torres Strait Islander Sunday will flow into the week when the children are back. What matters most is that this Sunday is **commemorated** . . .'

National Aboriginal and Torres Strait Islander Sunday

So what is the aim of this Sunday? According to its website, NATSICC views this annual commemoration as a celebration of the gifts that ATSI people bring to the life of the Australian Catholic Church.[18] An annual 'Resource kit' that includes 'Liturgy Resources' is produced for parishes and schools by NATSICC with participation from members of the Bishops Commission for Relations with Aborigines and Torres Strait Islanders and the Bishops Commission for Liturgy, especially the National Office for Liturgy.[19]

What follows is a summary of nine annual 'Liturgy Resources' from 2003 to 2011.[20] It broadly describes the content, structure and materials contained within the resource over the last decade and asks: What is the same each year? What is different? How has it evolved? The many suggested adaptations of liturgical objects, gestures and processions which remain constant over that period are noted. At the same time, observations of the resources based on the norms for celebration of the liturgy are made.

---

18. NATSICC Liturgy resources, <http://www.natsicc.org.au/resources/liturgy>. Accessed 20 February 2013.
19. This is mailed out to parishes across the nation and also sent electronically.
20. The resources for 2012, and continued in 2013, mark a major change in the liturgical resources, as will become apparent later in the paper, and so need to be commented on separately.

Resources for NATSICC Sunday

Elements that remain the same:

- A one-page document located at the beginning with images of the Aboriginal flag, the Torres Strait Islands flag and the NATSICC logo[21] designed by Mrs Olive Boddington from Western Australia;[22]
- Images ranging from selections of Kimberley clipart to a painting from an indigenous artist;
- A heading page close to the start of the Liturgy Resources identifies the Sunday of the liturgical year (for example, Thirteenth Sunday in Ordinary Time C) and gives the theme or the title.[23] This is in addition to the name of this special commemoration, 'Aboriginal and Torres Strait Islander Sunday';
- Letters addressed to parishes from various leaders involved with the annual celebration: the President of Australian Catholic Bishops Conference, the Chairman of the Bishops Commission for Relations with Aborigines and Torres Strait Islanders, the NATSICC Chairperson, the NATSICC Liturgy Team and the Executive Secretary of the Bishops Commission for Liturgy.[24]

---

21. The description of the logo is as follows: 'The NATSICC Logo depicts a willy willy, the wind force in the centre a symbol of God's Spirit. The round concentric circles at the top symbolise God and Life, the base depicts men and women receiving the Holy Spirit.'
22. NATSICC 2009 Liturgy Resource, NATSICC South Australia, 12.
23. Between 2003-2011, these have been as follows: 2003 The time for rebirth is now; 2004 'Go Forth on a Strong Faith Journey': Shepherd-Rejoice-Hope-Peace; 2005 Come—Listen—Live: Share the Bread of Life Together; 2006 Gathering Together in Faith: Sharing God's Love; 2007 Love one another as I Love You; 2008 Celebrate the Living Spirit; 2009 Spirit of our Ancestors; 2010 Justice and Peace for all; 2011 'Come to me, all you who are weary and are burdened'.
24. One of the writers and sometimes several of the writers describes the history behind the title/theme of the Sunday and offers a perspective for the consideration of the preparation team. The message from each leader or team is different year after year and reflects a wide variety of perspectives. Some striking examples of particular emphases over the last decade have included: John Paul II's Address in 1986 and his post-Synodal 'Ecclesia in Oceania'; the link between worship and justice for all, especially for indigenous Australians;

Within the 'introductory message' from the NATSICC Liturgy Team, one portion has remained standard over this nine-year period, even though it has sometimes been expressed in other wording. The text from the 2003 Liturgy Resource, entitled 'The Time for Rebirth is Now', serves as the clearest example:

> The liturgy group strongly urges that protocol and practice of both local and indigenous community and Christian traditions be respected.
>
> Where possible it is important to seek and invite local ATSI peoples to participate in the preparation of the liturgy. This practical process is critical to the nurturing of the deep rooted significance of appropriate symbol and prayer; and ensures respect for and enhanced sacredness of ritual and ceremony according to both local community and Christian traditions.
>
> If non-indigenous people are the only participants in the preparation of liturgy for NATSI Sunday we encourage the use of suggested prayers prepared by the NATSICC liturgy team.

What is occurring here? The parish liturgy preparation team is encouraged to 'seek and invite local' First Australians to be part of the preparation of the celebration of NATSI Sunday, alongside others in the parish. The resources stress deepening awareness, walking with one another and growing in unity. There is strong emphasis on learning, understanding and cooperating with protocols and norms of *both* the local indigenous community and the liturgy (as is found in the ritual books and as may have been determined by the local bishop and/or the episcopal conference). This echoes very strongly *SC* 37.

---

respecting indigenous spirituality; commemorations of historical events such as the fortieth anniversary of the 1967 Referendum that included Australian indigenous peoples in the Census and gave them the right to vote; the Australian Reconciliation Convention in 1997; naming injustices in the areas of indigenous health, education, and living standards; remembering movements within the international community such as the International Decade for a Culture of Peace and World Youth Day; and significant events in Australian society such as the 2008 Federal Apology to the Stolen Generations and their families.

Liturgical Texts

In the 2003 Liturgy Resource the presence of only non-indigenous people in the preparation of the liturgy is acknowledged as a possibility, and, if this is the local reality, encouragement is given to pray the prayers prepared by the NATSICC liturgy team. In the same resource, all the suggested texts are inclusive of everyone in the assembly, indigenous and non-indigenous alike, with the exception of the Closing Prayer (the Prayer after Communion).

There are two recommendations. The first is to be prayed only by an indigenous reader who is present:

> Father of all,
> you gave us the Dreaming.
> You have spoken to us through our beliefs.
> You then made your love clear to us in the person of Jesus.
> We thank you for your care.
> You own us,
> you are our hope.
> Make us grow strong as we face the problems of change.
> We ask you to help the people of Australia to listen to us and respect our culture. Make the knowledge of you grow strong in all people,
> so that you can be at home in us
> and we can make a home for everyone in our land.
> Amen.[25]

The second is an Alternative Prayer to be prayed by a non-indigenous person or an indigenous person:

> God of love,
> You are the Creator of this land and all good things.
> Our hope is in you because you gave your Son Jesus
> to reconcile the world to you.
> We pray for your strength and grace to forgive,

25. This prayer was prepared by Aboriginal people on the occasion of John Paul II's visit to Alice Springs in 1986.

accept one another,
as you love us and forgive and accept us in the sacrifice
of your Son.[26]

Both suggestions are problematic because the Prayer after Communion is prayed only by the priest as the setting is the Sunday Eucharist (GIRM 165). Given the fact that there are no indigenous priests in Australia the only assumption that can be made is that these prayers would be in addition to the Ordinary Prayer of the Sunday.

In the following year, within the 2004 Liturgy Resources, entitled 'Go Forth on a Strong Faith Journey: Shepherd-Rejoice-Hope-Peace', there are extensive additions to the rubrics with other texts provided. Those preparing the liturgy are encouraged to choose prayers for the local parish on the basis of 'Congregations with indigenous people present' or 'Non-indigenous congregations'. The new texts provided are:

- A Rite of Water Blessing (replacing the Penitential Rite)[27]
- Opening Prayer
- Aboriginal Our Father[28]
- Closing Prayer.

These remain in place as options within this special Sunday liturgy up to the present.

26. This prayer was prepared by Wontulp Bi-Buya Indigenous Theology Working Group. This alternative text in the 2003 Liturgy Resource was adapted from a longer prayer for National Aboriginal Sunday by the same Indigenous Theology working group and on a Queensland Churches Together (QCT) 'Prayercard' (Queensland Churches Together 'Prayercard', Milton BC, Brisbane, no date published). The date for the longer text is 13 March 1997 which was also the first year the Australian Catholic Bishops Conference mandated the celebration of National Aboriginal and Torres Strait Islander Sunday. In Brisbane, the Prayercard was published by QCT, which is the formal ecumenical body involving thirteen churches and Christian organizations in Queensland.
27. Water is of ceremonial significance and is used ritually in many aboriginal communities.
28. The Aboriginal Our Father (that is always sung) was written for Missa Kimberley <http://www.aboriginal.sydneycatholic.org/images/pdf/Aboriginal%20OUR%20Father.pdf>. Accessed 25 April 2013.

Introductory Rites

In the 2008 Liturgy Resources, entitled 'Celebrate the Living Spirit', there is a suggested text for acknowledgement of country and the traditional custodians and ancestors of the land. This is the first time this appears with the Liturgy Resources.

Within the 2009 Liturgy Resources, entitled 'Spirit of our Ancestors', there are several other suggestions for elements of the Introductory Rites that were made for the first time:

- Either 'A Welcome to Country by an Aboriginal Elder' or an 'Alternate Acknowledgement of Country by the Celebrant';[29]
- A welcome given to the gathered congregation intentionally connecting ATSI Sunday to the start of NAIDOC Week;[30]
- A rite of smoking (with texts for congregations with indigenous people present and for congregations with no indigenous people present);
- The playing of a didgeridoo[31] to accompany the Entrance Procession and the Recessional Procession;
- Aboriginal elders joining the Recessional Procession.

These suggestions remain within the 2010 and the 2011 Liturgy Resources. Further examples of inculturation have now been added to the previous suggestions of a water blessing and alternate prayers. These include the use of the didgeridoo. The smoking rite is a significant addition and is possibly the most innovative of the suggestions to date.

---

29. NATSICC, 2009 Liturgy Resources: Spirit of our Ancestors, 4.
30. In the 2008 Liturgy Resources, entitled 'Celebrate the Living Spirit', 3, Elsie Heiss, NATSICC Chairperson, wrote in her message: 'Aboriginal and Torres Strait Islander Sunday is one of our main celebrations of the year, where Australians come together in the church to celebrate with Aboriginal and Torres Strait Islander peoples. The first Sunday in July should not be confused with NAIDOC. This is a special liturgy prepared especially for Aboriginal and Torres Strait Islander Sunday, by our NATSICC liturgical team.'
31. A distinctive instrument that is traditional to some aboriginal communities and has become identified as a unique component of Australian music.

The Liturgy of the Word

The celebration of NATSI Sunday falls on a particular Sunday of the Liturgical Year in Ordinary Time. The texts for the Liturgy of the Word are the lectionary readings for the Sunday. There are no special scriptural texts assigned for this annual commemoration. Suggested additions to other elements of the Liturgy of the Word include:

Procession of the Book of the Gospel	From 2004 onwards, a suggestion is made of a procession of the Book of the Gospels that can be accompanied by an aboriginal message stick. 'A message stick could be carried forward with the Gospel. There are other symbolic actions that can be used according to local tradition and need to be discussed according to local practice. (The most important factor is to maintain the sacred tradition of the symbolism).'[32]
Homily Notes	Within the Resources, homily notes and reflection/reference material were prepared for 2003-2007 and 2010-2011. Each of these was written by an Australian bishop (from the Dioceses of Rockhampton and Townsville in Queensland, Broome in the Western Australia and Sale in Victoria); with one exception —one commentary was written by Peter Smith, a former NATSICC Chairman.
Prayer of the Faithful	Each year there are suggested texts for the Prayer of the Faithful. The petitions over this nine-year period are for various groups and people. The series of intentions provided in the resource does not always follow the order given in GIRM 70.[33] In addition, there are many different variations to the endings of the petitions from year to year that are not the familiar supplications at the end of each petition prayed in many Australian parishes.[34] The suggestions seem to assume that they would replace the parish prayers, rather than supplement locally-composed petitions.

32. NATSICC, 2004 Liturgy Resources, 6. In the 2004 resource, there is an addition of a Message Stick Activity designed for upper primary students. It is suggested that this completed 'Message Stick' 'may be given as a gift to Parishioners on their way out of the Church or distributed to students at a school Mass.'

33. '(a) for the needs of the church; (b) for public authorities and the salvation of the whole world; (c) for those burdened by any kind of difficulty; (d) for the local community.'

The Liturgy of the Eucharist

Over the nine years of resources considered, there is a consistent rubric regarding the 'Offertory Procession': 'In some areas the coolamon is used to carry the bread to the altar. In the absence of Indigenous people participating in the celebration, the coolamon can be placed on the altar as a symbol of the non-presence of Indigenous brothers and sisters at the table.'[35] The Resources after 2011 change this rubric to: '. . . the coolamon can be placed in front of the altar.'

The first part of this rubric is practical since the bread—which will soon become the Body of Christ—needs to be presented from the people in a worthy vessel. However, the second part of the rubric is not part of our eucharistic custom or practice. The Roman ritual never assumes that empty eucharistic vessels (including patens, communion plates and chalices) of any kind are placed on the altar or in front of the altar at the beginning of the Liturgy of the Eucharist, unless they are to be used in the ceremony. Additional gifts that have traditionally accompanied the bread and wine are 'to relieve the needs of the Church and of the poor'(GIRM 140). It is surprising that this ancient eucharistic practice is omitted as a suggestion on this Sunday.

Within the 2004 Resource and all subsequent years, there is a further unhelpful addition to this rubric. It is suggested that 'alternative Aboriginal gifts (a boomerang, woomera, Aboriginal painting)' be placed in front of the altar to signify the absence of Indigenous people at this eucharist.[36] Once again, there is no provision for anything like this at this part of the Sunday eucharist, but it could be included in the Opening Rite of the Mass, or such objects could be displayed in the foyer of the worship space, or some other suitable place.

---

34. 2003: Lord hear us—Lord hear my prayer; 2004: Lord hear us—Lord hear my prayer; 2005/6: Father you are good—Lord fill our hearts with love and Compassion; 2007: In love and trust—Lord hear my prayer; 2008: We seek the power of the Spirit—Lord hear my prayer; 2009: (all) We listen and pray the Holy Spirit is with us; 2010: (all) We pray for peace and justice for all; 2011: (all) We pray for all who are weary and burdened.
35. NATSICC, 2003 Liturgy Resources: The time for Rebirth is now, 4.
36. NATSICC, 2004 Liturgy Resources: 'Go Forth on a Strong Faith Journey' Shepherd-Rejoice-Hope-Peace, 9.

While the 2012 and 2013 resources have not been included in this study, it is interesting to note that they present a change in terms of the general flavour of the resources. A clear distinction is now made between what is possible during the liturgy and what must remain outside. For example, the 2013 resource states that 'The (water ritual and smoking) ceremonies can be used prior to or following Mass or, where appropriate, during other gatherings to celebrate Aboriginal and Torres Strait Islander Sunday'. In other words, two possible rituals of liturgical inculturation that were sanctioned by John Paul II in papal liturgies in 1995 have now been removed from the liturgy.

The Liturgical Inculturation of National Aboriginal and Torres Strait Islander Sunday: Questions and Possibilities

This annual commemoration—more or less successfully—acknowledges and celebrates the gifts that Aboriginal and Torres Strait Islander people bring to the life of the Australian Catholic Church. However, surely the celebration of the liturgy—especially the Sunday eucharist—is more than this? It seems that the affirming words of John Paul II to ATSI peoples: 'Jesus calls you to accept his words and values into your own culture. To develop in this way will make you more than ever truly Aboriginal' speak powerfully of the rich contribution of ATSI peoples to our Catholic culture. The Australian Church cannot become the Church 'that Jesus wants us to be' until it includes a joyful giving and receiving of Australian indigenous stories and symbols, music, gestures and words within the celebration of the Sunday liturgy itself to help all to understand what it means to be Church in Australia. The liturgical assembly is the subject of the liturgical action which celebrates the Paschal Mystery (SC 2, 6, 7, 10) incarnate in this time and place.

Almost twenty years ago, Tom Elich suggested a two-step process to liturgical inculturation in Australia.[37] He argues that firstly, understanding is needed about how an aboriginal symbol works and its range of meanings in an indigenous context. One symbol which is part of the everyday life of many indigenous peoples can have multiple meanings across the length and breadth of this continent. This

37. Tom Elich, 'Aboriginal Culture and Liturgy', in *Liturgy News*, 24/4 (1994): 2.

would suggest that extensive dialogue is called for. Secondly there is a need to determine where some kind of correspondence might occur with comparable liturgical gestures and symbols. How might indigenous rituals and symbols be incorporated into Christian ritual? For example: what is a message stick? What is its function? How is it suitable for liturgical use?

A review of the annual Liturgical Resources from 2003–2011 for this Sunday suggests that there have been many purposes for the material sent to parishes: educational, awareness-raising and liturgical. Completely omitted from these resources is any reference to inculturation in remote Australian indigenous communities. The liturgical parts of the Resource suggest the use of aboriginal symbols that are potentially liturgical: water rites, smoking rites, playing the didgeridoo, the coolamon and message sticks.

If we follow Elich's suggestion then necessary and critical questions must be asked of these symbols, especially in light of the disturbing fact that since 2012 a water rite and other ceremonial rituals are now deemed to be excluded from the liturgy. This seems to be a significant retrograde step that contradicts both John Paul's words and SC 37–40. Questions include: What is the symbolism of a rite of water blessing? Is the same meaning experienced for all indigenous peoples of Australia? What is the symbolism of a smoking ritual? Is it experienced as purification for all Australian indigenous peoples? Are message sticks common across indigenous communities? Is the use of the didgeridoo part of the musical heritage across the many indigenous cultures of Australia and the Torres Strait? What is the symbolism of using the coolamon as a vessel for carrying? And with these varying meanings might it still be possible, with sufficient dialogue, to include appropriate rituals in the Roman rite?[38]

38. The use and meaning of the smoking ceremony can vary amongst aboriginal communities. It is important to note that the inclusion of this ceremony at the papal Mass received no recorded criticism by aboriginal Catholics. Perhaps this was the case because the group of aboriginal people ensured that communities from all over Australia were included in the rite. Whether the smoking ceremony continues to replace incensation at significant Australian Catholic liturgy, or whether it replaces a penitential rite is a conversation that needs to continue between liturgists and aboriginal ceremony leaders.

A Way Forward

How might the annual resource for NATSI Sunday make a different contribution to the broad vision of SC and genuine liturgical inculturation in Australia? We propose a modest suggestion. What if we were to take the requirements of *SC* 37–40 and devote the entire resource for a particular year to one item: the coolamon or the water ritual, for example? The resource would explore the following questions: Who uses it? What is it used for? What areas or groups does it come from? How is it used? When is it used? What does the coolamon and its use mean? Are there variations from one people to another? What connections can be established with the Roman Rite? Where and how might it be used as a ritual object? In the following years, the resource would then explore 'the use of oil and perfumes, the use of colours and body marking, the use of fire or water or ash'.[39] Over a decade or more, we would then end up with a rich resource for the process of inculturation. This process itself would be an exchange of gifts between indigenous peoples and non-indigenous peoples. It would also be an exchange of gifts between First Australians and those who have come to the land of Australia in more recent times.

Such an exchange of gifts would encourage the 'Church herself in Australia' to become a little more readily 'the Church that Jesus wants her to be' since Australian indigenous people 'have made their contribution to her life and . . . that contribution has been joyfully received by others'.

39. Elich, 'Aboriginal Culture and Liturgy', 2.

Towards Inculturation: Traditional Seasonal Rites in Indonesia

Bernardus Boli Ujan

The area to be addressed in this paper is the section of *Sacrosanctum Concilium*[1] (*SC*) entitled: 'Norms for adapting the Liturgy to the culture and traditions of peoples', *SC* 37–40. The Second Vatican Council used the term 'adaptation' six times in this four-paragraph section that offers pastoral-liturgical norms for making liturgy suitable to the genuine culture of the local faithful. Since Vatican II 'liturgical inculturation' has been much discussed. Anscar J Chupungco—internationally known for his writings on liturgical enculturation—describes inculturation in liturgy as the process of a pre-Christian rite being reinterpreted or reformed and celebrated as a Christian rite.[2] The modification of received traditions of worship helps people of a particular culture enter into the liturgy in a 'full, conscious, and active' way.

The term 'inculturation' was used first in adjectival form by Joseph Masson in 1962,[3] then as a noun by Melville Herskovits in the nineteen seventies and GL Barney in 1973, though when speaking about missiology and theology rather than liturgy.[4] In 1979

1. The translation is from the text on the official Vatican website <http://www.vatican.va/archive/hist_councils/ii_vatican_council/documents/vat-ii_const_19631204_sacrosanctum-concilium_en.html>. Accessed 19 January 2013. All subsequent quotations from the Sacred Constitution are from this site.
2. Anscar J. Chupungco, *Liturgical Inculturation, Sacramentals, Religiosity, and Catechesis* (Collegeville, MN: Liturgical Press, 1992), 29–30.
3. Joseph Masson, 'L'église ouverte sur le monde' in *Nouvelle Revue Théologique*. 84 (1962):1038, referred by A. Sorter, *Towards a Theology of Inculturation* (Maryknoll: Orbis Books, 1988), 10.
4. G Barney, 'The Supracultural and the Church: Implications for Frontier Missions', in *The Gospel and Frontier Peoples* (Pasadena: William Carey Library,

Cypriano Valenziano used the term inculturation when he described the relationship between liturgy and popular piety. He said that inculturation is a way that makes possible the mutual interaction between liturgy and all kinds of popular religiosity.[5] While the term 'inculturation' is a relatively recent one not directly found in any of the documents of Vatican II, Chupugnco believes that Vatican II provided the theological starting point for enculturation, not as a concession but as 'an incarnational imperative'.[6]

The Council Fathers acknowledged and recognised the variety of cultures that gather to worship.

> Even in the liturgy, the Church has no wish to impose a rigid uniformity in matters which do not implicate the faith or the good of the whole community; rather does she respect and foster the genius and talents of the various races and peoples. Anything in these peoples' way of life which is not indissolubly bound up with superstition and error she studies with sympathy and, if possible, preserves intact. Sometimes in fact she admits such things into the liturgy itself, so long as they harmonize with its true and authentic spirit (*SC* 37).

With the primary aim to ensure 'full, conscious and active participation' the Fathers not only recognised the diversity of particular Churches and their way of life, but opened the way for local practices to be included in liturgical celebrations.

One particular Church, the local faithful in East-Flores and Solor Island, Indonesia has been actively involved in the process of adapting and inculturating its liturgical celebrations since the Coun-

---

1973); GD Napoli, 'Inculturation as Communication', in *Inculturation* 9 (1987): 71–98; Anscar J Chupungco, *Liturgical Inculturation: Sacramentals, Religiosity, and Catechesis*, 25.

5. Cypriano Valenziano, 'La religiosita Popolare in Prospettiva Antropologica', in *Ricerche sulla Religiosita Popolare,* Bologna (1979): 83–110.
6. Anscar Chupungco, *Cultural Adaptation of the Liturgy* (New York: Paulist Press, 1982), 62; quoted in Peter C. Phan, *Being Religious Interreligiously Asian Perspective on Interfaith Dialogue* (Maryknoll: Orbis Books, 2004), 233. In this chapter entitled, 'Liturgical Enculturation' Phan provides a useful summary of Chupungco's theory of liturgical enculturation, complete with a comprehensive bibliography.

cil. This paper will study 'with sympathy' the genius and talents of the local *Lamaholot* people and the celebration of traditional seasonal rites with a view to enculturating these rites as part of the Christian liturgical year.

Inculturating The Liturgy In Flores

Flores is an island in south-central Indonesia, next to the island of Timor. With no fewer than 1,548,328 adherents out of a total population of 1,811,874, Catholic Christians form a majority of about eighty-five per cent. There are four dioceses on the island. In west Flores the Diocese of Ruteng has 615,330 baptised persons out of a total population of 637,193.[7] In central Flores the Archdiocese of Ende has 442,446 members and the Diocese of Maumere some 251,778 out of a total population of 856,973.[8] In east Flores the Diocese of Larantuka has 238,463 faithful out of a population of 317,808.[9]

There are five major ethnic groups on the island each with its own ethnic culture, namely *Manggarai, Bajawa-Nagekeo, Ende-Lio, Sikka* and *Lamaholot*. The *Lamaholot* people are located in eastern Flores and also on the smaller nearby islands of Solor, Adonara and Lembata. Each cultural domain has its own seasonal celebrations according to the agricultural and fishery lifecycles, with its own customs expressed in distinct language, symbols and rites. However there are commonalities such as the timing, the meaning of the symbols and the aim of the celebration.

When Catholic missionaries came to the islands they tried to eradicate local cultic practices as they thought that such celebrations were full of *takhyul* (superstition and idolatry). Studies of the local cultures undertaken by the early missionaries aimed to understand how to evangelise the local people so they would, as far as possible, live out their Christian faith according to the incoming Roman Catholic culture rather than in line with local culture. Their studies were directed by negative attitudes towards local cultures as local celebrations and rituals were looked on as idolatrous.

---

7. Departemen Dokumentasi dan Penerangan Konferensi Waligereja Indonesia, Buku Petunjuk Gereja Katolik Indonesia 2005 (Jakarta: Kantor Waligereja, 2005), 215.
8. Departemen Dokumentasi dan Penerangan Konferensi Waligereja Indonesia, 91.
9. Departemen Dokumentasi dan Penerangan Konferensi Waligereja Indonesia, 133.

However in the 1940s and 50s a shift is observable in the aim of ethnographic research by some missionaries, particularly in Manggarai, west Flores. One prominent example is that of the late Willem van Bekkum SVD of Ruteng. Living closely with the local people while studying their culture, including their traditional rites, he understood that local celebrations contained many positive elements which were in no way contrary to Christian values or to the faith which is celebrated throughout the liturgical cycle. In the 1950s Van Bekkum introduced offertory processions with dancing in his 'Water Buffalo Mass' (*misa kaba*). Van Bekkum had long pioneered the use of local melodies in his hymn and prayer book *Dere Serani* where the earliest hymns date from 1937; in 1998 the tenth reprint contained 220 hymns, many with *Manggarai* motifs, all in the local language.

In 1956 Willem van Bekkum had the opportunity to address the first International Congress on Pastoral Liturgy in Assisi, where he outlined suggested changes to the rite of the Mass.[10] Later, as one of the participants at Vatican Council II, van Bekkum contributed personal and important experiences from outside Europe that convinced many other Council participants to be more open to positive elements in local cultures. It should be noted that each of the concrete suggestions van Bekkum had made some six years previously in Assisi[11] are found in *SC*. *SC* authorised and further encouraged missionaries and local Christian agents to retain positive local customs in liturgical celebrations.[12]

---

10. See John Prior with Eduard Jebarus *et al*, 'Old and New Christianity in the Southeastern Islands', in *A History of Christianity in Indonesia*, edited by Jan Sihar Aritonang and Karel Steenbrink, (Leiden: Koninklijke Brill NV, 2008), 229–344, especially 271: 'The church in Flores made a modest contribution to the Vatican Council (1962–1965)'.
11. Willem van Bekkum, 'The Liturgical Revival in the Service of the Missions', in *The Assisi Papers* (Collegeville MN: Liturgical Press, 1957), 95–112.
12. 'At the end of the century the liturgical adaptations of Van Bekkum in the 1950s had become routine throughout East Nusa Tenggara . . . Gabriel Manek of Ende and Paul Sani (from Flores but bishop of Denpasar, Bali) returned from the council intent on the indonesianisasi of personnel and pastoral approach.' John Prior with Eduard Jebarus *et al*, 'Old and New Christianity in the Southeastern Islands', in *A History of Christianity in Indonesia*, edited by KA Steenbrink and JS Aritonang (Brill E-Book, 2008), 271. <http://ebooks.brillonline.nl/view_pdf?id=nij9789004170261_nij9789004170261_i-1004-54>. Accessed 25 April 2013.

Efforts at adaptation-inculturation have continued to be undertaken widely in Flores since the Council, especially in the celebration of the Eucharist and the sacraments of matrimony and funerals. While these rites remain embedded in Roman Catholic culture, some elements have been adapted to local cultures. Elements that have been incorporated into Christian ritual during traditional annual celebrations include local languages, symbols, songs, music, decoration and liturgical vestments. Christians from Flores continue to follow the local traditional rite but at an appropriate point they celebrate the Eucharist as an integral part of the whole celebration. For example the Eucharist is celebrated in the fields, the presider wears the dress of his tribe, a large cross is placed in the ground, and the fields are blessed. While maintaining the seasonal rite with its local cultural symbols, the Eucharist is inserted into the celebratory program. There are strong parallels between the content of local seasonal celebrations and certain Christian rituals celebrated during the liturgical year. Christians from Flores celebrate annual traditional rituals where both local customs and the Roman culture are apparent.

There are a number of important annual celebrations integrated into the life cycle of the farmers and the fishermen on Flores Island. This paper will pay attention only to the annual agricultural celebrations of the farmers.

Agricultural Cycle In Flores

Flores, like the rest of Indonesia and other islands near the equator, experiences two main seasons—the rainy season which lasts from November to April and the dry season which lasts from May to October. For the people of the *Lamaholot* ethnic group, time not only marks the changing seasons, but also indicates the activities that accompany any given period of the year. The agricultural cycle (*mutatis mutandis*) is as follows:

July to September—Time to clear the garden
October—Time for planting
November to December—Time to clear the grass
April to May—Time for harvest

Months are named according to the working period of farmers.[13] August is called *Beolan* which means the initial period to cultivate dry land. November is the time for planting seeds in the field, so they call this month *Toben Nika* or *Nuba Baken* (to use tools for planting, usually bamboo). January is called *Mepik* (*mepik* means to collect leaves) because at this period the people collect a certain kind of leaf to plait sandals worn during the weeding of the fields during the rainy season. July is the time of thanksgiving for the new harvest. This month sees the climactic celebration of thanksgiving and so the month is called *Berauk* or *Wu'u Nuran* (new harvest).[14]

At certain times of the year the *Lamaholot* ethnic group also engage in specific activities such as making pottery (July to August), salt making (June to July), tapping palm trees (July to August), fishing (May to October) and constructing houses (July to October).

Rituals Accompanying The Working Period Of Farmers

In addition to ordering their activities according to the seasons, the *Lamaholot* believe that time is not only cyclical and spiral but also has a cosmic and existential dimension. The local community marks special activities with ceremonials and rituals.[15] The rituals that follow accompany the working periods of the farmers.[16]

---

13. Yosef Suban Hayon, 'Etika dan Moralitas Lamaholot bagi Pejabat Publik, Belajar dari Tradisi Pembangunan Koko Bale dan Pembukaan Eta (Etan)' in *Sketsa Budaya Lamaholot, Etika & Moralitas Publik,* Konsepsi Kearifan Lokal dalam Pembangunan Daaerah edited by Stanis Soda Herin (Larantuka: Yayasan Cinta Kasih, 2007) 128–129.
14. People in Ngadha, especially in region of Toda, name the months in a similar way. Petrus C Dhogo, *Memahami Religiositas Orang Toda dalam Ritus Su'i Uwi dan Relevansinya bagi Penghayatan yang benar akan Ekaristi sebagai Perayaan Syukur* (Ledalero: Tesis Pasca-sarjana STFK, 2008), 85–86.
15. Philipus Tule, 'Longing for the House of God, Dwelling in the House of the Ancestors', in *Studia Instituti Anthropos*, 50, (Anthropos Institute.V, Sankt Augustin, 2004), 45–46.
16. Yosef Suban Hayon, 'Etika dan Moralitas Lamaholot bagi Pejabat Publik, Belajar dari Tradisi Pembangunan Koko Bale dan Pembukaan Eta (Etan)' in *Sketsa Budaya Lamaholot, Etika & Moralitas Publik,* Konsepsi Kearifan Lokal dalam Pembangunan Daaerah, edited by Stanis Soda Herin, 132–145.

Rituals for preparing the farm—August-October:
In August, *Beolan*, the community arranges rituals to prepare for the cultivation of their fields. During this month they perform the rite *Dulu Elu Kenube* by sharpening the sword on the grindstone. The head of the ethnic group presides over the rite in the sacred clan house. The presider vows to serve others and prays to the owner of the land (the Supreme Being) to protect them in their work.

Rituals for planting seed—November-January:
In November the farmers perform the rite of collecting rice seed, *Maya Hode Besi Pare*. This rite is performed before seed planting. At first the farmers go to the clan house to call for some young women, *Ema Oa*, who represent the rice seed. They bring these young women along to the nearest seashore. There they sit together around a flat stone to pray. The presider asks for the return of the rice seed that had been previously wiped out. Then they return to the village.

Also in the month of November the farmers perform the rite of foreseeing the possibility of the rainy season and the harvest. For this rite the presider cuts in half the liver and bile of an animal, *Belo Wura Bake Mau*, to look for the signs and interpret its meaning. For example if the liver is yellow it means the rain will be enough—no scarcity—and if the bile is full it means there will be a good harvest.

The next rite in November is planting the seed called *Hika Tuba* or *Tuba Mula*. In this rite men make holes in the ground using bamboo sticks while women plant the seed into the holes. The farmers formally offer food to the Supreme Being as a sign of honour in the expectation that the soil is good, the rain sufficient and the harvest abundant. After a meal together, they continue to plant the seed.

From November to March the farmers need to maintain a peaceful atmosphere in the village and in the surrounding environment as they look forward to the harvest of their first fruits. They should not arrange any kind of feasting so as to let the crops grow peacefully. Certain persons such as old and dignified persons, the heads of clan and their wives, and young women representing the rice seed should fast during this time. They should not eat food from the new harvest until the appropriate times according to the rite that allows each category to eat, *Pi'in Wu'u Padan Uran*.

Harvest rituals—March-July:
During July, *Berauk*, the farmers arrange the rite of *Wu'u Nuran* as the climax of their activity as farmers. All the members of the village participate in this feast to give thanks to the Supreme Being and to the ancestors for protecting them during the previous agricultural cycle, for gifting the community a new harvest and prosperity, fraternity and solidarity, good health and peace, life and happiness. Usually there are two kinds of *Wu'u Nuran*—the annual celebration and periodic celebration.

The annual Wu'u Nuran:
On the appointed day, all the members of the village are invited to come, *Golan Mayan*, to the front yard of the traditional house, *Koke Bale*. After being together in the front yard, they listen to the message about being protected, *Lidung Lebe*, and united, *Abo At*, as a community. Then symbolically they shut the gates of the village and all the members of the community are forbidden to go out of the village and others (enemies) cannot enter and damage the village. They believe that those who do not follow this taboo will encounter disaster, even death.

The next rite is the slaughtering of animals for sacrifice. Prayers are said before the animal is slaughtered. At the time of slaughtering, gongs are sounded and drums beaten and all the people shout while a group of dancers perform. After the slaughtering of the animals, the meat is cooked with rice from the new harvest. Before the people eat together, the leader goes round giving food to the land by throwing some pieces of meat and rice and pouring out a little palm wine. Then all members of community receive some of the meat and other foodstuffs. The reception is followed by traditional singing and dancing with the active participation by all, accompanied by gongs and drums.

The periodic Wu'u Nuran:
This kind of celebration is arranged once every three to five years. The decision for this periodic celebration is made during a traditional assembly attended by all the principals of the clans. The need to rebuild the traditional clan house, *Koke Bale*, is one important reason for this periodic celebration. In fact the periodic *Wu'u Nuran* is virtually the

same as the annual one but with some special characteristics as follows:

- The celebration is prepared by repairing or rebuilding the *Koke Bale*, undertaken by the members of the village together.
- After the slaughtering of sacrificial animals, the rite of *Bau Baku* is performed, that is, filling the basket with cooked rice. All the wives of every clan bring cooked rice to the principal house of the clan. There they put the cooked rice in a big basket as their family contribution for all male members in their family (attending the celebration in the village or outside the village). No one should be forgotten. If they forget someone, it means that person has already died. They contribute cooked rice, too, for those who attend the celebration as visitors or outsiders. A smaller basket, *Baliken*, is prepared for them and it is put beside the big basket. When the contribution of cooked rice is completed, they collect all the baskets and put them in a litter or a sedan chair with special ornaments for the procession to the *Koke Bale*, accompanied by dancing and cheerful yells.
- The principals of the clan receive the baskets and place them on a flat stone, *Merik Bledan*. Before the meal, the presider gives food to the land and members of the community receive their portion, in the manner of usual annual festival.
- The *Bau Baku* rite expresses their desire to offer the harvest to the Supreme Being, thanking Him for gifting the good harvest. The rite indicates, too, the farmers' faithfulness to the Mother Land and their unity with Her.

The entire celebration of the periodic *Wu'u Nuran* forms the climax of the annual activities of the farmers, concluding one agricultural cycle, before commencing the next.

Some Observations

The inculturation of the liturgical cycle as celebrated by Christian farmers in Flores has been a long process. Being the majority in the island, Christians have the possibility to further the process of inculturation. There is no strong opposition from other world religions or even by the local people against efforts by Christians to use elements from local cultures in Christian liturgical celebrations. (It might be noted that on occasion strong opposition has been experienced on other islands where Christians are a minority). The leaders of the local Church in Flores have created an atmosphere which is conducive to people's active participation in the process of inculturation.

All the bishops in Flores are native Florenese who know and also live out local customs. Theirs is an important role in making correct and official decisions regarding the process of inculturation in celebrating the liturgical year imbued with Christian spirituality and adapted to local culture. The bishops understand the Christian faith, theology and Christian doctrine, particularly as regards the liturgical year. It is their role to make decisions on important issues for annual celebrations of the faithful in accordance with the agricultural cycle. The most important annual celebration is the thanksgiving harvest festival. Until now these celebrations have been undertaken by some priests in collaboration with the faithful. So far there has been no official decision taken by the bishops of Flores regarding the inculturation of the liturgical year, in particular regarding the harvest festival.

Some positive values expressed by farmers in their life cycle that are compatible with Christian ritual are:

1. Great respect for the land, the owner of the land, the living ancestors and most of all to the Supreme Being as the source of life, maintaining good relationships with all of them. The farmers are aware of the importance of living this respect in their daily life by creating good harmonious relationships with others as a *conditio sine qua non* for success in their work. The spirit of working together, solidarity with others in their extended families and with outsiders, particularly with the needy, is central.

2. The people fast from eating the new harvest until they are allowed to. Abstaining from the first fruits of the new harvest is a very positive aspect, a living out of the Christian spirit of the Lenten fast.
3. All the rituals undertaken by the farmers show that they believe in the Supreme Being as the giver of life, the source of strength to work and the source of every condition needed to have a good harvest for the prosperity of all the members of the clans and villages: soil, rain, seed, fire, wind, sun.
4. The community needs time both to work and to perform the rites (to pray and to bring offering to the Motherland, the ancestors and to the Supreme Being). It is important to do the right work at the proper time. They know the signs of the main seasons which help them to arrange their program of work at the appropriate time in order to succeed. But they are really dependent on the Supreme Being who arranges the seasons.
5. If they are overwhelmed by a natural catastrophe or disaster that damages their crops, land and village, the natives of Flores ask themselves whether they have done something wrong in their relationship with the Supreme Being, the Motherland and with other people. When they discover what went wrong that opened up the possibility for bad spirits to punish them, they arrange a reconciliation ritual to restore a better relationship with the source of life and with others. Such rituals help them to dispel the disaster from their village and their land, calming (cooling) the bad spirits. An adapted catechesis about sin and its personal and social consequence, and reconciliation based on biblical concepts, will bring out a better understanding of the Christian sacrament of reconciliation.[17] Such catechesis will be useful in evaluat-

17. See Boli Ujan Bernardus, *Dosa dan Upacara-upacara Pemulihan Menurut Orang Lembata, Suatu Tinjauan Antropo-religius untuk mengakarkan iman* (Maumere: Praskripsi Filsafat/Teologi, 1976), 30–38, 58–94, especially 6–69; Bernardus Boli

ing critically their concept of the direct connection between sin and disaster.

6. Their sense of being immersed in sacred time along the whole agricultural cycle is a positive concept which helps the people to be aware of the meaning of time as *kairos*, the time of salvation as accomplished in the Jesus Christ event. Therefore their active participation in harmony and collaboration both in hard work and celebratory rituals will help the people to live out the spirituality of the liturgical cycle celebrated in the Liturgy of the Hours and the liturgical year by paying attention to its very core—the Paschal Mystery.

A Way Forward

The annual celebrations are common for farmers on Flores. Christians take part in these traditional rituals primarily because they want to maintain these customs as part of their responsibility as local Florenese farmers. They also participate in the annual Christian celebrations according to the liturgical year (Advent, Christmas, Lent, Easter, Pentecost, and so on). It is important to see whether there is any danger of dualism or syncretism.

Christians may follow these two separate celebratory cycles—cultural and Christian—by paying attention to the main traditional rituals such as *Wu'u Nuran* and at an appropriate time celebrating the Eucharist using genuine elements from the traditional practices which are not contrary to the faith or to liturgical tradition.

The Church needs to integrate not only cultural elements but also the timing of the celebration. Some possibilities include:

- Celebrating Pentecost at harvest festival time, or maintaining the day of Pentecost in the Christian liturgical year while underlining the idea of thanksgiving for the harvest in relation to the first fruits of the act of salvation realised by Jesus Christ—the descent of the Holy Spirit. At the Mass on Pentecost the faithful could

---

Ujan, *Mati Dan Bangkit Lagi: Dosa Dan Ritus-Ritus Pemulihan Menurut Orang Lembata* (Maumere: Penerbit Ledalero, 2012), 71–116.

bring along the first fruits of their harvest to be part of the presentation of the gifts accompanied by singing and dancing to the altar.

- At the beginning of August the local faithful celebrate a Mass which includes the blessing of farmers' utensils. After the homily some representatives of the farmers present the utensils to be blessed.
- In November blessing of seeds after the homily. Before Mass, there could be a procession of farmers' utensils or seeds accompanied by appropriate singing and dancing towards the church or chapel. At the moment of dismissal, the principals of clans would distribute the utensils or the seed to the faithful giving them some messages of wisdom expressed in local language.

We need serious study on the annual celebrations according to the culture of local Christians such as those in Flores followed by workshops that look at possibilities for integrating this traditional cycle into the liturgical year.[18] More than that, the Church should offer an inculturative catechesis regarding the seasonal celebrations of the local farmers to help them better understand and live out the mystery of salvation in their own context.

Conclusion

Every year Asian liturgists, under the patronage of the Asian Catholic Bishops' Conference, gather to discuss liturgical enculturation around a particular topic. At these Forums a statement is produced and given to the bishops to guide National Liturgy Commissions. The thirteenth Asian Liturgy Forum (ALF) in September 2009 at Bahay Pari, Makati City, the Philippines, reflected on the liturgical year. The statement from that gathering acknowledges that the Roman tradition has continued to adapt according to cultures and circumstances:

> The history of the liturgical year shows that the calendar of feasts has been constantly adjusting itself to the political, cultural and religious environment of local Church-

18. *SC* #40.

> es. This should serve as a guiding principle in our work of enculturating the liturgical year.[19]

The statement goes on to indicate liturgical feasts whose symbols do not correspond to the seasons of nature for the particular Churches, for example Christmas and Easter. It recommends that feasts could be instituted from traditional practices and the statement refers to feasts that mark the cycle of human work and have shaped the notion of Rogation and Ember days.

There seems to be every reason why the particular Church in Flores should make efforts to integrate the traditional seasonal rites into the Christian liturgical year. Vatican II made provisions for this to occur and envisaged the possibility of even more radical adaptation. The Council entrusted to local ecclesiastical authorities responsibility to oversee this process and to draw upon experts in these matters.[20] As the delegates of the thirteenth ALF stated:

> Given that time is relative, that situations are provisional, and that culture and traditions are in constant evolution, the Church should continue to revise, reinvent, and create liturgical feasts that meet the actual needs of the faithful.[21]

This concurs with the thought of eminent Asian scholar, Peter C Phan, who believes that success or failure in the process of inculturation has a significant impact on the future of the Church.[22]

---

19. *The Liturgical Year and Inculturation 13th Asian Liturgy Forum* (ALF) South-East Asian Region. September 16–20, 2009 (Edsa, Makiti City: Bahay Pari, San Carlos Pastoral Formation Complex, 2009). <http://pilmalaybalay.wordpress.com/?s=ALF>. Accessed 19 May 13.
20. 'Within the limits set by the typical editions of the liturgical books, it shall be for the competent territorial ecclesiastical authority mentioned in Art. 22, 2, to specify adaptations, especially in the case of the administration of the sacraments, the sacramentals, processions, liturgical language, sacred music, and the arts' *SC* #39. (See also *SC* #40).
21. <http://pilmalaybalay.wordpress.com/?s=ALF>. Accessed 19 May 13.
22. Peter C Phan, In *Our Own Tongues: Asian Perspectives on Mission and Inculturation* (Maryknoll, N.Y: Orbis Books, 2003), xii.

Renegotiating Liturgical Leadership in Diverse Assemblies

Anthony Kain

This chapter focuses on leaders of liturgy who minister within complex communities. It identifies skills and attitudes required to 'do' liturgy in an inclusive way in the varied complexity of multicultural assemblies. In the past liturgical leaders relied on intuition, imaginative guesses or just dealt with things as they arose. This inquiry seeks to make liturgical practice more than just good guess work or intuition and so ensure that competent liturgical ministry is evident in our complex interactions. It will be argued that communication in liturgy is an important factor if the central goal of participation called for by *Sacrosanctum Concilium*[1] (*SC*) is to be achieved.[2]

The Church recognises that liturgy needs to be 'planned' not in a vacuum, but in the context of a particular faith community to ensure full participation.

> This (the celebration of the Paschal Mystery) will best be accomplished if, with due regard for the nature and the particular circumstances of each liturgical assembly, the entire celebration is planned in such a way that it leads to a conscious, active, and full participation of the faithful

1. The translation is from the text on the official Vatican website <http://www.vatican.va/archive/hist_councils/ii_vatican_council/documents/vat-ii_const_19631204_sacrosanctum-concilium_en.html>. Accessed 19 January 2013. All subsequent quotations from the Sacred Constitution are from this site.
2. 'In the restoration and promotion of the sacred liturgy, this full and active participation by all the people is the aim to be considered before all else … and therefore pastors of souls must zealously strive to achieve it, by means of the necessary instruction, in all their pastoral work'. SC #14.

> both in body and in mind, a participation burning with faith, hope, and charity, of the sort which is desired by the Church and demanded by the very nature of the celebration, and to which the Christian people have a right and duty by reason of their Baptism.[3]

Certain factors are to be taken into account to assist with the full and active involvement of worshippers. 'The nature and the particular circumstances of each particular assembly' includes such variables as culture, age, education, socio-economic status, to name but a few. In the words of the Council Fathers, leaders are to 'promote the liturgical instruction of the faithful, and also their active participation in the liturgy both internally and externally, taking into account their age and condition, their way of life, and standard of religious culture' (*SC* 19).Over the decades since the Council communication theory and semiotics[4] have been significantly developed by scholars.[5] This paper will offer some suggestions from such theories that might assist liturgical leaders to better engage with worshippers. But while communication theories help, liturgy is not simply a rational exercise but a matter of faith. A study of Mark's Gospel will also inform the presider to lead worship in a multicultural and diverse assembly.

---

3. *The General Instruction of the Roman Missal*, (Strathfield: St Pauls, 2012), #18.
4. Sciences of communication theory can also assist us as we seek better participation. Contextual theology, issues of identity and social change are addressed by this paper and lead to theories around identity and issues of 'competence/incompetence, anxiety' and 'uncertainty in social change'.
5. See *Handbook of International and Intercultural Communication* edited by William Gudykunst and Bella Mody (Newbury Park, CA: Sage Publications, 2002); Robert Schreiter, *Constructing Local Theologies* (Maryknoll NY: Orbis Books. 1985); Gerald Arbuckle, *Earthing the Gospel: An Inculturation Handbook for the Pastoral Worker* (Maryknoll NY: Orbis, 1990); Clifford Geertz, *The Interpretation of Cultures Basic Books* (NY: Harper and Collins, 1973); *Intercultural Communication Competence* edited by Richard Wiseman, (Newbury Park, CA: Sage Publications, 1993); Anscar Chupungco, *Liturgical Inculturation: Sacramentals, Religiosity and Catechesis* (Collegeville, MN: Liturgical Press, 1990).

The Participant-Observer Minister

As has already been suggested, communication theories inform our subject. A mode of participating and observing provides skills for the minister to attend to the complexity of the many subcultures that make up the Christian assembly. A theory/praxis model may be a simple and quick way for action but it is not necessarily accurate or helpful in the long-term. The liturgical leader might too easily choose a dominant group's approach or decision that gives the appearance of oppressing other groups within a worshipping community. The best minister is a 'participant-observer'[6]. Denham Grierson, in his study of Australian theological students, summarises his adaptation of the 'participant-observer' that is applicable also to liturgical ministers.[7] The participant-observer:

- shares in the activities and sentiments of the people. This involves face-to-face relationships, and direct contact;
- displays both a necessary detachment and personal involvement;
- does not come as an expert, but rather as a learner who, in order to learn, participates in the life of the people;
- acts consistently within the assembly, so no confusion is created by unexpected changes of behaviour or alternating of roles;
- is able to engage the assembly at a deeper level of understanding which cannot be gained from observing external behaviour alone, as would be in the case of the detached observer.[8]

Ministers are to be aware of the dialectic nature of interaction in a multicultural context. To avoid an ethnocentric response, they need to be able to move beyond cognitive simplicity when ministering in a multicultural assembly, to an understanding of the breadth of the

6. Bronislaw Malinowski, *Argonauts of the Western Pacific* (NY: Dutton, 1961).
7. Denham Grierson, *Transforming a People of God* (Melbourne: The Joint Board of Education of Australia and New Zealand, 1984), 43.
8. This theory, if ascribed to, questions the role of the priest who only visits an assembly to preside over its liturgy.

situation. An examination of these theories points to skills that engage people in the task of planning and leading worship.

Centrality of the Paschal Mystery

The Paschal Mystery is the central theological concept of the scriptures and is the interpretative key that unlocks the meaning of the whole liturgical reform. As Paul VI wrote in 1969: 'The Paschal Mystery and its celebration constitutes the essence of Christian worship in its daily, weekly and yearly unfolding. The Second Vatican Council clearly teaches this.'[9] It has been suggested that at least some of this insight can be attributed to the scholarship of Dom Odo Casel (1886–1948) who wrote extensively about Christian mystery.[10] He recovered the idea contained in the original Greek word *mysterion* of which the Latin word *sacramentum* is a translation. He seized on the idea of mystery as key to how humans participate in the liturgy. Casel argued that the liturgy is the means whereby Christians enter into the mystery; the liturgy is meant to communicate the mystery that is Christ.

Christians enter into Christ's passover from death to life in the liturgy; they participate in a transforming event: 'every liturgical celebration, because it is an action of Christ the priest and of His Body which is the Church, is a sacred action surpassing all others; no other action of the church can equal its efficacy' (*SC* 7). The liturgy holds the mystery. Christ is mystery but through the medium of worship Christ is both comprehensible and intelligible. Leaders can assist the assembly to enter fully into the mystery if they take into account the unique 'nature and circumstances' of each assembly. Skills in communication gained by, for example, a study of semiotics[11] help leaders understand how the liturgy expresses and formulates the content of the Paschal Mystery, so that they can engage people in deeper experiences of participation.

---

9. Paul V1, Motu Proprio, *Mysterii Paschalis*, On Liturgical Year and New Universal Roman Calendar, 1969. Text taken from <http://www.vatican.va/holy_father/paul_vi/motu_proprio/documents/hf_p-vi_motu-proprio_19690214_mysterii-paschalis_en.html>. Accessed 25 April 2013.
10. Odo Casel, *The Mystery of Christian Worship* (London: Darton, Longman & Todd, 1963). See Pius X11 Encyclicals *Mystici Corporis* (1943) and *Mediator Dei* (1948).
11. Semiotics—the study of signs and sign processes; indication, designation, likeness, analogy, metaphor, symbolism, and communication—is closely related to linguistics which explores the structure and meaning of language.

Mark: The Narrative

A study of Mark's Gospel also assists in this quest to understand how leaders communicate competently so that their interaction assists participants to more fully, consciously and actively engage with the Paschal Mystery. The author of the first recorded gospel (65–70 CE) set out to engage his community with the mission of Jesus. Mark wrote to 'insiders' to give a certain theology, to address the pastoral concerns of his community. He was not speaking to 'outsiders' whom he wanted to convert. The universal mission of the Gospel is not so much Mark's concern as the mixed composition of his community. Mark's Gospel is a mission document for the community which directed and authorised the community's life and worship on the basis of being authentic to the mission of Jesus.

Mark made a quilt of the oral tradition memories inherited by diverse people and patched together material of his choosing to serve the needs of his community. The literary genre that he invented spoke from the past into the contemporary scene.[12] The beauty of the dynamic of such narrative is that it continues to do this for any age—it can interpret the contemporary situation to direct, to authorise and to renew the mission of Christ's followers.

A reflection on the themes in Mark's Gospel—mindfulness, inclusivity, an initial lack of understanding leading to 'seeing' and a hoped-for end to the blindness of the disciples—can offer a way forward for liturgical ministry that is inclusive of and sensitive to the nature of the particular assembly. Jesus becomes the personification of 'variable mindfulness'. His mindfulness takes readers beyond using exclusive frames of reference to the frame of reference of 'others', especially those in crisis and conflict situations that need healing. Mark has Jesus moderate between those who were anxious and uncertain. In the events of Mark's Gospel he challenges the social milieu of his time and exposes its limitations, especially those that hamper the identity of people (and his own identity). Jesus shows how cultures and groups differ or are similar and negotiates the anxiety and uncertainty of people.

---

12. A classic resource was Paul Achtemeier, 'Mark as the Interpreter of the Jesus Tradition', in *Interpreting the Gospels*, edited by James Mays (Philadelphia: Fortress, 1981).

'Renegotiating' is the skill that opens up the question of ministering in the mixed society of Mark. The image of Jesus' determination for renegotiation is his relentless moving forward on the journey to Jerusalem, a journey that he constantly invites others to travel with him throughout the narrative. The paradox of his 'handing over' to the mystery of the cross is to become the 'root paradigm' of this renegotiating.[13] To understand Jesus is to follow his way that requires being prepared to fully enter into renegotiation and correction that leads to conversion. *Diakonia* and 'handing over' one's life in the journey to the cross is to be part of the inclusive ministry of Jesus who has gone 'ahead of' them (Mk 16:7). Renegotiating is also a skill clearly required by liturgical leaders as they lead assemblies that include diversity in all forms.

Mark clearly indicates to his community that their Christian heritage and engagement in the mission of Jesus lead to the cross. This mission is a challenge for Mark's 'in-group' (Mk 7:21)[14] and ultimately also for the 'out-group' (Mk 13:10).[15] Ministers cross boundaries and sign systems of outsiders/insiders with a 'listening heart'.[16] The boundary-breaking mission of Jesus deals with the murderous, disempowering authorities of his generation and the breaking in of the kingdom before the final 'handing over' of the cosmos and the coming of the Son of Man. Jesus' type of power,[17] as reflected in Mark's Gospel, gives a new perspective on meaning and leads to the inevitability of persecution and the cross.

---

13. William Biernatski SJ, *The Roots of Acceptance: The Intercultural Communication of Religious Meanings* (Rome: Editrice Universita Gregoriana, 1991), 24–28; Victor Turner, *Dramas, Fields and Metaphors* (Ithaca, NY: Cornell University Press, 1974); Victor Turner & Edith Turner, *Image and Pilgrimage in Christian Culture* (NY Colombia University Press, 1978).
14. Mk 7:21–22 'For from within, out of the heart of man, come evil thoughts, sexual immorality, theft, murder, adultery, coveting, wickedness, deceit, sensuality, envy, slander, pride, foolishness.'
15. Mk 13:10 'And the gospel must first be proclaimed to all nations'.
16. Robert Schreiter, *Constructing Local Theologies* (Maryknoll, NY: Orbis Books,1985), 39ff.
17. The 1980's classic biblical scholarship on power which is very relevant for today's Church. Donald Senior, 'With Swords and Clubs: The Setting of Mark's Community and His Critique of Abusive Power', in *Biblical Theology Bulletin*, 17/1 (1987): 10–20; Dorothy Lee-Pollard, 'Powerlessness as Power: A Key Emphasis in the Gospel of Mark', in *Southwestern Journal of Theology*, 40 (1985): 173–188.

The Jesus portrayed by Mark constantly challenges people away from their biases, their social constructs, their narrowness, whether it be the disciples who failed to appreciate the way of the cross as self-surrendering service, or the power-players of his society who defined 'insiders' and 'outsiders' in a narrow and limited way. One of the great twists of Mark's Gospel narrative is that those on the 'outside' become the 'insiders' and vice versa. The 'blind' Bartimaeus 'sees' and follows Jesus to Jerusalem and the cross. The nameless servant woman understands and anoints Jesus in Simon the Leper's house. The cured demoniac proclaims the reign of God. The taboo-breaking mother-in-law lives *diakonia*. The Roman centurion recognises the Christ. All are included in the narrative—those who are 'mindful' contrasting with those who show 'hardness of heart'.

Mark's methodology can be translated into contemporary times where it provides a model for the constant dialectic in multiculturalism that pays attention first to one group and then another and another and leads to a constantly expanding 'mindfulness' of the role and interaction of each of the interlocutors. This dialectic also calls for the skill of 'variable mindfulness' for those who participate in worship. The theme of 'boundary-crossing', of attending to those who make up the assembly, asks those involved to be active participant observers rather than merely passive recipients.

Failure Images: Trial and Error

Mark's account of the Last Supper provides the double-edged prediction of the failure of the disciples contrasted with the faithful action of the symbolic pouring of oil by the woman in Simon the Leper's house. Predictions of betrayal and denial sandwich the Last Supper narrative. Here Mark uses intercalation[18] as he seeks to help his community understand the nature of the mission of Jesus and discipleship. Jesus is the 'minister of inevitable paradox'. He is the 'empathiser' with the solitary woman pouring oil that seems to signal for Mark the beginning of the understanding that has been so missing from the entire Gospel story: 'she has done what she could; she has anointed my body beforehand for its burial' (Mk 14:8). The woman is a sign of hope, a harbinger of the Good News—'wherever the Good News

18. A story 'sandwiched' within another story.

is proclaimed in the whole world, what she has done will be told in remembrance of her' (Mk 14:9). In a surprise twist it is the woman who ministers to Jesus. Claude-Marie Barbour calls this 'mission in reverse'.[19]

By contrast the disciples show their fragility and lack of confidence in their response to the prediction of the betrayal, 'they began to be distressed … "Surely not I?"' (Mk 14:19). The bonding and unity of the final supper are breaking down even as they sit to eat and drink. The meal includes the betrayer, the denier, and the deserters. Mark moves from the disciples' incompetence to the contrasting competence that is found in Jesus who looks forward: 'Truly I say to you, I will never again drink of the fruit of the vine until that day when I drink it new in the kingdom of God' (Mk 14:25). He speaks of 'after I am raised up' (Mk 14:28). Yet it is not to be the 'raising up' of resurrection that is the ultimate: it is the 'raising up' on the cross.[20] Mark leads his community to see that in the very lack of understanding what Jesus does will be ultimately efficacious. There is ultimately room for 'renegotiation' even with (especially with!) violation and error. Jesus is the 'empathiser' who accepts ministry from the woman, and the 'minister of inevitable paradox' dealing with the lack of understanding of the disciples, in the final moments of the journey to the cross.

Mark inserts a story that provides a powerfully symbolic image of 'correction' in the narrative. A 'young man wearing nothing but a linen cloth (Gk: *sinon*)' (Mk 14:51), followed Jesus to the garden and is a witness to the beginning of the paradox of the cross. He is caught with Jesus but fearfully leaves the '*sinon*' and flees naked. In his fear the young man associates with the women who stand 'looking on from a distance' as Jesus hands his life over (*paradidemi*). Yet this is the 'young man dressed in a linen cloth (*sinon*)' (Mk 16: 5) at the tomb who announces the resurrection to those same women after Jesus' death. His fleeing is 'corrected': Mark has him witness to the handing over of Jesus and as the proclaimer of the resurrection

---

19. Claude-Marie Barbour, 'Seeking Justice and Shalom in the City', in *International Review of Mission*, 73/2 (1984): 302ff; Anthony Gittins, *Bread for the Journey: The Mission of Transformation and The Transformation of Mission* (Maryknoll, NY: Orbis Books, 1993).
20. Donald Senior, *Jesus and the Church's Mission. Biblical Foundations for Mission* (Maryknoll, NY: Orbis Books, 1984).

and a paradigm for those who have not understood and are in need of conversion. Liturgical leaders are sensitively aware that worship is mystery, an encounter with the mystery of Christ who invites 'correction'—conversion of heart.

The question for Mark and the community in Rome for whom he possibly wrote[21] is how the painful alienations of society and the early Christian communities could be healed and ultimately reconciled at the table fellowship of the Eucharist and in the inclusive ministry of *diakonia*, or 'handing over' of lives for God's purpose. In the original ending of Mark's Gospel the women move through terror, amazement and silence to fear (Mk 16:8). Reconciliation is promised for Mark's failed disciples who have abandoned, denied, betrayed and fled from the way of Jesus. Reconciliation is spirituality, not strategy. The source of hope in Mark's eucharistic community is not the fragile disciples but the compassion and strength of the Christ 'handed over' and 'raised up' on the cross. 'Mindfulness' of this aspect in the narrative is 'the beginning' of the Good News (see Mk 1:1). It calls faithful disciples to respond by participating in Christ's mission. Liturgical ministers are called to be people who echo this symbol of handing over, being raised up, being prepared to image the God who suffers with, the healing God of shared power, the God of divine empathy. There is much hope here for a fractured, flawed Church.

Diverse Oneness—The One Loaf

In the first chapter of Mark's Gospel, the evangelist portrays the extent of Jesus' appeal: 'all who were ill' (v 32), 'the whole city' (v 33), 'many were cured' (v 34). From the outset Mark portrays a Jesus who reaches out to all in an inclusive way. This continues throughout the subsequent narrative, with large crowds coming to Jesus (1:32; 2:2, 13; 3:9, 20; 4:1; 6:31, 55). There is sufficient bread, indeed extravagant bread for all people. The lake loses its power as a barrier as Jesus extends his ministry of preaching, healing, exorcising and feeding on both 'shores' (Mk 4:35–8:10). The whole of Mark's Gospel is a series of stories that reflect diversity and present Jesus especially as 'minister of inevitable paradox'.

In the narratives of the loaves it is Jesus who takes it upon himself to feed the crowds and who uses fragile disciples to distribute

21. Senior, 'With Swords and Clubs', 1987

the meagre offerings. The different groups, 'in fifties and hundreds' (Mk 6: 40), are fed from the same baskets and need to be part of one another, to be aware of the other 'fifties and hundreds'. This is not a miracle of feeding or multiplication, but the miracle of a people, a people united 'as this broken bread, scattered over the mountains, was gathered together to be one'.[22]

The miracle and the 'understanding about the loaves' is that, in the context of Jesus Christ, Christians can learn the power and the potential of his mission. 'You give them something to eat' (Mk 6:40) and 'How many loaves do you have?' (Mk 8:5). All the needs of such a diverse group are met in the reality of this inclusive response. Mark's Gospel offers a basis for liturgical inclusiveness. It concentrates on the reproach of the disciples by Jesus (Mk 8:14-21).[23] It is a plea to the disciples to be 'mindful', to understand the mission that Jesus is setting up. This text comes at the cross-roads of the story of Jesus' journey to the cross. It refers back, in its bread theme, to the two feedings of people, and to the healings that speak of Jesus' emerging identity. It refers forward to the understanding that is to come through the way of the cross, discipleship and the meal.

In Mark the resolution of the tensions of ministering in a worshipping assembly that is rich in diversity has to do with living *with* the paradoxes, the differences, the tensions and then being constantly reconciled with them through renegotiation, '*mestizaje*'.[24] It is not so much about conflict resolution but reconciliation where each party puts themselves in the shoes of the other. It requires a journey, a con-

22. The Didache 9:4 quoted from *Worship in the Early Church: An Anthology of Historical Sources*, edited by Lawrence Johnson (Adelaide: ATF Press, 2009), volume 1, 37.
23. 'Now the disciples had forgotten to bring any bread; and they had only one loaf with them in the boat. And he cautioned them, saying, 'Watch out—beware of the yeast of the Pharisees and the yeast of Herod.' They said to one another, 'it is because we have no bread.' And becoming aware of it, Jesus said to them, 'Why are you talking about having no bread? Do you still not perceive or understand? Are your hearts hardened? Do you have eyes, and fail to see? Do you have ears, and fail to hear? And do you not remember? When I broke the five loaves for the five thousand, how many baskets full of broken pieces did you collect?' They said to him, 'Twelve'. "And the seven for the four thousand, how many baskets full of broken pieces did you collect?" And they said to him, "Seven." Then he said to them, "Do you not yet understand?"' (Mark 8:14–21).
24. See Elizondo Virgilio, *The Future is Metizio* (Bloomington, Indiana: My Stone Books, 1978).

versation that is constant with hoped-for understanding that comes from on-going cyclical renegotiation.

The 'one loaf' that is the catalyst to the key text (8:14ff) speaks of the obtuseness of the disciples and of the unity Jesus envisions for all. From the dialectic between this obtuseness and unity a new reality is born, a constant boundary-renegotiating ministry of the cross. Those who come to understand the loaves are so 'mindful' that they can answer the question 'who do you say I am'. For Mark's community and for those that follow, the message is to be aware of the local Church and its *communio* with others and of the larger Church itself. Who is included in the 'lost sheep of the house of Israel'? There are ultimately no foreigners in the New Testament. The 'Gentiles'—Mark's 'outsiders'—are people of all faiths in pluralistic societies.

Eucharist in a multicultural setting is dependent on a ministerial approach that first reflects the 'meaning of the loaves' in Mark. 'Renegotiating ministers' are required to reconcile continuing tension concerning eucharistic hospitality.

The Cross: A Badge of Identity and Social Change

The Markan portrayal of Jesus who empowers people and society to shift and change, especially those discerned as 'evil', provides a way forward for liturgical ministers to bring about the primary goal of SC's reform. Focusing on the paradox of the cross takes the minister beyond the use of scientific theories. Mark adds directions which we cannot rationalise. The dimension of faith is what the Church—albeit a very flawed Church—has to offer a world in a time of violent change. If ministers are prepared to stand at the cross and constantly seek conversion for themselves, others and the world, they will journey in the way of the cross that is the Paschal Mystery.

The cross is the symbol of renegotiation. History indicates that rather than renegotiating fully, the Church uses its authority to give an official response to questions before renegotiation completes its process with the community as theologian.[25] Will the Church—that finds its fullness in the Eucharist—have the courage to renegotiate issues as radically as did the Jesus of Mark? Will the Church be prepared to name and lament issues of destruction and fracture in the context of worship?

25. cf. Schreiter, *Constructing Local Theologies*, 1987, 16ff.

Handing Over 'Diakonia'

Mark's true disciple 'hands over' his/her life to the *diakonia* of the cross. Mark does not hide the fact that this will be difficult. Even the *diakonia* women stand 'looking on from a distance' (Mk 15:40) completely uncomprehending and fearful, that leads them to say 'nothing to anyone' (Mk 16:8). Liturgical ministers are called to manage and deal with paradox, with violation of expectations, with incompetence, with threats. This is the current reality. The cross becomes a symbol *par excellence* that is interpersonal and cross-cultural.[26] The narrative of Mark is a narrative of the cross.

As ministers search for symbols that speak to and unite people, re-appropriation of the memorial sacrifice of the cross, a symbol used for generations, is an obvious start. Its full power needs to be renegotiated, constantly de-domesticated. There is no transformation or change in resignation. 'Mindfulness' of the Paschal Mystery is critical in a world of violence today, in a Church dealing with the abuse of power on many levels. Mark's Gospel that calls for *diakonia* attacks evil and seeks, through the very violence of the cross itself, to alert Christian followers to its transforming power.

Life for Christians in a multicultural, refugee society such as Australia could well concentrate on the root paradigm to unite peoples of different cultures. This journey begins with the dispossession of aboriginals, through the social and economic and political refugees of the nineteenth century, to the victims and survivors of wars. Conflicts and economic oppression both within what is now a largely secular society, and more recently within the Church itself, shape the contemporary worshipping assembly.

---

26. The Way of the Cross, has been explored at length by Victor Turner and Edith Turner, *Image and Pilgrimage in Christian Culture* (New York: Columbia University Press, 1978), 24ff. The cross reappears and shapes pilgrimage behaviour in many Christian cultures. Jesus actions and the actions of 'others' towards him, provide a set of patterned assumptions about the kind and sequence of actions the pilgrim should perform in the course of the pilgrimage, and even about the state of mind appropriate to the pilgrim and the content of the prayers said and meditations made in the journey. As the Turners point out, this root paradigm is evident in Christian pilgrimage behaviour over a long historical span and in many parts of the world where 'Christian culture'—or better, Christian 'partial culture' —has established itself.

The Ongoing Process of Competent Communication and Ministers' Needs

Leaders of liturgy and those who prepare liturgy could benefit from the following skills of communication:

- Observing as a participant listener
- Listening with empathy to other contexts, cultures and languages
- Leading with vulnerability and uncertainty resulting in openness
- Empowering that leads to the cross
- Facing the dilemma of leading diverse assemblies where no one is superior to another
- Openness to renegotiation after being aware of distinctions
- Being open to correction from others
- Recognising that the source of hope is not the fragility of discipleship but the compassion and strength of the Christ handed-over and raised-up.

Such skills would assist leaders to engage the worshipper in full, conscious and active participation in the Paschal Mystery. These would guide competent liturgical ministers into the on-going 'Beginning of the Good News' (see Mk 1:1).

Conclusion

This paper has suggested some 'beginnings' to assist leaders of liturgy who minister within diverse communities. It has suggested some skills and attitudes that might assist to 'do' liturgy in an inclusive way in the varied complexity of multicultural assemblies to achieve the central aim of the liturgical reform. More than one perspective is needed as they seek to help interpret what is happening in a given situation so that the liturgy is relevant and inclusive. Ministers' personal awareness of the multiple aspects of their own identity is a good beginning. This needs to be an ongoing discussion.

Eucharist: The Assembly Offers Sacrifice

Carmel Pilcher

I recently asked a friend who was a young priest in the wake of the Council, what he could recall of the introduction of the reformed Mass. He wrote in reply: ‘In the diocese, we had a series of talks on the Council decrees: perhaps one talk on each decree given in two or three places. I do not recall anything more than that specifically on implementing the liturgical changes. There may have been day-time sessions for the clergy. My memory is that we were each on our own, expected to read and take in and implement the various stages. No training for clergy about proclaiming aloud, proclaiming sacred scripture, and much less for the laity.’[1] This description seems to typify, with perhaps a few exceptions, the initial approach taken by bishops to implement the reform of the liturgy called for by *Sacrosanctum Concilium*[2] (*SC*).

With the introduction of the ‘new’ Mass—as it was colloquially known—it soon became evident that if the faithful were to participate ‘conscious of what they are doing, with devotion and full collaboration’ rather than as ‘strangers’ or ‘silent spectators’,[3] comprehensive programs of liturgical formation needed to be established, both in seminaries and parishes.[4] Liturgists were trained and diocesan liturgy

1. This was recorded by Fr John Woods, priest of the diocese of Maitland-Newcastle, NSW, teacher of liturgy.
2. The translation is from the text on the official Vatican website <http://www.vatican.va/archive/hist_councils/ii_vatican_council/documents/vat-ii_const_19631204_sacrosanctum-concilium_en.html>. Accessed 19 January 2013. All subsequent quotations from the Sacred Constitution are from this site.
3. *SC* # 48.
4. *SC* #43- 46.

commissions established. A proliferation of courses and workshops followed that ensured priests and other members of the worshipping faithful were formed, both in the performance of the ritual and, as importantly, in an understanding of the theology of the rites.

Chapter II of *SC* identified areas to be addressed in the reform of the Eucharist.[5] This paper will examine those areas and the extent to which reform has been achieved. Major areas that have not been developed appropriately will be indicated as well as implications for an ongoing theological understanding of the Eucharist. Throughout, the paper will reflect on documents that have provided direction and challenge to all those responsible for liturgical formation and suggest what still needs to be done for the participation in the celebration of the Eucharist envisaged by the Council Fathers to be fully realised.

Developments In Eucharistic Formation

Perhaps the greatest 'success' in terms of liturgical formation has been the opening up of the scriptures to Catholic Christians. The Liturgy of the Word has been restored to its former importance.[6] While the current lectionary bears some critique[7], it is markedly more lavish in content, and homilies—more or less successfully—apply the scriptures to the life of the assembly. Readers continue to be formed for their ministry of proclamation by study and personal reflection on the scriptures. While in many instances the assembly is yet to provide the intercessions, they at least announce them at Sunday Mass. eucharistic practice more clearly reflects the Conciliar Fathers' intention that 'the liturgy of the word and the Eucharistic Liturgy, are so closely connected with each other that they form but one single act of worship' (*SC* 56).

Considerable progress has also been made with regard to *SC*'s mandate that the rites be simplified and that they could be prayed in the vernacular. While the prayers of the Roman Missal (1969)

5. This paper will focus on the regulations listed in *SC* #50—58.
6. Prior to the Council, the proclamation of the scriptures at Mass was deemed so insignificant that Catholics were assured they had 'fulfilled their Sunday obligation' as long as they were present from the Offertory of the Mass to the Priest's Communion.
7. See for example Marjorie Procter-Smith, 'Lectionaries – Principles and Problems: Alternative Perspectives' in *Studia Liturgica*, 22/1 (1992): 84–89.

were only ever intended as an interim translation, they served the Church's worship for several decades until a 'Third Edition of the Roman Missal' (2010) was translated into English and subsequently implemented.[8] Also of importance is the development and expansion of lay liturgical ministries, among them extraordinary ministers of holy communion, musicians, servers, readers and ministers of hospitality. Formation in liturgy has often been a requirement before engagement in these ministries, prompting perhaps the most widespread liturgical formation for members of the assembly.

While much has been done, there is one area that has yet to fully engage the consciousness of the assembly—active participation in the sacrifice of the Mass. Many still believe that it is the priest who primarily—if not solely—offers the sacrifice. The Council gave particular instructions to ritually engage the laity in their baptismal duty to participate in the memorial sacrifice. These include occasional sharing of the cup and commending the 'more perfect form of participation in the Mass whereby the faithful . . . receive the Lord's body from the same sacrifice' (*SC* 55). While frequent communion has once again become the norm, in practice many of the faithful continue to be served communion from the sacrament reserved in the tabernacle and not from the sacrifice. Many are also denied the cup at Sunday eucharist. Communion can become distorted when separated from the sacrifice, and yet official Church recommendations continue to be largely ignored.[9] One can only conclude that presiders either fail to recognise the power of ritual, or fail to recognise that the whole assembly offers sacrifice and should partake in the memorial meal from bread and wine consecrated at that same sacrifice.

---

8. The third edition of the Roman Missal, with its return to a more literal translation of the Latin *editio typica* is yet to be truly tested at this early stage of its implementation, but critics fear that the unfamiliar vocabulary and verbose sentence structure might actually impede, rather than enable participation.
9. The most recent official documentation states: 'It is most desirable that the faithful, just as the Priest himself is bound to do, receive the Lord's Body from hosts consecrated at that same Mass and that, in the instances when it is permitted, they partake of the chalice so that even by means of the signs Communion will stand out more clearly as a participation in the sacrifice actually being celebrated' #85. *The General Instruction of the Roman Missal* (Strathfield: St Paul's Publication, 2012).

SC makes it clear that the faithful 'should give thanks to God; by offering the Immaculate Victim, not only through the hands of the priest, but also with him, they should learn also to offer themselves' (*SC* 48). It will be argued that only when the Church fully engages in Christian sacrifice will the Eucharist truly become the source and summit of the Christian life that the Church intended.[10] Only when Christians 'learn to offer themselves' will they make the link between the Sunday Eucharist and their daily lives.

Christian Sacrifice: Contemporary Notions[11]

More formation in this area is needed but there are obstacles. The notion of Christian sacrifice in contemporary western society is ambiguous and can be fraught with difficulty, carrying negative connotations. Christian sacrifice has—and continues to be—used to justify suffering as 'God's will', especially for women in situations of domestic violence and other forms of injustice and oppression. In the words of Anne Carr: 'Images of Jesus as sacrificial victim, of his sacrificial love and self-surrender on the cross … [are] destructive for women and amongst the most difficult for feminist Christians.'[12] Kevin Seasoltz cautions that 'the word "sacrifice" must be used with care, for it carries both biblical and historical overtones which are not only often offensive to contemporary people but which are subject to misunderstanding and consequent divisiveness and alienation.'[13]

---

10. 'Taking part in the Eucharistic sacrifice, which is the fount and apex of the whole Christian life, they offer the Divine Victim to God, and offer themselves along with It.' *Lumen Gentium* Dogmatic Constitution on the Church #11 at <http://www.vatican.va/archive/hist_councils/ii_vatican_council/documents/vat-ii_const_19641121_lumen-gentium_en.html>. Accessed 16 May 2013.
11. Much of this section is taken from Carmel Pilcher, 'The Sunday Eucharist: Embodying Christ in a Prophetic Act', in *Reinterpreting the Eucharist Explorations in Feminist Theology and Ethics* edited by Anne Elvey, Carol Hogan *et al* (Sheffield, UK: Equinox Publishing Ltd, 2013), 44 - 48.
12. Anne Carr, *Transforming Grace: Christian Tradition and Women's Experience* (New York: Harper Collins, 1988), 174; quoted in R Kevin Seasoltz, *God's Gift Giving in Christ and through the Spirit* (New York: Continuum, 2007), 43.
13. R. Kevin Seasoltz, *God's Gift Giving in Christ and through the Spirit*, 77.

One scholar who has helped correct this misconception is Erin Lothes Biviano.[14] In the introduction to her book 'The Paradox of Christian Sacrifice: The Loss of Self; The Gift of Self', the author poses the question: Is sacrifice always holy?'[15] She provides a detailed exploration and critique of a vast array of scholars on the complexity of the subject.[16] Biviano acknowledges that the idea of self-sacrifice is complex because it is often distorted. She identifies distortions of Christian sacrifice that lead to loss of self, a false understanding of suffering, and the potential for the erosion of identity in the name of sacrifice as a virtue.[17] She acknowledges that Christian sacrifice is always a paradox and concludes that the paradox can be either healthy or destructive, or contain elements of both. In her words, 'the complex role of sacrifice in realising genuine Christian self-hood calls for a theory of self that incorporates the value of wholeness, the reality of loss, and the paradox of their connection in the depth of the self.'[18]

Biviano argues that the apparent dichotomy of self-sacrifice and self-understanding as loss of self can find a resolution in the commandment to love one's neighbour as one loves oneself. To lose one's life is to save it when it is the gift of self. In the words of the author:

> The mystery of self-realising sacrifice partakes of the ethical paradox of solidarity with the neighbour—to love one's neighbour as oneself. Such sacrifice is holy if it seeks wholeness for the self and the other . . . Christian sacrifice is an offering of self to show love of God and neighbour, in response to the experience of God's love, that reflects the sacrifice of Jesus Christ on the cross and God's kenosis in creation. Being the image of God implies that our self-giving should reflect God's creative self-giving. It is God's way of being as Creator that renews the idea of sacrifice as creative self-giving. Chris-

14. Erin Lothes Biviano *The Paradox of Christian Sacrifice The Loss of Self: The Gift of Self.* (New York: A Herder & Herder Book, 2007).
15. Erin Lothes Biviano *The Paradox of Christian Sacrifice*, 2.
16. Erin Lothes Biviano *The Paradox of Christian Sacrifice*, 71–118.
17. Erin Lothes Biviano *The Paradox of Christian Sacrifice*, 3.
18. Erin Lothes Biviano *The Paradox of Christian Sacrifice*, 118.

> tian sacrifice realises one's identity as the image of the sacrificing God.[19]

She concludes that sacrifice is holy when it seeks wholeness and that is when it reflects God's creative self-giving expressed as the loving sacrifice of Christ on the cross. It is this self-giving that Christians memorialise each Sunday at the Eucharist.

Perhaps the single most important contemporary scholar of Christian sacrifice is Robert Daly. In his book *Sacrifice Unveiled: The True Meaning of Christian Sacrifice*,[20] Daly shares his conviction that authentic Christian sacrifice can only be understood as an expression of Trinitarian love. In the first part of his work, entitled 'To Unveil Sacrifice', he writes:

> Christian Sacrifice is a profoundly personal, eschatological, and Trinitarian event, an event in which we Christians, in the power of the same Spirit that was in Jesus, and in our concrete humanity, begin to do in this world what we will be able to do completely only in the next: we begin, namely, to enter into that perfectly self-giving and self-communicating relationship of Father and Son.[21]

Sacrifice Unveiled offers a careful development of Christian sacrifice that not only corrects distortions but offers a fresh possibility for the contemporary Church to engage in eucharistic sacrifice.

Daly confirms that Christian sacrifice is a 'personal event' that he describes as three 'moments' of dynamic activity by the Triune God and created humanity.[22] He labels these three moments 'the self-offer-

---

19. Erin Lothes Biviano, *The Paradox of Christian Sacrifice*, 231.
20. Robert Daly, *Sacrifice Unveiled: The True Meaning of Christian Sacrifice* (London: T&T Clark, 2009).
21. Expanded by Robert Daly from Edward J Kilmartin, SJ, whom the author credits to be the first scholar to attempt a liturgical theology from a Trinitarian perspective. See *The Eucharist in the West: History and Theology* (Collegeville, MN: Liturgical Press, 1998), 381–382. Daly, *Sacrifice Unveiled*, 8.
22. Elizabeth Johnson describes a similar God experience using different terms: 'the dynamic, inexpressible Sophia-God of compassionate, liberating love who is involved in history in multifaceted ways'. Elizabeth A Johnson, *She Who Is: The*

ing of the Father', the 'unique self-offering response' of the Son who becomes the Word made flesh, and 'the self-offering of the believers in the Spirit'.[23]

Daly describes the first 'moment' of Christian sacrifice as the 'initiative' of the Father[24] who sends the gift of Jesus the Word. The author begins with the premise that the mystery of the Trinity is that of one God. In sending Jesus, the Father is not sending someone else, but God's very self becomes human in Jesus. Daly is at pains to emphasise that sacrifice is not something that the Father does to the Christ. The Father is sending and giving of God-self—a self-offering while also sending the Christ. This self-sacrifice on the part of God is free and completely unconditional. This must be so, as Daly states, for 'authentic Christian sacrifice can never be something that someone does to, or demands from, someone else'.[25]

In the second 'moment', Christ responds to the 'invitation' of the Father by offering the unique self-gift of the incarnated humanity of the divine. 'Christ was innocent of sin, and yet for our sake God made him one with human sinfulness, so that in him we might be made one with the righteousness of God' (2 Cor 5:21). Christ's self-offering is a unique and loving response that is both intimately linked to the self-gift of the Father and a totally free gift of the 'Word made flesh' in and through the Spirit. This 'response' is not from another because: 'The Father and I are one' (John 10:30). As Daly concludes, the response is 'the perfectly free, responsive self-giving, self-communicating, en-Spirited love' of the Beloved to the Father 'and also to and for us'.[26]

It is in the third 'moment' that Christians, through a loving response in the same Holy Spirit that was in Jesus, become immersed into the divine Father-Beloved relationship. This response 'that ex-

---

Mystery of God in Feminist Theological Discourse (New York: Crossroads, 1994), 199.

23. Daly, *Sacrifice Unveiled*, 10–14. Daly remarks that these are not moments in time; rather the use of 'moment' is an example of the limitation of words when trying to illustrate a notion concerning the divine.
24. I did consider replacing Daly's God terminology 'Father' 'Son' and 'Spirit' with more inclusive terms, as Elizabeth Johnson cited above, but this invites a problem. To speak of the Father as Creator ignores the creative action of the Triune God.
25. Daly, *Sacrifice Unveiled*, 10.
26. Daly, *Sacrifice Unveiled*, 12.

plicitly commits Christians to emulate and to make their own the virtuous dispositions of the human Jesus in his response to the [Father]' is made possible 'only in the power of the Spirit'.[27] For Daly, only in this profoundly interpersonal event is there Christian sacrifice.

The author concludes that an understanding of Christian sacrifice as mutually self-communicating love corrects misconceptions of the past. Sacrifice is always at the initiative of God and not of humans. Therefore, it can never be something that is done to, imposed on, or required of someone else. Sacrifice will often involve suffering or hardship, but never for its own sake. It is less about giving up or doing without, than an act of deep and fully human love in response to the source of love. A loving response is gift, in and through the power of God's Spirit. Without love as the supreme motivation, some sacrifice is painful and demanding, but it is not by definition Christian sacrifice. Daly would agree with Lothes Biviano that Christians do not lose themselves in the offering, but rather give themselves in response to God and in this mutual self-giving the motivation is always love.

Augustine and Christian Sacrifice

Robert Daly and other contemporary scholars correct distortions of Christian sacrifice. Interestingly the Conciliar Fathers directed us to the writings of Augustine. The exhortation 'they should learn also to offer themselves' (*SC* 47) is a similar exhortation to that made many centuries before by the great homilist to the Carthaginian church: 'You were asking what you should offer for yourself. Offer yourself. What, after all, is the Lord asking from you, but you yourself? Because in the whole earthly creation he made nothing better than you. He asks yourself from you . . .'[28] This instruction might have been in answer to a simple question from his community concerning the nature of gift-giving at the Eucharist. It was a common practice in the ancient Church to bring gifts to the Eucharist, including the bread and wine.[29] The deacons chose the best bread and wine for the eu-

27. Daly, *Sacrifice Unveiled*, 14.

28. 'Sermon preached in the Celerina Basilica.48:2', in *The Works of Saint Augustine: A Translation for the 21st Century*, edited by John E Rotelle, translated by Edmund Hill (New York: New City Press, 1992–2008), III/2: 327–328 (hereafter 'Rotelle' will refer to this series of Augustine's work).

29. This custom that has its origin in the Jewish harvest ritual of offering 'first fruits'

charistic meal, while the remaining contributions were set aside to be distributed amongst the needy to sustain them in the coming week.[30] It was expected that all who could contribute would do so. That this was common practice is evidenced by the fact that the early Fathers commended those who brought gifts and chastised those who came to Eucharist empty handed.[31]

Augustine directly identifies the gift with the giver. Christians are to offer themselves, not as individuals but as one united body in Christ.

> This is the sacrifice of Christians: 'We, being many, are one body in Christ'. And this also, as the faithful know, is the sacrifice which the Church continually celebrates in the sacrament of the altar, by which she demonstrates that she herself is offered in the offering that she makes to God (City 10.6).[32]

Christ's broken and lifeless body in death took on new form as the body of the Church. In the act of assembling the members become one Church, one in Christ as they gather around the table.

According to Augustine, when Christians worship it is Christ's sacrifice that the Church offers. Christ is the mediator, Christ who is one with God, who took on human form and offered himself in service of humankind. Christ 'is both the priest who offers and the

---

to God. Irenaeus speaks of offering the 'first fruits' of creation. See Avers IV 17.5 in David N Power, *Irenaeus of Lyons on Baptism and Eucharist: Selected texts with Introduction,* Alcuin/GROW Liturgical Study #65 (Bramcote Nottingham: Grove Books Ltd, 1991), 15. See also Paul F Bradshaw, 'The Offering of the Firstfruits of Creation: An Historical Study' in *Creation and Liturgy: Studies in Honour of H. Boone Porter*, edited by Ralph McMichael, Jr (Washington, DC: 1993), 29–41.

30. For a detailed development of this connection between gifts brought to Eucharist and the poor see Carmel Pilcher, *The Prophetic Character of Eucharist.* (unpublished manuscript, Ph D, submitted to the Flinders University of South Australia, 2001).
31. See a reference to Cyprian of Carthage in Aime G Martimort *The Church at Prayer,* volume II The Eucharist edited by Robert Cabie (Collegeville MN: The Liturgical Press, 1986), 77–78.
32. *The City of God against the Pagans.* XX, 20. edited by RW Dyson (Cambridge: University Press, 1998), 919.

sacrifice which is offered' (City 10.20).[33] As priest offering the sacrifice, Christ becomes the mediator on behalf of humankind. It is this sacrifice that Christians offer at Eucharist. By presenting themselves as Christ's Body, it is Christ's sacrifice that they offer.

Christians come to the table bearing gifts, the gift of themselves. In the action of making memorial they engage in active remembrance. They enter into the four-fold eucharistic action of taking, blessing, breaking and sharing.[34] The Church gathered becomes more deeply transformed into the mystery of the Body and Blood of Christ in the action of communion.

> So if it's you that are the body of Christ and its members, it's the mystery meaning you that has been placed on the Lord's table; what you receive is the mystery that means you. It is to what you are that you reply *Amen*, and so by replying you express your assent. What you hear, you see, is *The body of Christ*, and you answer, *Amen*. So be a member of the body of Christ, in order to make that *Amen* true (Sermon 272).[35]

To remember Christ's ultimate act of love is to imitate him in loving response. Augustine calls Christians to love God and love their neighbour, a love that finds its meaning and purpose in Christ's ultimate loving sacrifice. 'We offer to him upon the altar of our hearts the sacrifice of humility and praise, kindled by the fire of love' (City 10.3).[36]

In the mind of Augustine all of life can be understood as Christian sacrifice if its focus is the cross. 'A true sacrifice, then, is every work done in order that we may draw near to God in holy fellowship: done, that is, with reference to that supreme good and end in which alone we can be truly blessed' (City 10.6).[37] From the table of the altar all go forth to be the Body of Christ, to live the sacrifice. The Council

33. In Dyson, *The City of God*, 422.
34. For a development of this see, among others, Xavier Leon-Dufour, *Sharing the Eucharistic Bread: The Witness of the New Testament* (New York/Mahwah: Paulist Press, 1987).
35. In Rotelle, *The Works of Saint Augustine* , III/7: 297.
36. In Dyson, *The City of God*, 395.
37. In Dyson, *The City of God*, 399.

Fathers argued that it is only when this participation at Eucharist is understood that the Church can be 'a sacrament of love, a sign of unity, a bond of charity' (*SC* 47).

Recent Teaching On Sacrifice

Christian sacrifice has continued to be connected to eucharistic celebration in the official writings of the Church since the Council. In a section of the Catholic Catechism[38] on the Eucharist (1345–1405), is stated:

> In the Eucharist the sacrifice of Christ becomes also the sacrifice of the members of his Body. The lives of the faithful, their praise, sufferings, prayer and work, are united with those of Christ and with his total offering, and so acquire a new value (CCC 1368).

Christians do not gather at the altar of sacrifice to recall a past event but are actively involved in the sacrifice. The restoration of the procession of the gifts of bread and wine into the post-Vatican II Eucharist offers the possibility for Christians to ritualise this gift giving. Those who carry the gifts to the altar do so in the name of the entire assembly. The bread and wine is 'the work of human hands' and represents those present: their lives, the activities of their week, their joys and sorrows, prayer, work and leisure. This bread and wine, this work of human hands, is placed on the altar of sacrifice. Through the power of the Spirit this bread and wine becomes the living sacrifice of Christ's Body and Blood, the living sacrifice of those who are Christ's Body. Christians are caught up into the dynamic action of God's love and the gift of their lives 'acquires a new value' in the mystery of the Eucharist.

As the Catechism states:

38. In his Apostolic Letter of 1997, *Laetamur Magnopere*, John Paul II introduces the Catholic Catechism as a 'full complete exposition of Catholic doctrine', that builds on the teaching of the Second Vatican Council. John-Paul II, Apostolic Letter. See *Catechism of the Catholic Church* (Strathfield: St Paul's Publication, 2000), xiv.

> The Eucharist is at the heart and the summit of the Church's life, for in it Christ associates his Church and all her members with his sacrifice of praise and thanksgiving offered once for all on the cross to his Father; by this sacrifice he pours out the graces of salvation on his Body which is the Church (CCC 1407).

The Eucharist, the memorial of Christ's sacrifice, is the centre, the pulsing life-blood of the Church. Christians are 'to learn to offer themselves' in the priestly ministry at the table of Eucharist. When Christians love in the manner of Jesus, their self gift becomes the living sacrament of Christ's sacrifice. In the words of Paul Philibert:

> The baptised as the Body of Christ are the visible, earthly expression of Christ's heavenly priesthood and eternal ministry. So the priesthood of the baptised—meaning both the faithful and their pastors—has as its content the struggle for justice, the toil of love, the labour for community, and the compassionate ministry of mercy of all the faithful. These values become priestly precisely when they are joined to the paschal sacrifice of Christ in the celebration of the Eucharist.[39]

The baptised exercise their priestly ministry when they offer sacrifice. This they do at the Eucharist and their daily 'toils of love' are also part of this priestly ministry.

In 1998, John Paul II wrote an Apostolic Letter, *Dies Domini* (On Keeping the Lord's Day Holy),[40] to remind Christians of the important tradition of Sunday as the 'Lord's Day'. A section of the letter is devoted to 'The Eucharistic Assembly: The Heart of Sunday'. John Paul writes:

> The rhythm of the week prompts us to gather up in grateful memory the events of the days which have just

---

39. Paul J Philibert, *The Priesthood of the Faithful Key to a Living Church* (Collegeville MN: Liturgical Press, 2005), 19.
40. <http://www.vatican.va/holy_father/john_paul_ii/apost_letters/documents/hf_jp-ii_apl_05071998_dies-domini_en.html>. Accessed 16 May 2013. Hereafter DD.

> passed, to review them in the light of God and to thank him for his countless gifts, glorifying him 'through Christ, with Christ and in Christ, in the unity of the Holy Spirit' (42).

In the context of daily life the rhythm of the week culminates in Sunday when Christians bring to the table of thanksgiving the events of their week. After affirming the Church's tradition that it is Christ's sacrifice that Christians offer, John Paul reiterates that 'to his sacrifice Christ unites the sacrifice of the church' (DD 43).

The restored manner of praying the Eucharistic Prayer has fostered participation of the whole priestly people. Not only the use of the vernacular, but also the dialogical nature of the prayer have added to this engagement. The presider begins the introductory dialogue to the Great Prayer by inviting the assembly to 'lift up your hearts' and the response affirms their priestly role in the thanksgiving. Indeed, according to the tradition, only when the people respond that 'it is right and just' and the ordained leader is assured he is praying in the Church's name can he can continue with the prayer.[41] The eucharistic sacrifice continues to be at the heart of Sunday, and the Eucharistic Prayer is the priestly prayer of the assembly. 'The truth that the whole community shares in Christ's sacrifice is especially evident in the Sunday gathering, which makes it possible to bring to the altar the week that has passed, with all its human burdens' (DD 43). Augustine would say that every loving action in the life of the Christian becomes continual worship, for 'sacrifice is a divine matter'.[42]

Some years after writing *Dies Domini*, John Paul II wrote an encyclical *Ecclesia de Eucharistia* that is more devotional in flavour. It

41. In the words of John Chrysostom: 'But there are occasions in which there is no difference at all between the priest and those under him; for instance when we are to partake of the awful mysteries, for we are all alike counted worthy of the same things . . . before all one body is set and one cup. And in the prayers also, one may observe the people contributing much . . . the prayers are made in common . . . the offering of thanksgiving again is common: for neither does he gives thanks alone, but also all the people, for having first taken their voices, next when they assent that it is 'meet and right so to do', then he begins the thanksgiving' (Homily on 2 Corinthians 18:3.) in *Nicene and Post-Nicene Fathers of the Christian Church,* volume 12, edited by Philip Schaff, (Grand Rapids, MI: Eerdmans, 1975), 36.
42. In Dyson, *The City of God*, 10. 6, 399.

makes the link between the 'sacrament of the altar' and the Church, and stresses the importance of the ordained priest as leader of the Eucharist.[43] That same year, in an apostolic letter *Mane Nobiscum Domine,* the pontiff announced a 'Year of the Eucharist' with the appeal:

> Can we not make this Year of the Eucharist an occasion for diocesan and parish communities to commit themselves in a particular way to responding with fraternal solicitude to one of the many forms of poverty present in our world? I think for example of the tragedy of hunger which plagues hundreds of millions of human beings, the diseases which afflict developing countries, the loneliness of the elderly, the hardships faced by the unemployed, the struggles of immigrants. These are evils which are present—albeit to a different degree—even in areas of immense wealth. This will be the criterion by which the authenticity of our eucharistic celebrations is judged (28).[44]

The benchmark for authentic eucharistic celebrations is not attention to a particular translation of the liturgical texts, the gestures used, or the act of worship itself;[45] rather authentic Eucharist will be judged to the extent that the Church engages in loving service for the poor, the lonely, the oppressed and anyone in need.[46]

43. John Paul II, Encyclical Letter, *Ecclesia de Eucharistia*, On the Eucharist in its relationship to the church, 2003, #1. <http://www.vatican.va/holy_father/john_paul_ii/encyclicals/documents/hf_jp-ii_enc_20030417_eccl-de-euch_en.html>. Accessed 16 May 2013.
44. <http://www.vatican.va/holy_father/john_paul_ii/apost_letters/documents/hf_jp-ii_apl_20041008_mane-nobiscum-domine_en.html> . Accessed 9 June, 2013.
45. Earlier that same year, 2004, the Congregation for Divine Worship and the Discipline of the Sacraments released *Redemptionis Sacramentum*, On certain matters to be observed or to be avoided regarding the Most Holy Eucharist. This subtitle makes clear its purpose. <http://www.vatican.va/roman_curia/congregations/ccdds/documents/rc_con_ccdds_doc_20040423_present-card-arinze_en.html>. Accessed 16 May 2013.
46. John Paul II is returning to the tradition of prophetic Eucharist that finds expression in a loving community that reaches out to the poor. See Carmel Pilcher, *The Prophetic Character of Eucharist*. (unpublished manuscript, Ph D submitted to the Flinders University of South Australia, 2001).

Benedict XVI continued this theme. In his encyclical letter *Deus Caritas Est*[47] he writes:

> Faith, worship and ethos are interwoven as a single reality which takes shape in our encounter with God's agape. Here the usual contraposition between worship and ethics simply falls apart. 'Worship' itself, eucharistic communion, includes the reality both of being loved and of loving others in turn. A Eucharist which does not pass over into the concrete practice of love is intrinsically fragmented (14).

A fragmented Eucharist occurs when the assembly fails to engage fully in the eucharistic sacrifice. And a fragmented Eucharist runs contrary to the very essence of the mystery truthfully remembered, the loving self-gift of God in Christ to the Church.

The Eucharist is the source and summit of the Church's life when all its members participate in the sacrifice by offering themselves. It has been established that 'learning to offer themselves' has been a regular theme, not only amongst significant scholars but in the official teaching of the Church. The Catholic Catechism and two recent popes, John Paul II and Benedict XVI, have continued to link participation in the Church's worship with an ethical witness that the eucharistic sacrifice is engaged in beyond the table of memorial.

Christians come to the table of thanksgiving bringing the only gift they have to offer, the gift of their lives: their burdens and praise, their suffering and work, indeed all the activities of their week. When caught up in the sacrifice of thanksgiving and praise, their very selves are joined to Christ. By giving they receive. Christians receive, in Augustine's words, 'the mystery of who we are', or as John Paul names it, 'communion with Christ is deeply tied to communion with our brothers and sisters' (DD 44). Christians go forth to live the unity they proclaim, to 'return to their everyday surroundings with the commitment to make their whole life a gift, a spiritual sacrifice pleasing to God' (DD 45).

---

47. <http://www.vatican.va/holy_father/benedict_xvi/encyclicals/documents/hf_ben-xvi_enc_20051225_deus-caritas-est_en.html>. Accessed 16 May 2013.

A Way Forward

There is a clear connection between Eucharist as the source and summit of the Church's life and the self-offering that full participation requires. Without active engagement in the sacrifice, the ethical dimension of Eucharist is absent. Christians fail to make the link between Eucharist and life unless they are aware that *they* are the gift they offer. This requires continuous priestly participation in the Sunday Eucharist from the gathering to the sending forth. This requires also that the whole Church recognises the Eucharistic Prayer as more than just the prayer of the presider, but 'the vocation of the baptised'.[48] So what still needs to be done?

First and foremost, education is needed. With a renewed understanding of Christian sacrifice that invites Christians to recognise their calling as a priestly people[49] and that their gifts are not only worthy but sacred, they are empowered to bring their lives to the altar. It is through Christ and by the Holy Spirit that their loving actions take on a new value when presented at the table of sacrifice. Christians receive 'the mystery of who we are' and are charged to go and continue to serve Christ, especially in the poor of our world.

But ritual understanding is also important. The Church is a sacrament of ritual and symbol and the tradition invites Christians to use this language to communicate with God. The revival of the presentation of gifts at Sunday Mass highlights the 'offerings' that are brought in procession to the table. Worshippers bring bread and wine and they also bring gifts for the poor. It is important that the collection takes place as the table is prepared so that all the offerings are brought forward in procession. The procession is reverent, the gifts can be seen, and those bearing gifts process through the entire assembly. In this way the presentation of gifts ritualises the offering of self that Christians make. The procession of gifts from the assembly to the table finds its corollary in the procession of the assembly to the table to share the consecrated gifts in communion.

The Roman Missal contains more than a dozen Eucharistic Prayers: Eucharistic Prayers for Reconciliation, a series of 'Prayers for Special

48. Richard McCarron, *The Eucharistic Prayer at Sunday Mass* (Chicago: Liturgical Training Publications, 1997), 50–62.
49. See D Orr, chapter 11 of the present collection, 'Confirmation: Ordered to Sacrifice', 161–172.

Occasions' and provision for a series of Eucharistic Prayers especially designed for use when there are many children present. This makes it possible for the faithful to offer thanks and praise in a variety of ways, and to suit the prayer to the occasion or liturgical season. It is vital that those preparing the liturgy—representatives from the assembly and the priest—choose carefully the Eucharistic Prayer that will be prayed by a particular assembly on a particular Sunday. It is important also that the richness of our prayers be explored and used.

In the Western world the Eucharistic Prayer is considered long by contemporary standards. Some are tempted to employ technology as a means to focus the attention of the worshippers but this prayer is meant to be 'live'. Presiders need special preparation to ensure that they truly are the voice of the Body of Christ. This includes preparation of the presidential texts, especially given the verbose and complex nature of the current translation, but also attention to a presiding style that is inclusive of the assembly. From time to time it would be opportune to preach about aspects of the Eucharistic Prayer, its structure, various themes, why it is a trinitarian prayer and how that relates to our offering. It would also be important, now that English-speaking Catholics have a more literal translation of the Eucharistic Prayer, to preach on the meaning of words such as 'oblation' and 'victim' that are either unfamiliar to the ears of the assembly or suggestive of a different meaning.

As has already been said, the Council Fathers, and every liturgical instruction since, recommend that the assembly should 'receive the Lord's Body from the same sacrifice' (*SC* 55) and that—at least on significant occasions—they share from the cup.[50] When the faithful receive communion from the bread and wine offered at that same sacrifice the ritual sense of participation is clearly evident.[51] With the generosity of the people of God in accepting the role of assisting with ministering communion and with their co-operation, it should be possible to ensure that both these practices are implemented. This is vital, not only so that the sign of the action of the sacrifice may be more complete, but to distinguish between the Mass and celebrations

50. *The General Instruction of the Roman Missal* #283.
51. 'Even by means of the signs Communion may stand out more clearly as a participation in the sacrifice actually being celebrated.' *The General Instruction of the Roman Missal*, #85.

of the Word and Communion that are becoming all too prevalent in Sunday worshipping communities in Catholic parishes. Communion offered at a Service of the Word does not directly involve the action of the sacrifice that is possible during the celebration of the Mass. For this reason John Paul II wrote in *Ecclesia de Eucharistia* of 'the sacramental incompleteness of these celebrations'.[52]

There are a number of barriers to full participation of the assembly in the eucharistic sacrifice. There is confusion regarding posture—the presider (and concelebrants) stands during the Eucharistic Prayer while the rest of the assembly kneel or sit. A common posture helps to express a common mind and purpose. Spatial church settings where the altar is separated either by steps or physical distance serve to visually distance the assembly from its active role. It is important that these limitations are attended to so that the Eucharistic Prayer, the central moment of the Mass, can truly become the vocation of the people of God.

Conclusion

Although catechesis might have been minimal or even non-existent immediately after the Council, the implementation of the reform of the Eucharistic Liturgy has enjoyed some modicum of success, thanks in no small part to the ongoing dedication of diocesan commissions and liturgical educators. It is of major concern that some Church leaders are convinced that the conciliar reform of the liturgy will be complete with the advent of the implementation of the Third Edition of the Roman Missal (2010) and the subsequent literal translations of the other texts of the sacraments. This is a dangerous and erroneous opinion that is already becoming a reality with the disappearance of many diocesan liturgical commissions and liturgy offices.

At this time in history, when the pendulum seems to be swinging back to the details of rubrics and the style of liturgical dress rather than the significance of ritual behaviour, the words of the great American liturgical pioneer Virgil Michel seem timely: 'If the liturgical worship is properly understood and lived it will be quite impossible to enter its participation without having its influence carry over

52. *Ecclesia de Eucharistia* #32.

into daily life'. Michel defined this as 'intelligent participation'.[53] Only when the whole body of Christ recognises that baptism brings with it the priestly responsibility to offer the sacrifice of thanksgiving and praise and they 'learn to offer themselves' will Eucharist truly be at the 'heart of the Christian life' and the 'sacrament of love, a sign of unity, a bond of charity' that the Council intended (SC 47).[54]

53. Virgil Michel, *The Liturgy and Catholic Life,* unpublished manuscript (Collegeville MN: St Benedict's Monastery), 110.
54. *SC* #47 quoting Augustine, in *Ioannis Evangelium Tractatus* XXVI, chapter 6, # 13, PL 35, 1613.

Eucharist: Scripture in Prayer and Song, Action and Sign

Gerard Moore

This reflection on *Sacrosanctum Concilium*[1] (*SC*) seeks to explore a singular excerpt on the biblical nature of worship: '. . . the prayers, collects, and liturgical songs are scriptural in their inspiration and their force, and it is from the scriptures that actions and signs derive their meaning'(SC 24). The intention is to apply this passage to the current edition of the Roman Missal (2010) and the Mass it serves, recovering something of the biblical basis of our worship and opening up questions of our interpretation of this scriptural foundation. First some comments about the passage of the Constitution and its later interpretation. It is important to quote the article in full. The text reads:

> Sacred scripture is of the greatest importance in the celebration of the liturgy. For it is from scripture that lessons are read and explained in the homily, and psalms are sung; the prayers, collects, and liturgical songs are scriptural in their inspiration and their force, and it is from the scriptures that actions and signs derive their meaning. Thus to achieve the restoration, progress, and adaptation of the sacred liturgy, it is essential to promote that warm and living love for scripture to which the venerable tradition of both eastern and western rites gives testimony (SC 24).

1. The translation is from the text on the official Vatican website <http://www.vatican.va/archive/hist_councils/ii_vatican_council/documents/vat-ii_const_19631204_sacrosanctum-concilium_en.html>. Accessed 19 January 2013. All subsequent quotations from the Sacred Constitution are from this site.

The context of the paragraph within the Constitution gives significance to what follows. The paragraph contains the third of four general norms (*SC* 22–25) for the renewal of the liturgy (*SC* 21). This gives emphasis to the role of scripture in the very reform of the liturgy itself. From within this larger context in the section the scriptural inspiration is one of the criteria for renewal. It is set alongside the processes of discerning what has been divinely laid down, what can change, what is now less suitable or appropriate to the innermost character of the liturgy, and what helps the people understand the holy things and to enter into them fully and actively (*SC* 21).[2]

This essay will deal in detail with only a section of the paragraph: 'the prayers, collects, and liturgical songs are scriptural in their inspiration and their force, and it is from the scriptures that actions and signs derive their meaning'. There will be two broad lines of approach. The first investigates how clearly the prayers and collects draw their inspiration and force from the scriptures, and actions and signs their meaning. The second asks whether the way the scriptures are used matches the genius and intent of the sacred texts themselves.

The General Instruction of the Roman Missal

The ongoing importance of the paragraph is reflected in the revisions of the *General Instruction of the Roman Missal* (hereafter GIRM) as part of the Third Edition of the Roman Missal of Paul VI, where *SC* 24 is the inspiration for a new paragraph in the Instruction. The paragraph urges Conferences of Bishops to take great care in the provision of translations of biblical texts due to the reasons given in *SC* 24, and goes on to repeat the *SC* text almost *verbatim*. Nevertheless there is a modification to the Latin text of *SC* and a consequent change of

---

2. Paragraph 21 reads: In order that the Christian people may more certainly derive an abundance of graces from the sacred liturgy, holy Mother Church desires to undertake with great care a general restoration of the liturgy itself. For the liturgy is made up of immutable elements divinely instituted, and of elements subject to change. These not only may but ought to be changed with the passage of time if they have suffered from the intrusion of anything out of harmony with the inner nature of the liturgy or have become unsuited to it. In this restoration, both texts and rites should be drawn up so that they express more clearly the holy things which they signify; the Christian people, so far as possible, should be enabled to understand them with ease and to take part in them fully, actively, and as befits a community.

interpretation. There have been two different translations of the passage. The first from the 2001 edition of the Instruction reads:

> . . . For it is out of the Sacred Scripture that the readings are read and explained in the homily and that psalms are sung, and it is drawing upon the inspiration and spirit of Sacred Scripture that prayers, orations, and liturgical songs are fashioned in such a way that from them actions and signs derive their meaning (GIRM 391).[3]

In this reading the actions and signs of the liturgy are understood to derive their meaning from the texts of prayers and songs, which in turn are inspired by the scriptures. This is marked deviation from the content of the Vatican II document. If intentional, it would mark a significant departure in Catholic liturgical theology in that it appears to subordinate ritual action and symbol to accompanying words and songs, scripturally inspired. This has resonance with what may be described as the 'classic' Protestant position, in which the dogmatic norms of belief govern the rule of prayer[4].

The revised translation in the 2010 edition of the *General Instruction* tries to retrieve something of the original sense of *SC*. While this is encouraging, the meaning of the English translation is obscure and perhaps somewhat unintelligible. The revision reads:

> . . . For it is out of the Sacred Scripture that the readings are read and are explained in the Homily and that Psalms are sung, and it is by the influence of Sacred Scripture and at its prompting that prayers, orations, and liturgical chants are fashioned in such a way that it is from Sacred Scripture that actions and signs derive their meaning.[5]

3. Translation from the United States Conference of Catholic Bishops, *General Instruction of the Roman Missal*, Liturgy Documentary Series 2 (Washington DC: United States Conference of Catholic Bishops, 2003).
4. For a summary of the 'classic' Protestant approach see Geoffrey Wainwright *Doxology: The Praise of God in Worship, Doctrine and Life* (New York: Oxford University Press, 1980), 251–2.
5. From the translation on the Unites States Conference of Catholic Bishops:< http://www.usccb.org/prayer-and-worship/the-mass/general-instruction-of-the-roman-missal/girm-chapter-9.cfm>. Accessed 4 February 2013. All texts of

Yet there is good reason to set aside both readings from the revised GIRM. The Latin version of the Instruction follows the original text of *SC* faithfully except for one word, more precisely one letter of the alphabet. *SC* reads: *atque ex eius afflatu instinctuque preces, orationes et carmina liturgica effusa sunt, et ex ea significationem suam actiones et signa accipiunt.* However, where the text of *SC* reads *et* ('and'), the GIRM has *ut* ('in such a way that'). Further, this use of *ut* would require changing the mood of the verb to the subjunctive[6], but this has not been done to the text. It seems that this is a typographical error, one with unwanted consequences. In light of this, the interpretation of *SC* 24 by the current Instruction can be set aside.

Inspiration, Force and Meaning

The Constitution sets prayers and collects first, and then signs and actions. This may not be the most felicitous approach, given that the liturgy is first and foremost made up of actions and symbols, amongst which are prayers and collects. Despite this cavil the order will be followed as given. Unfortunately, there are restrictions on space, so the discussion of the scriptural force and inspiration of liturgical songs will have to be taken up at another opportunity. It parallels much of what is said below.

The English version of *SC* from the Vatican website translates *preces [et] orationes* as 'prayers [and] collects'. This is useful, but may be too precise. The prayers of the third edition of the reformed Missal now styled as 'collects' were known in the Roman family of worship books as either *preces* or *orationes*[7]. *SC* retains the breadth of the language in the liturgical tradition, and incorporates all the prayers of the liturgy[8]. For the purpose of this paper the collects will be treated separately from the other prayers.

---

the *General Instruction* are taken from this official ecclesial site, though the text does contain elements that apply in the United States only.

6. The subjunctive form of *accipiunt* is *accipiant*. My thanks to Paul Turner for his help in delineating this problem.
7. For an analysis of the various names used for various missal prayers see Patrick Regan, 'The Collect in Context, in *Appreciating the Collect: An Irenic Methodology*, volume 1 Documenta Rerum Ecclesiasticarum Instaurata edited by James Leachman and James McCarthy (Farnborough: St Michael's Abbey Press, 2008) 84-91.
8. The Tanner translation has a more generic, but perhaps more accurate, translation as 'the various kinds of prayers'. See Norman P Tanner, *Decrees of the Ecumenical Councils*, volume II (London: Sheed & Ward and Georgetown University Press, 1990), 825.

Influential studies have cast doubt on the scriptural qualities of Roman prayers in general. Klauser was emphatic in his discussion of the biblical qualities of Roman liturgical texts: 'there is none of this in the Roman Collects and only occasionally does one find traces of it in the other Roman prayers. I hope I shall not be misunderstood if I say that, fundamentally, the Roman liturgy is far removed from the Bible'[9]. Yet he called for more studies of the vocabulary of the collects, resulting in research that has made his position look extreme. Highly respected scholar Christine Mohrmann has written that Roman collects in particular were quite incomprehensible to the ordinary believer because the language was highly stylised, following conventions of classical Roman rhetoric. The value of the prayers was that they conveyed a sacral style that was deemed by all to be appropriate to worship[10]. In effect, any scriptural inspiration in a prayer can be seen as irrelevant since it would not be 'heard' by the worshipper, and did not necessarily contribute to the 'sacrality' of the prayer.

The Prayers

There are a number of ways in which the prayers of the Mass reflect the scriptures, though it is not always clear that worshippers hear or appreciate this. This section will take up the Sign of the Cross, the *Kyrie Eleison*, the General Intercessions and the Communion Rite.

In the Missal of Paul VI the Sign of the Cross is the first action of the assembly gathered[11]. Through it the community marks on its body that together they form a people gathered in the cross. It is only since the fourteenth century that this sign of blessing has been accompanied by the words of Baptism based in the final command of Jesus to his disciples before his ascension (Mt 28:19). In the Tridentine Mass the Sign of the Cross was the first of the prayers the priest said at the foot of the altar. The priest alone was designated to make the blessing and pronounce the formula in a clear voice. In the revisions arising

9. Theodore Klauser, *A Short History of the Western Liturgy: An Account and Some Reflections*, translated by J Halliburton (Oxford University Press, 1979), 41–42.
10. Christine Mohrmann, *Liturgical Latin: Its Origin and Character, Three Lectures*, (Washington DC: The Catholic University of America Press, 1957), 60–61.
11. 'When the Entrance Chant is concluded, the Priest stands at the chair and, together with the whole gathering, signs himself with the Sign of the Cross'. GIRM #50

from Vatican II, the blessing was set as the first action of the gathering as a whole, ritually announcing the cross, discipleship and baptism as defining marks of the Christian assembly. For our purposes, it is clear that the Mass begins with a resounding scriptural image (the cross), text (Mt 28:19) and action (the blessing/signing).

A less acknowledged scriptural allusion underpins the litany known as the *Kyrie eleison*. The prayer is a petition, common across the ancient world and found in the biblical texts.[12] In that sense, the prayer is not so much directly influenced by the scriptures. Nevertheless there is an important resonance between the singing of the petition in Christian worship and particular gospel passages, especially given that in the Mass the prayer was always sung in Greek and, though introduced into the Latin liturgy, never translated into that vernacular. The Gospel of Mark features Bartimeaus (Mk 10:47–48), a blind beggar who is healed by Jesus. To gain the attention of the itinerate prophet, he calls out 'Jesus, Son of David, have mercy on me (*eleison*)!' Matthew gives virtually the same plea in his recounting of the cure of two blind men (Mt 9:27): 'have mercy on us, Son of David!' The most exact correspondence is found further on in Matthew. A Canaanite woman pleads with Jesus: 'Have mercy on me, Lord (*eleison me kyrie*), Son of David. My daughter is tormented by a demon' (Mt 15:22).

This resonance gives the prayer a particular force. The unnamed woman has no standing in that society, and no right to call upon Jesus. Immediately, she is identified as a foreigner, not a member of the people of Israel. She is a woman, a second-class citizen. She has the misfortune to have a daughter, not a son. The child is ill, a sign that the mother or family has sinned. Yet it is her plea, her prayer that is echoed in worship. And in singing her song, the Christian community is opting not only to take up her words but to stand beside her and identify with her sufferings. She has become one of the teachers of faith.

12. For a comprehensive study of this prayer see Peter Jeffrey, 'The Meanings and Functions of *Kyrie eleison*' in *The Place of Christ in Liturgical Prayer: Trinity, Christology, and Liturgical Theology*, edited by Brian Spinks (Collegeville, MN: Liturgical Press, 2008), 127–194. For the classical and scriptural foundation of the prayer see 144-149. One regret is that he makes too little of the New Testament influences.

The Bishops at Vatican II instructed that the Prayer of the Faithful be restored to the Mass after centuries in abeyance (*SC* 54). The inspiration was the passage 1 Timothy 2:1–2: 'First of all, then, I urge that supplications, prayers, intercessions, and thanksgivings be made for everyone, for kings and all who are in high positions, so that we may lead a quiet and peaceable life, in all godliness and dignity.' The prayer is given even greater force through its interpretation as one of the liturgical manifestations of the royal priesthood of the faithful:

> In the Universal Prayer or Prayer of the Faithful, the people respond in some sense to the Word of God which they have received in faith and, exercising the office of their baptismal Priesthood, offer prayers to God for the salvation of all (GIRM 69).

This is a direct reference to 1 Peter 2:9, 'But you are a chosen race, a royal priesthood, a holy nation, God's own people, in order that you may proclaim the mighty acts of him who called you out of darkness into his marvelous light.'

While the actual petitions ought to be written afresh for each act of worship, reflecting local language and style, the inspiration for the rite is scriptural and likewise is the rite's liturgical force as a key manifestation of the priesthood of all believers.

Almost every prayer in the rite of Holy Communion has a direct scriptural origin. It is as though human words falter at this point, and the word of God guides the faithful to Communion in the Godhead. Matthew's version of the Lord's Prayer requires no comment regarding its scriptural origin. Interestingly the version in Luke's Gospel does not appear to have been used liturgically. The embolism that follows seems to take its cue from the Letter to Titus: '. . . while we wait for the blessed hope and the manifestation of the glory of our great God and Saviour, Jesus Christ' (Titus 2:13). While the acclamation 'For the kingdom . . . ' is not immediately biblical, it has been found as a conclusion to the Lord's Prayer in some of the oldest manuscripts of Matthew's Gospel. It would seem that the copyist thought it belonged there![13] Without labouring the point, the greeting of peace (Mt 5:23–24), the breaking of bread (1 Cor 10:16–17) and the Lamb of God (Jn

13. Lucien Deiss, *The Mass*, (Collegeville, MN: Liturgical Press, 1992), 91.

1:29) are all immediately scriptural, and allow the entire rite to be understood as biblical in inspiration and force.

While not every rite in the Mass has been opened up, the examples above show a deep sense of scripture across the eucharistic liturgy as a whole, with a reliance on the biblical text in the face of deepest mystery.

The Collects[14]

Three collects shall suffice for uncovering the biblical basis of the prayers. The collect for the Third Sunday in Ordinary Time offers us an example of how a prayer encapsulates a particular biblical passage and applies it to a concrete situation.[15] The current official translation reads:

> Almighty ever-living God,
> direct our actions according to your good pleasure,
> that in the name of your beloved Son
> we may abound in good works.

In structure, content and vocabulary, the collect corresponds to the Vulgate translation of the passage Ephesians 1:3-2:11. The prayer sets together the divine favour of God (Eph 1:9), God's guidance of all things (Eph 1:11), the power of the name of Christ (Eph 1:21), the abundance of grace (Eph 1:8, 2:27) and the good works designated by God for the faithful (Eph 2:10). As well, the original eighth century setting of the prayer within a Mass for January or during the octave of Christmas applied this Pauline passage in two ways. It referred both to the mystery of the incarnation just celebrated, and to the power of the divine name of Jesus over the pagan deities whose power and influence were seen as heightened at the turning from the old year into the new year. It is clear that the prayer is an accurate reflection of the biblical passage and, in original context, an astute application to a pressing pastoral situation.

---

14. I am offering here a summary of an earlier work. See Gerard Moore, 'The Vocabulary of the Collects: Retrieving a Biblical Heritage', in *Appreciating the Collect*, edited by James Leachman and James McCarthy (Farnborough: St Michael's Abbey Press, 2008), 175–196.
15. For an extensive study of the prayer see Gerard Moore, *Vatican II and the Collects for Ordinary Time: A Study of the Roman Missal (1975)* (San Francisco: International Scholars Press, 1998), 444–456.

A more general biblical influence can be seen in the collect for the Twenty-Third Sunday Ordinary Time.[16] The current official translation reads:

> O God, by whom we are redeemed and receive adoption,
> look graciously upon your beloved sons and daughters,
> that those who believe in Christ
> may receive true freedom
> and an everlasting inheritance.

The outstanding feature of the prayer is its reflection of the Pauline matrix of redemption, adoption, baptism, inheritance and freedom. The structure, vocabulary and content of the prayer closely resemble certain passages in the Letter to the Galatians: the conjunction between redemption and adoption; the association between baptism and inheritance; the conjunction of inheritance and liberty; the relationship between the pair redemption/adoption and the pair inheritance/liberty. Various combinations of these are also present in other Pauline writings. In effect, the collect presents a concise version of key Pauline teachings, found throughout the Letter to the Galatians in particular, but not restricted to it.

Whereas not all collects are so explicitly scriptural, some exhibit interplay between well-known scriptural verses and tensions current at the time of writing. This is especially the case in the collect for the Fourth Sunday in Ordinary Time[17]. The current official translation reads:

> Grant us, Lord our God,
> that we may honour you with all our mind,
> and love everyone in truth of heart.

Here the translation does little justice to the Latin text. At the heart of the oration is a play on the biblical injunction to love God and neigh-

---

16. For a detailed analysis see Moore, *Vatican II and the Collects for Ordinary Time* 223–235.
17. For a close analysis of this, despite appearances in translation, highly complex prayer, see Moore, *Vatican II and the Collects for Ordinary Time*, 99–115. The prayer is a masterpiece of subtle theology and immediate pastoral impact.

bour (Mt 22:37–40). With this passage providing the touchstone for the hearers, the writer has juxtaposed 'honour' with 'love' of God. This was no abstract discussion. Rather, the prayer arose in response to a specific and highly controversial pastoral question. Was the on-going participation in the somewhat lascivious festival of Lupercalia by the faithful in the city of Rome worthy of their Christian faith? Did it compromise their theology of the love and honour owed God, and did it match the demands of Christian charity? Challenged about the purity of their response to God, the faithful are further driven to seek to love their neighbour fully. The Latin verb 'to love' used in this second petition has trinitarian connotations in that it is usually found when referring to the love of God for Christ. The phrase 'truth of heart' is an attempt to capture a sense of love reflecting the love bestowed by the Holy Spirit, an aspect not readily available in any translation. Here, then, is a scripturally inspired prayer that builds on a biblical mandate, but interprets and applies it to a pressing community need.

Just three examples are sufficient to show the depth and variety of scriptural influence. In sum, the collects display a remarkable scriptural virtuosity. Unfortunately it is a heritage that is somewhat hidden from general view. There are insufficient studies of the prayers in depth to enable translators to hone the texts in light of their scriptural content. As well, there is no single biblical translation that holds sway across the many countries where English is the language of worship, making it harder for translators to render the biblical allusions for a common audience. What is now clear is that the first tool a translator should reach for when dealing with a collect is a Vulgate concordance.

Rites and Actions

From the perspective of liturgical theology, the biblical inspiration of actions is more important than of prayers and collects in that the liturgy is first and foremost an action. If the ritual itself does not have a scriptural foundation, then the biblical nature of any prayers is masking a possible disconnection between the word of God and the worship of the community. This sense of biblical underpinning is reflected in the teaching that the sacraments are direct commands from

Christ.[18] Working from the Roman Missal, with a focus solely on the Eucharistic Prayer, I will attend only to the warrant for the Eucharist, and the ritual shape of the celebration.

There is a clear and compelling biblical warrant for the celebration of the Eucharist. The Last Supper narratives in the three synoptic gospels, and the writings of Paul, contain a mandate from Jesus that the community bless and share in loaf and cup as the memorial of his presence. This sense of memorial, *anamnesis*, is more than a calling to mind, and is equivalent to what is known in Catholic theology as sacrament. It is a blessing in which the very presence of the risen Jesus is realised: 'when he was at table with them, he took the bread, blessed it and broke it, and gave it to them. Then their eyes were opened and they recognised him' (Lk 24:30–31). This blessing rite was an essential action of the early communities (Acts 2:46), and remains the defining action of the Church.[19]

Given that there is a biblical warrant for the eucharistic celebration, is there a scriptural inspiration for the shape of the rite? Here the focus on the Last Supper narratives[20] as exemplars of a ritual structure is unhelpful, though understandable. There are reasons for this from within the texts, and also from longstanding interpretations of these texts (which will be covered below). The various supper narratives have elements in common and inconsistencies. In common are blessing, the use of bread and wine, and the sharing by all in this as the memorial of Christ. However there are differences in ritual pattern, particularly in the order of cup and loaf, and in the number of cups. The setting for the blessing is a meal, and clearly the Eucharist maintains its character as a meal. Yet these passages are not simply eyewitness accounts. Rather they are the end product of two to three generations of Christian practice. It is better to look at them as finely honed texts, reflecting the practices and questions of later commu-

18. This is unmistakable from the Council of Trent, which anathematises anyone who rejects that the [seven] sacraments of the new law were not all instituted by our Lord, Jesus Christ. See *Dogmatic Canons and Decrees* (Rockford, Ill: Tan Books and Publishers, 1977), 59 Session 7 canon 1.

19. See GIRM #112 where the preeminent expression of the Church is understood to be the Mass where the Bishop presides surrounded by the presbyterate, the deacons, lay ministers, and with all the community participating fully and actively.

20. 1 Corinthians 11:23–36; Matthew 26:26–29; Mark 14:22–25; Luke 22:15–20.

nities rather than simply as descriptions of the actions of Jesus and the disciples on the night before his death. During the period when these passages were being given shape, already in Paul there is a falling away from 'breaking of the bread' as a common meal and the development of a symbolic ritual meal, one which offered the participant wine and bread, but satisfied their spiritual hunger, not the pull of empty bellies (1 Cor 11:20–22).[21]

All this serves to emphasise further the centrality of the supper narratives as the warrant for the Eucharist over and against its contribution to the ritual structure. The usual place to seek the shape of this ritual is in the writings of Justin Martyr, who offers a fairly comprehensive shape for the liturgy: Sunday gathering, word, preaching, intercessions, peace, gifts presented, the thanksgiving, communion, the collection for the poor, dismissal.[22] Is there biblical influence behind this? The narrative of the disciples on the road to Emmaus provides a valuable touchstone (Lk 24:13–35). The passage has four key moments. Firstly, the disciples, disillusioned as they are, are gathered, and soon accompanied by Jesus himself. A second point is that they are attentive to the word, so much so that their hearts burn within them and they provide Jesus with the best hospitality they can muster. Thirdly, they recognise the presence of Jesus in the blessing and breaking of bread. The final moment is that they are impelled on mission. This is the first recorded celebration of the Eucharist, and witnesses a simple ritual shape; gathering, word, blessing (and communion), dismissal/mission. This architecture is reflected in the descriptions of Justin Martyr, and has retained its influence through to the present.

In sum, it can be seen that the celebration of the Eucharist is inspired by the scriptures, and has a shape that is reflected in the scriptural records, particularly the post resurrection narratives of Luke's Gospel.

---

21. For discussion of the separation of the Eucharist from a community meal see Frank Senn, *Christian Liturgy: Catholic and Evangelical* (Minneapolis: Fortress Press, 1997), 61.
22. The relevant texts are found in Justin's *First Apology*, 65–67. They are collected in *Prayers of the Eucharist: Early and Reformed*, edited by RCD Jasper and GJ Cuming, (New York: Pueblo Publishing Company, 1987), 28–30.

Biblical Interpretation

SC sets out an understanding that the scriptures provide inspiration and force to prayers and collects, and meaning to actions and signs.

Our study of the orations shows a variety of biblical influences. Some prayers and collects are immediately biblical, others build on biblical teachings and sayings, some engage with more lively 'play' with the texts. The Communion Rite seems to have been surrendered to the compelling power of the word to aid the faithful as they enter into participation in the table. The overt biblical nature of these texts allows them to inspire the faithful, keep their worship close to the inspiration of the scriptures, and carry something of the force and power of the word into many of the aspects of worship. There is an important corollary here. The biblical inspiration and force is only apparent when the prayers and collects are in the language of the worshipping community, and the translations give prominence to the scriptural references in the text in ways that ensures worshippers easily recognise them. The current Roman Curial strictures around liturgical translation do not provide adequately for the way that the prayers use and reflect biblical themes nor for the need for the hearers to be able to recognise biblical allusions in a familiar vernacular biblical idiom.[23]

The question of meaning, however, raises more complex concerns around interpretation. It is possible to have biblical interpretations of the Mass that actually distort the nature of the liturgy, and contribute to systemic misinterpretations. One of these is seen in the allegorical interpretation of the Mass.[24] In this approach each part of the liturgy was assigned a particular circumstance of the life of Jesus. It is worth quoting a little from one exponent, Honorius of Autun (c. 1100):

> Thus when the celebrant says the *orate* he expresses Christ placed for us in agony, when he commanded

---

23. The literalist bent in the translation regimen established under *Liturgiam Authenticam* does not allow well for translators to capture the scriptural 'play' found in prayers.
24. A comprehensive discussion of this approach is found in 'The Mass as Sacred Drama', in *Christian Rite and Christian Drama in the Middle Ages: Essays in the Origin and Early History of Modern Drama*, by OB Hardison (Baltimore: The Johns Hopkins Press, 1965), 35–79.

> His apostles to pray. By the silence of the *Secreta* he expressed Christ as a lamb without voice being led to the sacrifice. By the extension of his hands he represents the extension of Christ on the Cross . . . Through the secret prayers of the Canon he suggests the silence of Holy Saturday . . . [25]

Pious worshippers could attend the liturgy and see in the actions of the Mass the life of Jesus played out before them. This clearly provided a scriptural meaning for signs and actions, yet was overlaid upon the liturgy, and did little to bring about engagement with the actual texts and actions themselves. It gave a biblical solution to the dislocation of the worshippers from participation in the liturgy itself, and allowed them some spiritual sustenance as they were reduced to the role of passive onlooker. Nevertheless this interpretative lens gave impetus to systemic distortions. As a minor example, the embolism 'for yours is the kingdom, the power and the glory . . . ' inserted after the Lord's Prayer came to be recited in silence as it was seen to stand within that portion of the Mass which represented the Passion of Christ.[26] The allegorical approach gave impetus to the reduction of the focus of the Great Prayer of Thanksgiving to the death of Christ, allowing for an exclusive emphasis on theologies of sacrifice and the over-identification of the priest celebrant with Christ.

A highly significant biblical text that has a complex history of interpretation is the passage commonly described as the consecratory words of Jesus. This singular passage is found in all the Eucharistic Prayers in the current Roman Missal, and highlighted in capital letters within the text itself, both in the Latin *editio typica* and translations. The section reads:

> Take this all of you and eat of it, for this is the Body which will be given up for you . . . take this, all of you and drink from it, for this is the chalice of my Blood, the Blood of the new and eternal covenant, which will be poured for you and for many for the forgiveness of sins. Do this in memory of me.

25. Hardison, *Christian Rite and Christian Drama*, 40.
26. See Joseph Jungmann, *The Mass of the Roman Rite: Its Origin and Development*, volume II (Westminster: Christian Classics, 1992), 289.

Particularly since the middle ages, this text has been characterised as the 'very words' of Jesus, which bring about the transformation of the bread and wine into the Body and Blood of Christ. At a further level of interpretation, through his authority to pray these words in the Eucharistic Prayer, the priest acts in the person of Christ, and is identified as (another) Christ.

How does this interpretation stand up in light of contemporary biblical and liturgical research? There are a number of reasons to call this view into question. As with many liturgical texts, the biblical reference is precisely a reference to a biblical text but not the exact text itself. It is misleading, though common, to see this excerpt as the 'very words' of Jesus when closer examination reveals it does not follow any Vulgate text exactly but rather is a liturgical approximation from the many Supper texts.[27] While the passage is scriptural in inspiration and force, what does it add to the meaning of the Eucharistic Prayer? The best response is that it belongs in the prayer as the culmination of the things for which thanks is given, and as a warrant for the celebration itself.[28] As well, more recent liturgical scholarship has shown the text is not essential to authentic eucharistic praying: indeed an ancient text whose current use is recognised by the Curia as legitimate does not contain these words.[29]

The change in interpretation of this text affects the way the prayer is understood and prayed by the worshipping community. It signals a shift from the Eucharistic Prayer as mainly a vehicle for the con-

27. For convenience the references are repeated here: 1 Corinthians 11:23–36; Matthew 26:26–29; Mark 14:22–25; Luke 22:15–20.

28. For a study of the place of the dominical words in the Roman Canon itself, see Dominic E Serra, 'The Roman Canon: the Theological Significance of Its Structure and Syntax', in *Primary Readings on the Eucharist*, edited by Thomas Fisch (Collegeville, MN: Liturgical Press, 2004), 129–156, particularly 144 ff.

29. The Roman Church has recognised the legitimacy of the Liturgy of the Saints Addai and Mari, and even contributed that though the Institution Narrative is absent, the consecratory words are integrated in the prayers of the text. The fact remains that the text has no tradition of containing the Last Supper words of Christ. See Pontifical Council for Promoting Christian Unity, *Guidelines for Admission to the Eucharist Between the Chaldean Church and the Assyrian Church of the East* (2001), <http://www.vatican.va/roman_curia/pontifical_councils/chrstuni/documents/rc_pc_chrstuni_doc_20011025_chiesa-caldea-assira_en.html>. Accessed 10 February 2013.
The text of this Eucharistic Prayer can be found in Jasper and Cuming, *Prayers of the Eucharist*, 39-44.

secration of the bread and wine, to the oration as the great prayer of thanksgiving in which the blessing of bread and cup is effected. Further it offers an opportunity to review the theology of priesthood and revise the devotional habits of ordained and lay alike. There is much to discuss on this issue, but for the purpose of this paper it is important that close and continuous attention be given to the way scripture is used in the assignation of meaning to actions and signs.

Concluding Remarks

There is a comprehensive case to be made for the role of the scriptures as an inspiration for the prayers and collects. Further, the more these orations are at play with the scriptures, the more they seem capable of empowering worshippers and enlivening worship. A similar case can be made for the liturgical songs, though that has not been substantiated here. In the case of the Eucharist, there is an undeniable biblical warrant for the celebration itself, along with strong evidence for grounding the basic structure of the rite in the scriptures themselves.

Yet it is not sufficient to use or mimic the biblical text to claim a prayer, collect, song, action or sign is scriptural. As seen with our discussion of the Eucharistic Prayer, it is the critical appreciation of how a scriptural passage is being interpreted by the worshipping community that is also at play. One of the criteria for renewal of the liturgy mentioned above was changing those elements that are out of harmony with the inner nature of the liturgy or become unsuited to it (*SC* 21). While the profound biblical nature of the liturgy of the Mass has been revealed, the community needs to turn its efforts to uncovering strongly held theological and devotional positions that have resonance because of their use of the biblical text but whose meaning is no longer able to be sustained due to more recent biblical and liturgical scholarship.

Eucharist: Inclusive of all Women and Men

Carol Hogan

Sacrosanctum Concilium[1] (*SC*) proclaimed the liturgy, especially the Eucharist, to be a vital means of supporting the growth of Catholics in Christian living and in their capacity to preach Christ. It was also seen as a sign by which 'the Church was raised above the nations'. *SC* unequivocally recommended that changes be made 'to adjust certain elements of the liturgy to make it more functional and its rites more appropriate to the times'.[2] It emphasised the 'paramount' importance of scripture, the need for it to be 'more varied and suitable, and a more representative portion of it to be read over a set cycle of years'.[3] These goals seemed to indicate that the way was open for new theologies and a praxis that had the potential to bring changes to the Eucharist that would reflect a wider variety of human experience, especially women's experience of participation in the Church's rituals. In examining some fundamental theological issues that are integral to the Eucharist, some current practices and fragments of liturgical history, I shall indicate ways that would support and enable women to attain 'full, conscious and active participation' in the eucharistic celebration.[4]

Vatican II—Renewed Theology

The Second Vatican Council (1962–65) initiated unexpected and unimagined changes to Catholic communities worldwide. It opened the

1. *SC* #1 & 2. The text of this document is taken from <http://www.vatican.va/archive/hist_councils/ii_vatican_council/documents/vat-ii_const_19631204_sacrosanctum-concilium_en.html> Accessed 24 April 2013.
2. *SC* #61.
3. *SC* #51.
4. *SC* #14.

way for a significant revision of the format of the Eucharist.[5] Where the language of the Eucharist had been Latin, and the priest officiated with his back to the congregation, it was now characterised by features such as the presider facing the congregation, and greater participation of the people in the whole celebration as well as in ministries such as reading and distributing communion. Having the readings proclaimed in the vernacular became integral to the eucharistic rite. Emphasis on the table of the bread and wine, together with twelve new Eucharistic Prayers of praise and thanksgiving, balanced an understanding of the Mass as the Holy Sacrifice by restoring the notion of the Mass as a meal. Rich biblical themes such as memorial, covenant, thanksgiving, passover, and Paschal Mystery informed eucharistic theology. *SC* emphasised that the presence of Christ was to be found not only in the transubstantiated bread and wine and in the person of the priest, but also in the word and in the worshipping assembly.[6]

The vast majority of the faithful very happily welcomed the reforms, which enabled them to participate more fully in the rituals, not only by understanding what was being said but also by participating in the many roles that were made available to them. At that time, the sexism of the language passed unnoticed. It would be some years before the feminist theological movement would begin to bring a critical perspective to theology and to the liturgical praxis of the Church.

A Feminist Perspective[7]

The early 1980s saw a number of female Catholic theologians begin to challenge traditional theologies and scripture interpretations in a way that opened up new perspectives and understandings.[8] One of

5. The Sacred Congregation of Divine Worship, *The Order of Mass*: English Translation (Sydney: E.J Dwyer, 1970).
6. *SC* #7.
7. See Elizabeth Schüssler Fiorenza, *Wisdom Ways: Introducing Feminist Biblical Interpretation* (Maryknoll, New York: Orbis Books, 2001), 209.
8. Mary Daly, *The Church and the Second Sex* (London: Geoffrey Chapman, 1968); *Woman Spirit Rising*, edited by Carol P Christ & Judith Plaskow (San Francisco: Harper & Row, 1979); Elizabeth Schüssler Fiorenza, *In Memory of Her: A Feminist Reconstruction of Christian Origins* (New York: SCM Press, 1983); Letty M Russell, *Human Liberation in a Feminist Perspective—A Theology* (Philadelphia: Westminster Press, 1974); Rosemary Radford Ruether, *Sexism and God-talk:*

these key writings was Rosemary Radford Ruether's seminal study on feminist theology, 'Sexism and God-Talk: Towards a Feminist Theology'. Ruether introduced a central theological axiom (which has been accepted generally in English speaking countries) with which to work in defining feminist theology. She argued that 'the critical principle of feminist theology is the promotion of the full humanity of women. Whatever denies, diminishes, or distorts the full humanity of women is, therefore, appraised as not redemptive.'[9] Thus Ruether and others began to provide a new perspective for interpreting Christianity. They pointed out that the Jesus of the gospels did not oppress women. Indeed he had women friends and the gospels are replete with stories of his friendship with and affirmation of women, as well as the many ways in which they were involved with his ministry. Clearly, women were at the heart of decisive salvific events foundational to the Christian faith: they were present at the birth, death and resurrection of Jesus and in the upper room at Pentecost

While Vatican II had brought enormous and transformative changes to Catholicism, some decades later it became increasingly obvious that a feminist critique which had the capacity to develop and enhance those changes even further had not influenced them. In Australia the growth and importance of feminism was eventually recognised and formalised with the publication by the Australian Catholic Bishops Conference in April 1999 of 'Woman and Man: One in Christ Jesus. Report on the Participation of Women in the Catholic Church in Australia' (hereafter 'Woman and Man').[10] While the focus of this research project was more extensive than women and liturgy it is pertinent to our subject. The project was commissioned by the Australian Catholic Bishops Conference and jointly undertaken by its Committee for Justice, Development and Peace, the Australian Catholic University, and the Australian Conference of Leaders of Religious Institutes (later renamed Catholic Religious Australia).[11] The work addressed four key questions:

Toward a Feminist Theology (Boston: Beacon Press, 1983).

9. Ruether, *Sexism and God-Talk*, 18.
10. The Australian Catholic Bishops Conference, *Woman and Man: One in Christ Jesus*. Report on the Participation of Women in the Catholic Church in Australia (Australia: Harper Collins, 1999).
11. Dr Marie Macdonald chaired this committee of three men and three women.

1. What are the ways in which women participate in the Catholic Church in Australia?
2. What assistance and support are currently offered to women to participate in the Church?
3. What are barriers to women's participation in the Church?
4. What are some ways in which women's participation in the Church can be increased?

One of the important conclusions was that the Church was seen to be unaffected by Australian society's recognition of the changing role of women and affirmation of their equality with men. The limited involvement of women in decision-making was another key issue and relates to liturgical reform.[12] An increasing number of women had become more aware of the apparent equality of the sexes that was evident in the early Church and was now attained in secular society. Both factors gave more and more women insight into how the male-focused Church worked to the exclusion of women. Those who adopted a feminist perspective felt impelled to examine the basic theological concepts of the Catholic tradition, including those of sacramental theology. Of the many problematic issues in eucharistic theology, I suggest that three critical concepts need to be addressed—the meaning of sacrifice, the role of gender, and the place of symbol—as key defining eucharistic themes that are seriously considered in any sacramental dialogue.

The Holy Sacrifice of the Mass[13]

Although the themes of the Lord's Supper, community and thanksgiving were carried over from the tradition of the Jewish meal, focusing on the Mass as a Holy Sacrifice has long predominated in the Catholic Church's official teaching. Frank O'Loughlin describes it unambiguously:

> Since the Council of Trent (but originating before it) sacrifice became the sole category that Catholics used to

12. *Woman and Man*, viii.
13. For a further discussion on this subject see Carmel Pilcher, Chapter 8, 'Eucharist: The Assembly Offers Sacrifice', pages 109–129 in this collection.

> describe the Mass as an action. They identified the Mass with the notion of sacrifice. So we often used such terms for the Mass as 'the Holy Sacrifice' identifying it simply as a sacrifice. Catholics had no other term with which to describe the action of the Mass. To deny or question it was tantamount to denying or questioning the value of the Mass.[14]

That the sacrifice of the Mass continues to be central to the Magisterium's teaching on Eucharist is reflected in recent documents such as *Ecclesia de Eucharistia*, *Mane Nobiscum Domine*, *Redemptionis Sacramentum* and the 'Eucharist, Source and Summit of the Life and Mission of the Church'.[15] However, this theology of the Mass, as I have already suggested and Vatican II demonstrated, has not been the only one operative in the history of Christianity.

Three authors from different disciplines have written of ritual sacrifice from another perspective. They support the argument that the theology of Eucharist as sacrifice is linked to men's fear of and resentment towards women. Their arguments are a critique of the belief that there are ontological differences between men and women.

Firstly, anthropologist Nancy Jay demonstrated that in most cultures the remedy for having been born of a woman is to engage in blood sacrifice. In a sense, men repudiate the physical birth that incurs mortality and impurity by engaging in sacrificial rites that establish religious-social genealogies and bonds between generations of men.[16] Through sacramental rituals, patriarchal lines replace matriarchal lineage.

Psychologist William Beers draws on Jay's theory to argue that men's need to establish cultural lineages has its source in unresolved

14. Frank O'Loughlin, *Christ Present in the Eucharist* (Homebush: St Pauls Publications, 2000), 81.
15. John Paul II, *Ecclesia de Eucharistia*; John Paul II, *Mane Nobiscum Domine*; Congregation for Divine Worship and the Discipline of the Sacraments, *Redemptionis Sacramentum*: Instruction on certain matters to be observed or to be avoided regarding the Most Holy Eucharist; Synod of Bishops: *The Eucharist: Source and Summit of the Life and Mission of the Church,* Lineamenta. <http://www.vatican.va/roman_curia/synod/documents/rc_synod_doc_20040528_lineamenta>. Accessed 27 July 2005.
16. Nancy Jay, *Throughout your Generations forever: Sacrifice, Religion, and Paternity* (Chicago: Chicago University Press, 1992), 112.

male anxiety and narcissism arising out of separation from the mother.[17] He explains how narcissistic anxiety fuels rituals and social structures that subordinate women.[18] His analysis of the Episcopal Eucharist leads him to the conclusion that 'the male function of sacrifice psychologically precludes a woman from performing the act, because at a profound level of the male psyche lie fear and resentment of women's femininity'.[19] Philosopher and psychoanalyst Luce Irigaray argues that sacrifice has brought about the original sin of the disassociation of the human and the divine, and more specifically the robbing of women of their subjectivity by 'both disavowing and appropriating the mother'.[20]

If Jay, Beers and Irigaray are correct, then hierarchical structures are sustained and maintained by liturgy to meet men's emotional needs, and sacrifice is a means of establishing and maintaining the Father-Son relationship. If no other strategies for establishing these relationships are available, then the Magisterium is likely to maintain its focus on Eucharist as sacrificial atonement, thus continuing to exclude women from some ministerial roles, the ordained ministry, and by implication a voice in decision-making in the Church. This understanding is contrary to a theology and experience of the God who healed the breach between divinity and humanity, a God who so loved humanity as to give God's life for them. Sadly, the Magisterium appears to ignore significant current eucharistic theologies that have the potential to create inclusive and dynamic eucharistic celebrations.[21]

---

17. William Beers, *Women and Sacrifice: Male Narcissism and the Psychology of Religion* (Detroit: Wayne State University Press, 1992), 123-179.
18. Beers, *Women and Sacrifice*, 139–147.
19. Beers, *Women and Sacrifice*, 167.
20. Luce Irigaray, *Marine Lover of Friedrich Nietzsche* (New York: Columbia University, 1991), 173.
21. Louis-Marie Chauvet, *The Sacraments: The Word of God at the Mercy of the Body* (Collegeville MN: Liturgical Press, 2001); Andrea Bieler and Luise Schottroff, *The Eucharist: Bodies, Bread and Resurrection* (Minneapolis MN: Fortress Press, 2007); William T Cavanaugh, *Torture and Eucharist: Theology, Politics and the Body of Christ* (Oxford, UK: Blackwell Publishers, 1998).

Anthropology/Complementarity

If, as the French sacramental theologian Louis-Marie Chauvet claims, anthropology is a 'co-essential aspect of the sacrament',[22] then the Church's teaching on women is also pertinent to its stance on sacramentality. In the face of evidence presented by contemporary developmental theorists and theologians, the Magisterium's teaching on the complementarity of the sexes cannot be sustained. Irigaray, among others, offers insights on this issue.[23] She values 'irreducible sexual differences between the sexes' but draws other insights from these differences.[24] Arguing from the Magisterium's own ground, she challenges its conclusions and, by implication, its understanding of the Eucharist.

Irigaray names our patriarchal culture 'phallocentric', because the worldview that it represents and symbolises is one that justifies and validates only male power. Although there are two sexes there has been 'only one subjectivity, one voice and one normative experience'.[25] In Christian culture, women are perceived as 'the Other' of the 'phallocentric Same'. Hence, to successfully enter Western culture, women have had to act according to its masculine and heterosexual symbols, language and norms, the 'law' or 'name' of the Father. This is in keeping with the point made by Beers, that Christianity is embedded in a symbolic system which views complementarity of gender relationships as a product of right order. Thus Christianity claims divine approbation for its viewpoint.

Irigaray concludes that if women as a whole are to become a unified subject they have the right to name and claim their own female

22. Louise-Marie Chauvet, *Symbol and Sacrament: Sacramental Reinterpretation of Christian Existence* (Collegeville MN: Liturgical Press, 1995), 403–404.
23. Frances Carol Hogan, *Eucharistic Metamorphosis: Changing Symbols—Changing Lives*. Doctoral Thesis submitted to the Melbourne College of Divinity, 2007. For supporting arguments, see for example, Elizabeth Johnson, *She Who Is: The Mystery of God in Feminist Theological Discourse* (NY: Crossroad Publishing Co, 1992).
24. Grace M Jansen, 'Luce Irigaray (b 1930); Introduction'. In *The Post-Modern God: A Theological Reader*, edited by Graham Ward (Oxford: Blackwell Press, 1997), 102-103.
25. Jansen, 'Luce Irigaray (b 1930); Introduction', 102–103.

symbolic order.[26] Basing her argument on Ludwig Feuerbach's 'Essence of Christianity', Irigaray explores the implications for the female subject of his notion that God is essential to help 'man' define 'his' gender.

> In order to become, it is essential to have a gender or an essence (consequently a sexuate essence) as horizon. Otherwise becoming remains partial and subject to the subject . . . Divinity is what we need to become free, autonomous, and sovereign. No human subjectivity, no human society has ever been established without the help of the divine. There comes a time for destruction. But, before destruction is possible, God or the gods must exist.[27]

Women not only need a divine of their own, they also need their own divine horizon. Men have a multitude of images to mirror back to them what a divine or divinised man looks like throughout the male life cycle, from the baby Jesus in the crib to the resurrected Christ.[28] However, 'Women have no such mirror, because until now, maleness has been normative philosophically, theologically and socially.'[29] Irigaray's theory of the female divine also demands the figure or symbol of a divine Mother-Daughter relation equivalent to the present Father-Son relation, and a Father-Daughter, as well as Mother-Son.[30] Thus, women would eventually:

> establish their own symbolic structure with its own language significations and terms; develop a new value

26. Jansen, 'Luce Irigaray (b 1930); Introduction', 102–103.
27. Luce Irigaray, '*Divine Women' in Sexes and Genealogies* (New York: Columbia University 1987), 61–62.
28. Kim Power, *Woman: Image of God or Image of Man? Artists Representations of Women and the Sacred*, unpublished lecture given at Australian Catholic University, 26 August 2003.
29. Kim Power, *Luce Irigaray and the Emergence of a Divine Horizon for Women*, Penny Magee Memorial Lecture (Australian Association of Scholars of Religion, 2000) CD Rom 9.
30. Jenny Daggers, 'Luce Irigaray and "Divine Women": A Resource for Postmodern Feminist Theology?', in *Feminist Theology*, 14 (1974): 47.

> system in which an emerging genealogy based on the mother-daughter relationship is prized; develop a new or deeper understanding of Divinity with the former as its symbolic constituents . . .[31]

Irigaray's argument for women's own divine symbolic does not imply two separate permanent cultures. When individual women have established their own divine symbolic they will be ready to dialogue with men about their roles and functions, thus creating the possibility for the emergence of a richer overall symbolic that is always in process, always flexible and fluid. However, the integrity of the masculine and feminine symbolics will always be preserved, as a becoming, not a being. So the symbolic that emerges is a single symbolic that is dialogical and fluid. How individual women might begin to link their symbols with official liturgy in the present climate is a fraught but critical question if our sacraments are to invite women to 'full, conscious and active participation'.[32]

Chauvet's Symbolic Sacramental Theology

One possible way to begin a conversation that coheres with feminist concerns is offered by Louis-Marie Chauvet's radical new ways of exploring eucharistic theology. He claims that a metaphysical theology no longer meets contemporary cultural needs and that the theory of divine causality is no longer viable. It puts at risk the supreme importance of God's personal relationship to humanity and isolates this presence from its liturgical context. As Robyn Horner explains: 'To think of the Eucharist in a substantial way is to think of a person as an object. Real Presence thought of in metaphysical terms is a presence that becomes subject to technical manipulation, a presence that can be used and controlled.'[33]

---

31. Frances Gray, *Jung, Analytical Psychology, and the Question of the Feminine* (London: Routledge, 2007), 178.
32. *SC* #14.
33. Robyn Horner, 'The Eucharist and the Postmodern', in *Eucharist: Experience and Testimony: A Colloquium*, edited by Tom Knowles (Melbourne: David Lovell Publishing, 2001), 18–19.

Symbolic theology teaches that Christ's presence is not that of a thing—an *esse*—but the gift of his life and 'his coming into presence'.[34] Chauvet argues that symbolic theology addresses meaning, relationships, the bodily and the local.[35] As Christians we believe that we go to God not in spite of our bodies but with the very core of our bodies—of desire, of tradition, of culture, of the universe. Bodies, female and male alike in their common humanity and their gendered differences, are the site of sacramental encounter with the gift of Christ's life and 'his coming into presence', *adesse*.[36] Chauvet does not mention that both society and tradition are patriarchal and androcentric, but he does note that liturgical power remains in the hands of clerics and that liturgical language is formulated in 'an almost esoteric way'. The conversation has begun among women and between women and men who share Chauvet's symbolic theology. Can this dialogue include open-minded members of the hierarchy?

Current Liturgical Praxis

Feminist theology has gradually begun to affect women's attitudes to liturgical praxis. Over the past thirty years, women have realised that traditional liturgical celebrations do not reflect either women's concerns or the richness of research in women's studies.[37] The liturgy continues to be formed by the dualities that the category of gender provides.[38] Catholic liturgies are usually led by men; God is habitually imaged and addressed almost exclusively in the masculine.[39] Exclusivist language is too often used by homilists, male clerics who rarely have a feminist or feminine perspective and certainly do not share women's experience.[40]

34. Chauvet, *Symbol and Sacrament*, 403–404
35. Chauvet, *The Sacraments*, 113–114. For further development of this issue see Hogan, *Eucharistic Metamorphosis*, 49–58.
36. Chauvet, *Symbol and Sacrament*, 403–405.
37. Teresa Berger, *Women's Ways of Worship: Gender Analysis and Liturgical History* (Collegeville: Liturgical Press, 1999), 2.
38. Berger, *Women's Ways of Worship*, 152.
39. See Elizabeth Johnson, *She Who Is*; Gail Ramshaw, *God Beyond Gender: Feminist Christian God-Language* (Minneapolis: Fortress Press, 1995); Sally McFague, *Models of God: Theology for an Ecological, Nuclear Age* (Philadelphia: Fortress Press, 1987).
40. Mary Catherine Hilkert, 'Feminist Theology: A Review of Literature', in

Male bias is clearly evident in the choice and treatment of lectionary readings. Even when the scriptures feature women's voices, history or experience, verses that refer to women are often omitted in the liturgical readings. For example, the midwives Shiprah and Puah who saved the lives of Hebrew baby boys (Exod 1:15–21) are deleted from the reading for Monday of the Fifteenth Week of Ordinary Time, Cycle A, in the lectionary. Only 20.9 per cent of references in the lectionary are to women: 14.7 per cent of those are significant and 6.2 per cent are peripheral. Many do not portray women appropriately.[41] Women are usually praised for a limited number of virtues, such as virginity, humility and self-effacement. Stories of women's faith and courage, exemplified in Shiprah and Puah and in Esther, are found in the lectionary only on weekdays, when the assemblies are small. Furthermore, translations have been misleading. For example, for a millennium the female apostle Junia has been referred to as Junias, and represented as the male apostle referred to by Paul.[42]

In sum, it appears that the lectionary's hermeneutical principles fail to take women seriously as significant active agents in salvation history. They are regarded as adjuncts to male actors, important only in relation to marriage and as birthing mothers. Otherwise they appear to be expendable.[43]

This is not surprising given the fact that the Congregations for Divine Worship and for the Doctrine of the Faith do not employ women and do not appear to consult them. Thus women are automatically excluded from input into Vatican documents on liturgy and theology.[44] Clearly, these influential agencies do not consider that women's experience of communal worship could make a valuable contribution to the liturgical practice of the Church.

Theological Studies, 56/2 (1995): 341–342.

41. Margery Procter-Smith, 'Images of Women in the Lectionary', in *The Power of Naming: A Concilium Reader in Feminist Liberation Theology*, edited by Elisabeth Schüssler Fiorenza (Maryknoll, New York: Orbis Books, 1996), 179. The Common Lectionary adopted the Catholic Lectionary's choice of New Testament readings, but its Hebrew readings contain more suitable readings about women; see Procter-Smith, 'Images of Women in the Lectionary', 177.
42. Eldon J Epp, *Junia: The First Woman Apostle* (Minneapolis, MN: Fortress Press, 2005).
43. Marjorie Procter-Smith, 'Images of Women in the Lectionary', 183.
44. Robert Mickens, 'Revealed; the True Role of Women in the Vatican', in *The Tablet*, 26 August 2006: 28.

Yet, since the Council, women's ministry as readers, cantors, liturgical educators and leaders of the celebrations of the sacraments has not only been of practical assistance to the Church, but in places such as South America the only way the Church's traditions and practices are maintained. This ministry carries high symbolic value.[45] One might even argue that it has prepared women for ordination. In 1976, when attempts to allow women to be ordained failed,[46] many left the Catholic Church and began their search for women's ways of worship in small groups. Professional liturgists, members of Christian communities or 'women churches', and participants in women's conferences or associations are using their creative imaginations to celebrate Eucharist in rituals that give expression to their beliefs, their images of the divine, their stories and their dreams.[47]

These rituals address God in biblical terms that are female, use texts that focus on women, invite women to interpret the scriptures, celebrate contemporary women's works and writings, use female symbols, enable women to share their experiences and sing women's songs. Members of one women's group in Melbourne, Australia, have spoken of their experience in a variety of ways. One has grown into 'a deep sense of pride in her womanhood as readings, images and symbols which are exclusively feminine touch into my very being'. Another has felt 'the new sense of a spiritual community that has developed over the years that has never been present in the parish'. For another it is the presence

45. Susan A Ross, *Extravagant Affections: A Feminist Sacramental Theology* (New York: Continuum 2001), 34.
46. In 1976 the Sacred Congregation for the Doctrine of the Faith discussed the issue of the ordination of women and issued a Declaration on the Question of the Admission of Women to the Ministerial Priesthood which concluded that for various doctrinal, theological, and historical reasons, the church 'does not consider herself authorized to admit women to priestly ordination.' 100 <http://www.vatican.va/roman_curia/congregations/cfaith/documents/rc_con_cfaith_doc_19761015_inter-insigniores_en.html>. Accessed 18 May 2013.
47. *Dissident Daughters: Feminist Liturgies in Global Context*, edited by Teresa Berger, (Louisville: Westminster John Knox Press, 2001); Sheila Durkin Dierks, *Women Eucharist* (Colorado: Woven Word Press, 1997); Kathleen M Henry, *The Book of Ours: Liturgies for Feminist People* (Jamaica Plain, MA: Alabaster Jar Liturgical Arts, 1980); Miriam Therese Winter, *Woman Prayer, Woman Song* (Oak Park, IL: Meyer Stone, 1987); *Woman Word* (New York: Crossroad, 1991); *Woman Wisdom* (North Blackburn, Vic: Collins Dove, 1992) and *Woman Witness* (North Blackburn, Vic; Collins Dove, 1992); Gloria Ulterima, *Drawing from Women's Well* (Notre Dame, Indiana: Ave Maria Press, 2002).

of a God, who is 'Sophia, Creator Spirit, Life and Grace Giver, Sustainer'. For two others this worship is their sole link with the official Church and for one of them has engendered a new understanding of God. Such rituals offer women the opportunity to be nurtured in a community spirituality that is based on women's personhood and psychology and a specifically feminine symbolic system.

Three Eucharistic Fragments

Support for feminist liturgies that use female images and symbols of God can be found in recent biblical and liturgical research. Drawing on contemporary German studies, Teresa Berger has 'lifted the veil' on rich feminine scraps of liturgical history that have the potential to shape an Irigarayan symbol system.[48] Firstly, she explores ancient traditions that describe the making of bread as a distinctive communal and labour-intensive female occupation that Jesus assumed in his many feedings of the multitudes. She notes the Sirach female image of Sophia as host and food at her banquets to which she invites all.[49] Yet another compelling image in early Christianity was the linking of Jesus shedding his own blood with nourishment through breast milk. In a number of his writings, Clement of Alexandria (c 150–c 215) describes the Church as providing 'milk that is holy' and suggests that Christ is the maternal breast of the Father nursing the believers with his shed blood turned into breast milk.[50] Historically, the image of the eucharist as mother's milk, especially at baptismal eucharists when the sacrament was distributed with honey and the bread and wine, appeared across Syrian, Greek, and Latin Churches, as well as in France and North Africa.[51] Metaphors of breast-nursing and milk are found in mystical writings, especially in those of women such as Julian of Norwich (1342–1416) and Teresa of Avila (sixteenth century).

Berger has also found evidence in a fourth or fifth century Greek treatise by a female ascetic on virginity, entitled 'Discourse on Salvation to a Virgin' (*De virginitate)*, which describes the daily round of her

48. Teresa Berger, *Gender Differences and the Making of Liturgical History: Lifting a Veil on Liturgy's Past* (Burlington, VT: Ashgate Publishing Ltd, 2011).
49. Berger, *Gender Differences*, 71.
50. Berger, *Gender Differences*, 74ff.
51. Berger, *Gender Differences*, 72-75.

prayers. It lists detailed instructions to 'eucharistise' the bread on her table, sign the bread three times, and speak a concluding prayer and thanksgiving which includes a petition for 'heavenly nourishment'.[52] Berger concludes that it is not a prayer of a heretical group, nor a prayer specifically written for women. It indicates that ascetic women were celebrating 'domestic' eucharists at the same time as basilica eucharists were developing. This practice provides evidence of women as eucharistic presiders, as indeed they could well have been in the early Church. It would seem to open the way for women to 'eucharistise' in contexts where a priest is not available.

The above eucharistic fragments—the link between Jesus and Sophia, the eucharist as mother's milk, and the ascetic virgin's Eucharistic Prayer—are valid and rich, if little known, threads in our liturgical/eucharistic tradition. They are also differently gendered and bring into focus the idea that gender has always operated as a privileged category in the Church. This is only fully realised if one starts using the female body and women. It is then that the maleness becomes transparent. It is the male gendered body that has been the paradigm, with the female body side-lined. With Berger we can conclude, firstly, that those who gather for eucharist are gendered bodies.[53] Secondly, the fragments she has gathered can be understood only within their attention to the materiality of broader life which includes food production and nursing practices. Finally, given the variety of early eucharistic practices one may ask what is normative and who decides? Clearly, the inclusion of Lady Wisdom as host and food, the image of God as nourishing and nursing mother, and the symbol of milk are rich and appropriate symbols for the Church to adopt.

Thus, a feminist reinterpretation of liturgical history indicates that within the sacramental/liturgical sphere women are clearly perceived or treated as second-class Christians. They have had restricted access to the formulation of the Church's doctrine and its history. More seriously, the Church itself is being deprived of a feminine symbolic and liturgies that could become more relevant and inclusive, and thus life-giving. If women had the opportunity to contribute to the renewal of liturgy, in particular a eucharist that embodied some of Berger's findings, women's experience, and newly-found biblical themes and the-

52. Berger, *Gender Differences*, 88-92.

53. Note: Berger does not use the traditional binaries of male and female, but widened her definition of gender to include, for example, eunuchs.

ology, then a different model of eucharist more inclusive of women could be possible.

A Way Forward

I believe that 'Woman and Man' has given us a starting point (however indirect) for a more inclusive eucharist. The data clearly indicates that the most important ways of promoting women's participation are prayer, increasing involvement in decision-making and Church administration, reforming those beliefs and practices that do not promote equality, appointing women as spokespersons for the Church, and creating opportunities for theologically qualified women to make a greater contribution to the Church.[54]

Prayer that is shaped by women, celebrates women, provides women as models for the younger generation and uses inclusive language and images and a homily preached by women would widen the parameters and meet the requirements of *SC* for full participation.

While increasing women's involvement in decision-making within the Church is a valid form for increased participation, one needs to constantly be mindful that the structures of the Church are patriarchal, and not those within which feminist thinkers function easily with integrity and effectiveness. Some feminists would even argue that to join them is a betrayal.

Reforming beliefs and practices that do not promote equality is critical to any forward agenda. The issue here is that of the Church's theology of complementarity, which is a subtle form of inequality and oppression, and which cannot remain a foundational concept for a renewed eucharistic theology. The theology of sacrifice is also related to the issue of gender, as I have pointed out with reference to the theories of Jay and Beers. Irigaray's call for a feminine symbolic is essential to the dialogue. Sacramental and liturgical history as unveiled by Berger is a rich site for further study and potential change.

Inclusion does not mean equality, but what is really demanded is a complete transformation of the way the Church understands itself within its masculine, paternal symbolic. Appointing women as spokesperson is a hazardous issue. Generally, the women who are ap-

54. *Woman and Man*, 386.

pointed are chosen simply because they are loyal to the hierarchical Church. Women who would choose to give a women's point-of-view have the potential to be a catalyst in bringing another perspective to the public face of the Church, and deconstructing the false universalisation of male experience.

The recommendation to provide theological education for women was potentially helpful in 2000 with the launch of 'Woman and Man'. Indeed, for many years, women—mostly lay and in the teaching profession at both undergraduate and graduate level—have been in the majority in the theological institutes. However evidence of teaching of feminist theology and related subjects is scarcely visible. It is only when faculties open their teaching to feminist theology and associated subjects which include feminist theories that progress will be made.

The full implementation of the recommendations of 'Woman and Man' would be a welcome and effective means of bringing the aims and ideals of SC to fruition.

Confirmation: Ordered to Sacrifice[1]

David Orr

> The Rite of Confirmation is to be revised and the intimate connection which this sacrament has with the whole of Christian Initiation is to be more lucidly set forth: for this reason it will be fitting for candidates to renew their baptismal promises just before they are confirmed .*Sacrosanctum Concilium*, 71 *(SC)*

With this brief comment, the Council began a period of searching by the pastors of the Church for the 'intimate connection' of confirmation within the whole of Christian Initiation. In the pastoral practice of that time, confirmation was usually celebrated as a sacrament during adolescence, often several years after the celebration of first communion. The publication of the Rite of Christian Initiation of Adults reflected the research that had been done on the integrity of the Sacraments of Initiation: along with all the rites of the catechumenate, this ritual includes the 'celebration of the sacraments of baptism, confirmation and Eucharist' in one celebration.[2] Thus the sacraments of initiation are seen as a unified celebration. This then puts pressure on a theology that seeks to explain the separate celebration of each of these sacraments of initiation, and the order in which they

1. 'The sacrament of confirmation makes us *subjects* of the eucharistic action, changing us from passive observers of a religious ritual into active participants receiving anew, during every Eucharistic Prayer, the power of the Holy Spirit invoked both on the bread and wine and *upon those who have assembled to share it.*' Bruce Morrill, 'Holy Communion as Public Act: Ethics and Liturgical Participation', in *Studia Liturgica*, 41/1 (2011): 33.
2. *Rite of Christian Initiation of Adults.* (1987) #2.

are celebrated. 'To celebrate the sacrament of confirmation on its own sometime after a Christian has begun sharing in the Church's eucharistic communion is theologically incomprehensible and liturgically corrupt'.[3] This has been particularly evident in the ordering of the celebration of confirmation. In fact, there has been little work done on directly linking confirmation to Eucharist, 'the climax of their initiation and the centre of the whole Christian life'.[4] Morrill reminds us that 'the sacrament of confirmation makes us *subjects* of the eucharistic action, changing us from passive observers of religious ritual into active participants'.[5] What then is lacking that will enable us to move from being passive participants to being active? How can this intimate connection between confirmation and Eucharist 'be more lucidly set forth'?

Emerging from a study of the history of confirmation, there has been a call to restore the traditional order for the celebration of the sacraments of initiation. Consequently many local churches have restored the traditional order with confirmation now being celebrated either before or with first communion. The driving force for this change has often been a respect for the normative value of ancient practice. It may be helpful to review the history of this ancient practice to shed light on possible solutions. A brief overview of this history is provided by Morrill, with particular emphasis on the Bishop's role.[6] He concludes: 'Confirmation and first Communion both lost any effective connection to baptism which had come to function as a 'clinical' ministration to each infant's moral soul'.[7] The present paper will build on his work but focus particularly on confirmation as the giving of the priesthood to the faithful[8] leading to Eucharist.

Often the reading of history is skewed by a study seeking to identity confirmation as a separate sacrament. The separation of confir-

3. Bruce Morrill, 'The Meaning of Confirmation: Searching with the Bishop, the Liturgy, and the Holy Spirit', in *Liturgical Ministry*, 9 (2000): 57.
4. *Rite of Christian Initiation of Adults*. (Sydney: EJ Dwyer, 1987), #233.
5. Morrill, 'Holy Communion as Public Act: Ethics and Liturgical Participation', 33.
6. Morrill, 'The Meaning of Confirmation: Searching with the Bishop, the Liturgy, and the Holy Spirit', 50ff.
7. Morrill. 'The Meaning of Confirmation: Searching with the Bishop, the Liturgy, and the Holy Spirit', 55.
8. Denis Orr, *The Giving of the Priesthood to the Faithful* (Rome: Pontifical Liturgical Institute, 1991).

mation from baptism (and consequently from Eucharist) is linked with the loss of the understanding of the priestly role of the baptised in the celebration of the Eucharist. The work of the faithful in the celebration of the Eucharist gradually became taken over by the cleric. Consequently the Mass became the work of the cleric only, when it should be the action of all the baptised. In its history as the role of the baptised was diminished, the celebration of Eucharist was no longer the action of Christ and the Church, but seemingly only the work of the presider.

In their early research, Lampe[9] and Thornton[10] approached the sacrament of confirmation with an understanding of the sacrament being essentially linked to the Spirit. They draw upon the working of the Spirit in the life of Christ 'anointing him in power for his messianic mission'.[11] Christ's birth is the work of the Spirit and then at baptism Christ is given the Spirit. At Incarnation Christ is born among us as the Son of God through the power of the Spirit (Lk 1: 35). Then at baptism Christ is anointed by the same Spirit for mission (Lk 4: 22; John 1:32–34). 'In the Spirit's coming to rest on Jesus at the Jordan, the Church Fathers saw that the three functions identified with anointing were now united in Jesus: in his person and ministry, the Spirit was presently at work building the new Israel'.[12] It will be into this Paschal Mystery that Christians are to be initiated.

History

Hippolytus' 'Apostolic Tradition'[13] provides liturgical form for the celebration of initiation. Its context is the celebration of the Eucharist by the bishop and community where the candidates are washed (in baptism), have hands laid upon them by the Bishop (confirmation) so that their oblation may be consecrated as the Body and Blood of Christ (in eucharistic communion) which they receive for the first

9. GWH Lampe, *The Seal of the Spirit* (London: Longmans, Green and Co, 1954).
10. LS Thornton, *Confirmation. Its Place in the Baptismal Mystery.* (Westminster: Longmans, Green and Co, 1955).
11. C Masters Keightley, '*Summorum Pontificum* and the Unmaking of the Lay Church', in *Worship*. 86/4 (2012): 296.
12. Masters Keightley, '*Summorum Pontificum* and the Unmaking of the Lay Church', 296.
13. Reference will be made to *La Tradition Apostolique de Saint Hippolyte*, edited by B Botte (Műnster: AVH, 1963).

time at this celebration.[14] The prayer accompanying the episcopal imposition of hands names the working of the Spirit so that the neophytes will receive the gift of the Spirit to serve God according to God's will.[15] Thus the gift of the Holy Spirit, made possible by baptism and ritualised in the episcopal imposition of hands, enables them to take their rightful part in the celebration of the Eucharist: to pray with the assembly, give and receive the sign of peace, and offer and receive the oblation. Ordered by the anointing of the Spirit, the initiated now make their spiritual sacrifices in union with the mystical Body of Christ (the assembly) to be the Body of Christ.

Augustine describes this journey by invoking the image of baking bread:

> unless wheat is ground . . . it cannot possibly get into the shape which is called bread. In the same way you too were being ground and pounded (as a catechumen[16]), as it were, by the humiliation of fasting and the sacrament of exorcism. Then came baptism and you were, in a manner of speaking, moistened with water in order to be shaped into bread. But it's not yet bread without fire to bake it. So what does fire represent? That's the chrism, the anointing. Oil, the fire-feeder, you see, is the sacrament of the Holy Spirit.[17]

Notice the movement from formation to celebration in water and anointing (which he identifies as the Holy Spirit) so that they may be the bread of Eucharist. Being the bread of Eucharist is linked with the words of Paul in Romans 12:1—'offer your bodies to him as a living sacrifice'. Christ takes flesh in the Eucharist which has been made

14. Botte, *La Tradition Apostolique*. Chapter 21 De la tradition du saint baptême: 45–59.
15. Botte, *La Tradition Apostolique*, 53.
16. 'When as catechumens, you were held back, you were being stored in the barn'. *Sermon 229 On Holy Easter Sunday about the Sacraments of the Faithful*. In *The Works of Saint Augustine: A Translation for the 21st Century*, edited by John E Rotelle, translated by Edmund Hill (New York: New City Press, 1992–2008), III/6: 265 (hereafter 'Rotelle' will refer to this series of Augustine's work).
17. *Sermon* 227 'Preached on the holy day of Easter to the Infants, on the Sacraments.' In Rotelle, *The Works of Saint Augustine*, III/6:254.

possible by the sacrifice of each member of the assembly because they have been anointed with the gift of the Holy Spirit. Each member comes to the Eucharist both to offer their spiritual sacrifices and receive anew 'the power of the Holy Spirit invoked both on the bread and wine and *upon those who have assembled to share it*'.[18]

Augustine notes that the gift of the Spirit is not a physical one, but rather spiritual: 'It is written of (Christ) more openly in the Acts of the Apostles that God anointed him with the Holy Spirit (10:38), not of course with a visible oil but with the gift of grace which is signified by the chrism the Church anoints the baptised with'.[19] He goes on to remind them that 'visible oil is a sign; invisible oil is a sacramental mystery'.[20] It is because of this mystical anointing, an invisible oil, that the baptised are priests: 'just as we call all Christians "*Christs*" in virtue of their sacramental anointing (*chrisma*) so we call them all "*priests*" because they are members of the one Priest. The apostle Peter says of them that they are "a holy people, a royal priesthood" (1 Peter 2: 9)'.[21] SC will also take that quote from First Peter as its basis for affirming the priesthood of the faithful[22]—a theme that will be later acknowledged by the Council in the document on the Church: 'the baptised, by regeneration and the anointing of the Holy Spirit, are consecrated into a spiritual house and a holy priesthood'.[23] Thus the Christian is transformed in the water of baptism and the sacramental anointing by the Spirit to be 'priests' with Christ. By initiation we become a new creation for mission.

The question of who is the ordinary minister of confirmation was to dominate the development of confirmation in the Western Church–unlike the development in the East where the presider at baptism, either Bishop or Priest, would celebrate confirmation. With insistence on the Bishop being the celebrant in the West, the celebration of confirmation was separated from baptism and emerged in its own right. This is well documented as developing the separation of confirmation from Eucharist. The pastoral decision of Pope Pius X

18. Morrill, 'Holy Communion as Public Act: Ethics and Liturgical Participation', 33.
19. *On the Trinity* XV, 46, Rotelle, *The Works of Saint Augustine*, I/5, 431.
20. *Ennaratio in Ps 44*, 19, Rotelle, *The Works of Saint Augustine*, III/16, 297.
21. *The City of God against the Pagans*. XX, 10, edited by RW Dyson (Cambridge: University Press, 1998), 919.
22. *The City of God against the Pagans*, XX #14.
23. *Dogmatic Constitution on the Church*, #10.

to encourage young children to receive communion formalised this separation so that the order for the celebration of initiation then became baptism, Eucharist and confirmation. This inversion has understandably put pressure on the celebration of confirmation as an opportunity for adolescents to affirm the faith professed in baptism by their godparents.

The Anglican celebration of confirmation,[24] which is not viewed as being a sacrament but as an opportunity to profess personally one's faith, provided a helpful pastoral tool for Catholic catechists preparing children for confirmation. However they did not consider the Anglican linking of this profession to admission to communion. Confirmation therefore was seen as a separated celebration, independent of baptism and Eucharist, in which the candidates could give public profession to their baptismal faith.

The Catholic Church however always links confirmation with the gift of the Holy Spirit. Even with their diverse rituals, in the Eastern and Western traditions the Church always maintained 'the significance of a conferring of the Holy Spirit'.[25] This tradition is to be distinguished from the previous catechesis which focused upon one's receiving of the gifts on the Spirit to strengthen one's faith. This notion finds its origin in Fautus of Riez (CE 495) who first speaks of the 'gifts of the Spirit'. 'Through the coming of the Holy Spirit the gifts of strength [*virtutum munera*] are given, and miracles are performed by those who have been strengthened [*confirmatis*]'.[26] Fautus then goes on to invoke the image of military service to explain the purpose of a ritual separated from baptism and Eucharist and sees that 'confirmation arms us and instructs us on how we are to keep ourselves safe from the struggles and battles of this world'.[27] Thus the focus of confirmation moved from the eucharistic purpose of the reception of the Spirit to the military role of being strengthened by the 'gifts' to battle for the faith.

---

24. 'As one of passage into maturity and adulthood.' Morrill, 'The Meaning of Confirmation: Searching with the Bishop, the Liturgy, and the Holy Spirit', 55.
25. Paul VI Apostolic Constitution *Divinae Consortium Naturae*. 1971 in *Documents on the Liturgy 1963–1979* (Collegeville MN: Liturgical Press, 1982), #2502.
26. 'On the Holy Spirit # 11', in *Worship in the Early Church*, edited by Lawrence Johnson (Adelaide: ATF Press, 2009) #3053.
27. 'Sermon 28. On Pentecost', in *Worship in the Early Church*, edited by Lawrence Johnson (Adelaide: ATF Press, 2009) #3060.

It is interesting to find evidence in the ninth century of the earlier patristic teaching that linked the giving of the Holy Spirit with the priestly people of God offering their oblation in the celebration of the Mass. Florus of Lyon (CE 860) explains the term, 'the gifts which we offer', in the Roman Canon as referring to the oblation of the whole Church, made by all standing around the altar: presider and assembly. The Church is rightly called 'the holy priesthood who, through the Holy Spirit, comes immaculate before God'.[28] This teaching is in marked contrast with the allegorisation of the time which tried to give meaning to the Eucharist for the laity who were excluded from participating in the action of Eucharist itself but who were still present at its celebration.

Our patristic tradition saw that we are initiated into Christ—initiation is not just a ritual celebration of joining the Church: it is encounter with Christ. As Christ was formed in the womb of Mary so the newly initiated were formed in the womb of the Church. As Christ took flesh in the womb of Mary, through the power of the Holy Spirit, so Christ is given to us through the power of the same Holy Spirit. Being rightly called 'Christ', the new-born Christian is one with Christ the Priest and so can be called 'priest'. For Augustine 'if there is no sacrifice there can be no priest; but we know we have a priest in heaven who intercedes for us'.[29] Thus the journey of initiation leads one to the priestly service of offering sacrifice. The significant priestly service of the newly initiated (besides intercessory prayer) is to offer the sacrifice of Christ. For this reason the newly initiated 'now raised to the rank of the royal priesthood have an active part in bringing the gifts to the altar'[30] as part of their ritual of offering sacrifice.

Called to Sacrifice

Sacrifice is often a difficult term for our contemporary world. The notion of sacrifice has often been taken from the pagan context in which a victim is slaughtered to placate an angry God. Fortunately in our generation, Robert Daly[31] has restored a trinitarian understanding of

28. P Duc, *Étude sur l' «Expositio Missse» of Florus de Lyon* (Belley: 1937). LII: 1-2: 126.
29. *Ennation in Ps. 130*, 4 I Rotelle, *The Works of Saint Augustine*, II/20, 141.
30. *Rite of Christian Initiation of Adults*, #210.
31. Robert Daly, *Sacrifice Unveiled: The True Meaning of Christian Sacrifice* (London:

sacrifice to enable us once again to pastorally employ the Christian understanding of sacrifice as being, in Christ, a life of self-giving. Confirmation is part and parcel of this journey. Like all sacraments in the Catholic Church, it is orientated to Eucharist. 'Liturgically this means that confirmation can only function properly in sequence between baptism and Eucharist'.[32] If then we take the meaning of confirmation in terms of being ordered to offer sacrifice—which does not compete with the meaning of ministerial ordination, but rather complements it—how does it help us in reading our history of confirmation and aid us in our celebration of this sacrament today?

Since the invitation of Vatican II to establish the 'intimate connection' of confirmation to initiation, the restoration of the traditional order of celebrating the sacraments of initiation has become common and well founded in historical research and pastoral practice. Still, it has to be asked what is the significance of celebrating confirmation without reference to the Eucharist? Many dioceses will still celebrate confirmation after first communion, a practice described as 'theologically incomprehensible and liturgically corrupt'.[33] From the present study this criticism can find its explanation in terms of the giving of the priesthood of the faithful in confirmation. This gift of the Spirit is directly linked to the celebration of the Eucharist where the faithful can fully take part in the oblation of the celebration. Without that formal participation in the priesthood of Christ through the giving of the Spirit in the celebration of confirmation, can they be said to fully participate and exercise their priestly role in the Eucharist?

Pope Paul VI in his 'Apostolic Constitution on the Sacrament of Confirmation' states explicitly that the newly baptised 'for the first time become sharers in the priesthood of their Saviour'.[34] He then goes on to speak of the sacrament of confirmation as 'the inexpressible gift, the Holy Spirit himself'.[35] It is often understood that in Baptism we take on 'our special incorporation into the priestly, prophetic

---

T&T Clark International, 2009).

32. Morrill, 'The Meaning of Confirmation: Searching with the Bishop, the Liturgy, and the Holy Spirit', 57
33. Morrill. 'The Meaning of Confirmation: Searching with the Bishop, the Liturgy, and the Holy Spirit', 57.
34. Paul VI, Apostolic Constitution *Divinae Consortium Naturae*, 1971 in *Documents on the Liturgy 1963–1979* (Collegeville MN, Liturgical Press, 1982), #2502.
35. Paul VI, *Divinae Consortium Naturae*, #2502.

and kingly roles of the risen Christ'.[36] According to the Rite of Christian Initiation of Adults if confirmation immediately follows baptism, the post-baptismal anointing with chrism (which names our being 'a member of Christ who is Priest, Prophet and King') is omitted.[37] This direction to omit the reference to 'Christ the Priest' reflects Augustine's identification of our being priests through the mystical anointing of the Spirit. Paul VI did speak of the giving of the Spirit in confirmation as endowing 'special strength . . . to spread and defend the faith'.[38] This strength is then 'closely linked with the holy Eucharist'.

Taking the wisdom of Augustine it is possible to make this link with Eucharist through an understanding of confirmation as the giving of the Spirit so that our incorporation into Christ the Priest enables us as priests to offer sacrifice. Thus with this full, active participation of all the assembly 'the Eucharist shows itself to be the source and the apex of the whole work of preaching the gospel'.[39] Then this call by Paul VI for those being confirmed 'to spread and defend the faith' becomes fully eucharistic.

If we are to abandon our understanding of confirmation as the giving of the Spirit, a gift which had not been given in baptism—a differentiation based on the example of Christ who was born through the power of the Holy Spirit and anointed by the giving of the Spirit at his baptism in the Jordan for mission—then we risk losing the specific purpose of confirmation. If the Spirit is in fact given in baptism and we are fully empowered to exercise our eucharistic role as the royal priesthood, then confirmation would lack any sacramental content—particularly it would lose the 'intimate connection' to Eucharist. In this context it would be appropriate to accept the Anglican understanding of confirmation as a catechetical moment for the personal affirmation of infant baptism.

While seeking to separate the giving of the Spirit from the working of the Spirit in baptism, it is important that we hold onto the unity of the sacraments of initiation. Some authors have argued that confirmation should only be celebrated immediately with baptism (as in

36. Kevin Seasoltz, *A Virtuous Church. Catholic Theology, Ethics, and Liturgy for the 21st Century* (Maryknoll, NY: Orbis Books, 2012), 172.
37. *Rite of Christian Initiation of Adults*, # 222.
38. Paul VI, *Divinae Consortium Naturae*, #2502.
39. Vatican II. *Decree on the Ministry and Life of Priests*, #5.

the practice in the Maronite Catholic Church), but because this is not possible within the contemporary Roman Church there can be pastoral value in naming clearly the priestly role given in confirmation so that our catechesis and pastoral practice are well informed. Clearly this will require a new approach to catechesis for confirmation and Eucharist.

Benedict XVI had expressly requested the Bishops of the world 'to examine the relative effectiveness of the two sequences of confirmation and first communion'[40] on their experience of celebrating Eucharist. For the first time[41] a pope actually raised the issue of the order of celebrating the sacraments of initiation. Previously the question had been left for individual dioceses to decide and provide pastoral responses. It is important to note his eucharistic focus: 'concretely, it needs to be seen which practice better enables the faithful to put the sacrament of the Eucharist at the centre, as the goal of the whole process of initiation.'[42] Pope Benedict clearly focused his interest on Eucharist as 'the centre and goal of the whole process of initiation.' 'Now that the Roman Catholic Church has had some years of experience with the restored catechumenate, with deferring the age of confirmation, and with weathering the struggles of this sacrament, perhaps the time is indeed ripe for a decision to be made.'[43]

Another pastoral question begins to emerge in this discussion. Generally the Bishop has lost his role of presiding at Baptism and first communion as both roles have been given to local pastors. Consequently the Bishop will only be present for the celebration of confirmation. Sadly his presence is not linked with the celebration of first communion where the bishop's role as minister of initiation could be firmly named. For some bishops confirmation is the only opportunity to participate in the celebration of initiation in some meaningful way. If confirmation is to be celebrated with very young children, to en-

40. Paul Turner, 'Benedict XVI and the Sequence of the Sacraments of Initiation', in *Worship*, 82/2 (2008): 132.
41. 'This is a unique development in the history of confirmation in the Latin Rite'. Turner, 'Benedict XVI and the Sequence of the Sacraments of Initiation', 133.
42. Benedict XVI, Apostolic Exhortation *Sacramentum Caritatis*. (2007), # 18. <http://www.vatican.va/holy_father/benedict_xvi/apost_exhortations/documents/hf_ben-xvi_exh_20070222_sacramentum-caritatis_en.html>. Accessed 10 June 2013.
43. Turner, 'Benedict XVI and the Sequence of the Sacraments of Initiation', 132.

able them to receive first communion as the final stage of initiation, then pastorally the bishop may feel he is not able to fully engage with the very young candidates. To ensure a fruitful encounter with their bishop, confirmation would then be delayed until the children are older. But does this delay for pastoral reasons respect the 'intimate connection' of confirmation to the sacraments of initiation, as desired by the Council?

Conclusion

Through the generated by *SC* our generation has fortunately begun to restore the participation of the assembly in the celebration of the Eucharist: the assembly are not simply passive spectators but active participants. This active participation would find its full expression if we could catechise confirmation as the gift of the Spirit drawing us into the heart of Christ's priesthood, and we would then be forming the candidates for their full, active and conscious role in Eucharist. Confirmation cannot stand alone from either Baptism or Eucharist.

> Those who have been baptised continue on the path of Christian initiation through the sacrament of confirmation. In this sacrament they receive the Holy Spirit, who was sent upon the apostles by the Lord on Pentecost. This giving of the Holy Spirit conforms believers more perfectly to Christ and strengthens them so that they may bear witness to Christ for the building up of his body in faith and love.[44]

The Church sees the role of its members in the celebration of Eucharist as building up the Body of Christ which is central to the journey of initiation. The restoration of confirmation as the second stepping stone to Eucharist would enable candidates to fully participate in the Eucharist by exercising their transformative priesthood through their offering and receiving the sacrifice of Christ.

So why not return to the priesthood of the faithful as a key to catechising for and celebrating of confirmation? Vatican II had opened up this possibility in drawing our attention to the sacraments of ini-

44. *Rite of Confirmation*, #1 & 2.

tiation. Consequent scholarship has provided further knowledge in this area. It would be significant to continue to take this scholarship to the pastoral life of the Church. In this context the hope of John Paul II that the ministerial priest 'can help the People of God to exercise faithfully and fully the common priesthood which it has received'[45] would be fulfilled. In this way the ministerial service role of the ordained would realise the transformative priesthood of the faithful.

45. John-Paul II, Apostolic Exhortation: *Pastores Dabo Vobis* (1992), # 17. < http://www.vatican.va/holy_father/john_paul_ii/apost_exhortations/documents/hf_jp-ii_exh_25031992_pastores-dabo-vobis_en.html>. Accessed 10 June 2013.

Reconciliation: Ever Evolving Sacrament

Julia Upton

It was a simple sentence in *Sacrosanctum Concilium* (hereafter SC): 'The rite and formulas for the Sacrament of Penance are to be revised so that they more clearly express—or 'give more luminous expression to,' as another translation put it[1]—both the nature and effect of the sacrament.'[2] However, it set off years of painstaking work resulting in powerful experiences of reconciliation for many and concern and confusion for others. Now, fifty years later, the rite and formulas have been revised but have not been fully implemented. There is still work to do if they are to give more luminous expression to the awesome presence of our merciful Lord in the sacrament. Standing in the shadow of Vatican II, this essay will look at where we are, where we have been, and where we might go to revitalise the Sacrament of Reconciliation today.

When we compare sacramental penitential practice today with that of fifty years ago, it is obvious that a drastic change has taken place. Eric Luijten reported that in the Netherlands the practice of regular confession disappeared almost completely in the course of only a decade from 1960 to 1970.[3] In 1972, Francis Buckley SJ wrote, 'during the last few years there has been a sharp drop in confession: about fifty per cent in Europe and up to seventy-five per cent in some parts of the United States'.[4]

1. *The Documents of Vatican II* edited by Walter M Abbott, SJ (New York: America Press, 1966), 161.
2. *SC* #72 to be found <http://www.vatican.va/archive/hist_councils/ii_vatican_council/documents/vat-ii_const_19631204_sacrosanctum-concilium_en.html>. Accessed 24 February 2013.
3. Eric Luijten, *Sacramental Forgiveness as a Gift from God: Thomas Aquinas on the Sacrament of Penance* (Utrecht: Peeters Publishers, 2003), 1.
4. Francis J Buckley, SJ, *'I Confess': The Sacrament of Penance Today* (Notre Dame:

A survey of Catholic practice in the United States undertaken by the Committee for Pastoral Research and Practice of the National Council of Catholic Bishops in 1988 reported that four per cent of the laity surveyed celebrated the sacrament weekly; five per cent monthly; seventeen per cent every two or three months; fifty-five per cent once or twice a year; nineteen per cent never.[5] Without comparable data for any other specific time period, any conclusions drawn are based only on our perceptions of Catholic practice at the time of the Council. Furthermore, since the survey did not question any of the respondents on their prior experience with the sacrament, or draw out their mystagogical reflections on becoming reconciled with God and community, we do not even have a complete picture of the state of the sacrament in that country in 1988. This much seems obvious, however: people were simply not availing themselves of the Sacrament of Penance to the same degree they once did.

More recent studies confirm the trend. Data from the Center for Applied Research in the Apostolate [CARA] at Georgetown University reported (2008) that thirty-seven per cent of those who attend Mass celebrate the Sacrament of Reconciliation monthly, six per cent even less often while sixty-two per cent of weekly Mass attendees say they celebrate the sacrament at least once a year.[6] This leads us to wonder if the *sensus fidelium* is informing us that the Sacrament of Penance as we now know it is no longer fundamental to the life of Catholic Christians or if it is evidence of yet another transformation of this sacrament.

To assume that the Church's practice of Sacramental Reconciliation was always restricted to or even included private individual confession to a priest is to be completely off target. Nothing could be farther from the truth. Yet this is a common assumption held by many Catholics today—both those who continue to seek reconciliation with the Church through this sacrament and those who reject it as archaic or irrelevant.

Ave Maria, 1972), 21.

5. NCCB Committee for Pastoral Research and Practices, *Reflections on the Sacrament of Penance in Catholic Life Today: A Study Document* (Washington, DC: NCCB, 1990), 7. [Hereafter referred to as *Study Document*.]
6. <http://cara.georgetown.edu/sacraments.html>. Accessed 24 February 2013.

A Backward Glance

Jesus expected his followers to forgive one another. When he taught them to pray and when he taught in parables he emphasised forgiveness as a core value in the community. How that developed over time is both colourful and dynamic. There was no uniform practice until the fourth Council of the Lateran in 1225, and not until the Council of Trent in 1551 was private individual confession first mandated as the only 'orthodox' understanding of penance. James Dallen has observed that what we call the Sacrament of Reconciliation has changed so markedly over time 'that it seems only a convention that we regard it as the same sacrament in each era'.[7]

There have been many fine histories of the Sacrament of Reconciliation (Penance) written in recent years,[8] and the intention here is not to go into detail, but rather to glance at history in order to better inform the topic at hand. The purpose of studying the history of the Sacrament of Penance, as Catherine Dooley notes, is not 'to restore the past but rather to enrich the present and the future through the interaction of the tradition with contemporary theology and pastoral practice'.[9]

Despite Jesus' constant encouragement to forgive one other, as the early Church began to take shape it did not allow for sinners to be reconciled. Baptism was *the* Sacrament of Reconciliation and given the seriousness with which the early Church approached the catechumenate and initiation, they did not expect members to fall into serious sin. Although there is evidence in the first-century Didache of a practice of 'confessing sins,' no ritual is described. In time, however, a ritual developed that allowed for those guilty of serious sin to be reconciled with the community *once*. Theologically, we have to look at this development alongside initiation practice. Bishops saw that,

7. James Dallen and Joseph Favazza, *Removing the Barriers: The Practice of Reconciliation* (Chicago: Liturgy Training Publications, 1991), 5.
8. See James Dallen, *The Reconciling Community: The Rite of Penance* (New York: Pueblo, 1986); Monika Hellwig, *Sign of Reconciliation and Conversion: The Sacrament of Penance for Our Times* (Wilmington: Michael Glazier, 1984). A briefer historical treatment of the sacrament can be found in Catherine Dooley, 'The History of Penance in the Early Church: Implications for the Future', in *Reconciliation: The Continuing Agenda*, edited by Robert J Kennedy (Collegeville, MN: Liturgical Press, 1987), 83–95.
9. Dooley, 'The History of Penance in the Early Church', 84.

by sinning, people lost the graced relationship they had with God and the community, so that the practice for reconciling penitents that emerged looked very much like the catechumenate.

The penitent would present himself or herself to the bishop and confess his or her sins. The bishop would assign some works of repentance aimed at convincing the community of the sinner's change of heart. These practices varied from place to place and often involved some special attire with cultural or scriptural associations, such as dressing in sackcloth made of goat hair or having their hair cut short like slaves. Penitents were prayed over at the weekly celebrations of the Eucharist but were not permitted to receive communion. The period of penitence, from weeks to years, depended on the nature of the sin. In many places Holy Thursday was the official day for the reconciliation of penitents. The bishop would then wash their feet and welcome them to receive communion at the Eucharist that day.

By the end of the fifth century this form of penance, known as 'canonical penance', had all but disappeared from Christian life in Europe, even though some rigid regulations were relaxed to encourage people to practise it. Lent is actually a vestige of the practice. Besides being very severe and public in nature, canonical penance also required the presence of the local bishop to reconcile penitents. In mission countries, particularly in Ireland where there were initially no bishops, another penitential practice developed.

Since there were no cities in Ireland, Christian life centred on the monasteries. Monks went out from them to minister to people in the area, but wild clans folk did not readily adjust to the moral norms of Christian life; in everyday life, they behaved as they had before. As a remedy, the monks prescribed for the people the same practices that were used in the monastery to overcome sin and make satisfaction for failings. In monasteries it was common for monks and nuns to confess their infractions of community law to their superior and receive some penance in return. Unlike canonical penance which could be received only once, these confessions could be repeated each time the penitent fell into sin.

In time this 'monastic penance' came to be preferred because it promised salvation that baptism itself no longer assured; and like canonical penance it could even offer forgiveness for less than serious sins. Initially it was condemned as detestable by the Council of Toledo in 589 and several other Councils that sought to return to the practice of canonical penance.[10] Despite such repeated condemnations, however, the practice continued to spread, and in 650 a Council in Chalon-sur-Saône approved confession to priests as 'a medicine for the soul' and 'helpful to people'. Future Councils, most notably the Council of Trent in its fourteenth Session, continued to affirm the practice of auricular confession to a priest. Confessionals became common in churches and Catholics regularly availed themselves of the practice of regular confession.

The Way We Were

The 'Baltimore Catechism' taught that the Sacrament of Penance was necessary only for the forgiveness of mortal sins. Venial sins could be forgiven in other ways, in particular through devout reception of Eucharist. Yet, week after week Catholics at the time lined up to confess the same list of venial sins, just to be sure that they were forgiven, or perhaps to get extra grace. Today, before approaching the altar to receive Eucharist, as with one voice the assembly faithfully and urgently prays, 'Lord, I am not worthy that you should enter under my roof, but only say the word, and my soul shall be healed.' Before the Council the very same phrase was prayed by the priest in Latin, '*Domine non sum dignus ut intres sub tectum meum, sed tantum dic verbo et sanabitur anima mea*'. With the vernacular and with the people praying, the words themselves came transformation. They believed and experienced God's loving mercy more confidently.

In the early 1960s the tone of articles about 'confession' appearing in religious magazines in the United States shifted. The assurance that devotional confessions were a practice to be encouraged began to wane as questions about the ecclesial dimensions of this practice grew. The image of Church as the 'People of God', so central to the documents of Vatican II, had begun to emerge in Europe in the decades leading to the Council, and American theologians who had studied abroad began to raise serious questions about sacramental practice in the United States.

Reports began to spread in the United States about what was happening in other countries with regard to the Sacrament of Penance.

10. See Luitjen, *Sacramental Forgiveness as a Gift from God*, 17.

The 5 April 1962 issue of the Davenport, Iowa *Catholic Messenger*, for example, carried an article reporting on public celebrations of the Sacrament of Penance taking place in France and the Netherlands. Writing in the May 1962 issue of *Paroise et Liturgie*, Dom Thierry Maertens of Saint-André Abbey in Bruges described in great detail a communal service used in the Archdiocese of Malines in Belgium.[11]

During Advent in 1976 Bishop Carroll T Dozier of Memphis, Tennessee made headlines in the United States when he presided over Reconciliation Services using the Third Form of the Rite with General Confession and Communal Absolution. In the stadium, 13,000 Catholics—over one-quarter of the Memphis diocese—experienced the embrace of forgiveness in sacramental reconciliation. The mood was reported to be exciting, electrifying even. As shepherd of Memphis Catholics, Bishop Dozier was most concerned about inactive Catholics, particularly those who for whatever personal or psychological reasons were unable to take the first step in returning to the Church. He wanted the Rite of Penance to be a bridge, an 'extended hand'.[12]

On a personal note, I remember quite clearly the first communal penance service I ever attended. It was during Lent of 1972, when I was a not-very-active Catholic myself. I read about the upcoming service in our parish bulletin. Intrigued by the concept and drawn probably more by guilt than contrition, I arrived at the parish church that Saturday afternoon to find it filled with people. Because there was no 'official' form of a communal rite of penance at that time, the ritual took the shape of a Liturgy of the Word focused on sin and repentance, a communal examination of conscience, individual confessions, concluding with common absolution. It was very much like the service described in Belgium ten years earlier, and an accurate response to the reform mandated by the Second Vatican Council. These celebrations gave clear expression to the Church's witness that God welcomes the repentant sinner—cause for rejoicing, not shame.

My father had a dictum, 'Praise in public, criticise in private'. It is regrettable that such earthy wisdom was not followed by Church of-

11. Cited in Frank B Norris, SS, 'Reform of the Rite of Penance: Public Celebration and Confessions of Devotion', in *Worship*, 37/2 (1963): 107.
12. For a complete account of the diocesan program see Albert Kirk, 'Reconciliation in Memphis: A Diocese Prepared', in *America*, 136/5 (1977): 146–148.

ficials in their outright condemnation of Bishop Dozier's celebrations or in the thousands of other reverent and faith-filled celebrations of the third form of the Rite of Penance.[13]

The Memphis program involved several months of preparation, beginning with the Advent celebrations and continuing through the Easter season. Confessors were named and regional sites were specified for all those interested in following general absolution with private consultation with a confessor. Careful to nuance this recommendation, Bishop Dozier believed 'the grace of the sacrament will take care of them from then on . . . I am counting on Jesus being there and I'm counting on him doing his job. I'm counting on that spark in human nature that really wants to know and love God.'[14] In addition to providing extensive education, a day of prayer and eucharistic adoration was held in every parish. Several days before the first celebration, the entire diocese observed a day of prayer and fasting, and the bishop prepared himself by an eight-day retreat.[15] All these years later, this author can see no better model for a diocese to adopt. It gives vivid ritual expression to the circumstances of sin, penance and reconciliation as described in the 'Catechism of the Catholic Church'. There it is written that 'sin is before all else an offense against God, a rupture of communion with him. At the same time it damages communion with the Church. For this reason conversion entails both God's forgiveness and reconciliation with the Church.'[16]

The recent dismissal of Bishop William Morris as Bishop of Toowoomba, Queensland, Australia, troubled and discouraged many Catholics since one of the concerns the Vatican seemed to have with him was his use of the third form of the rite of reconciliation in his geographically sprawling diocese.[17] Jesus did not teach us to race to condemnation, but rather first to seek and understand. Many would have taken a different approach than the Vatican did, wondering if the Spirit might be leading the Church in a different direction with

13. See 'General Absolution: Were the Norms Followed in Memphis?', in *Origins*, 7/2 (1977): 1, 3–4.
14. Mark Winiarski, 'Reconciliation in Memphis', in *National Catholic Reporter*, 13 (17 December 1976) 3.
15. Kirk, 'Reconciliation in Memphis', 148.
16. *Catechism of the Catholic Church*, #1440.
17. See Frank Brennan, SJ, 'John XXIII's Half Century Challenge', <http://www.eurekastreet.com.au/article.aspx?aeid=30635>. Accessed 24 February 2013.

regard to this sacrament. Although the third form of the rite was intended by its authors for battlefield kinds of situations, what harm could come from considering that this might be a work of the Spirit at this time? The Church might have a lot to gain from such discernment.[18]

In my work as a university professor, trying to educate and prepare young men and women for their role in the Church of tomorrow, I have given much attention to the pastoral situation of sacramental reconciliation today. That has led me to many parish settings where I have presented workshops on the Sacrament of Reconciliation, for general audiences, and for the parents of children preparing for first communion. I have also had the privilege of participating in the process of catechesis with adults preparing for entrance into full communion with the Roman Catholic Church. Each of these three groups has a different agenda, one might say, but the core issues remain the same: fear, confusion, and discomfort.

The Way We Are

The changing pattern of going to confession was accompanied by a changing concept of God. Something began to transform an image of God from a pseudo-benevolent despot to a loving parent in the 1960s, perhaps an indirect result of beginning to celebrate the Eucharist in the vernacular. Perhaps it was that once Catholics began to ponder our sinfulness in the Penitential Rite, to pray the Lord's Prayer in common, and to exchange the sign of peace, they became more aware of other meaningful ways in which reconciliation occurs between God and the members of the Church.

It can be argued that the Roman Catholic community now has a much better sense of how the Eucharist is (or can be) a Sacrament of Reconciliation. Each of the ten formulae for the Penitential Rite that

18. In many dioceses throughout Australia the third form of Penance was celebrated during the Advent and Lenten seasons each year. This practice proved extremely popular and churches were filled at these times over a period lasting almost two decades until an edict by John Paul II effectively ceased this practice. See John Paul II, *Motu Proprio Misericordia Dei on certain aspects of the Celebration of the Sacrament of Penance 2002.* <http://www.vatican.va/holy_father/john_paul_ii/motu_proprio/documents/hf_jp-ii_motu-proprio_20020502_misericordia-dei_en.html>. Accessed 15 May 2013.

appeared in the Sacramentary (1985) concluded with the rubric, 'The priest says the absolution' followed by the words:

> May almighty God have mercy on us,
> forgive us our sins,
> and bring us to everlasting life.

In the revised (3rd) Edition of the Roman Missal (2010) although there are fewer formulae in the front section,[19] the prayer concluding what is now called the Penitential Act is the same, and is still referred to as 'the absolution'. Before the Council, the assembly did not pray the Confiteor. Rather it was recited by the priest and servers: first the servers recited it to the priest, then the priest recited it to the servers. Now 'the Priest calls upon the whole community to take part in the Penitential Act', which, after a brief pause for silence, it does by means of a formula of general confession. The rite concludes with the Priest's absolution, 'which, however, lacks the efficacy of the Sacrament of Penance.'[20] Perhaps here is another reason that fewer people access the Sacrament of Reconciliation. The Lord's Prayer, the sign of peace, and the Communion Rite all have a penitential and reconciliatory thrust to them. It should come as no surprise, therefore, that many people today perceive themselves to be reconciled with God and the community through their celebration of Sunday Eucharist. Rather than argue with peoples' experience, this is a fine opportunity for the Church to use what is already fertile sacred ground. I will return to this concept in the concluding section.

The revised rite was available in 1973 and made mandatory in the United States on the First Sunday of Lent in 1976. Since then there has been very slow, sometimes non-existent implementation. Why? The perception seems to be that 'the people don't want it', but it is time to re-examine that attitude. With homage to Chesterton, it is not that the revised Rite of Penance has been tried and found wanting; it has not been tried.

The reality is that the Rite of Penance puts demands on both confessors and penitents. In the old system, confessors sat in the shad-

19. All the formulae are found in the 2010 edition, but most have been moved to the Appendix.
20. *General Instruction of the Roman Missal* (Strathfield: St. Pauls, 2013), #51.

ows, sometimes hour upon hour, hearing the recital of a seemingly endless list of sins or pseudo-sins to which many responded with the same canned penance and mumbled words of absolution. Similarly, the anonymous penitent could slip into the confessional, recite the same sins each week, firmly intending not to commit them again, receive absolution, leave assured of redemption at least for a little while, and return to life as usual.

Rite of Penance

It took two Commissions seven years of research and discussions through more than a dozen draft documents to implement that simple statement made in *SC*. Their work began with an attempt to determine difficulties inherent in present practice. Questionnaires completed in France, England, Scotland, the United States, Australia, and Africa were analysed. The writings of numerous scholars were collected and studied as well. All the research indicated 'a growing dissatisfaction with the Sacrament of Penance as well as a desire to restore vitality to it by means of a less mechanical and formal practice that would bring out more clearly the social and communal aspect of both sin and reconciliation.'[21] A communal ritual to complement the individual ritual was also cited as a desire. Throughout the process the Commissions maintained the focus that: 'sin is by its nature both an offense against God and a wound inflicted on the Church; sacramental reconciliation is reconciliation with both God and the Church; and the entire Christian community works together for the conversion of sinners.'[22]

In 1973 Paul VI approved the *Ordo Paenitentiae* [Rite of Penance] which gives a better expression of celebrating that reconciliation between God and the sinner and is more consistent with the way the community prays in common today. In the *Praenotanda*, or Pastoral Introduction, we are given an overview of the reform in six sections. The text begins with situating the 'mystery' of reconciliation in the history of salvation. 'The Father has shown forth his mercy by reconciling the world to himself in Christ and by making peace for all

21. Annibale Bugnini, *The Reform of the Liturgy 1948–1975* (Collegeville, MN: Liturgical Press, 1990), 664–665. For a thorough discussion of the various stages, documents and difficulties encountered in this process, see 664–683.
22. Bugnini, *The Reform of the Liturgy*, 665.

things on earth and in heaven by the blood of Christ on the cross.'[23] Immediately made clear are the two dimensions of Jesus' mission. Jesus walked the way with his followers, first calling them out of darkness and then into his wonderful light. He not only preached repentance; he also welcomed sinners. Similarly this Pastoral Introduction also emphasises two dimensions: immersion in the 'mystery' of reconciliation first through baptism, and only later through the Sacrament of Penance. Quoting Saint Ambrose, the first section concludes: 'The Church possesses both water and tears; the water of baptism, the tears of penance'.[24] This provides a smooth transition into the second section of the introduction, which discusses the reconciliation of penitents in the life of the Church.

Of its very nature, as the ongoing presence of Christ on earth, the Church is holy. However, by including sinners within its company, in addition to being holy it is at the same time always in need of purification. The Church seeks this continual repentance in many different ways: by enduring difficulties, carrying out works of mercy and charity, and adopting ever more fully the outlook of the Gospel message. In this way the people of God stand before the world as a sign of conversion expressed in their lives and celebrated in the liturgy.[25] This section continues with a description of the nature of contrition, confession, satisfaction, and absolution, and the importance of frequent confession.

The third section of the introduction describes the offices and ministries in the reconciliation of penitents, beginning with a description of the role of the Christian community in the celebration of penance, and a discussion of the dispositions required in both ministers of reconciliation and penitents.

The celebrations themselves are discussed next in the Pastoral Introduction, followed by two concluding sections on penitential celebrations and adaptations.

Celebrating Reconciliation

The *Rite of Penance* consists of three different forms that the celebration may take: one individual form and two communal forms. The

23. Rite of Penance [*RP*], #1.
24. Letter 41:12; PL 16, 1116.
25. *RP*, #3–4.

Praenotanda makes no reference to one preferred form, although the first form is most commonly used. 'Just as the wound of sin is varied and multiple in the life of individuals and of the community,' the rite states, 'so too the healing which penance provides is varied.'[26]

All three forms have the same common elements, but these differ in size and shape.

The proclamation of the word of God, or the reading of scripture, is an important element of each form of the rite for it is 'through the word of God the Christian receives light to recognise his (sic) sins and is called to conversion and to confidence in God's mercy'.[27]

Confession of sins, 'which comes from true knowledge of self before God and from contrition for those sins',[28] is a second common element of the rite. The confession follows the penitent's examination of his or her own conscience and presumes the penitent's openness to God's grace through the spiritual ministry of the priest.

A third common element is prayer, beginning with the prayer of both priest and penitent before approaching the sacrament. 'The priest should call upon the Holy Spirit so that he may receive enlightenment and charity,'[29] and during the rite the penitent prays to God for forgiveness. All conclude with absolution[30]:

> God, the Father of mercies,
> through the death and resurrection of his Son
> has reconciled the world to himself
> and sent the Holy Spirit among us
> for the forgiveness of sins;
> through the ministry of the Church
> may God give you pardon and peace,
> and I absolve you from your sins
> in the name of the Father, and of the Son,
> and of the Holy Spirit.[31]

---

26. *RP*, #7.
27. *RP*, #17.
28. *RP*, #6b.
29. *RP*, #15.
30. In the third form of the rite the absolution is more extensive.
31. *RP*, #46.

Moving to Mystagogy

When the rites of Christian Initiation were revised in the 1970s, I feared two things: that translators would find a more 'relevant' word than mystagogy and that the last stage in the process would be eclipsed entirely. While the Church has survived the first hurdle and the word 'mystagogy' remains in the official texts if not in the hearts of Christians, I am not so sure that there is an understanding of the spiritual significance of the last stage. Mystagogy is far beyond the pale of the present cultural horizon and moving even farther away at a lightning pace.

Liturgically, the term 'mystagogy' is used to refer to the time immediately following the reception of the Sacraments of Initiation. In the early Church this was the time when the newly initiated first learned about the mysteries of the faith. They received Eucharist before learning how the community understood and explained the transformation of the elements. They had all their sins washed away in the waters of Baptism before they learned to analyse sin and its impact on the community.[32]

Today most of the mysteries of the faith are explained quite exhaustively during the time of the catechumenate and the terminology of mystagogy is retained in name only. It could be described as similar to a 'honeymoon' for the new members of the community.[33] More regular practice of reflecting on the mysteries of faith in general would surely enliven preaching in the community and enable the Church to live more balanced lives, to celebrate common beliefs more robustly, and to hand on the faith to children and their children's children.

In all of the books and articles on the subject of sacramental reconciliation I have read in the last thirty years (and my reading has been extensive), no priest has ever described his experience of being a sinner and the object of sacramental reconciliation himself. Even at an international ecumenical symposium focused specifically on

---

32. For a complete treatment of this subject see Enrico Mazza, *Mystagogy: A Theology of Liturgy in the Patristic Age* (New York: Pueblo, 1989).
33. See Julia Upton, RSM, *A Church for the Next Generation: Sacraments in Transition* (Collegeville, MN: Liturgical Press, 1990), 37, 45–46; *Becoming A Catholic Christian: A Pilgrim's Guide to the Rite of Christian Initiation of Adults* (Washington, DC: Pastoral Press, 1993), 77–81.

the Sacrament of Penance, not one cleric in the English-speaking discussion group referred to his or her personal experience of being reconciled. In all such discussions, however, that is the bottom line: all members of the Church—including those who are ordained—are sinners.

That observation has led me to invite a guest speaker into my graduate course on 'The Sacraments of Healing' whenever and wherever I teach it. I usually invite one of my priest-colleagues, but remind him that he must join the conversation as a sinner as well as a confessor. As a result we have had some extraordinary classes in which everyone walked away with a deeper experience of God's merciful embrace. The model works for Alcoholics Anonymous. Why should we not expect it to work for us sinners who stand in need of God's mercy?

The work of reclaiming reconciliation will be more successful if seeds are planted in fertile ground, as I noted previously. Tilling the soil, therefore, is an important task because there still lies ahead many years for allowing the power of the Spirit unleashed through Vatican II to breathe freely in the Church and beyond. This will draw Christians closer to their true identity as the People of God joined in the Mystical Body of Christ.

> The People of God believes that it is led by the Spirit of the Lord, who fills the earth. Motivated by this faith, it labours to decipher authentic signs of God's presence and purpose in the happenings, needs, and desires in which this People has a part along with others of our age. For faith throws a new light on everything, manifests God's design for our total vocation, and thus directs the mind to solutions which are fully human.[34]

By fertile ground is meant clear indicators of a readiness to receive the word of God and reflect on it. The exceptional popularity of *Les Miserables* is a good example. Written by Victor Hugo in 1862, in recent years the musical version of the story which condemns social injustice in nineteenth-century France has given new life to this work. The London production has run continuously since 1985, making it the world's longest running musical which has been seen by sixty mil-

34. GS, #11.

lion people in forty-two countries.[35] The film adaptation of the musical was released worldwide in 2012. The central motif is mercy, exhibited early in the play by the bishop who shows forgiveness and mercy and not vengeance to the thief Jean Valjean. What fertile ground for preaching on forgiveness and reconciliation that could be!

The world around us offers many other themes—floods, wildfires, mass shootings, sometimes the ordinary wear and tear of daily life that causes people to be short-tempered or unkind. Many contemporary Christians suffering silently and alone when the Sacrament of Reconciliation could bring them pardon and peace. Some parishes are now making use of Penitential Celebration, such as the nine outlined in Appendix II of the Rite of Penance. These celebrations are not intended to include sacramental reconciliation and so do not need to be led by a priest. They are excellent outlines for celebrations that might serve as a way into the sacrament for people who might be reluctant to enter into the sacramental celebration. In a recent article published by 'Catholic News Service' priests offered other suggestions that might help people return to the sacrament.[36] One pastor suggested people not prepare too intensely before coming to the sacrament, that in conversation they would work it out together. That seemed like such a wise suggestion made to people often carrying heavy burdens or bearing deep scars.

In Conclusion

Is reconciliation a lived reality? What Christians ritualise sacramentally is the living human experience of conversion and encounter with God they have already had. If the human experience has not happened, then the sacramental ritual makes little or no sense; it becomes an empty gesture.

Are conflicts addressed and reconciled or are they denied before they conveniently 'blow over'? Can reconciliation be experienced with God and the Church if people have never known reconciliation with another? Are parents reconciled with their children or are children expected to learn about reconciliation in a vacuum?

---

35. This author saw the New York City production four times, entranced by the theme of forgiveness and greatness of soul that is at its heart.
36. <http://www.catholicnews.com/data/stories/cns/1300399.htm>. Accessed 24 February 2013.

I still believe that we are in a period of evolution—a sure sign of life not death. At the moment, at least in many Western countries, reconciliation is being sought in a whole host of other ways—through spiritual direction, therapy, interpersonal conflict resolution, retreats, and 12-step programs. It is important to recognise that while the rites have been revised, the people (including confessors) have not uniformly been 'revised'. Here is opportunity and fertile ground.

Among my students and in audiences the most frequently asked question is 'Why confess my sins to a priest?' From God's perspective, perhaps there is no reason, but from the human point of view, there certainly is one. All of humanity needs to see, hear and feel forgiveness, and not just to think about it. Sacramental reconciliation, celebrated well, gives Christians that deeply personal experience. Issuing more statements will not restore this sacrament to the life of the community. Mystagogy has a much better chance. It seems to be what Benedict XVI called for in a reflection on the Sacrament of Reconciliation, which he called 'a path to take for the work of the New Evangelization' and urged the minister first to renew himself, 'his own awareness that he is a sinner and is in need of receiving sacramental pardon. In this way may be renewed the encounter with Christ, which was begun in Baptism . . .'[37] Christians live in hope!

37. Benedict XVI, Address to the Annual Course on the Internal Forum Organized by the Apostolic Penitentiary (9 March 2012) <http://www.vatican.va/holy_father/benedict_xvi/speeches/2012/march/documents/hf_ben-xvi_spe_20120309_penitenzieria-apostolica_en.html>. Accessed 24 February 2013.

The Divine Office in the Contemporary Church

Catherine Vincie

The Constitution on the Sacred Liturgy, *Sacrosanctum Concilium*[1] (*SC*), of Vatican II mandated reforms across the whole spectrum of Catholic liturgy by publishing general norms for all liturgical practice and making specific recommendations for the sacraments, sacramentals, the liturgical year, music and art. In addition, *SC* devoted an entire chapter to the reform of the Divine Office, proposing some structural changes regarding the hours to be prayed, extending the Psalms over a longer period, recommending a revision of the office of readings, and calling for a richer selection of scriptural readings. Perhaps the most important statement of the chapter is that the Divine Office is the public prayer of the entire Church (*SC* 90, 100). This had the potential for a major impact on the liturgical reforms of the Office in the post-conciliar period.

The history of the Divine Office or the Liturgy of the Hours, as it is now called, is complex and rich.[2] While it is not possible in this paper

1. The text of this document is taken from <http://www.vatican.va/archive/hist_councils/ii_vatican_council/documents/vat-ii_const_19631204_sacrosanctum-concilium_en.html> Accessed 24 April 2013.
2. See the following for an extensive history of the Liturgy of the Hours. Balthasar Fischer, 'The Common Prayer of Congregation and Family in the Ancient Church', in *Studia Liturgica*, 10/3-4 (1974): 106–24; William Storey, 'The Liturgy of the Hours: Cathedral Versus Monastery', in *Christians at Prayer*, edited by John Gallen (Notre Dame: University of Notre Dame Press, 1977), 61–82; Paul Bradshaw, 'Cathedral and Monastic: What's in a Name?', in *Worship*, 77/4 (2003): 341-53; Paul Bradshaw, *Daily Prayer in the Early Church: A Study of the Origin and Early Development of the Divine Office*, Alcuin Club Collection 63 (London: Alcuin SPCK, 1981); Pierre Salmon, *The Breviary Through the Centuries* (Collegeville, MN: Liturgical Press, 1962); Robert Taft, The Liturgy of the Hours in East and West (Collegeville. MN: Liturgical Press, 1986); Stanislaus Campbell,

to treat this history in any detail because of the limits of space, it is possible to trace that history in broad strokes attending to three main issues: participation of the whole Church, the focus on the monastic form of the Office and the sung nature of the Latin Office. I will then look at the reforms of Vatican II and raise six issues related to contemporary practice.

A Brief Historical Overview

The earliest recorded data concerning the Divine Office comes from the fourth and fifth centuries where there is evidence of a popular Office under the leadership of the bishop (known as the Cathedral Office) that was simple and repetitive, and a more complex but austere Office that was celebrated by the city or desert monastics. At the risk of reducing the history of the Office to a caricature, the Office gradually became monasticised during the medieval period in that the simpler Office gave way to the more complex and frequently sung version of the Hours that excluded the secular clergy and laity from full participation. One notable aspect of the monastic Office was the development of a huge body of Gregorian chant that demanded significant musical resources; of particular importance was the creation of antiphons that accompanied sung Psalms and responsories that followed the readings.

While there were some reforms over the centuries that tried to address the needs of the secular clergy and the laity, immediately prior to the Second Vatican Council the secular clergy 'said' the Office privately from their Breviaries, praying it when they could, even if that meant saying Morning Prayer at night. Those religious bound by their Constitutions to celebrate the Office sang the Hours in choir. Other religious not bound to the Office said a smaller version—called

---

From Breviary to Liturgy of the Hours: The Structural Reform of the Roman Office 1964–1971 (Collegeville, MN: Liturgical Press, 1995); Dominic Scotto, *The Liturgy of the Hours: Its History and Its Importance as the Communal Prayer of the Church After the Liturgical Reform of Vatican II* (Petersham, MA: St Bede's Publications, 1987); George Guiver, *Daily Prayer and the People of God* (New York: Pueblo, 1988); Carlo Braga, *La Liturgia delle ore al Vaticano II* (Rome: CLV-Edizioni Liturgiche, 2008); Philip Timko, 'The Background and Rationale for the Liturgy of the Hours: Paluch Lecture III', in *Chicago Studies* 49/2 (2010): 211–220; Stanislaus Campbell, 'The Paschal Mystery in the Liturgy of the Hours', in *Liturgical Ministry*, 15/2 (2006): 53–57.

the 'Little Office of the Virgin'—and the laity said the Office not at all, or at least by way of exception. The laity was mostly left to fend for itself as none of the official reforms from Trent onwards addressed their specific needs. With the declaration in *SC* that the Liturgy of the Hours was the prayer of the whole Church, it became necessary to address the needs of all three groups. These reforms will now be examined.

Reforms of Vatican II

SC set forth five norms for the reform of the Divine Office.

1. Morning Prayer and Evening Prayer were to be the two 'hinge' hours of the day, the chief hours, and were to be celebrated as such.
2. Compline was to be retained as a suitable prayer for the end of the day.
3. Matins (known also as Nocturns) or the office of readings was to be retained as a night office when celebrated in choir, but it was to be adapted to be celebrated at any hour of the day.
4. Prime was to be suppressed.
5. The other three minor hours—*terce, sext and none*—were to be observed if done in choir, or a choice of one of these hours was to be made (*SC* 89).

Above all, the 'truth of the hours' was to be maintained (*SC* 94). This meant that the Hours were always to be celebrated at the designated time; no longer would one celebrate Morning Prayer at night to fulfil an obligation. Those bound to the Office as well as clerics and the laity were all encouraged to pray the Office as the public prayer of the Church.

The group charged with the actual revision of the Roman Office in the time immediately following the close of Vatican II (Group 9 of the Concilium) struggled with either a strict interpretation of *SC* regarding a structural reform of the Office or a more radical revision.[3] Fr Juan Mateos, an Oriental liturgical scholar, who was a consulter to

3. See Campbell, *From Breviary to Liturgy of the Hours*, for a close study of the reform of the Hours by Group 9, especially chapter 4.

the Concilium but not a member of Group 9, recommended a return to the cathedral style Office at which the laity and their respective clergy could celebrate together. Unfortunately, to this author's mind, his suggestion was rejected out of hand. The majority of the consulters felt that too few laity would be involved to make such a revision reasonable and their concern was mainly for the spiritual life of secular clergy. Another proposal was to have two different Offices, a more fulsome one for monastics and a simpler one for clergy and laity. This too was rejected because the consulters did not want laity and clergy to have a 'second class' version of the Roman Office as had been the case before the Council. According to Stanislaus Campbell, this hesitancy to engage in a more radical revision amounted to a failure of vision 'to risk moving much beyond current practice in order to achieve the major, general goals of liturgical reform as stated in *SC* 14, 26–27, namely, communal celebration of all liturgical rites by all members of the Church'.[4]

While significant structural changes were made to the Office, particularly to address the needs of secular clergy—but not in a pastoral context with their parishioners—what remained unclear was how a single edition of the Liturgy of the Hours could be suitable for all three groups—secular clergy, monastics and the laity. This has plagued the effort of reform since the Council. While monastics have adapted the Liturgy of the Hours to their specific traditions, clergy and laity — along with those religious not bound to choir—have struggled with the official version of the text.

The Sung Tradition of the Hours

It is important to realise that before the Council the Office, as it was sung in choir, was not only in Latin, but for over a thousand years it was sung to Gregorian chant. The Office would not have been what it was without the simultaneous development of the Gregorian chant repertoire. The Psalter was sung to relatively simple chants, but there was an enormous body of musical literature for the antiphons and the responsories that were tonally linked to the chants. Thus not only did the antiphons and the responsories express textual interpretation of the Psalms or readings that they accompanied, but the musical set-

4. Campbell, *From Breviary*, 250.

tings of these antiphons and responsories provided elaborate musical interpretation of the texts that preceded them. To speak about 'music wedded to text' is to speak of the intimate connection that is possible when language and music work in concert with one another. The Gregorian chant tradition was a superb example of such a 'wedding'.

From Latin/Gregorian Chant to Sung English Texts

Anyone who has tried singing English texts to Gregorian chant knows that one simply cannot move from Latin to English and maintain the same musical form. Gregorian chant is what it is because it was composed with the Latin text in mind. The translation of the Liturgy of the Hours into the vernacular in the post–Vatican II reform is not the first time the Church has faced the issue of translation and adaptation of musical forms. The Reformation traditions made significant efforts to translate the Psalms into the vernacular and to find new musical forms that would express their meaning and increase participation. Of particular note are the efforts of the French Calvinists and the English Reformers.

Following Luther's example, John Calvin set about providing metrical Psalmody for his community in Strassburg in 1537. Over the period of the next twenty-five years Calvin and Clement Marot, a poet of the French courts, translated all 150 Psalms and set them to music in '110 different metres, with 125 tunes edited by Claude Goudimel'.[5] This Genevan Psalter called *Les Pseaumes mis en rime, Par Clement Marot & Theoldore Beza* (1562) had an enormous effect throughout the reformation world as nearly every European language group imitated this metrical Psalter. What was clear for them was that translating the Psalms from Latin into the vernacular required a new and different musical form. The reformers' solution was to create a body of hymn tunes that suited the metrical translation of the Psalms.

The English reformers made a similar effort. They, too, followed Luther's lead, and in 1530 Miles Coverdale translated fifteen Psalms and other songs in *Goostly Psalmes and Spirituall Songes* (London, c 1535). This effort was continued in 1547 by Thomas Sternhold who

5. Robin A Leaver, 'Liturgical Music as Corporate Song 1: Hymnody in Reformation Churches', in *Liturgy and Music: Lifetime Learning*, edited by Robin A Leaver and Joyce Ann Zimmerman (Collegeville, MN: Liturgical Press, 1998), 287.

wrote poetic versions of the Psalms. He intended to complete the one hundred and fifty Psalms but died before he could finish them. John Hopkins, however, continued his work, publishing in 1549 forty-four metrical Psalms. This was further expanded and completed by exiled English protestants in Geneva during 1556. According to musicologist Robin Leaver, these revisions 'were made in accordance with Calvinist ideals: the biblical text of the psalm was primary and poetry secondary. Rhyme and metre were acceptable but poetic paraphrase was not'.[6] After the reign of Queen Mary I, the exiles returned to England and in 1562 completed what became known as the English metrical Psalter (The Whole Book of Psalmes, collected into Englysh metre by T Sternhold I Hopkins & others: conferred with the Ebrue, with apt Notes to synge them withal). This Psalter was used with minor revisions well into the nineteenth century. The English tradition of psalm singing was brought to the Colonies, and in 1640 the Bay Psalm Book was published, the first book of any kind published in the English Colonies. Reflecting the Calvinist influence, the emphasis was on faithful translation from the Hebrew while allowing full participation through accessible hymn melodies.

Within the contemporary Catholic context, there is some evidence that progress is being made on the issue of setting English texts to music. The International Commission on English in the Liturgy (ICEL) engaged in a project in the 1980s and 1990s to translate the Psalms into contemporary English for singing and recitation. As part of this project, the composer Howard Hughes contributed a series of musical chants that were matched with particular Psalms and Canticles. These chants provided a base level expression of what might be done musically with these new English Psalm texts. The project ran into difficulties when, even though it was approved by the National Conference of Catholic Bishops of the United States (USCCB) in 1995, it was rejected by the Congregation for Divine Worship and the Discipline of the Sacraments and consequently had to be withdrawn. A little more than a decade later a Grail translation of the Psalter was completed and published in accordance with the translation guidelines of *Liturgiam authenticam* (2001). The translation was approved by the USCCB in 2008 and was granted *recognitio* (recognition) by Rome in 2010. It will be the only approved version of the Psalter for

6. Leaver, 'Liturgical Music', 289.

liturgical books for the American Church and perhaps for all English-speaking countries for the foreseeable future. In 2010, GIA Publications produced a musical setting of the new Revised Grail Psalter composed by the monks of Conception Abbey. It is too early to make any judgment on the success of this project, and one would expect to find many more versions attempted in the years to come.

There is more to singing the Hours than just psalmody, and composers have turned their hand to this larger project as well. To celebrate the Hours in a more festive manner, there are a number of publications of musical settings for Morning and Evening Prayer.[7] These provide new hymnody, a musical setting for an Evening Thanksgiving, Psalm 141 and the canticles, and in some cases antiphons for the Psalms. Multiple settings of the *Magnificat* are also surfacing, often as independent compositions which are inserted into Evening Prayer that is either 'said' or partially sung. What is missing is any attention to setting the responsories for the readings. Shortly after the Liturgy of the Hours was promulgated, composers such as Chrysogonus Waddell and Richard Proulx published collections of antiphons and responsories, but these have not seen wide circulation, at least outside of the monastic context. While these responsories in the Gregorian chant tradition were extremely elaborate and an important means of interpretation, it remains to be seen if more composers will turn their hands to this element, and if such settings in English catch the imagination of the contemporary Church.

This effort to provide for sung versions of the Psalter, in particular, and the Hours in general is strongly supported by the General Instruction of the Liturgy of the Hours (GILH). The Instruction devotes eighteen paragraphs to the appropriateness of singing the Hours. As a general norm, it states that 'the sung celebration of the Divine Office is more in keeping with the nature of this prayer and a mark of both higher solemnity and closer union of hearts in offering praise to God . . . Therefore the singing of the Office is earnestly recommended to those who carry out the office in choir or in common'.[8] This applies to clergy, monastics and laity.

7. See for example David Haas, *Light and Peace* (Chicago, IL: GIA Publications, 1986); Michael Joncas, *St Francis Evening Prayer* (Chicago, IL: GIA Publications, 1999); Cyprian Consiglio, *Lord Open My Lips: Music for the Hours* (Portland, OR: Oregon Catholic Press, no date); *God of Light Be Praised: Music for Evening Prayer* (Shiller Park, IL: World Library Publications, no date).
8. *General Instruction on the Liturgy of the Hours* (hereafter GILH) #268.

Unofficial Versions of the Liturgy of the Hours

One of the difficulties in the renewal of the Liturgy of the Hours has been the tendency to see it as a relic of the past rather than a living tradition that needs reform and revitalisation. The GILH reminds us of this reality. 'The Liturgy of the Hours should not be looked on as a beautiful monument of a past age, to be preserved almost unchanged in order to excite our admiration. On the contrary, it should come to life again with new meaning and grow to become once more the sign of a living community.'[9] Efforts are being made toward this goal in the unofficial Hours that are being published.

Various religious communities have starting producing their own versions of the Liturgy of the Hours in order to address such contemporary issues as inclusive language and a more inclusive version of the calendar of saints—both of which are left unaddressed in the official version. Among the many communities doing this are the Sisters of Mercy of the Americas[10] and the several Dominican communities of women[11] who have collaborated on a new translation of the Psalms. Both have provided simple tones for chanting the Psalter. The Carmelite Sisters of Indianapolis have created a setting of the Liturgy of the Hours that has been used by many communities of religious women who do not have the resources to mount a full scale reform of the Hours themselves.[12] Of particular importance is their use of readings from more contemporary sources; new intercessions that are quite specific to the contemporary context and have an accent on justice; and the use of inclusive language. They also include modern holy people, who are often founders of religious communities and contemporary martyrs such as the four American women killed in El Salvador in 1980.

What is missing from this last revision is any attention to music. The transition from choral sung celebration to a spoken version of the Office was a vast change even when everything was in Latin. Reading texts and singing texts are not the same thing. The added layer of

9. GILH #273.
10. *Morning and Evening Prayer of the Sisters of Mercy*, 1998.
11. *Dominican Praise: A Provisional Book of Prayer for Dominican Women*, 2005.
12. *Peoples Companion to the Breviary*, volume I and II. Revised and Expanded Edition of the New Companion to the Breviary with Seasonal Supplement (Indianapolis, IN: The Carmelites of Indianapolis, 1997).

interpretation with the concomitant expression of joy, pathos, sorrow, delight, *etc etera.* that music provides makes the celebration a vastly different experience. Especially when the Liturgy of the Hours is celebrated in community, should it be merely 'said' with no attention to musical forms and no attention to the principles of progressive solemnity? In addition, very little if any attention is given to ritual context in these publications, although in the actual celebration of the Hours communities are paying attention to environment and the use of candles and incense. On the other hand, an important addition to the Hours is that lay preaching has begun to find a place. While the non-ordained are not allowed to preach in a eucharistic context, no such limitations are placed on the Liturgy of the Hours, and women are taking advantage of this situation to bring their experience to bear on the scriptures.

The Liturgy of the Hours and the Laity

Another major concern is how well the revised Hours suit the laity. There were some efforts in the early twentieth century to modify the structure of the Hours to enable the laity and those not bound to celebrate the whole Office to participate in this prayer form.[13] This effort was promoted in the Vatican II reforms which state that the communal celebration of the Hours is to be preferred to that of individual recitation. The GILH states that 'celebration in common, however, expresses more clearly the ecclesial nature of the liturgy of the Hours . . . Hence, whenever it is possible to have a celebration in common, with the people present and actively taking part, this kind of celebration is to be preferred to one that is individual and, as it were, private.'[14] As stated in paragraph 100 of *SC*, pastors are instructed to gather the laity in parishes at least on Sundays and feasts for corporate celebration of the Hours. Anecdotal evidence suggests this is happening in a very limited number of settings. Before daily Mass some parishes are saying Morning Prayer from 'Christian Prayer', an abbreviated publication of the official Liturgy of the Hours that contains Morning and Evening Prayer as well as prayer during the day. Other parishes are

13. The monks of St. John's Abbey at Collegeville MN had published *A Short Breviary for Religious and Laity* in 1941. In this version the number of Psalms was reduced, and later editions even distributed the Psalms over a four week period.
14. GILH #33.

beginning to use the Liturgy of the Hours for the Sundays of Advent or Lent. Sunday Celebrations in the Absence of a Priest provides the option for Morning or Evening Prayer as does the Vigil Rite for a Funeral, but there is not much evidence that they are being used.

The Presence of Christ

Since the publication of *SC*, paragraph seven has stood as a beacon in speaking of the various presences of Christ in the liturgy. In addressing the eucharistic liturgy, it noted that Christ is present in the two traditional ways: in the person of the priest presiding and *par excellence* in the eucharistic species. To these it added that Christ is present when the Church gathers and prays, and when the word is proclaimed and preached. In addition, it speaks of Christ's presence in the sacraments. It is helpful to expand this understanding of Christ's presence to the Liturgy of the Hours. Indeed, when the Church gathers for the corporate prayer of the Hours, Christ is present, and when the word is proclaimed and preached, he is also present. If the Hours are to be esteemed by the laity, this fact needs to be taught and emphasised. It is not necessary to celebrate Eucharist at every pastoral occasion. The Hours have the advantage of not requiring an ordained presider, allowing for the leadership of the laity to come to the fore.

Patricia Ramsey makes an important point in her writing on the Hours. 'The Liturgy of the Hours', she says, 'is not going to assume its rightful place in the lives of the faithful which the Fathers of Vatican II desired unless they (the faithful) are convinced of the positive value of the Divine Office. Just as the believing Christian is changed into the Body of Christ by means of the Eucharist, so the praying Christian is changed into Christ by means of the Liturgy of the Hours.'[15] Once again, this fact needs to be impressed upon the laity if the Hours are to receive the attention they deserve.

The Hours and the Sacredness of the Cosmos

Since the beginnings of the Hours in the fourth century, the Church has experienced a paradigm shift in its way of relating to the world. For some monastics in the early Church there was a world-denying

15. Patricia M. Ramsey, 'The Different Concepts of Sacred Time Underlying the Liturgy of the Hours', in *Worship* 78/4 (2004): 302.

aspect to their spirituality. The monks interceded for the salvation of the world which they had 'left'. While intercession for the needs of the world remains a mandate for the Christian, the world embraced in *Gaudium et spes* is a world already sacred by virtue of its creation by God. While not being naïve about the forces of evil in the world, Christians have no other choice but to work out our salvation in this blessed creation. As theologian Edward Schillebeeckx was fond of repeating, 'There is no salvation outside the world'.

But the world that is currently being embraced has in recent years expanded beyond anything ancestors in the faith would have imagined. Because of the new science, the 'world' has become the 'cosmos'—ever expanding and growing in complexity. Humans are the world come to consciousness; capable of reflecting on existence and on the God that believers understand has created all things and holds all things in being. Through the explorations of the Hubble telescope and other scientific instruments of the current time, understanding of the size of the cosmos has expanded beyond anything ever imagined even a decade ago. This explosion in the concept of the universe has necessarily enlarged an understanding of God and decentred the human person as the focal point of the universe. The understanding that all of creation is related even at the molecular level binds all, not just to other humans, but to all that exists. The insight that humans are star dust has changed a perspective of what it means to be human. All of these new realities—the goodness of creation, the extent of creation, and the changing understanding of God and the human—must make some difference in the way Christians pray the Hours.

The traditional Liturgy of the Hours was formatted according the unfolding of the hours on earth as the earth rotated and revolved around the sun. (Even if our ancestors in the faith did not understand the scientific nature of this reality, they understood the movement of the sun across the sky and the rhythms of day and night.) Today Christians stand in a different place. The challenge is how to take into account the rhythms of our galaxy which exists amongst one hundred and twenty-five billion galaxies in the known universe. How can Christians bring this to prayer, and how do they pray for the immensity of the cosmos?

The Christian Interpretation of the Psalms

From the earliest days of the Church, the Psalms were a privileged form of prayer for the Christian community. Inherited from Judaism, Christians continued to use the Psalms but began to interpret them christologically. As the GILH noted, 'the Fathers of the Church saw the whole Psalter as a prophecy of Christ and the Church and explained it in this sense'.[16] In the medieval Church, captions were attached to each psalm to aid in this christological interpretation. This is continued in the official version of the Liturgy of the Hours. Antiphons were also added before and after each Psalm to focus the meaning and the prayer of the community. According to chant scholar Willi Apel, 'A small number of antiphons borrow their text from the Psalms with which they are, or originally were, connected'.[17] On the other hand, the great majority (three quarters) are drawn from other parts of scripture, mainly the prophecies, the historical books, and the gospels.[18] It was through these antiphons that another layer of christological interpretation was made. In the later medieval Church psalm prayers were added, which, again, were a means to interpret the psalm in a Christian perspective. In the current form of the Liturgy of the Hours, these psalm prayers are published in a supplement.[19] In practice this means that most people who pray the Hours do not pray these Psalm prayers.

The issue for today is twofold: do the Psalms continue to hold a place of honour in the Christian repertoire of prayer, and are the multiple layers of christological interpretation completely appropriate at this time when there is a renewed appreciation of the integrity of the Hebrew scriptures. Regarding the former, the GILH places great emphasis on the Psalms, but I am not sure whether the people of God themselves hold the Psalter as dear as they did in the past or as the documents suggest they ought.

---

16. GILH #109.
17. Willi Apel, *Gregorian Chant* (Bloomington, IN: Indiana University Press, 1958), 96.
18. Apel, *Gregorian Chant*, 97.
19. GILH #12.

Conclusion

Structurally, the Liturgy of the Hours has been modified so as to enable multiple groups within the Church to adapt the Hours according to their needs. No longer is a monastic structure normative for secular clergy and laity. Rather than structure being the primary obstacle to the Church's celebration of the Hours, pastoral issues are the determining factor for making the Hours a celebration of the whole people of God. The laity is just beginning to understand that the Hours are not just the prayer of clergy and religious; much work needs to be done to convince them of the importance of the Hours and the role of praise and sanctification that is a part of Christian prayer. Christ is truly present when the community gathers, and the Church is changed ever more deeply into the Body of Christ when it joins Christ in praise and intercession. What remains is how to persuade the laity that this is true and how to persuade pastors that joining the laity in this prayer form at least on Sundays and feasts is preferable to saying the Hours by themselves.

The translation of the Hours into the vernacular has been a first step towards inculturating it into specific contexts. Within the North American Church, issues such as inclusive language within the Psalter, the prayers and the intercessions has become an important consideration. In addition, extending the calendar of saints have also become important for women's communities and for the laity. Since there are no efforts along these lines in the official Liturgy of the Hours, unofficial versions of the Hours are being created and used.

Musical issues are part and parcel of the reform of the Hours, and Christians are clearly at the beginning of a process of turning vernacular texts into sung prayer. They cannot expect to create in just a few years a full-blown musical tradition that would match the thousand-year tradition of Gregorian chant or of the hundreds of years of setting vernacular psalmody. Setting the Psalter is one issue; setting antiphons and responsories is quite another. It remains to be seen if the contemporary Church will develop anything approximating the Gregorian tradition of interpretive antiphons and responsories. One important adaptation of the Hours for Evening Prayer in parishes or other such settings is the creation of *Lucernarium* services—blessings of the lights, evening thanksgiving and incensing that were not included in the official Hours. This would have been more typical of Cathedral Hours in the early Church, and since this option was rejected as seen above, it is not surprising that it was left out of the official Hours. Sensitivity to progressive solemnity is also typical of this effort at reform through the creation of more elaborate musical settings and greater attention to environment, posture and movement.

Overall, it can be said that the reform of the Hours is a work in progress and will be for the next several decades. As given, the form is reasonably flexible, but much more thought needs to be given to the use of the Hours by the laity. Religious communities, monastic and otherwise, have made their own adaptations to the Hours, but the laity has not yet taken the project in hand and adapted it for its use. It remains to be seen if any changes will be made along these lines as ICEL takes on the Liturgy of the Hours as one of its next revision projects.

Liturgical Time: Celebration and Interpretation

Guy Hartcher

This paper examines the liturgical cycle as set out in the document *Sacrosanctum Concilium*[1] *(SC)* where a set of overall attitudes were assumed and how these have changed over time and place. Our worldviews vary as do our relationship to liturgy and the place of the liturgical year to our sense of time and the extent to which individuals have any sense of belonging to the local worshipping community. This is examined particularly in the context of Australia and its multicultural context and its socio-cultural context where the work structure has so many different shapes. It also considers the challenges for liturgy in the southern hemisphere when all the cycles are tied to the seasons of the northern hemisphere and are contradictory for the Australian context which needs to find new meaning for liturgies whose language refers to darkness in mid-summer. The issues are considered from a practical pastoral perspective.

The World of *Sacrosanctum Concilium*

Some of the less positive critiques of the work of Vatican II have taken the view that the Fathers at the Council had too optimistic a view of the world and of the work of the Church within the world. Whatever one's view of that opinion, it is certainly true that as a work of the Spirit, the Council manifested a great sense of hope, and in varying ways that virtue shines in all the documents of the Council.[2]

1. <http://www.vatican.va/archive/hist_councils/ii_vatican_council/documents/vat-ii_const_19631204_sacrosanctum-concilium_en.html>. Accessed 14 April 2013.
2. Such memoirs as Gerald O'Collins, *Living Vatican II* (NY: Paulist, 2006) convey vividly the air of hope and joy common during the Council years, and mood changes since.

That sense of hope is strongly evident in *SC* which is underpinned by the sense of our worship as a foretaste of the everlasting loving and awe-filled worship of Heaven. *SC* 8 articulates that point: 'we take part in the foretaste of that heavenly liturgy which is celebrated in the holy city of Jerusalem towards which we journey as pilgrims'. That hope-filled awareness of the worshipping action of God's people as a life-giving bridge towards the eternal invests the whole Constitution with energy and life.

That investment underlies the chapter on the Liturgical Year,[3] and the chapter echoes that sense of joyful hope as it develops the theme of the year as the vehicle for the Church's living again Christ's Paschal Mystery. That is to happen within the whole context both of his life and of broader salvation history. This must be our starting point in any examination of the liturgical year. Each year of our lives as people and as children of God we see as 'celebrating this annual cycle of the mystery of Christ'.[4]

So our world-view is fundamentally different. The individual cycle of birthdays and anniversaries of each of us and our individual families is one dimension of our lives, but only one. Every individual and every family has its life cycle swept up into the cycle of reliving Christ's mystery. This is our Christian viewpoint. The daily grind, the school year, the tax year, the waiting for the annual vacation, the wrenching reliving of past tragedies as their anniversaries recur—all these and more become part of the story of Christ's Body celebrating the annual cycle of his mystery. It is the mystery of Christ's life, death and resurrection in which we participate and which brings each of us as members of Christ to the God who is our beginning and our end.

The most powerful basis for that worldview is the scriptural message aptly summarised in Romans 12: 4, 5 and then elaborated in verses 6–8: 'We, who are many, are one body in Christ, and individually we are members one of another.'[5] And the variety of gifts which we share is given for the benefit of each member. Prophecy, ministry, teaching, exhorting, giving, leading and being compassionate: all these are gifts to be exercised for one another.

---

3. *SC* #102 to 111.
4. *SC* #103.
5. Romans 12: 5.

This explanation of the essential relationship of belonging to one another and to Christ is then further elaborated in I Corinthians,[6] the lengthiest of a number of explanations of how God's people are connected in Christ. The explanation is preceded immediately by the crucial reminder that the particular relationships and gifts we possess are all manifestations of the one Spirit, and that we are each given manifestations of the Spirit 'for the common good'[7]. This is not an auxiliary grouping together of individual believers; it is an essential membership of the one body for the good of that body.

Without that mega-view of reality and of life,[8] our lives and our worship shrink down to the small scale of our own individual life and our imagination. We can lose the grandeur of our destiny and the hope that gives us purpose. But with that sense of the year, each and every year, as a vehicle conveying all of us with Christ towards the Father, our individual lives are given a context, a purpose and a means to operate in Christ and with one another. For we are all participants in the unfolding of salvation history, and our worshipping activity within the Eucharist and sacraments has to be seen within that patristic context of the economy of salvation,[9] the journey of the whole body which will only be completed in the *parousia*.

That communal sense of journeying together in Christ and with one other is at the core of our Christian identity. But it is more than that. At the human level, we all have a deep need for community.[10] Both history and anthropology demonstrate that the formation of community, its preservation, and when necessary its rebuilding, are central to human evolution and development. It can be argued that recent post-enlightenment trends in Western societies towards individualism,[11] and towards the individual's choices made for the

6. I Corinthians 12:12–27.
7. I Corinthians 12:7.
8. Which forms such an intrinsic part of the mega-history of salvation in the chapter 'The Mystery of the Church' in *Lumen Gentium.*
9. Pamela EJ Jackson 'Theology of the Liturgy', in *Vatican II: Renewal Within Tradition,* Matthew Lamb (NY: Oxford University Press, 2008), 111.
10. Avery Dulles in his seminal *Models of the Church* (New York: Doubleday, 1974): in the chapter 'The Church as Mystical Communion', 43–57 centres on the community which is and which becomes communion.
11. Sylvana Tomaselli, 'Individualism', in *The Blackwell Companion to the Enlightenment,* edited by John W Yolton (London: Blackwell, 1991), 242–244.

benefit of the individual, have generated social isolation and a loss of a sense of communal identity. It is evident that in so many contexts people almost automatically find themselves building village-sized communities and community groups as a countervailing influence in their lives. Properly handled, and with the assistance of the Spirit, the parish and its component parts can and do become life-giving community for their people. The wider community within which the parish lives is strengthened by the communal influence of the parish community. The key components in the building of such community are Spirit-given grace, leadership and liturgy that bond us all to Christ; and give us a sense of that pilgrimage we are all making together.

At the level of the divine, that pilgrimage is part of a cosmic movement from the flawed present towards a fulfilled future. The process of becoming God's world, of becoming a creation totally imbued with grace (as distinct from a creation partly imbued with grace, struggling with the alien forces of sin and selfishness) is the task not only of all humanity, but of all creation led by humanity. At the beginning of the Third Eucharistic Prayer we pray:

> You are indeed holy O Lord
> and *all you have created* rightly gives you praise,
> for through your Son our Lord Jesus Christ,
> by the power and working of the Holy Spirit,
> *you give life to all things and make them holy,*
> and you never cease to gather a people to yourself
> so that from the rising of the sun to its setting
> a pure sacrifice may be offered to your name.[12]

This is a clear description of the task. It is a gathering of all living things, made holy through the power of the Spirit, led by the people God has gathered, whose task is to give voice for all creation in giving praise to God, and to make a pure sacrifice to God's name.

In God, through Christ and with the power of the Spirit lie our future, and the future of all creation. That is the total context within which human life is lived, human society is developed, and the world and universe around us achieve their purpose for being. It is not some

12. *The Roman Missal* (London: Catholic Truth Society, 2011), 684. Emphasis added.

airy-fairy theological daydream. It is the real and practical goal of Christianity as lived by Christians individually and collectively. At least in theory this is truly what separates us from the rest of humanity. We have the goal, we have been given the method, and we have the guidance to use the method to achieve the goal.

The goal is a communal goal.[13] The method is a communal method. The guidance is divine, given to the Body and through the Body to the members of the Body. The whole process is communal. Each individual must consent, must cooperate, must be reborn in the Spirit, must become part of the Body, for the Body is Christ, the giver of grace and of the Spirit. That is our context.

So liturgy as the focus for all this human involvement with God is at the core of Christian life. It injects Christ's mystery into the lives of all of us, and it injects us into the mystery.

Hence the building of this community, this Body, is counter-cultural in the Western world of the twenty-first century, but in accord with the deep needs and instincts of people. As grace builds on nature, so Christ's Body works through the natural human desire for community.

The Role of the Liturgical Year

The role of the liturgical year becomes clearer. It is to be a structural framework within which the journey takes place.[14] The people who are becoming the Body of Christ gradually become more deeply conscious of him with whom we are connected. Who he is and what he calls us to grow on us and in us. And it is in living again and again, year by year, the mystery that was his life and covenant and sacrifice, that we become part of the one to whom we are committed. So the cycle is not just a cyclic one, around and around. It is more like a spiral, around and deeper, and around and deeper still.

More than that even, it is the whole people who move ever deeply. At the individual level, there are those who are distracted for some

---

13. Bernard Haring *My Hope for the Church* (Liguori, Miss: Liguori, 1999), 65–69. In particular 67 & 68 Christ's 'all-embracing salvific solidarity', to be 'understood in a radically communitarian way'.

14. *Varietates Legitimae: The Fourth Instruction for the Right Application of the Constitution on the Sacred Liturgy Of the Second Vatican Council* # 26 in Kenneth J. Martin, *The Forgotten Instruction* (Chicago: Liturgy Training Press, 2007), 168.

years by the demands of family and job and simple survival. These may simply hang on at the level they had previously attained. Some lose the sense of what they are involved in, and simply hang on to forms that give them comfort and hope. Others lose even that and wonder why they are there at all, but even so, at least periodically, they find themselves struggling to be part of what the community is doing. Some grew up as members of that community but never grafted it onto their individual lives, so only find themselves part of it, almost by proxy, at weddings and funerals and other family gatherings. But they are there, and in many cases, without stopping to analyse it, they feel obscurely strengthened and re-integrated into their family by that involvement. Some unfortunately drop by the wayside entirely and do not participate in any way at all.

In those distracted and difficult years, which occur in the lives of most people, even in some manner in the lives of clergy and religious, those people are carried by the rest of the community. While in other years these might become the ones deepening their own part in the cycle, while helping to carry the others who are still hanging on. It is a deeply communal activity, this pilgrimage of the people of God, and in the Western world we almost always err on the side of being too individualistic in our approach to it, and insufficiently focused on the life-giving movement of the whole body swirling around us. The Council stated: '[God] has however willed to make men and women holy and to save them, not as individuals without any bond between them, but rather to make them into a people who might acknowledge him and serve him in holiness.'[15] All those who look to Christ have been gathered together by God into 'this saving unity', the Church, which will advance until it arrives at 'that light which knows no setting'.

The Lord's Day

It is within the context of that annual movement of the people towards their God that the Council Fathers place the celebration of the Lord's Day. Not only do they remind us that this celebration comes down to us from the apostles, and that it originated in the 'very day of

15. *LG* #9.

Christ's resurrection',[16] but further elaboration specifies the celebration of the Lord's Day as the original feast day, a day of rejoicing and of freedom from work.

Everyone involved in the planning and celebration of liturgy is well aware that it is far easier to annually highlight the Annunciation, Christmas, Holy Week, Easter and Pentecost, than to make a weekly celebration truly celebratory. Even with well-celebrated liturgy and a well-formed community the regularity of the weekly gathering tends to mute the power of the rejoicing. Human nature can be overtaken by routine, making it difficult to sustain the particular effort needed to revive the full sense of rejoicing each week. But on the other hand we have inherited a strong early tradition specifying that the Christian community must celebrate the Lord's Day.[17] There is a sense of need, of a powerful communal urge to assemble on the first day of the week to worship together.[18]

Seen from the other end of the spectrum, the weekly celebration is the individual brick which, added to similar bricks, builds the structure which becomes the annual celebration of the mystery of Christ's saving work. The last few words of the *Dies Domini* document give powerful expression to the notion that Sunday is the 'foundation and the kernel of the entire liturgical year'.[19] The Council is in no doubt that the celebration of Sunday is the core of our whole worshipping lives. It is important that we acknowledge formally that there is no alternative to this basic principle. The Church's tradition that the Lord's Day is the continuation of the Jewish Sabbath observance makes the Sunday Eucharist the centrepiece of the Church's life.

So Sunday is the starting point, and the annual cycle is the elaboration and the full expression of the mysteries of salvation history in Christ. Both are necessary, and both interact to build that spiralling cycle which draws the people to their God and to the transformation towards which creation is being drawn.

And let us not forget that that cycle of growth and transformation is built of multiple celebrations of the covenant supper and participa-

16. *SC* #106.
17. Peter Cobb, 'The Calendar', in *The Study of Liturgy*, edited by Cheslyn Jones *et al* (London: SPCK, 1978), 405.
18. John Paul II developed this theme in his Apostolic Letter: *Dies Domini: Guide to Keeping Sunday Holy* (1998)
19. *SC* #106.

tions in the Lord's sacrifice. The liturgy is the 'summit towards which the activity of the Church is directed'[20] and the source of its power. So as each Sunday we are fed with God's word, remember with Christ his dying and rising, and eat the flesh and drink the blood of our Saviour, 'grace is poured upon us as from a fountain',[21] and we join with all creation in giving praise and glory to God.

Multiple Ways of Celebrating

It is because the spiralling cycle of the pilgrimage of God's people is such a communal activity that we can all participate at different levels, in different ways, at different stages of our lives. In multicultural societies such as Australia, ways of participation will reflect the differing cultural understandings that come from those backgrounds, but over time and the turns of the cycle, the capacity for a common understanding grows. Just as migrants gradually become bi-cultural themselves, living the culture of their birth in their new home, but also caught up in the culture of the workplace and the town or suburb in which they live, so over years and decades they become new persons, grafting on to their original persona elements of their new culture. And the deeper absorption into the new culture which their children achieve gradually interprets for them aspects of that culture which initially they did not comprehend. A simple example is the plethora of Australian words which have crept into the Italian spoken by Italo-Australians and gradually made their spoken Italian almost a separate dialect.

The variations grow even wider as clergy and religious from the migrant cultures (Italian and Vietnamese prominent among them) take up ministry within the Australian Church, so that the cultural approaches to Catholic worship and life which they absorbed as children they later teach as the Australian Catholic pattern. The adaptations happen in both directions, but gradually, deeply and slowly. This includes not only the particular devotions which were important in the original homelands of migrant peoples, but their basic Christian attitudes towards worship and the cycle of the liturgical year that become part of the fabric of the pilgrimage of the people of God.

---

20. *SC* #10.
21. *SC* #10.

Seasons in the South

The other dimension of the worship cycle which has not been addressed adequately is the seasonal issue. Where the new life dimension of spring reinforces the celebration of resurrection at Easter in the northern hemisphere, there is no such reinforcement with the beginning of the autumn in the South. When Easter is early, there exists the possibility of celebrating the rich fullness of harvest life at the end of summer. Resurrection life in Christ is after all the fullest phase of life, and certainly the ripe fecundity of harvest time in a good year does reflect the gift of full life from the creator God.

When Easter occurs later, and especially if the autumnal weather arrives early, the obvious lead-in to winter does not speak to us of resurrection life, our religious symbols speak not in parallel to the symbols of the season but in contrast. An autumnal Easter can still symbolise new life.[22] To Australians (at least in the southern half of the continent), the coming of cooler weather and arrival of rain are reasons for rejoicing in revival, even resurrection.

The season of Christmas in the southern hemisphere brings with it even further challenges. For more than a century non-indigenous Australians—heavily influenced by Europe—have celebrated with images of snow and northern trees in the midst of burning heat and totally dissimilar greenery. One explanation is that 'because the climate, the people and the landscape were so totally outside their experience newly arrived Europeans had to struggle to make sense of celebrating Christian festivals in such a strange context'.[23] It is possible for Australian Christians to compare the blazing summer sun to the dazzling Christ our Light, but this image can become limp when that sun is accompanied by such searing and debilitating heat.[24] There is need for a far fuller discussion than has yet taken place to adapt the traditional European cycle to the reversed seasons of the South, but the limitations of this discussion prevent us from further comment here. It is vital that we note that the fullness of worship and its symbols cannot be properly expressed until the expressions of our faith

22. Carmel Pilcher, 'Poinsettia: Christmas or Pentecost—Celebrating Liturgy in the Great South Land that is Australia', in *Worship*, 81/6 (2007): 516.
23. Pilcher, 'Poinsettia', 509.
24. Pilcher, 'Poinsettia', 515.

in our worship do integrate with all the world, not just the northern hemisphere.[25]

So to bring to fulfilment the promise which *SC* holds out to us, we, the collective body of the People of God, need to enrich our understanding of our communal task of growing through the worship cycle into Christ. That enrichment can be helped by the absorption of our many migrant cultures and Christian traditions into our local worship, and by working to better integrate the southern hemisphere's seasonal patterns into the liturgical cycle.

The World of Work

In modern life, the work patterns of society have powerful impact on the Church's ability to celebrate its worship and live the worship cycle through the year. There have been recent changes to employment and work conditions in the Western world which have arisen in part out of the triumph of capitalism over communism more than two decades ago. The balance of power has moved decisively away from labour and towards capital, and this has led to changes in work patterns such as the diminishment of the concept of a weekend, an adjustment to remuneration of workers, longer working hours, and the weakening of trade unions' ability to organise and defend the rights of workers.[26]

The set hours in a working week has increased in Australia and in the west generally, with heightened expectations on professionals and skilled personnel to routinely work longer and longer hours. As organisations become global in nature they take on a twenty-four hour cycle, with a seven day a week rotation made possible through increased technology. Shifts for workers are likely to be driven more by economic factors rather than human or cultural concerns.

---

25. This is particularly evident when *Varietates Legitimae* (Martin, *The Forgotten Instruction)* is examined. Even in an Instruction specifically dealing with inculturation and legitimate adaptation of the liturgy, the issue of the Southern Hemisphere is not even mentioned, even though South America is the home of a significant majority of the world's Catholics.
26. A useful though biased study reflecting on this whole area of employment and social change is *Insecure Work, Anxious Lives: the growing crisis of insecure work in Australia* , a 2011 ACTU report. <http://www.actu.org.au/Images/Dynamic/attachments/6637/Secure_Jobs_Better_Future_paper.pdf>. Accessed 10 April 2013.

With rosters that demand longer shifts it is more efficient to plan these on a seven day week where weekends become just normal workdays. This tendency is reinforced in industries where continuous operation is more viable than 'on-off' use of equipment. Owners of industries such as smelters, refineries, and oil and gas mining, in which the equipment is technically difficult and expensive to shut down, are well aware that continuous operation, and therefore continuous workforce presence, is more feasible both in terms of output and economics. According to the needs of the plant and industry cycles, contracts can then be developed to allow for longer periods of work time and down time, for example ten days working and four days away, or other more 'efficient' divisions of time.

In Australia, particularly in outback mines and offshore drilling rigs, the further development of a 'fly-in-fly-out' system enables managers to employ workers otherwise not procurable in remote and harsh work locations. This provides yet another variation on what used to be a much more standardised situation. The remuneration to the worker is high, but so are the costs, with added pressure on family, social and Church life where routine is disrupted and commitments difficult to honour.

Such an extended statement on current employment situations in Australia and parts of the western world may seem odd, but one of its dimensions is weakening of the tradition of Sunday as a day of rest, and for Christians as the Lord's Day. The power and complexity of the forces aligned against the Lord's Day are increasing. To develop the Church's approach to the liturgical year and the worship cycle, we must first wrestle with the growing trend to make the weekend and Sunday 'disappear'.

How we Involve the Absent

Both pastorally and catechetically, there is growing requirement for sensitivity to the needs of individuals and families caught in different and sometimes erratic work patterns and thereby absent from, or minimally present to, Sunday worship and the cycle of liturgical time. The Church can no longer afford to ignore the factors that militate against these non-attenders. The new evangelisation is aimed in part at such believers, although it seems to focus more on people whose absence is from choice rather than necessity.

With minimal or no attention paid to the changed realities of so many people's lives, effective preaching as part of the new evangelisation[27] will fail to produce the desired effect on people who are absent, because their employment and other pressures deny them the freedom to worship on Sundays. Building parish revival around Sunday Eucharist is only helpful for those who are free to be present on the Lord's Day.

There have always been minorities who have been constrained from full participation in Sunday worship, through no fault of their own. An element in the new evangelisation needs to be a widespread and focused enrichment and welcoming[28] of the occasional presence of those unable to participate every Sunday. They should be made to feel a valued part of the gathering and encouraged in the efforts they make to be present.

More than that, a clear focus on identifying those who are unable to be part of the parish's Sunday worship will provide the basic data upon which to build alternatives on other days for them. Once the group has been identified, their availability can be canvassed and an alternative structure set in place at the parish and diocesan levels to provide worship and community specifically for that group.

Catechesis for a Dynamic Understanding

A primary principle to be applied if the Church is to enrich its living of the liturgical year is the idea of the liturgical cycle as a structural foundation of pilgrimage of the people of God. The concept of our worship lives as a movement by all of us together, towards God and the reign of God is the key. This marks a crucial shift from a relatively static view of worship to a dynamic one. Our worship is not just part of a cycle, it is part of a mass movement. If each individual act of Sunday worship, each individual Eucharist, is of immeasurable value as an act of Christ towards His Father, how crucial is the totality of

27. *Synodus Episcoporum Bulletin XIII Ordinary General Assembly of the Synod of Bishops 7–28 October 2012*, especially Propositions 34, 35, 45 at <http://www.vatican.va/news_services/press/sinodo/documents/bollettino_25_xiii-ordinaria-2012/02_inglese/b33_02.html>. Accessed 10 April 2013.
28. Keith F Pecklers, '40 Years of Liturgical Reform: Shaping Roman Catholic Worship for the 21st Century', in *Worship*, 79/3 (2005): 200–201.

worship of Christ's Body, spread over time and space.[29] Only when we understand the overall movement, only when we understand each of our acts of worship as an integral part of that entire pilgrimage of life, love and hope, can we be fully part of it.

That understanding, its growth and 'depthing', is not arrived at only by a catechetical process alone.[30] Living the liturgy through its cycle involves a process of listening and absorbing,[31] of allowing the liturgy to penetrate the inner consciousness of each individual in the worshipping community.

It is also true that clergy at all levels can be as short-focused and as individualistic in their thinking as their faith community. So, building on the liturgical catechesis of the last forty years there has to be a new educational effort (experiential as well as theoretical) towards knowing and feeling that sense of communal progression towards God through the liturgical cycle.

This will be reinforced by the individual prayer lives of Christians who are aware of our interconnectedness with one another as well as with God, and by the other activities of life and charity of Christian communities. Works of charity, education and prayer interlock with works of worship, and all facets of the Body's life mutually enrich one other. A deeper understanding of the communal dimension of our worship will also enrich these other facets of the community life of Christians.[32]

This movement is the other side of the coin of the individual pursuit of virtue for the Christian. Neither movement is adequate on its own; each depends on the other. But in particular the individual pursuit of holiness implies contributing to the virtue and the salvation of one's brothers and sisters in Christ. Virtue cannot be a selfish quality. Christian love has at its core desire for the salvation of everyone else. Hence the need for the individual to be involved in the communal progress towards God's reign, manifested importantly in the re-production of the covenant and the sacrifice.

29. Glen Olsen, 'Time and Expression in the Eucharist', in *Worship*, 80/4 (2006): 317.
30. Pecklers '40 Years of Liturgical Reform', 197. 'Believers grow up as it were "speaking liturgy"'.
31. Godfried Cardinal Danneels 'Liturgy Forty Years After the Second Vatican Council: High Point or Recession', in *Liturgy in a Post-modern World*, edited by Keith Pecklers (London: Continuum, 2003), 14.
32. *SC* #105.

The people of God on pilgrimage with Christ to the Father need to become more conscious of that dynamic process in which they are involved. Discovering that dynamic in their lives and their communities through actual worship and through catechesis, and discovering ways to include the individuals and families who are not able to participate on Sundays in the worship lives of the People are the tasks ahead for the Church to implement *SC*.

Postconciliar Church Music: Dissonance and Development

William A Jordan

Chapter Six of the Constitution on the Sacred Liturgy *Sacrosanctum Concilium*[1] (*SC*) addressed in very broad terms the all-important role of music in worship, its purpose, and its qualities. Later documents, especially the 1967 Instruction of the Congregation of the Rites *Musicam Sacram*[2] (*MS*), would give more specific norms for implementing the principles given in *SC*. This chapter will treat the tensions surrounding the whole area of music in Christian worship before and after the Second Vatican Council and the implementation and reception of the Council's norms. It will address in particular the important aspect of liturgical music formation and the shortage of Church musicians which in turn has led to the use of recorded music in the liturgy instead of live music. Some suggestions will be made regarding the future directions of liturgical music.

The definition of what constitutes 'sacred music' has varied in the different Church documents in terms of musical style, language, and individual genres. *SC*'s use of the term 'sacred music' merely reflects the conventional usage of previous Church documents but does not

1. The translation is from the text on the official Vatican website <http://www.vatican.va/archive/hist_councils/ii_vatican_council/documents/vat-ii_const_19631204_sacrosanctum-concilium_en.html>. Accessed 19 January 2013. All subsequent quotations from the Sacred Constitution are from this site.
2. Congregation of Rites, Instruction *Musicam sacram* on Music in the Liturgy, 5 March 1967 #4b where its description of 'sacred music' uses the distinction *liturgical or religious music* of the people. See *Documents on the Liturgy 1963–1979 Conciliar, Papal, and Curial Texts* (Collegeville, MN: Liturgical Press 1982) #4125.

give a formal definition of sacred music. Paragraph 4 of the 1958 'Instruction on Music and Liturgy' added two further categories of sacred music to those in earlier documents, namely popular religious singing and religious music, which are mentioned also in *SC* 118 and MS 4b. This last category, religious music, refers to music that is not meant for liturgical worship but would be suitable for sacred devotions, bible services and in other ways helpful for religion.

Since the Council, and especially since the introduction of vernacular languages and inculturation possibilities in the liturgy, academics in liturgy, theology, philosophy, aesthetics and music as well as pastoral liturgists and musicians have explored much more extensively this whole area of music in worship and its ministerial function. There are new descriptions of Roman Catholic ritual music, liturgical music, worship music and a deeper understanding of the sacramentality of liturgical music. The term 'sacred music' is a rather incomplete description which does not have to be completely abandoned because there are aspects about the term that are worth keeping.

The opening article of *SC* chapter six states that sacred music is a 'necessary and integral part' of the liturgy particularly because it is bound so closely to the text. The same article refers to the ministerial function supplied by sacred music in the service of the Lord, and very significantly states that the Church admits all forms of genuine art (music) into divine worship (*SC* 112).

Seven of the ten articles in Chapter six touch on some aspect of the Council's dominant theme for the liturgical reform namely the 'full, conscious, active participation' of all of the assembly, especially that of the congregation. This emphasis is reiterated many times throughout *SC*. It suffices to quote *SC* 14:

> this full and active participation by all the people is the aim to be considered before all else, for it is the primary and indispensable source from which the faithful are to derive the true Christian spirit.

Consequently the Council recognised the need for a certain inculturation and adaptation of the reformed rites under the guidance of the local bishops' conferences, the most significant one being the use of the vernacular languages in the liturgy.

Other matters concerning music raised in *SC* were the Council's desire to preserve the rich treasury of Catholic sacred music, particularly Gregorian chant and sacred polyphony, whilst at the same time fostering new music whose texts should be drawn chiefly from holy scripture and from liturgical sources (*SC* 121). It was concerned also about the need for formation in liturgical music (*SC* 115).

Prior to Vatican Council II

The period following *Tra le Sollecitudini* of Pius X in 1903 saw the gradual development of modern liturgical music and modern hymn texts that reflected the new theological and liturgical insights that were emerging. The biblical inspiration of many of the new hymns was accompanied also by a rediscovery of the psalms. Some composers were also writing choral settings of the Ordinary that included parts for the people in Latin. While there would have been various levels of musical development across parishes, nevertheless many liturgists, liturgical musicians, composers and parishes were pastorally ready for Vatican II's liturgical reform of sacred music.

It may be helpful to younger readers to explain why the reform of the liturgy was needed. The Mass was celebrated by the priest in Latin with his back to the people whilst altar servers responded in Latin on behalf of the congregation. In many cases the people were silent for the whole of the Mass unless they were attending the main Sunday Mass which was usually a sung Mass with choir. The musical repertoire in the vernacular language such as hymnody was very limited in many countries. As the liturgical movement progressed the people themselves took part in the Latin dialogues with the priest and sang hymns sometimes in a more modern responsorial style with texts that reflected the fruits of the latest liturgical studies. The only musical instrument allowed was the organ.

Tensions Surrounding the Changes in Sacred Music

However, alongside the positive anticipation for liturgical reform prior to the Council there were many liturgical musicians who were concerned about the future of sacred music with the probable downgrading of Gregorian chant and choral polyphony, especially the Roman school of polyphony. The difficulties encountered in the drafting of Chapter six are well documented.

> Sacred music was unfortunately the most unsettled area of the reform both before and after the Council. The hostile attitude of music directors and distinguished composers prevented the reform from introducing renewal and pastoral participation into sacred music. This background of negative reaction explains the confusion of the postconciliar period, which saw a mushrooming of compositions that were not always inspired works of art and yet were widely received because they were more in keeping with the reform spirit of the postconciliar liturgy.[3]

It must be acknowledged that the difference of opinion amongst liturgists and liturgical musicians was much deeper than that of musical taste or the desire to preserve the Catholic Church's rich patrimony of sacred music. After the Council, the debate was very much polarised between the traditionalists, many of whom were members of the *Consociatio Internationalis Musicae Sacrae* established in Rome in November 1963 and those in the spirit of Vatican II and *aggiornamento* such as members of *Universa Laus*, founded in April 1965. Tensions were inevitable between the eschatological and incarnational aspects of liturgy, the conservative and evolutionary nature of ritual. The strongest point of contention is the tension between beauty and functionalism.[4] The polemics against *Universa Laus* were so acrimonious that the Consilium issued a clarification *Nell'aprile scorso* which stated that the members of *Universa Laus* have 'earned the Church's commendation' for their valuable work.[5]

The Implementation and Reception of the Liturgy Reforms Regarding Sacred Music

The bishops' conferences around the world saw the need for the formation of clergy and the laity in the theological-liturgical prin-

3. Annibale Bugnini, *The Reform of the Liturgy 1948–1975* (Collegeville, MN: Liturgical Press, 1990), 22.
4. For an overview see Anthony Ruff, *Sacred Music and the Liturgical Reform, Treasures and Transformations*, (Mundelein, IL: Hillenbrand Books, 2007), Part 1.
5. 'Necessary Clarification:*Nell'aprile scorso*, on "Universa Laus and the Consociatio Internationalis Musicae Sacrae"', in *Notitiae 2/21–22* (1966): 249–251.

ciples and norms to be followed in liturgical celebrations. Dioceses revamped where necessary their liturgical commissions, opened new liturgy centres and offices, ensured that places of tertiary education and seminaries offered appropriate courses in liturgical studies and liturgical music, and organised seminars and workshops for parish liturgy teams, clergy and musicians. Professional bodies such as the National Association of Pastoral Musicians and Church Music Association of America were formed to help pastoral musicians and clergy. Many publications and journals dedicated to promoting the liturgical reforms appeared. National and regional pastoral music conventions in various countries gave considerable impetus to the promotion of liturgical music. In this period there was a sharing of expertise ecumenically that was of mutual benefit to all Christian Churches.

Over 100,000 hymn titles appeared in a few years, a phenomenon described by some as the 'hymn explosion'. Music publishers were very busy and helpful in disseminating new music which had to be relevant to contemporary life, using modern English and having the quality of universality and accessibility for the congregation that often crossed social and cultural boundaries. The first twenty years after the Council was a very exciting time for both liturgy and music.

In 1972 the US Bishops Committee on the Liturgy produced a very significant statement, based on the conciliar and post-conciliar documents, entitled 'Music in Catholic Worship'[6] (MCW) which greatly influenced the liturgical music scene, not only in the USA but also in other English-speaking countries such as Australia. MCW was very readable, clear, practical and inspirational and it became a key non-Roman pastoral document on sacred music in the English-speaking world. The section on the threefold liturgical, musical and pastoral evaluation of music in celebration aroused considerable and worthwhile discussion.[7] Ten years later a second document 'Liturgical Music Today' appeared that treated of music in sacramental celebrations

---

6. The 1983 text of this document originally published in 1972 by the United States Catholic Conference, Washington DC appears in *The Liturgy Documents: A Parish Resource* (hereafter *TLD*) (Chicago: Liturgy Training Publications, 1991), 274-93.
7. In the 2007 revision, this section was reordered as a threefold evaluation: one judgement, thus, liturgical-pastoral-musical, that is, each judgement was not to be isolated from the others, and to take into consideration the overall flow and rhythm of the liturgical celebration.

and the Liturgy of the Hours.[8] In 2007 these two documents were revised and combined in 'Sing to the Lord: Music in Divine Worship' (STTL).[9]

Different Evaluations of Liturgical Music in the Reformed Liturgy

During the 1990s, there appeared in the USA two important documents that summarised reflection and discussion amongst musicians about the musical and liturgical developments since the Council from different theological points of view. These were the 1992 Milwaukee Report (*MR*)[10] and the 1995 Snowbird Statement (SS)[11]. They were the result of various symposia and meetings of highly regarded expert musicians, composers and liturgists. It is significant that there were no signatories in common.

MR stressed functionality as the foremost quality of the holiness of ritual music, along the lines of *SC* 112:

> as sacred song united to the words, it forms a necessary or integral part of the solemn liturgy . . . Therefore sacred music is to be considered the more holy in proportion as it is connected with the liturgical action.

It stated that 'holiness' does not inhere in music but arises from the joining of music and text in the enactment of the rite, hence the adoption of the term 'ritual music' (*MR* 6). The next paragraph states that 'Christian ritual music, as a sacramental event, expresses and shapes our image of God' (*MR* 17). The Report makes no specific mention of beauty in its list of criteria for ritual music. 'It is not simply a matter of discovering how much the musicians or even the community itself likes the music. Rather, there needs to be a ritual evaluation, discovering how the music enables the community to enter into its liturgy and common life' (*MR* 36).

8. *TLD*, 295–312.
9. *Sing to the Lord—Music in Divine Worship* (Washington DC: United States Catholic Conference, 2007).
10. *The Milwaukee Symposia for Church Composers : A Ten-Year Report* (Washington DC: The Pastoral Press, 1992).
11. *The Snowbird Statement on Catholic Liturgical Music* (Salt Lake City, Utah:The Madeleine Institute, 1995).

SS took a different perspective and explicitly focused on the importance of the aesthetic beauty in expressing our eschatological hope. SS 3 states that 'Beauty is essential in the liturgical life and mission of the Church. Beauty is an effective—even sacramental—sign of God's presence and action in the world'. *SS* 5 welcomes the Christian ritual music concept but laments that much modern Catholic Church music today focuses too much on utilitarian functionalism with an inadequate attention to the beautiful and artistic. SS 6 acknowledges that the musical judgement is a complex one that needs more development in order to identify the objective elements involved in this judgement that cross over musical styles and transcend personal preference or social or historical convention.

Both *MR* and *SS* present highly important statements that can be regarded as complementary rather than irreconcilable. Taken together hopefully it will be possible to develop some sort of measure of objective beauty in Catholic liturgical music that serves the rite appropriately whilst being at the same time musically artistic and pastorally sensitive. The later *Universa Laus* document affirms:

> In Christian worship it is not music which is sacred but the live voices of the baptized singing in and with Christ. In liturgy, what makes up the beauty of a type of singing or instrumental music does not exist by itself, independently of the celebration, the place, the ritual, the rite or the assembly which includes such singing or music.[12]

In his book on the need for a reform of the reform Thomas Kocik summed up the strong dissatisfaction felt by a vocal group of musicians wanting the recovery of Gregorian chant, polyphony and organ music and lamenting the dire state of contemporary liturgical music which was 'a bundle of banalities adapted from pop music and other extravagant sources'.[13] Various suggestions were made that a new pontifical body was needed to oversee sacred music and that the implementation of *SC* was flawed. The aim of the movement was to

12. 'Universa Laus, *Music in Christian Liturgies: Document II*' (May 2002) in Music and Liturgy Issue, 30/1, (2004): 20-21.
13. Valentino Miserarchs Grau, *Chiesa, Musica Sacra: passato, presente e futuro* (Rome: Pontificio Istituto di Musica Sacra, 2002).

restore 'a pronounced sense of the sacred and transcendent dimensions of worship'.[14]

Chirograph of John Paul II (2003)

The Chirograph of John Paul II (Chiro) written to mark the Centenary of Pius X's Motu Proprio *Tra le Sollecitudini* on Sacred Music took the opportunity to address unrest in the liturgical music world by confirming the fundamental principles of *SC* and *MS*. The document addressed the benefits to be derived from the wise use of past musical treasures and the new vernacular compositions that were demanded by the inculturation process inherent in the liturgical reform. Important though they are, there was no mention of a large-scale restoration of Gregorian chant, polyphony and the organ requested by the proponents of the reform of the reform. At the same time John Paul II certainly stressed that it was necessary 'to purify worship from ugliness of style, from distasteful forms of expression, from uninspired musical texts which are not worthy of the great act that is being celebrated to guarantee dignity and excellence to liturgical compositions' (Chiro 3). Elsewhere he affirmed the notion that sacred music must possess a 'beauty that invites prayer'.[15] In other words, it must be not just pure, genuine art, but art that is also functional: leading to prayer and the liturgical assembly's faith response to what is being proclaimed and celebrated in the liturgy.

With regard to the composition of new liturgical music, the general rule enunciated by Pius X that composers should be inspired by Gregorian chant does not mean that they are to imitate Gregorian chant but rather be imbued with the same spirit that inspired and shaped it (Chiro 12). Composers will need formation centres in order to gain this specialised knowledge.

The document speaks of the importance of artists, including composers, being profoundly steeped in the *sensus Ecclesiae* if they are to perceive and express in melody the truth of the Mystery that is celebrated in the liturgy (Chiro 12).

---

14. Thomas M Kocik, *The Reform of the Reform? A Liturgical Debate: Reform or Return* (San Francisco: Ignatius Press, 2003), 15.
15. John Paul II, *Address to the professors and students of the Pontifical Institute of Sacred Music*, 19 January 2001, #4 Available at <http://www.vatican.va/holy_father/john_paul_ii/speeches/2001/documents/hf_jp-ii_spe_20010119_musica-sacra_en.html>. Accessed 8 May 2013._

Chiro 13 reiterated the importance of continuing formation of clergy and laity in liturgy and music organised by the bishops through their diocesan commissions and seminaries, as well as through other institutes and associations. The Congregation for Divine Worship and the Discipline of the Sacraments was asked 'to increase its attention . . . in the sector of liturgical music, utilising the competencies of the various commissions and institutions specialized in this field'. Hence there was no need for a new pontifical body to oversee liturgical music as requested earlier by proponents of the reform of the reform.

The pope encouraged the Pontifical Institute for Sacred Music to embrace the work of the new evangelisation which called for new artistic expressions of the faith.[16]

Looking back over the last fifty years of liturgical reform, one can see that the tensions between creativity and regulation, between function and art, between modernity and tradition have not abated.

Areas for Further Reflection

Some areas that require ongoing reflection and discussion include the following:

a) Criteria for making a musical judgment about a composition that could be more objective and that would be valid across musical styles.
b) The theological, philosophical and liturgical understanding of aesthetics and beauty in Christian worship and especially in liturgical music.
c) The development of a stable, core repertoire of ritual music and hymnody (metrical and non-metrical) to be known throughout all parishes and schools in every diocese within each nation. Nationally published or adopted hymnals are useful for this purpose.
d) The treasury of sacred music can be used in today's worship and can be included in the core repertoire in

16. Re the role of sacred music and art in the new evangelisation, see John Paul II's Post-Synodal Apostolic Exhortation *Ecclesia in Europa - On Jesus Christ alive in His Church the source of Hope for Europe* (28 June 2003), #60. Available at <http://www.vatican.va/holy_father/john_paul_ii/apost_exhortations/documents/hf_jp-ii_exh_20030628_ecclesia-in-europa_en.html>. Accessed 8 May 2013.

ways that foster the participation of the cantors, choir and congregation.[17]

e) The need for new musical compositions for the entrance and communion songs. The General Instruction of the Roman Missal (GIRM) gives several sources for these but no reference is made to the antiphons given in the Roman Missal which presumably are intended for recitation rather than song.[18]
f) The real need for architects involved in building or renovating churches to be properly briefed about the spatial and acoustic requirements for choirs, cantors, leaders of song, instrumental ensembles and larger instruments such as pipe organs. The musicians' requirements need to be factored into the church design from the beginning. Often this oversight cannot be rectified satisfactorily at a later stage.
g) The importance of reminding celebrants, liturgy planners and musicians about the place for moments of sacred silence, an essential ingredient in prayerful participation in the liturgy.
h) The quality of the use of technology, including recorded transmissions of liturgical celebrations.

On-Going Education and Formation

The Council recognised the importance of liturgical formation of both clergy and laity, not only in the spirit and content of the liturgical reforms of the rites, but also the unique place of liturgy in Christian life and mission of the Church (*SC* 44–46, 115; *MS* 68–69). The key to the implementation of the liturgical reforms was the formation of present and future parish priests and should include also lay or

17. The importance given by *SC* #114 & 116 to the preservation of the rich tradition of sacred music, especially Gregorian chant and polyphony needs revisiting. The collective musical memory of the Church is a significant way of passing on the Catholic faith and tradition. MS #53 amplifies what is said in *SC* #114.
18. *General Instruction of the Roman Missal (2010)*. (Strathfield: St. Pauls, 2012) #48 & 87. A good summary of various post conciliar attempts to address this matter can be found in John Ainslie's article 'The Entrance Song—Antiphon or Hymn?', in *Music and Liturgy, the Journal of the Society of Saint Gregory*, 39/1 (2013): 52–56.

religious pastoral associates and school religious education co-ordinators.

The enthusiastic acceptance of the changes, especially those of language, music and the different liturgical ministries, points to the success of this early work of formation and implementation. Now that the texts, rites and music have been revised, one can be tempted to relax as if there is now no need for such intensive activity on the part of liturgical commissions and music committees as before. In fact, unfortunately, it seems that in some places this has been the case. The need for effective diocesan commissions, well trained seminarians taught by a new generation of experts in liturgy and sacred music, well informed parish liturgy teams, formation programs for parish liturgy teams, composers and musicians will be on-going. Congregations also need to be educated about the purpose and structure of the liturgy and its music and to be shown how to interiorise the sacred mysteries being celebrated as the summit and source of the Christian life.[19]

Ongoing Strategies Needing Attention

a) Leadership

Leadership by the bishops is essential in ensuring that their diocesan liturgical commissions and music committees are promoting effectively the liturgical apostolate in parishes and schools.[20]

Tertiary Institutes and dioceses need to ensure that formation courses in liturgy and music continue to be available for music ministers and liturgy planners as well as clergy and lay presiders, who are all responsible for making liturgical, musical, pastoral and theological judgements about the suitability of music for the liturgy. The need for formation applies also to text writers and composers, so that they are aware of the function and purpose of what they create for the liturgy (*SC* 121). Parish priests have the responsibility of ensuring that those responsible for the music in their liturgical celebrations make use of the opportunities offered by their diocese.

---

19. *SC* #10.
20. *SC* #43-6, *MS* #68-9.

b) The growing shortage of both musicians and training opportunities

One of the major challenges facing many dioceses and parishes is the ever-growing shortage of musical personnel both at the professional level and at the parish volunteer level, who are truly formed in the spirit of the liturgy and who can also minister at a sufficiently competent musical standard so that the musical participation by the congregation, choir, cantors, organists, instrumentalists will add greater understanding, spiritual richness and beauty to the celebration.[21] This shortage is related also to the declining Mass attendance in recent years. Obviously contemporary lifestyles make it more difficult for parish musicians to find time for music lessons, continual rehearsal sessions, and impact on the long-term availability of competent music directors, singers and instrumentalists.

In some countries there are insufficient places or courses of formation in liturgical music at a professional level, whether tertiary or at a certificate level. The Australian Catholic University and other universities and institutions that previously offered liturgical music courses have been forced to close down for lack of students. The reasons for this acute shortage of students applying for these courses need to be identified.

In many places, an important disincentive for musicians taking on professional training in church music is the lack of a career path in Catholic church music. In other words, there are few opportunities for a full-time or even part-time career as a church musician in countries such as Australia. In the United States, the full-time music director is a professional position which is highly valued by the parish. This role is often shared between the parish church and school which employs the music director as part of the music staff.[22] Another option is

21. Deirdre Browne IBVM & Paul Taylor, *The Influence of the LITURGICAL MOVEMENT on MUSIC in key Australian Catholic Dioceses following Vatican II. A Report submitted to the Australian Research Theology Foundation Inc* (Private Publication, 2012), 57.
22. The 1958 *Instruction on Sacred Music and Sacred Liturgy*, Sacred Congregation for Rites 3 September 1958 mentioned the importance of salaries for church musicians and of dioceses providing pay scales for musicians, Chapter III-5, #101–103. Available at <http://www.adoremus.org/1958Instro-sac-mus.html#anchor36301306>. Accessed 8 May 2013.

to encourage those professional musicians or graduates from secular institutions to undertake a specially designed curriculum such as a diploma course in liturgical music giving them the necessary liturgical and pastoral background to complement their musical studies.

Given that full-time study and full-time musical careers are going to be undertaken by very few, a more creative look at ways of providing skills in music making or conducting is required. A progressive series of intensive short courses for musicians is one option. Some of the more theoretical subjects could be offered on-line. Ecumenical sharing of musical skills training would help overcome the shortage of Catholic music teachers. Other possibilities are collaboration between neighbouring parishes in sharing expertise and ideas or mentoring by musically well-resourced parishes of those struggling with their liturgical music.

An enthusiastic collaboration between parishes and neighbouring Catholic schools and colleges would provide not only an important source of enthusiastic singers and instrumentalists for parish liturgies but also ensure a certain amount of common repertoire between school and parish.

c) Financial resources for the ministry of liturgical music[23]

One main practical reason given for the present shortage of musical ministers and choirs is the lack of finance to fund music resource centres or a music resource person on the part of the diocese, and/or the lack of financial resources in parishes for church music resources and musicians. One wonders if this is at times a valid reason. It depends on the importance the parish or diocese attaches to liturgy and music. Given the need for musicians, for resources (music, instruments), for training (for instance, by attendance at music workshops or courses), there must be a place in the parish budget if good liturgy and good liturgical music is desired. Parish choir members and many instrumentalists are usually unpaid volunteers who still value being well resourced by the parish by way of purchases of music, well-maintained instruments and suitable facilities for rehearsals. One way the parish

23. Paul Taylor, *The Ministerial and Congregational Singing of Chant: A Study of Practice and Perceptions in the Catholic Archdiocese of Melbourne*. PhD Thesis. (Melbourne: Australian Catholic University, 2010), 309–10, 332.

can reward these volunteers is to help with in-service or tuition fees when they are upgrading their musical and liturgical skills. Effective leadership by the priest as singing presider must be accompanied by well-prepared and adequately-resourced liturgical and music ministers.

Some parishes or individual parishioners may be financially able to help their musical ministers take lessons, or to offer commissions to composers and text writers, or to upgrade their organ or other instruments. It would also be possible to build long term personnel resources by offering tertiary level scholarships for liturgical music studies. It is necessary to raise the awareness of Catholics about ways in which those interested in good church music can help financially, for instance by bequests.

d) The use of recorded music

SC did not address the matter of recorded music in the liturgy, whether on its own or as an aid to congregational singing. But the mind of the Consilium was very clearly spelt out in a 1967 editorial forbidding its use. 'To introduce such recordings would be artificial and, in fact, a lie.'[24] One exception to this general principle can be found in the Directory for Masses with Children.[25] The United States Conference of Catholic Bishops addressed this issue briefly in STTL 93–4. It stated that 'recorded music should not, as a general norm, be used within the liturgy'. They mentioned some exceptions, for instance during Masses with children to accompany their song, during outdoor processions, or as an aid to prayer during long periods of silence at a communal celebration of reconciliation. 'However, recorded music should never become a substitute for the community's singing'.

Unfortunately, the shortage of church musicians mentioned above has forced many parishes in recent years to rely on recorded music because of the lack of live music. From being an emergency measure, this practice will become accepted unless something can be done to reverse the situation.[26] There are other social and cultural reasons for

---

24. 'Mécanique et Liturgie', in *Notitiae* 3/25 (1967): 3–4.
25. *Directory for Masses with Children* (1973), #32. See *TLD*, 180.
26. On this point, *SS* has expressed its view in these terms: 'The use of recorded music is a great temptation in Catholic worship today, especially where adequate musical resources are lacking. This opinion, attractive as it may appear, should be discouraged as antithetical to the nature of liturgy as a living act of God's people

this reliance on recorded music. Contemporary culture and technology have made it much easier to have access to music anywhere at any time in any style.

It should be pointed out that strong unaccompanied congregational singing can be a powerful and uplifting form of communal participation even without musical accompaniment. It helps also to have a good leader of song when the instrumentalists are missing. However, this is all dependent upon the availability of training.

The 'iPod' has given people the wonderful benefit of easy instant access to music but not without some less desirable effects for liturgical music. Listeners can, and often do, exclude being engaged with any other person or activity around them. The listener has complete control over what they wish to hear. They do not have to consider anything other than their personal likes and dislikes. They form a 'community of one'.[27]

Another consequence of the developments in technology is that listeners can become very critical of performance quality and selective regarding the sort of musical styles they want to listen to. They are used to instantly starting or stopping a piece of music as they wish. Liturgy is really counter cultural to what 'iPod' users do. For worship to be expressive and transformative, those present need some predispositions such as an openness to God and their fellow worshippers and to engage in musical idioms that may sometimes be different from that to which they are accustomed.

There are other aesthetic considerations about the over-use of recorded music. For instance, constant repetition of the same version of a song leads to the expectation that a particular interpretation involving choice of instruments, tempo, pitch, and sometimes with the vocalist's idiosyncrasies must be followed as a matter of course, without any allowance for differences of mood, type of congregation, available cantors and musical accompaniment.

Certainly modern technology can be of great service to musicians

---

. . . The use of recorded choirs, organs and cantors, though they can seem to serve an immediate need, has the effect of discouraging local communities from marshalling the resources necessary for the authentic celebration of the liturgy' (*SS* #25).

27. James Brauer's article, 'The Challenge of the iPod Tribe to Liturgical Music', in *Liturgy, Quarterly Journal on Pastoral Liturgy of the Liturgical Conference*, 24/ 4 (2009): 21.

and congregations by making pre-recorded music available in the process of learning repertoire or in the provision of accompaniments when the organist or instrumentalist is unavailable.

> It enables communities to reproduce a repertoire and quality level seldom achievable on a local level. It is not only the considerations of expanded repertoire and superior quality, however, that are the criteria for deciding whether or not pre-recorded music should be employed within worship. Rather, it is first and foremost whether the recording will enable or impede the community's participation.[28]

Conclusion

Despite the inevitable and unresolved tensions between the proponents of old and the new music in liturgy today, the liturgical music reforms of SC have been greeted very positively because of the introduction of music in the vernacular and the recognition that the Church welcomes all forms of art and musical styles provided that they serve the liturgy in an integral way. Recent scholarship has paved the way for a more enlightened complementarity in the different schools of thought about liturgical music. Continuing national and diocesan leadership in ongoing education and formation in liturgy and music is vital if worshipping communities are to use effectively the evocative power and beauty of music in the service of a life-giving, mission-oriented liturgy.

28. *MR* #78.

Postconciliar Church Design: Continuity and Contradiction

Stephen Hackett

In December 1963 Pope Paul VI promulgated *Sacrosanctum Concilium*[1] (*SC*), thereby enacting the reform and promotion of the liturgy as envisioned by the bishops of the Second Vatican Council. Earlier in that same year the Benedictine monk R Kevin Seasoltz (1930–2013) published a remarkably prescient book entitled 'The House of God: Sacred Art and Church Architecture'.[2] In 'The House of God', the index of which reveals the influence of the Liturgical Movement on church design, Seasoltz observed that:

> Although all over Christendom one can sense a deepened understanding of the liturgy and its expression in a dynamic architecture, it is necessary that one be discriminating. In itself, there is no virtue in an unconventional plan, and it would seem that the great diversity in the planning of post-war churches . . . is not always due to a concern for liturgical function. The builder must begin with a clear understanding of the liturgy of the church and the nature of the liturgy which takes place there, and then he should design the church accordingly. He should not design a fascinating structure, and next

1. The translation is from the text on the official Vatican website <http://www.vatican.va/archive/hist_councils/ii_vatican_council/documents/vat-ii_const_19631204_sacrosanctum-concilium_en.html>. Accessed 19 January 2013. All subsequent quotations from the Sacred Constitution are from this site.
2. R Kevin Seasoltz, *The House of God: Sacred Art and Church Architecture* (New York: Herder and Herder, 1963).

> attempt to adapt the liturgy to the structure he has already planned.[3]

Were 'post-war' to be replaced with 'postconciliar' this assessment would regrettably still hold true.

The years that have passed since Seasoltz set forth his observations correspond with the years during which *SC* has been implemented. Yet the reform and promotion of the liturgy as manifested in church architecture throughout these years does not stand out as one of the great postconciliar accomplishments. How has this situation come about? What has been achieved? And what remains to be done to better fulfil the conciliar vision?

The Conciliar Injunction, its Implementation, and Diverse Influences

In *SC* the bishops had much to say about the nature of the liturgy, its reform and promotion, the Eucharist and other rites, the liturgical calendar, music and the arts. In contrast, when they came to treat of the architectural setting for the liturgy, their words were few but significant: 'And when churches are to be built, let great care be taken that they be suitable for the celebration of liturgical services and for the active participation of the faithful.' (*SC* 124). The bishops' concern for the 'full and active participation' of the faithful had already been identified as 'the aim to be considered before all else' in the restoration and promotion of the liturgy (*SC* 14). The active participation of the faithful would influence the entire process of liturgical renewal, particularly the reform of the liturgical rites and the design of churches for the celebration of these rites. Yet whereas the reform of the liturgical rites was undertaken methodically and its progress monitored, considerably less coordination and scrutiny was afforded the reform of church architecture. Indeed, the implementation of this injunction and postconciliar developments in church architecture were influenced by diverse factors, some quite unrelated to *SC*.

The conciliar injunction came in the seventh chapter of *SC*, entitled 'Sacred Art and Sacred Furnishings'. In the implementation of the liturgy constitution, it became commonly accepted that the prin-

---

3. Seasoltz, *The House of God*, 122.

ciples set forth regarding sacred art applied by extension to church architecture. Accordingly, postconciliar church design was to be informed by conciliar affirmations that everything set apart for the liturgy 'should be truly worthy, becoming, and beautiful, signs and symbols of the supernatural world' (*SC* 122); that the Church has not adopted any particular style as its own but has admitted styles from every period and culture, including those of our own days (*SC* 123); that what is created for liturgical use be characterised by noble beauty rather than sumptuous display (*SC* 124); and that moderation and right order be observed in the placing of sacred images in churches. The bishops further decreed a revision of laws governing the design and construction of churches, the shape and material fabrication of altars, the nobility and placing of the tabernacle, the dignity and suitability of the baptistery, and the proper ordering of sacred images, vessels and liturgical items, and vestments (*SC* 128).

These affirmations were reiterated in liturgical documents, instructions and introductions to the rites and liturgical books, and papal pronouncements. In many instances these same authoritative sources specified in greater detail what was affirmed or indicated in the liturgy constitution, nowhere more so than in the 'General Instruction of the Roman Missal'. Here, though, even the Church's own instruction reflects a confusion of the reform principles enunciated in *SC*.[4] It decreed that the liturgical rites were to be distinguished by a 'noble simplicity'[5] (*SC* 34) and the liturgical arts and architecture by 'noble beauty'[6] (*SC* 124). However in implementing the liturgical reform, 'noble simplicity' rather than 'noble beauty' frequently came to be applied to church design; and the adjective 'noble' was all too often neglected. Notions of 'simplicity' gave rise to churches that were variously stark, monochromatic, unadorned and 'unbeautiful', ill-suited for enacting the liturgical rites, and effectively incapable of inspiring the Catholic imagination. This is not to suggest that beauty and simplicity are mutually exclusive; some postconciliar churches

4. *SC* #124 prefers 'noble beauty rather than mere sumptuous display'. In what would seem to be an unfounded paraphrase, *The General Instruction of the Roman Missal* (Strathfield: St Pauls, 2013) GIRM #292 prefers 'noble simplicity rather than ostentation'.
5. 'Ritus nobili simplicitate fulgeant . . .' (*SC* #34).
6. '. . . potius nobilem intendant pulchritudinem . . .' (*SC* #124).

clearly manifest the mutuality of simplicity and beauty.[7] Rather, it is to observe that simplicity is not, *per se*, synonymous with beauty. Moreover, even if both ritual text and church architecture were to be informed by noble simplicity, what constitutes the former does not correspondingly constitute the latter. Noble simplicity in liturgical rites may be realised by limiting repetition, whereas noble simplicity in liturgical architecture may be enhanced by repetition.

The twentieth century Liturgical Movement had been the catalyst for adaptation and innovation in the design of Catholic churches from as early as the 1920s. After four centuries of a standardised liturgical ordering which derived from Charles Borromeo's *Instructiones Fabricae et Supellectilis Ecclesiasticae*[8], the Liturgical Movement gave rise to new spatial arrangements in churches. These arrangements, both adaptations in continuity with earlier church forms as well as new developments, were incorporated into plans for the construction and reconstruction of churches following the devastation of World War II. The conciliar injunction provided the impetus by which new and adapted liturgical ordering in the architecture of Catholic churches quickly became widespread.

The implementation of the conciliar injunction coincided with late architectural modernism and the emergence of postmodern architecture. Long before Vatican II, churches had been built in accordance with the principles of modernism, both with the prevailing shape and standardised liturgical ordering and with novel shapes and spatial arrangements. During the early postconciliar period the design of new churches continued to be informed by these same principles, but more often with exterior forms consistent with new and adapted liturgical ordering of the interior. Postmodern architecture offered new possibilities for the design of churches, without preferring a particular style, and some expected that the philosophical and aesthetic limitations of modernism might be overcome as postmod-

7. Consider, for example: the Church of Our Lady of the Ark of the Covenant in Paris, France; the Chapel of the Cistercian Monastery of Nový Dvur at Plzen, Czech Republic; the Cathedral of St Mary and St Helen at Brentwood, UK; the Chapel of St Ignatius in Seattle, USA; the Church of St Mary of the Angels in Singapore; and St Francis Church at Regensburg, Germany.

8. *Instructions on the architecture and furnishings of churches*, issued by Charles Borromeo, Archbishop of Milan 1560–1584, as part of his response to the counter-reformation initiatives of the Council of Trent.

ernism reappropriated 'traditional idioms of church architecture'.[9] This expectation has been borne out in the re-emergence of the design principles and architectural style of classicism, often couched in terms of continuity with pre-modern church architecture. However, whether this development is an authentic act of *ressourcement* or simply an instance of historicism[10] is debatable.

Another contested question, occasioned by the departure from traditional forms of church architecture during the twentieth century and certainly in the postconciliar era, concerns the iconic character of Catholic churches. Put simply: ought a church today look like a church from eras past? Here the appeal is to historical referents: a basilican or cruciform plan; narthex, nave and sanctuary; dome or spire; tower with bells; and recognisable styles. Yet this is a limited and perhaps disingenuous response to the question of how a church ought to look. In the evolution of church architecture, every epoch began with something new. When Romanesque architecture emerged, what did those familiar with the older basilican forms make of it? When those familiar with Romanesque churches found that this style was being gradually supplanted by the new pointed architecture, they called it 'gothic' to show their disdain. In turn, those familiar with the Gothic eventually witnessed the re-emergence of classical architecture in the design of Renaissance churches. Every epoch in the history of church architecture began with a century or more of overlap between the familiar old and the emerging new. Is it that twentieth and early twenty-first century church forms differ too extremely from those of the past and must therefore be rejected, or that a normative architecture for the current epoch is still evolving?

Complementing the conviction which favours a traditional form or 'look' for a Catholic church is a re-appropriated historicist approach to church architecture which diverges from the conciliar injunction and instead emphasises the theology of the church building as the foremost design principle.[11] Thus a church is built not primar-

9. M Francis Mannion, 'Toward a New Era in Liturgical Architecture', in *Studia Anselmiana*, 131 (2001): 71.
10. See Michael S Rose, *In Tiers of Glory: the Organic Development of Catholic Church Architecture Through the Ages* (Cincinnati: Mesa Folio Editions, 2004), 112–113.
11. Duncan Stroik, 'Domus Dei et Domus Ecclesiae: The Church Building as Sacred Place', in *Sacrosanctum Concilium and the Reform of the Liturgy*, edited by Kenneth D Whitehead (Chicago: University of Scranton Press, 2009): 80–81.

ily for the celebration of liturgical services and for the active participation of the faithful, but to be an image of the '*Domus Dei*', the 'New Jerusalem', the 'Temple of the Lord', the 'City of God' or the 'Body of Christ'.[12] Each of these theological images has precedent in scripture, tradition, and the history of church architecture. In light of what *SC* decreed about church building, the question posed by these theological images is whether each image presumes a predetermined liturgical ordering or whether the liturgical ordering can be adapted so as to fulfil what the Council Fathers decreed. For the most part, the proponents of this approach to church design tend to indicate not.[13]

In contrast to such standpoints, some architects have sought a contemporary approach to church architecture that preserves 'a fundamentally precise and distinctly recognisable architectural language' and is subject neither to postmodernist or vetero-modernist ideologies.[14] This 'language' is informed by both architectural and liturgical traditions yet avoids returning to an earlier architectural style. Though the beginnings of this architectural language predate Vatican II, it is exemplified in some postconciliar churches in Germany and Italy.[15]

Ultimately, the implementation of the conciliar injunction, coinciding as it has with differing architectural, hermeneutical and even ideological influences, has demonstrated that competing standpoints do not serve church architecture well. The design of churches in this

12. Steven J Schloeder, 'Sacramental Architecture: Body, Temple, City', in *Faith & Form*, 36/3 (2003): 8–10; Stroik, 'Domus Dei et Domus Ecclesiae', 81, 84–86.
13. Duncan Stroik, *The Church Building as Sacred Place: Beauty, Transcendence and the Eternal* (Chicago: Hillenbrand Books, 2012), 138–142, 158–161; Steven J Schloeder, *Architecture in Communion: Implementing the Second Vatican Council through Liturgy and Architecture* (San Francisco: Ignatius Press, 1998), 132–134. A more nuanced view is found in Philip Bess, *Till We Have Built Jerusalem: Architecture, Urbanism, and the Sacred* (Wilmington: ISI Books, 2006), 140–148. A notable exception is the Cathedral of St Mary and St Helen at Brentwood, UK; see David Watkin, *Radical Classicism: The Architecture of Quinlan Terry* (New York: Rizzoli, 2006), 240–245.
14. Giancarlo Cataldi & Gian Luigi Maffei, 'Tradition and Modern in the Twentieth Century Roman Liturgical Architecture', in *Reconquering Sacred Space 2000: the Church in the City of the Third Millennium*, edited by Cristiano Rospini, Giampaolo Rossi & Duncan G Stroik (Rome: Il Bosco e la Nave, 2000): 187.
15. See, for example, Gisberth Hülsmann, *Emil Steffann* (Bielefeld: Kunsthalle Biekefeld, 1980), 28–39, 70–79, 92–97; Cataldi & Maffei, 'Tradition and Modern', 187–211.

postconciliar era will be better informed by a sound grasp of the fundamental truths evident in every form of church architecture, an appreciation of tradition that does not dissolve into historicism, and a clear understanding of the essential principles and convictions that undergird the liturgical renewal decreed by the Council.

The Primacy of Liturgy in Church Design

The conciliar injunction does not stand alone. Following upon six preceding chapters in the liturgy constitution, it encompasses and builds upon the liturgical principles and norms enunciated there and which have been foundational in the reform and promotion of the liturgy ever since.[16] In turn, the implementation of these principles and norms in the reform of the liturgical rites established directives for the celebration of the rites which have spatial implications. These directives are elaborated in the instructions and rubrics of the liturgical books. In some instances they provide or presume particulars regarding elements of the architectural setting for the liturgy; most often they need to be interpreted with respect to the overall design of a church and the liturgical ordering of the church for enactment of the rites.

Though the liturgical principles and norms, and the related instructions and rubrics, are too many to expound upon here, those that are foundational for the design of the liturgical setting can be outlined. First among these, as already noted, is the priority given by the Council Fathers to full, conscious and active participation. This presumes a church that is ordered in such a way as to engage the entire liturgical assembly—congregation and ministers—in a corporate liturgical act in which everyone celebrates, a dynamic coordination of different orders and ministries which upholds and expresses the unity of the Church while simultaneously honouring the hierarchical ordering of the Church community (*SC* 26, *SC* 29).[17]

16. In this regard, had *SC* #23 been applied to the reform of church design, at least some contemporary architectural inadequacies and controversies might not have arisen.

17. Aidan Kavanagh, *Elements of Rite: A Handbook of Liturgical Style* (New York, Pueblo Publishing Company, 1982), 45.

If, as the Church teaches, 'liturgy is an "action" of the whole Christ (*Christus totus*) . . .'[18] and 'it is the whole community, the Body of Christ united with its Head, that celebrates . . .'[19], then the liturgical setting must be designed in such a way as to facilitate this action, this celebration. The prevailing ordering of churches at the time of Vatican II was designed for liturgical celebration that was primarily enacted by the ministers within the sanctuary while the participation of the congregation remained passive. Postconciliar church plans deriving from performing arts and sport venues, while well intentioned, perhaps unsurprisingly give rise to a style of liturgical celebration akin to performers and audience, players and spectators, rather than to liturgical celebration in which everyone participates as a full, conscious and active doer of the liturgy.[20] The *ressourcement* (return to the sources) and *aggiornamento* (updating) that were the leitmotiv of the Council, applied to the liturgical setting, led to both adaptation and innovation in church design, only some instances of which adequately promoted the Council Fathers' aim to be considered before all else of 'full and active participation by all the people' (*SC* 14).

Another foundational principle that should inform church design concerns the manifold presence of Christ in the liturgy. The liturgy constitution sets out four ways in which Christ is present: in the person of the ordained minister; in the eucharistic elements of bread and wine which sacramentally become Christ's body and blood; in the word, that is in the proclamation of the scriptures; and in the gathered assembly (*SC* 7). The 'General Instruction of the Roman Missal' has subsequently sequenced these modes of Christ's presence as they are 'gradually made clear'[21] in every celebration of the Eucharist: ' . . . Christ is really present in the very assembly gathered in his name, in the person of the minister, in his word, and indeed substantially and uninterruptedly under the eucharistic species' (GIRM 27). The spatial implication of Christ's manifold liturgical presence is to highlight the significance of the places for the assembly or congregation, the chair for the priest celebrant, the ambo, and the altar as the key litur-

18. *Catechism of the Catholic Church*, #1136.
19. *Catechism of the Catholic Church*, #1140.
20. Tom Elich, 'Churches Back to Front', in *Liturgy News*, 35/3 (2005): 10.
21. Everett A Diederich, 'The Unfolding Presence of Christ in the Celebration of the Mass', in *Communio*, 5/4 (1978): 330.

gical places or centres in the design and layout of a church. Moreover, the altar has from the earliest times signified Christ and traditionally stands as the preeminent architectural presence of Christ in the church building.[22]

Incorporating the modes of Christ's presence in church design is not simply a matter of arranging the furniture, but requires clear understanding of the relationships that exist between these liturgical places or centres which highlight Christ's unfolding presence in the liturgy, as well as with other elements of the church building such as the entrance, baptistery and place of eucharistic reservation. These relationships operate at both functional and symbolic levels. Functionally they enable engaging and graceful enactment of the liturgical rites; symbolically they communicate Christ's presence by evoking the recognition and memory of the assembly.[23]

The design of the liturgical setting ought also to be informed by the sacramentality of the liturgy (*SC* 6, 7 and 10). This sacramentality is multivalent. Certainly it concerns those liturgical rites that celebrate one of the seven sacraments of the Church. Yet the sacramental principle also underpins the other rites as well, in the sense that they reveal or make present a reality that is otherwise hidden. The funeral rites, for example, manifest the Paschal Mystery of Christ's death and resurrection, in which we first come to share through baptism, which is nourished in us through the Eucharist, and which attains its fullness in us through death. The Paschal Mystery thus has implications for the place in the church where the body of a deceased person is brought for the funeral rites and the relationship between that place, the baptismal font and the altar. The Paschal Mystery, celebrated in every Eucharist yet eschatological in the destiny it presupposes, also has particular implications for the location of the altar, which needs to be at once the liturgical centre of the church and a sign of our destiny in Christ.

The sacramentality of the liturgy extends to the church building in which the liturgy is celebrated. This occurs through the participation of the architecture in the action of the liturgy and the effect of the

22. Cyril of Alexandria, *De Adoratione in Spiritu et Veritate* 9: PG 68, 647; *Roman Pontifical*, 'Rite of Dedication of a Church and an Altar' (1977) chapter 4, #4.
23. David Torevell, *Losing the Sacred: Ritual, Modernity and Liturgical Reform* (Edinburgh: T&T Clark, 2000), 177.

liturgy upon the architecture:[24] 'Material place symbolically amplifies the liturgical action, and the liturgy, in turn, draws itself into the spatial and material.'[25] The church building understood in this way signifies our dwelling with God.[26] Moreover, the celebration of the liturgy within the church building can be said to attain the fulfillment of architecture as it becomes an 'an epiphany of the sacred'.[27]

The sacramental principle is further expressed in the iconographic program of a church. Images of Jesus Christ, Mary and the saints, rendered in glass, sculpture, mosaic, textiles, painting, and other contemporary media—whether readily seen or somewhat obscure—sacramentally mediate those who are represented.[28] These representations in figurative form remind us that the liturgy is celebrated not only by those gathered within the church, but that 'those who even now celebrate it without signs are already in the heavenly liturgy, where celebration is wholly communion and feast'[29] and that 'it is in this eternal liturgy that the Spirit and the Church enable us to participate whenever we celebrate the mystery of salvation in the sacraments'.[30] These images also serve to 'manifest the truth that the worshipping community does not live in and from itself'[31] but is called into being by God in Christ and finds its identity and mission in him.[32] Thus the figurative representation of Jesus Christ serves to call to mind the historical Jesus of Nazareth who is the Christ proclaimed in the Gospel; the same Jesus Christ in whose name the community of the Church gathers to celebrate the Eucharist; the same risen Christ received sacramentally in the consecrated bread and wine; and the One

24. Michel Remery, *Mystery and Matter: On the Relationship between Liturgy and Architecture in the Thought of Dom Hans van der Laan OSB (1904–1991)* (Leiden: Brill, 2011), 243.
25. Mannion, 'Toward a New Era', 46.
26. Hans van der Laan, *The Play of Forms: Nature, Culture and Liturgy* (Leiden: Brill, 2005), 32.
27. Paul Evdokimov, *The Art of the Icon: a Theology of Beauty* (Redondo Beach: Oakwood Publications, 1990), 117.
28. Christopher Irvine, *The Art of God: the Making of Christians and the Meaning of Worship* (London: SPCK, 2005), 115–117.
29. *Catechism of the Catholic Church*, #1136.
30. *Catechism of the Catholic Church*, #1139.
31. Mannion, 'Toward a New Era', 55.
32. John Paul II, *Dies Domini* (1998), #31; Kevin R Irwin, *Models of the Eucharist* (New York: Paulist Press, 2005), 70.

into whose image we are reconfigured through our participation in the liturgy.[33]

Designing churches to be 'suitable for the celebration of liturgical services and for the active participation of the faithful' demands much more than a spatial conceptualising of the renewed liturgical rites. It calls for a clear and faithful appreciation of the principles and norms which underscore the entire work of the reform and promotion of the liturgy. The liturgy and the architectural setting in which it is celebrated need to be as one; there should exist a functional and symbolic coherence between them. This is evident in the foundational principles that have been outlined; and it becomes evident in the ordering of the church building for liturgical celebration.

Ordering the Church for Liturgy

The evolution of the spatial arrangement of Catholic churches down through the centuries reveals an organic connection between the liturgy and liturgical ordering. Indeed, the history of Catholic church architecture clearly shows that the liturgy has been the foremost influence in the evolution of the ordering of churches; and it attests to the genius of the Catholic Church in innovating and adapting architecture for its liturgy. This same history confirms that the ordering of church buildings for the liturgy is not static but continually evolving.[34]

No era demonstrates this more clearly than our own. From the emergence of new and adapted church forms and liturgical ordering some thirty years prior to Vatican II, to the conciliar decree that churches be built 'suitable for the celebration of liturgical services and for the active participation of the faithful', and throughout the postconciliar era during which this injunction has been implemented, we have witnessed the construction of churches built to diverse plans. These many and varied plans are indicative of popular awareness of the Council's reform and promotion of the liturgy. At they same time they indicate a lack of clear understanding of both the functional and symbolic spatial requirements of the revised rites and of the prin-

33. Irvine, *The Art of God*, 116–117.

34. Stephen Hackett, 'The Architecture of Liturgy: Liturgical Ordering in Church Design; the Australian Experience in Perspective,' PhD thesis, (Sydney: The University of New South Wales, 2011), 40.

ciples and norms that informed their revision. Accordingly, many churches were planned in accordance with a general notion of the postconciliar liturgy and a sense of the interplay between liturgy and the ecclesiology of Vatican II. New and adapted churches were quite often inspired by the designs of other recently erected and renovated churches. Architecture, after all, is mimetic. So too did architects who specialised in church design often repeat in their plans a preferred architectural style, design characteristics and motifs, understanding of liturgical enactment, and sense of what ought to constitute a Catholic church informed by the liturgical renewal initiated by the Council.

The range of postconciliar liturgical ordering has been widely surveyed and numerous commentaries have been published since Vatican II.[35] However there has been considerably less research into this crucial facet of church design since the Council.[36] Nor has a commonly accepted set of types of liturgical ordering become established, so the content of surveys, commentaries and research cannot be readily correlated. Consequently, flawed designs and plans with inherent limitations have been oft-repeated. The types of liturgical ordering identified in church design since Vatican II range in number from two to fourteen, often with variables within a given type.[37]

The two basic types, observable throughout the evolution of liturgical ordering, may be variously described as sociofugal and so-

35. See, for example: W Jardine Grisbrooke, 'The Shape of the Liturgical Assembly: Some Third Thoughts,' in *Research Bulletin*, University of Birmingham Institute for the Study of Worship and Religious Architecture (1972): 30–41; Bill Beard, 'Seating for Catholic Worship: a Primer', in *Environment and Art Letter*, 1/1 (1988): 2–3; Richard Hurley, '20th Century', in *Sacred Places–The Story of Christian Architecture in Ireland*, edited by R Hurley & P Larmour (Dublin: The Royal Institute of Architects in Ireland, & Belfast: The Royal Society of Ulster Architects, 2000), 14–31; and Rudolf Stegers, *Sacred Buildings: a Design Manual*, translated by J Reisenberger (Basel: Birkhäuser Verlag AG, 2008), 28–29.
36. See, for example: Maurizio Bergamo & Mattia Del Prete, *Espacios Celebrativos: Estudio para una Arquitectura de las Iglesias a partir del Concilio Vaticano II* (Bilbao: Grafite Ediciones EGA, 1997), 70–77; and Richard Hurley, *Irish Church Architecture in the Era of Vatican II* (Dublin: Dominican Publications, 2001), 40–101.
37. See, for example: Richard S Vosko, *God's House is Our House: Re-imagining the Environment for Worship* (Collegeville, MN: Liturgical Press, 2006), 56–59; Dennis McNally, *Sacred Space: an Aesthetic for the Liturgical Environment* (Bristol: Wyndam Hall Press, 1985), 51–65; and Bergamo & Del Prete, *Espacios Celebrativos*, 66–67, 74-77.

ciopetal, longitudinal and circular, axial and centralised.[38] The first type, found in most preconciliar churches and in some postconciliar churches, orders the assembly in a mono-directional configuration so that the faithful are gathered to the altar but less to each other. The second type, found in most postconciliar churches, orders the assembly in multi-directional configurations so that the faithful are gathered to the altar and to each other. A survey of Catholic churches built since the Council indicates that eight types of church plan or liturgical ordering are broadly and adequately representative: the basilican, longitudinal, axial, processional, sociofugal or hall ordering (Figure 1); the fan arrayed, radial, auditorium, theatre or semicircular ordering (Figure 2); the centralised, central, concentric, or sociopetal ordering (Figure 3); the antiphonal, monastic, communio, choral or choir ordering (Figure 4); the transverse or juxtaposed ordering (Figure 5); the crucifrom, cross shaped, Greek-cross, Latin-cross or Gothic ordering (Figure 7); and the *circumstantes,*[39] *circumadstantes* or elliptical ordering (Figure 8).

The first of these types, the basilican ordering, with its frontal sanctuary setting, is often assumed to be the prototypical Catholic church. In the sense that it replicates the basic floor-plan of the ancient Christian basilica and is represented in every architectural style, this may be true. However, the advent of rows of seating in churches for the assembly as relatively recently as the seventeenth century has radically altered the way in which the faithful engage in the liturgy, effectively changing the basilican church from a participative processional space to a passive auditorium space.[40] Fundamentally, the functioning of the regimented basilican type of liturgical ordering with which we are familiar does not correspond with the functioning of the ancient basilican church, in which there was minimal seating and the faithful moved within the church as the liturgy progressed.[41]

38. Vosko, *God's House is Our House*, 58; McNally, *Sacred Space*, 65; Bergamo & Del Prete, *Espacios Celebrativos*, 66–67.
39. *Circumstantes*, literally 'standing around', derives from a project undertaken in 1923 by Dominikus Böhm who, working with fellow architect Martin Weber, designed a church informed by this principle.
40. Louis Bouyer, *Liturgy and Architecture* (Notre Dame: University of Notre Dame Press 1967), 81; Edward Foley, *From Age to Age: How Christians have Celebrated the Eucharist* (Chicago: Liturgy Training Publications, 2008), 257.
41. Seasoltz, *The House of God*, 137, 142–143.

The fan-arrayed, centralised, antiphonal and transverse types of liturgical ordering represent innovation or adaptation of other church usage or other building types. Each represents an attempt to gather the faithful to the altar and to each other, to convey the manifold liturgical presence of Christ in the spatial arrangement of the church. The antiphonal setting perhaps manifests the greatest continuity with existing liturgical ordering, in that its configuration of the assembly is found in monastic and collegiate churches, and in cathedral choirs. However the various permutations of altar, ambo and chair utilised in postconciliar antiphonal churches, while found in a few instances prior to Vatican II, are essentially a recent phenomenon. The centralised form of church can be identified throughout the history of church architecture, but mostly with a frontal or basilican liturgical ordering. Historically the only significant centralised liturgical setting is found in church designs which blended the longitudinal and centralised plans, locating the sanctuary at the intersection of the two, such as in the Basilica di Santa Maria del Fiore in Florence. Locating the sanctuary at the centre of a postconciliar centralised-plan church is, like the antiphonal ordering, an innovation arising out of the influence of the twentieth century Liturgical Movement. The fan-arrayed and transverse plans constitute innovations in church design that are without precedent prior to the twentieth century. Each represents a phase in the evolution of postconciliar church design, but neither has proven to be of enduring value.

The cruciform, U-arrayed and circumstantes plans represent a merging of the two basic types of liturgical space, the longitudinal and the centralised. To varying degree these types of liturgical ordering manifest innovation and adaptation in the evolution of liturgical ordering and history of church design. All three plans gather the faithful to the altar and to one another; and all three locate the altar as liturgical centre while simultaneously signifying eschatological destiny. That is, the assembly is gathered to the altar which sits at the head of the liturgical setting and is also gathered in some form around it. In the cruciform ordering the assembly is gathered around the altar, usually on three sides but sometimes on four, yet there usually remains physical and visual separation between the faithful. While they may be united in the liturgical act, the sense of unity from being gathered to one another is diminished. In the U-arrayed ordering the assembly is configured around a central processional and liturgical enactment space. This ordering gives clear emphasis to the places that signify the modes of Christ's liturgical presence while creating a strong sense of the faithful being gathered to the altar and to one another, and of the assembly being united (Fig. 9). The circumstantes ordering, whether symmetrical or asymmetrical in plan, conveys a sense of the faithful being gathered to the altar and to each other in unity, and has a strongly processional character (Fig. 10).

The contemporary cruciform ordering constitutes an adaptation of the earlier cruciform plan, with the sanctuary drawn forward into the crossing of nave and transept, and transept seating reoriented to face the new sanctuary. The curving U-arrayed and *circumstantes* types of liturgical ordering are innovations in the evolution of liturgical ordering and history of church architecture. Yet each in its own ways can be said to constitute an authentic act of *ressourcement*: both U-arrayed and *circumstantes* plans, through the relationship between the configuration of assembly seating and the places for the altar and other sacred furnishings, mirror the gathering of the faithful to the altar and to one another in the early basilican church. And each in its own way can be said to constitute an authentic act of *aggiornamento*: both U-arrayed and *circumstantes* plans, through their thoughtfully conceived ordering for the celebration of the revised liturgical rites and for the full, conscious and active participation of the faithful, thereby fulfil the conciliar injunction to a significant degree.

Designing churches in which the foremost consideration is that they be 'suitable for the celebration of liturgical services and for the active participation of the faithful' is a multifaceted task. That so many postconciliar churches manifest liturgical, functional, aesthetic and iconographic deficiencies indicates that the implications of the conciliar injunction have been neither adequately understood nor implemented. There has been no want for creativity in the architecture of Catholic churches built and reordered since Vatican II, but there has been significant want for this architecture to be informed by the principles and norms that are integral to the Council's reform and promotion of the liturgy.

Conclusion

While there is much to be learned from evaluating church design since Vatican II, there is perhaps even more to be learned by returning to the foundations of postconciliar church design in the liturgy constitution, the revised liturgical rites and related directives, the history and evolution of architecture for the liturgy, and the tradition of the liturgical arts. A more rigorous engagement with these seminal elements will surely lead to a better architecture for liturgy. So too will setting aside standpoints which contradict or underplay the conciliar injunction and are often articulated in dismissive and polemical discourse: what the Council Fathers decreed must be adhered to or we neglect the most authoritative point of reference for church architecture today. National and diocesan guidelines for church architecture and art, deriving from the conciliar injunction and postconciliar pronouncements, ought to be regarded as a necessary resource for every church project.

The church design process needs to become more attentive to both the functional and symbolic attributes of the edifice which houses the Church and is named for it. These attributes find intentional expression in the form of the building, the ordering of the church for liturgy, the design of sacred furnishings, the program of iconography, the accommodation of personal prayer and devotions, and the capacity for hospitality and witness. Some forty years after R Kevin Seasoltz published 'The House of God', he reprised its themes in 'A Sense of the Sacred: Theological Foundations of Christian Architecture and Art'.[42] In 'A Sense of the Sacred', which assessed the evolution of postconciliar church architecture in light of the diverse influences that have shaped it, Seasoltz concluded that:

> As the history of architecture and art clearly shows, the church has been responsible for the birth and development of a great architectural and artistic treasury. In our own time and place, architects and artist should be given relatively free scope in the church, but they must have both a clear understanding of the requirements of the sacred liturgy and a profound understanding of the paschal mystery of Jesus Christ and the dignity and role of the community of the faithful who celebrate that sacred mystery.[43]

His conclusions ring true if contemporary church design is to fulfil the Council's vision.

42. R Kevin Seasoltz, *A Sense of the Sacred: Theological Foundations of Christian Architecture and Art* (New York: Continuum, 2005).
43. Seasoltz, A Sense of the Sacred, 346.

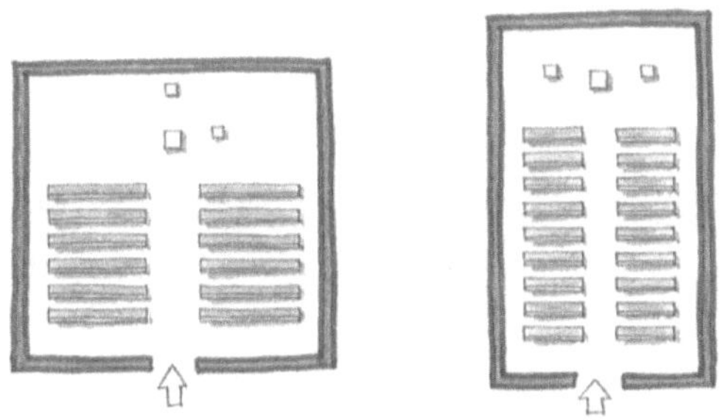

(Figure 1) Basilican liturgical ordering (David Toohey 2012).

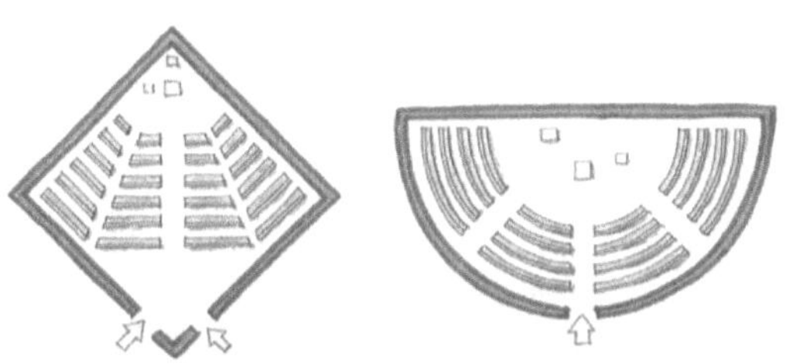

(Figure 2) Fan-arrayed liturgical ordering (David Toohey 2012).

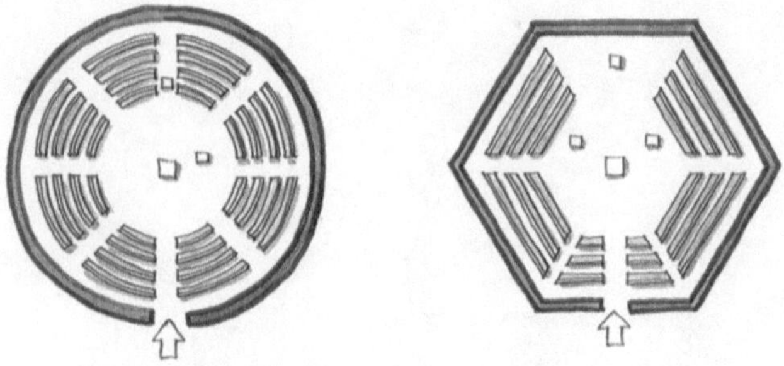

(Figure 3) Centralised liturgical ordering (David Toohey 2012).

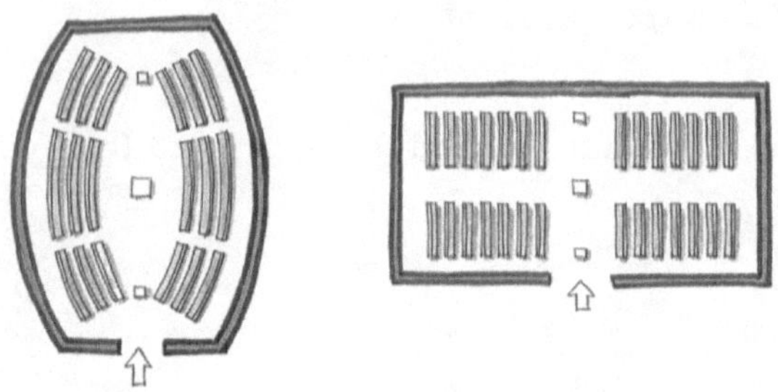

(Figure 4) Antiphonal liturgical ordering (David Toohey 2012).

(Figure 5) Transverse liturgical ordering (David Toohey 2012).

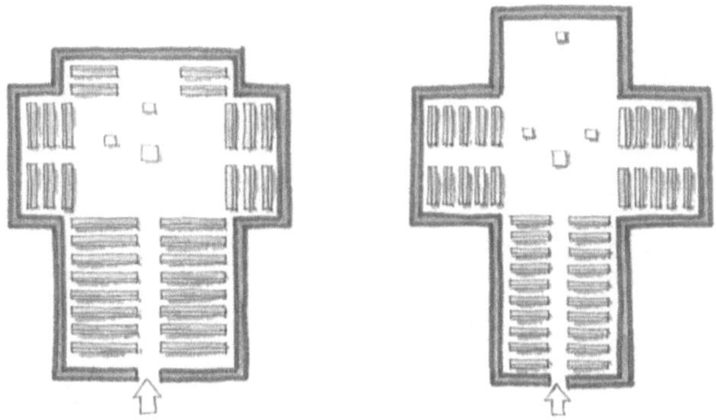

(Figure 6) Cruciform liturgical ordering (David Toohey 2012).

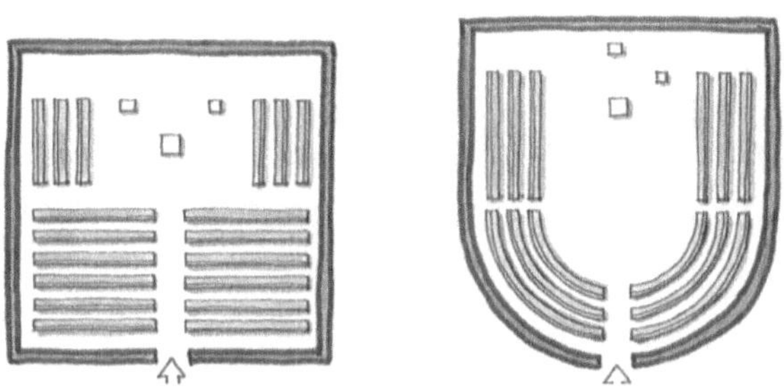

(Figure 7) U-arrayed liturgical ordering (David Toohey 2012).

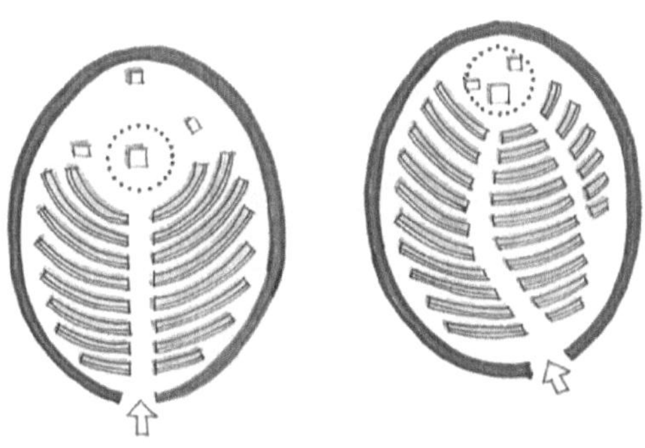

(Figure 8) *Circumstantes* liturgical ordering (David Toohey 2012).

(Figure 9) U-arrayed liturgical ordering in St John the Baptist Church, Woy Woy, Australia (Stephen Hackett 2011).

(Figure 10) *Ciurcumstantes* liturgical ordering in St Franziskus Church, Burgweinting, Germany (Stephen Hackett 2005).

The Impact of *Sacrosanctum Concilium* on Protestant Traditions

Stephen Burns

Writing in a collection on twentieth-century developments in Christian spirituality—a collection which defines its orbit as 'an ecumenical age'—the liturgical theologian Don E Saliers calls the Second Vatican Council 'the most important thing to affect the Protestant traditions in the twentieth century'.[1] This essay will suggest that this large claim stands up to some scrutiny—and the following pages explore the deep, if somewhat piecemeal, appropriation of key themes in the Council's first and perhaps most far reaching document, *Sacrosanctum Concilium* (*SC*), across a range of Protestant traditions and their ritual books. Inevitably, my reflections are selective, unsystematic, and only partial, but nevertheless may offer clues to the bases on which wider appropriation of *SC* in Protestant practice and understanding of liturgical celebration has been built. They will close with a focus, close to a lament, on what twenty-first century shifts in Roman liturgy imply for a new era of ecumenism.

Of course, a very great diversity marks Protestant traditions, and it is salutary to remember at the outset of such reflection just how widely, with regard to worship, the Protestant churches stretch in their styles and convictions. James White's book, *Protestant Worship*, makes the point that in the fifty years from 1520, five lasting traditions emerged: the Lutheran, Reformed, Anabaptist, Anglican and Puritan. Since then, he asserts, durable traditions have emerged at the more sedate pace of about one per century: the Quaker in the seventeenth, Methodist in the eighteenth, Frontier (a North American

1. Don E Saliers, 'Christian Spirituality in an Ecumenical Age', in *Christian Spirituality III: Post-Reformation and Modern*, edited by Louis Dupre and Don E Saliers, volume 18 (London: SCM Press, 1989), 538.

development with origins in revivalism, since transmuted in various ways) in the nineteenth century, and the Pentecostal in the twentieth century.[2] This essay makes reference to a range of Protestant communities, though it cannot possibly take in the full spectrum indicated in White's sketch; and its is limited to English-speaking contexts, albeit with reference to developments on at least three continents (Europe, North America, and Australia) this is by no means a full picture, given the exponential growth of Christianity in both Catholic and Protestant expressions in Africa, Asia and South America.

The First Principle: 'Above all Else'

> Mother Church earnestly desires that all the faithful should be led to that full, conscious, and active participation in liturgical celebrations which is demanded by the very nature of the liturgy. Such participation by the Christian people as 'a chosen race, a royal priesthood, a holy nation, a redeemed people' (1 Pet. 2:9; cf. 2:4-5), is their right and duty by reason of their baptism.
>
> In the restoration and promotion of the sacred liturgy, this full and active participation by all the people is the aim to be considered before all else; for it is the primary and indispensable source from which the faithful are to derive the true Christian spirit; and therefore pastors of souls must zealously strive to achieve it, by means of the necessary instruction, in all their pastoral work.[3]

Of course, *SC* 14's central insistence on 'full, conscious and active participation' as 'the aim to be considered above all else' has had a most extraordinary influence on the life of Roman Catholic communities and liturgical scholars. Gabe Huck, the North American liturgical theologian who oversaw the work of the Chicago-based Catholic press Liturgy Training Publications through a time when it gave perhaps the most vivid expression of *SC*'s first principle and encouragement to its enactment, made a most lively appropriation of *SC*'s central mandate:

---

2. James F White, *Protestant Worship: Traditions in Transition* (Lousiville, KY: Westminster John Knox Press, 1989), 209-210.
3. *SC* #14. <http://www.vatican.va/archive/hist_councils/ii_vatican_council/documents/vat-ii_const_19631204_sacrosanctum-concilium_en.html>. Accessed 3 April 2013. All subsequent references to *SC* are drawn from this web archive.

> Why full and conscious and active participation? The answer is: That's liturgy. The answer is not: Because the Church has always taught this. The answer is not: Because the bishops say so. The answer is not: Because in some golden age of liturgy it was this way. None of this. Rather: Such participation—the full and active and conscious kind—is what we are after because that is 'the very nature of the liturgy'. In other words, no such participation, no liturgy.
>
> That means that it is the nature of the liturgy to be done by the people. It is not done to people. It is not done for people. It is not done in the presence of people. People do it and the plural is correct because it is as a Church assembled that people do liturgy.
>
> A liturgy has not 'worked' simply because people leave uplifted, made peaceful, made cheerful, made warm, made smarter, or all of the above. When we look to liturgy to be primarily about such things, we miss this clear but hard saying that the bishops [of the Second Vatican Council] got straight: The kind of human activity liturgy is can't tolerate an audience, can't tolerate those who do and those who are done to. . .
>
> . . .The 'it' ['for it is the primary and indispensable source . . .'] is not the liturgy but 'full and active participation'. So we have: Full and active participation by all the people is 'the primary and indispensable source from which the faithful are to derive the true Christian spirit'. In doing the liturgy—over many Sundays, many seasons and festivals, many weddings and initiations and anointings and funerals—whatever is the 'true Christian spirit', Christ's own spirit, seeps and creeps into us, into the person, into the people. That is the way it works.[4]

As Gordon W Lathrop has suggested, *SC* 14 has become highly significant in ecumenical exchange. Indeed, he calls it a piece of 'ecu-

4. Gabe Huck, 'The Very Nature of the Liturgy,' in, *Finding Voice to Give God Praise: The Many Languages of the Liturgy*, edited by Kathleen Hughes rscj (Collegeville, MN: Liturgical Press, 1999), 301.

menical treasure'.[5] It has been deeply appropriated across Protestant traditions, such that, for example, the British 'Methodist Worship Book' insists that 'the congregation is not an audience',[6] and the Uniting Church in Australia's 'Uniting in Worship 2' echoes this very same phrase.[7] Similar convictions are not difficult to find across the range of Protestant ritual books. Notwithstanding numerous ongoing doctrinal differences and controversies between the Roman Catholic Church and Protestant traditions, the past fifty years have seen a remarkable appreciation of liturgy as 'the work of the people'—albeit perhaps to the detriment of other venerable renderings of the word 'liturgy', such as 'public service', with its outward-orientation, arguably most easily lost along the way when muddled with notions of the so-called 'priesthood of all believers' which attempts to turn everyone in the assembly into a potential presider at the expense of the church's witness in the rest of the world.[8]

The 'Central Things' of Word and Sacrament

The phrase 'Central Things' comes from Gordon W Lanthrop's *Central Things: Worship in Word and Sacrament* (Augsburg, 2006).

> . . . the liturgy is the summit toward which the activity of the Church is directed; at the same time it is the font from which all her power flows. For the aim and object of apostolic works is that all who are made sons of God by faith and baptism should come together to praise God in the midst of His Church, to take part in the sacrifice, and to eat the Lord's supper (*SC* 10).
>
> The liturgy in its turn moves the faithful, filled with 'the paschal sacraments', to be 'one in holiness'; it prays that 'they may hold fast in their lives to what they have grasped by their faith'; the renewal in the Eucharist of

5. Gordon W Lathrop, 'Strong Center, Open Door: A Continuing Vision of Liturgical Renewal,' in *Worship*, 75/1 (2001): 35–46.
6. *Methodist Worship Book* (Peterborough UK: Methodist Publishing House, 1999), 5.
7. *Uniting in Worship 2* (Sydney NSW: Uniting Church Press, 2005), 131.
8. See Andrew Dutney's illuminating essay, 'A Worldly Calling: The Uniting Church Begins a Second Debate,' in *St Mark's Review* 135 (1988): 15–21.

> the covenant between the Lord and man draws the faithful into the compelling love of Christ and sets them on fire. From the liturgy, therefore, and especially from the Eucharist, as from a font, grace is poured forth upon us; and the sanctification of men in Christ and the glorification of God, to which all other activities of the Church are directed as toward their end, is achieved in the most efficacious possible way.

SC 10 has been much-lauded for speaking of liturgy as 'font/source and summit' of the church's life.[9] How frequently Eucharist is celebrated is just one indication of its centrality, but of course this varies widely in Protestant practice, making for a challenge to 'source and summit' imagery as a discernibly accurate descriptor of the breadth of Protestant worship. However, among a great many Protestant communities, there is likely, since and under the ecumenical influence of the Second Vatican Council, to be at least a growing conviction that the 'service of the Lord's day' includes communion, and that the Eucharist involves both word and sacrament. Robert W Gribben narrates the sense of progress that has been made:

> What is characteristic of Christian worship is neither a service of the Word, nor the sacrament of the Lord's supper, but both. Looking back, we can see how church history has divided what God has joined together. The medieval church made the sacrament a thing in itself, and celebrated it on every conceivable occasion. The place of the Word was severely diminished. The Reformation was in part a reaction against that. But equally, and for a complex of reasons, the reformed churches swung to the other extreme, and overdid the Word to the diminution of the sacramental means of grace. But Word and sacrament belong together. Both faithful preaching and the obedient breaking of bread are signs of Christ's living presence.[10]

9. See also, editors of *Source and Summit: Commemorating Josef Jungmann,* edited by Joanne M Pierce and Michael Downey (Collegeville, MN: Liturgical Press, 1999) for reflection about a main protagonist in the Council.
10. Robert W Gribben, *A Guide to Uniting in Worship* (Melbourne, Vic: Uniting Church Press, 1990), 43.

Both word and sacrament are 'central things', as Lathrop has said. Key to promoting that recognition has been the advocacy of an 'ecumenical *ordo*', indebted to Justin Martyr's witness to the shape of worship in Rome circa 150 CE. Justin's testimony may or may not depict the actual practice of liturgy in even one ancient Roman assembly, however, what he tells the emperor about the gathering of Christians gives the best clues we have to go on. As a text which broadly coheres with the patterns of the Roman Catholic Mass, Justin's testimony has drawn numerous Protestant traditions closer to a shared shape for Sunday worship. And as a text with at least certain resonance with scriptural pericopes (the Emmaus road story most notably), which also seems to highlight some sense of word and sacrament—at least scripture and meal (see Lk 24:27, 34), as key to the Lucan community's practice—it has commended itself to many Protestants. As an early text, it has also allowed consensus to gather around a narrative which is both antecedent and roundly regarded as authoritative in relation to the controversies of the reformations—either Protestant or Catholic. It includes little if any doctrine, but points to the presence of 'writings of the prophets,' 'records of the apostles,' preaching, and prayer—including prayer over the gifts of the table. These gifts ares received by a presider, depicted as 'a guardian to all who are in need,' and are sent out as a collection for the poor. The shape that Justin's witness gives to later Christian liturgy is one which has yielded numerous attractive distillations, such as, notably, the Church of England's *Common Worship*. 'The journey through the liturgy has a clear structure with signposts for those less familiar with the way. It moves from the gathering of the community through the Liturgy of the Word to an opportunity of transformation, sacramental or non-sacramental, after which those present are sent out to put their faith into practice.'[11] Protestant, as Catholic, traditions have come to acknowledge the centrality of scripture and sacrament in this 'journey.' The United Methodist Church of the United States of America calls its Sunday service simply 'a service of word and table.'[12]

Such moves can be noted by comparison of the World Council of

11. *Common Worship: Services and Prayers for the Church of England* (London: Church House Publishing, 2000), x.
12. *United Methodist Book of Worship* (Nashville, TN: Methodist Publishing House, 1992).

Churches' highly influential document *Baptism, Eucharist and Ministry* of 1982 and its 1995 document *Eucharistic Worship in Ecumenical Contexts*, the latter of which speaks of an ecumenical *ordo*. In 1982, BEM admittedly spoke of the eucharistic liturgy as 'essentially a single whole', but one which 'consist[s] historically of the following elements in varying sequence and of diverse importance':

- hymns of praise;
- act of repentance;
- declaration of pardon;
- proclamation of the Word of God, in various forms;
- confession of faith (creed);
- intercession for the whole Church and for the world;
- preparation of the bread and wine;
- thanksgiving to the Father for the marvels of creation, redemption and sanctification (deriving from the Jewish tradition of the *berakah*);
- the words of Christ's institution of the sacrament according to the New Testament tradition;
- the *anamnesis* or memorial of the great acts of redemption, passion, death, resurrection, ascension and Pentecost, which brought the Church into being;
- the invocation of the Holy Spirit (epiklesis) on the community, and the elements of bread and wine (either before the words of institution or after the memorial, or both; or some other reference to the Holy Spirit which adequately expresses the 'epikletic' character of the Eucharist);
- consecration of the faithful to God;
- reference to the communion of saints;
- prayer for the return of the Lord and the definitive manifestation of his Kingdom;
- the Amen of the whole community;
- the Lord's prayer;
- sign of reconciliation and peace;
- the breaking of the bread;
- eating and drinking in communion with Christ and

with each member of the Church;
- final act of praise;
- blessing and sending.[13]

By 1995, the list is ordered in a 'Justin-esque' turn, as

GATHERING of the assembly into the grace, love and *koinonia* of the triune God

WORD-SERVICE
Reading of the scriptures of the Old and New Testaments
Proclaiming Jesus Christ crucified and risen as the ground of our hope
(and confessing and singing our faith)
and so interceding for all in need and for unity
(sharing the peace to seal our prayers and prepare for the table)

TABLE-SERVICE
Giving thanks over bread and cup
Eating and drinking the holy gifts of Christ's presence
(collecting for all in need)
and so

BEING SENT (DISMISSAL) in mission in the world.[14]

Even when not celebrating communion, Protestant traditions may now accent thanksgiving in the third section of the *ordo*, as an intentional 'eucharistic echo', as it were.[15] Other traditions have greatly enriched their word-services with many possibilities for what they

---

13. BEM, E27. <http://www.oikoumene.org/fileadmin/files/wcc-main/documents/p2/FO1982_111_en.pdf>. Accessed 1 April 2013.
14. *Eucharistic Worship in Ecumenical Contexts: The Lima Liturgy–and Beyond*, edited by Thomas Best and Dagmar Heller (Geneva: World Council of Churches, 1995), 35.
15. Examples include the *Methodist Worship Book* and *Uniting in Worship 2*. Others, such as the Anglican Church of the Province of Kenya's *Our Modern Services* (Nairobi: Usima Press, 2002), for example 14, 26, have strengthened this section of the *ordo* with rubrics inviting 'prayerful choruses' and such like.

might call quasi-sacramental observances: baptismal remembrance[16] and sometimes dramatic interest in healing liturgy.[17]

All this being said, it remains that Protestant denominations vary in their expectations of the use that local congregations will make of whatever official resources their centralised bodies produce. Some provide norms and models (as such), without requirement that the texts provided are used. An example is the Uniting Church in Australia's *Uniting in Worship 2*, which is asserted as normative, in the sense of setting a 'standard against which other services can be measured,' not least in terms of congruence of doctrinal expression. So even as there is no 'requirement that it is always used,' *Uniting in Worship 2* provides services and resources for the 'core of the Uniting Church's liturgical life.'[18] Others that have inherited notions of 'common prayer' are revisiting and revising the meanings of such a notion as they face new missionary challenges. Common prayer is now sometimes defined in terms of a 'common core' and provides a marker to which directory resources are brought.[19] Hence, the Church of England, whilst remaining firmly committed to the ecumenical *ordo* has defined some marks of Anglican style as a core which has loosened its sense of common prayer. These are said to be:

> -a recognisable structure for worship;
> -an emphasis on reading the word and on using psalms;
> -liturgical words repeated by the congregation some of which, like the creed, would be known by heart;
> -using a collect, the Lord's Prayer and some responsive forms in prayer;

---

16. For example the Presbyterian Church of the USA's *Book of Common Worship* (Louisville, KY: Westminster John Knox Press, 1993), 471–477; numerous examples from the Church of England's *Common Worship* series (London: Church House Publishing, 2000), *Uniting in Worship 2*.
17. The work of the Scottish Iona Community seems to have done much to promote this. See their *Wee Worship Book* (Glasgow: Wild Goose Publications, 1989).
18. *Uniting in Worship 2*, 8–9.
19. Regarding Anglican developments, see, for example, Paul Bradshaw, 'Liturgical Development: From Common Prayer to Uncommon Worship', in *Comfortable Words: Polity, Piety and The Book of Common Prayer*, edited by Stephen Platten and Christopher Woods (London: SCM Press, 2012), 121–131. This is an interesting chapter that elides discussion of the means by which Anglican churches have continued to affirm notions of common prayer.

> -a recognition of the centrality of the Eucharist;
> -a concern for form, dignity and economy of words . . .;
> -. . . a willingness to use forms and prayers which can be used across a broad spectrum of Christian belief.[20]

Most notably, however, some churches which may have thought of themselves as 'non-liturgical' (a misnomer) have embraced the *ordo*, at least at the level of their official denominational resources. An interesting example is the Baptist Union's *Gathering for Worship*,[21] which not only takes a clear hold of the *ordo*, but also a wide range of pastoral services, and calendar and lectionary.[22]

Some Protestant traditions are harder to map in terms of the *ordo*, but nevertheless, significant studies have emerged which have at least sometimes convinced members of such churches that their liturgies are not only deeply patterned but often so in ways with clear resonance with the *ordo*.[23] In terms of the unfolding of the 'frontier' legacy, its contemporary expressions in 'alternative/emergent' worship have particularly brought to the fore the fact that at least some free-forms are intentionally searching for patterns indebted to deep tradition, albeit if employing it in analogy to sampling.[24]

20. *Patterns for Worship* (London: Church House Publishing, 1989), 6. The 2008 edition omits the last point, *New Patterns for Worship* (London, Church House Publishing, 2008), 53.
21. *Gathering for Worship: Services and Prayers for the Community of Disciples* (Norwich: Canterbury Press, 2005).
22. Also most notable are developments in non-western settings in which traditions of worship had grown around distinctive missionary legacies but which are now moving to the *ordo*. For the Presbyterian Church of Korea as example, see Kyuong-Jin Kim, 'The Contexts, Contours and Contents of Worship in the Korean Church: Focused on the Presbyterian Church', in *Korea Presbyterian Journal of Theology*, 44 (2012): 65–92.
23. Two of the most interesting examples are Daniel Albrecht, *Rites in the Spirit: A Ritual Approach to Pentecostal/Charismatic Spirituality* (Sheffield: Sheffield Academic Press, 1999), and Christopher J Ellis, *Gathering: A Spirituality and Theology of Worship in Free Church Tradition* (London: SCM Press, 2005).
24. See Jonny Baker, Doug Gay, *et al*, *Alternative Worship* (London: SPCK, 2003), which invokes the analogy of sampling in electronic music to depict its relationship to the wider tradition. Doug Gay, *Remixing the Church: Towards an Emerging Ecclesiology* (London: SCM Press, 2011) continues the use of related metaphors. Mary Gray-Reeves and Michael Perham, *The Hospitality of God: Emerging Worship for a Missional Church* (London: SPCK, 2011) is a recent example—

As the Protestant churches approached the third millennium since Christ, many have faithfully reflected a pattern which they share also with the Roman liturgy. Shifts within the Roman Church may have left the shape more or less intact but have nevertheless cut across other points of convergence, as we shall see.

'The Table of God's Word'

> The treasures of the bible are to be opened up more lavishly, so that richer fare may be provided for the faithful at the table of God's word. In this way a more representative portion of the holy scriptures will be read to the people in the course of a prescribed number of years (*SC* 51).

Convergence has also been expressed in terms of use of common lectionary patterns. The way many Protestant communities read the bible in their assemblies now has much to do with the Roman Lectionary for Mass, with its origins in *SC* 51: the bishops' call for 'richer fare at the table of God's word'. The Common Lectionary and later Revised Common Lectionary (RCL) emerged from this, with some notable changes, such as the RCL allowing for two ways of reading the Hebrew bible portions, one more thematic and the other more sequential—the former more closely related to the Roman lectionary, the latter less so. Likewise, the RCL often provides somewhat longer portions than its Roman counterpart.[25] Such factors notwithstanding, there is very evident relationship between the lectionaries.

Still, what Protestant traditions expect of their congregations by way of following the lectionary varies. The Church of England, for example, requires allegiance during certain seasons, but permits local construction of reading schemes for pastoral and teaching reasons at other times in the calendar.[26] Most notable, however, is that some churches which have 'traditionally' resisted centralised read-

---

written by two bishops—of the influence of 'alternative worship' on an old-line tradition—in this case, Anglican.

25. See Gail Ramshaw, *A Three-Year Banquet: Lectionary for the Assembly* (Minneapolis, MN: Augsburg Press, 2004) and Gail Ramshaw, *Treasures Old and New: Images in the Lectionary* (Minneapolis, MN: Fortress Press, 2002).
26. See *New Patterns for Worship*, 104.

ing schemes have embraced the RCL.[27] Their doing so has involved a more expanded use of scripture than the past tendency for the public reading of scripture to be the choice of the preacher of the day. It may now perhaps take in more readings in any one service, but also more of the canon over time. Moreover, shifting to using the lectionary has started to enable different kinds of scriptural hermeneutics, given the lectionary's privileging of gospel portions, 'giving the last word to Jesus' as it were in the sequence of readings. This is perhaps upturning earlier tendencies to privilege certain canonical epistles. This expansion opens up new avenues of education and formation in Protestant churches, just as greater exposure, 'richer fare,' from the bible has opened Catholic communities to paths to renewal. At the same time, RCL has also not escaped criticism from a range of Protestant quarters—feminist critique has been notable, and recently, other 'marginalised' questions have been voiced.[28]

Other opportunities of learning in Protestant circles might also be looped back to *SC* via the second paragraph of *SC* 14, on pedagogy. The shift to directory provisions of liturgical resources, for instance, has been a major move requiring more careful formation of clergy, as greater trust is placed in their abilities to shape liturgy to form local communities well, than was the case in earlier, older 'prayer book' approaches. Protestant seminaries and lay training institutes have given greater attention to liturgical studies as part of a more general shift from more-or-less inchoate 'pastoralia' to more methodically-sophisticated approaches to various strands of the so-called 'fourth area of practical theology (that is, 'fourth' after biblical, historical and systematic theological studies.) Protestant scholars are now firmly embedded in scholarly circles of liturgical studies, such as the international *Societas Liturgica* and the Australian—and North American Academy of Liturgy. *SC* 14's concern with the formation of local congregational life has also been mirrored in many Protestant traditions.[29]

27. For example, *Gathering for Worship* and *Worship from the United Reformed Church* (London: United Reformed Church, 2003).
28. See, for example, Jione Havea, 'Local Lectionary Sites,' in *Christian Worship in Australia: Inculturating the Liturgical Tradition,* edited by Stephen Burns and Anita Monro (Strathfield NSW: St Pauls, 2009), 117–128.
29. See, for example, *Worship-Shaped Life: Liturgical Formation and the People of God,* edited by Ruth A Meyers and Paul Gibson (Norwich: Canterbury Press,

'Present in the Sacraments'

In some cases, there has been renewal of sacramental sensibility, drawing more widely on the Vatican Council II sources, notably *Lumen Gentium*, and associated notions of 'primordial' and 'fundamental' sacraments, of Christ and Church, as prior categories in consideration of specific sacraments: either seven or two, or as some Protestant distinguish the two and seven, those deemed to be of either the 'gospel' or 'common' kind.[30] In any case, it is important to recognise that however Protestant traditions do or do not invoke wider notions of sacramentality, their ritual books invariably represent resources that map closely to the Roman rituals' provisions for the seven sacraments. Wider moves have also been encouraged by hospitable readings of *SC* 7 on, as it were, 'dispersed presence' in assembly, word, presiding minister and sacramental action as well as sacramental thing ('eucharistic species').

> . . .Christ is always present in His Church, especially in her liturgical celebrations. He is present in the sacrifice of the Mass, not only in the person of His minister, 'the same now offering, through the ministry of priests, who formerly offered himself on the cross', but especially under the Eucharistic species. By His power He is present in the sacraments, so that when a man baptises it is really Christ Himself who baptises. He is present in His word, since it is He Himself who speaks when the holy scriptures are read in the Church. He is present, lastly,

---

2010). The struggle for liturgical formation in seminaries is reflected in *Common* Worship *in Theological Education,* edited by Siobhan Garrigan and Todd Johnson (Eugene, OR: Wipf Stock Publishers, 2010).

30. For a wide view of sacramentality, see Ann Loades, 'Finding New Sense in the Sacramental', in *The Gestures of God: Explorations in Sacramentality,* edited by Geoffrey Rowell and Christine Hall (London: Continuum, 2004), 161–172; and Ann Loades, 'Sacramentality and Christian Spirituality,' in *The Blackwell Companion to Christian Spirituality,* edited by Arthur Holder (Oxford: Blackwell, 2005), 254-268. On the sacraments of Catholic tradition see, for example, John Macquarie, *A Guide to the Sacraments* (London: SCM Press, 1997)—an Anglican work—and John E Colwell, *Promise and Presence: An Exploration of Sacramental Theology* (Milton Keynes: Paternoster, 2005)—a fascinating work by an evangelical Baptist.

> when the Church prays and sings, for He promised: 'Where two or three are gathered together in my name, there am I in the midst of them' (Matt 18:20) (*SC* 7).

Notwithstanding numerous remaining points of doctrinal difference, Roman Catholic theology and the Protestant churches, but among the Protestant traditions themselves, these developments have been very significant turns towards ecumenical consensus.

The Future

In an article first published in *The Christian Century*, and later posted on the Liturgical Press blog PrayTell,[31] Gail Ramshaw writes about the new (2010) translation of the Mass as 'yesterday's language'. She writes as one of the major contemporary thinkers about liturgical language, whose texts for prayer have shaped not only her own Evangelical Lutheran Church in America, but also ritual books across a range of other traditions.[32] In focusing on her critique of recent Catholic liturgical developments, I take her concerns to be representative of other Protestant scholars, and it must also be noted that they overlap with significant critique by Catholic scholars also.[33]

In 'yesterday's language' she opens with her conviction that 'because of the unity of the body of Christ, the health of one arm affects the entire body', and so wades into the debate. She writes of her work to make the words of Christian worship 'communally approved, biblically inspired, theologically alive and masterfully crafted', and then speaks of her 'sadness' that the new translation 'wounds not only many of [her] Catholic friends'. Ramshaw parallels the process of producing the new translation to the sometime Protestant phenomenon of a single minister composing texts for Sunday, foisting such upon

31. <http://www.praytellblog.com/index.php/2011/08/27/yesterdays-language/>. Accessed 1 April 2013.
32. For example, her Eucharistic Prayer 'Triple Praise' is found in the United Church of Canada's *Celebrate God's Presence* (Etibicoke: United Church Press, 2000), 299–301. Note, among numerous possible examples, her *Words Around the Fire, Words Around the Font* (Chicago: Liturgy Training Publications, 1990), and her *Words Around the Table* (Chicago: Liturgy Training P,ublications, 1990).
33. Note, for example, John B Baldovin SJ, *Reforming the Liturgy: A Response to the Critics* (Collegeville, MN: Liturgical Press, 2008), which should by no means be collapsed into others critiques, but is robust in making its own.

the gathered assembly. Moreover, she is 'saddened' that the translation and its implementation, in 'outshouting an emerging ecumenical consensus', has reflected recent Roman Catholic moves to 'heighten its denominational distinctiveness' by rejecting use of ecumenical translations of shared texts'—the so-called 'prayers we have in common'.

Ramshaw is particularly scathing of the new translation's measure against 'words masterfully crafted': 'the rhetorical style of the complex Latinate sentences suggests that masterful English cannot carry the mystery.' Ramshaw also charges the new translation with 'resurrecting the archaic', calling it a 'compendium of the antiquated', and she criticises its unnecessary capitalisation as hierarchy-reinforcing (so 'Priest' gets a capital letter, but 'deacon' does not, and nor do 'people'). The author's most chastening comments are reserved for the words of the Eucharistic Prayer around the cup, when Jesus is said to have taken 'this precious chalice in his holy and venerable hands'—a depiction she finds simply 'unfathomable'.

Ramshaw's assessment of this 'lamentable new rite' discerns that it 'does not represent liturgical language that is communally acceptable, biblically accurate, theologically helpful or linguistically masterful', giving articulate if acid slants on widespread exasperation, from within and beyond Protestantism, about the so-called reform of the reform.

Whatever such views indicate about the prospects of an ecumenical future, it remains that one very significant irony of recent developments with the Roman liturgy is that although it has been edged from the centre of Catholic prayer and practice, fruit from *SC* has transmuted in a range of ways into Protestant terrain. For example, the International Commission on English in the Liturgy (ICEL) collects were published in England and are widely used by Anglicans and others,[34] and the ICEL psalms have been incorporated into the daily prayer resources of the Uniting Church in Australia.[35] Such movements are at least part of the future of *SC*!

34. *Opening Prayers: Collects in Contemporary Language Scripture related prayers for Sundays and Holy Days, Years A, B and C* (Norwich: Canterbury Press, 1999). The volume is dedicated to Michael Vasey, an evangelical Anglican who before his death in 1998 strongly advocated for the use of the prayers in the Church of England.

35. <http://assembly.uca.org.au/theology/worship-resources-and-publications/item/download/302_b9476de6a0b4c4ab062b6af24755afcb>. Accessed 10 June 2013.

Issues for a Twenty-First Century *Sacrosanctum Concilium*

Frank O'Loughlin

Sacrosanctum Concilium (*SC*) changed the Church. The reforms included in that document and those that flowed from it changed the shape and spirit of the Church. It was the source of those changes which most impacted on the faith and everyday lives of Catholics. It dared to envision that things could be otherwise than they were. It took up things that were already happening or being proposed; it critiqued, refined and developed these things and set a vision and task for the future.

We now live in a different time to that of the Second Vatican Council. The seeds of what has now come about were certainly at work at that time and were being discerned by many of the Council Fathers and the experts assisting them. These seeds have now come to flower among us and are changing the shape of society and consequently of the Church. Thus the first task of this essay is to look at this new context in which we live.

A Time of Transition

In Western societies we are at a critical point in a long term transition from the society of Christendom to societies which are pluralist in character. Beginning in the fourth century with the Christianising of the Roman Empire and reaching its apogee in the Middle Ages, a societal structure developed in which Christianity and those societies fused to form what we call Christendom. This was a form of Christianity in which being a citizen and being a Christian coalesced. To be a European was to be a Christian. In fact, people of that time would have called themselves Christians rather than Europeans.

The basic means by which one became a Christian in such a society was by socialisation into that society and culture. One became a Christian by osmosis with the society and culture one lived in. The social processes at work making people Christian in those times are at work in Australian society in the twenty-first century making people Australian, making them part of a pluralist culture.

The social and cultural structures of Christendom were the same social and cultural structures that are at work in a strictly Islamic society today: citizenship and religion merged. If you were not a Christian in the Middle Ages or are not a Moslem in a strictly Islamic society today, you could not and cannot be properly a citizen.

This Christian social structure no longer exists. In the course of the last few centuries the fusion of Western societies and Christianity has been gradually diluted until Christianity is no longer a presumed factor of that structure. We can clearly identify something of the beginnings of this dilution in the Reformation when the one Christendom became many Christendoms. We can identify this transition in the very principle which was used to resolve the wars following the Reformation—the people of each region would follow the religion of the ruler (*cuius regio eius religio*).

Western Christendom has disappeared and we live now in societies in the twenty-first century which are, in principle, pluralist. That means that there is in principle no alliance between the society we live in and any particular religious tradition or indeed between the society and any particular worldview. This is so at least in principle, if not always in practice.

By belonging to a contemporary pluralist society one does not imbibe any particular religious tradition in the process of one's socialisation. One's religious belonging becomes a purely private matter with which the society does not interfere. Becoming a Christian by socialisation is now out of the question. It does not happen. This removes that very powerful means of becoming Christian. It leaves a gap which we have to learn to fill. This leads into the question of evangelisation which we see being raised not just in theological and pastoral circles but also by the teaching office of the Church.

Pastorally the perception of this new situation has been in evidence for some time in the many pastoral initiatives that have arisen in the last sixty or seventy years. We have seen the rise of initiatives such as the preparation of parents before their children's reception of the sacraments, the re-introduction of the catechumenate and countless programs of adult education and formation in faith. As suggested already, the coming of this pluralism was at work in the deliberations and the documents of Vatican Council II and the work of many theologians whose thought was formative of the Council's work.

It is in this contemporary situation that I would like to ask the question which is the title of this article: If *SC* was to be published in 2013, what issues ought it address?

An Evangelising Liturgy

The first thing I would like to suggest is that our liturgy itself should be evangelising. On the one hand, the liturgy presumes evangelisation; on the other it needs to have an ongoing evangelising dimension.[1]

This is of particular importance to people who inhabit a pluralist culture because that pluralist culture is within them. Cultures go into the make-up of the people who live them and live in them. Cultures are not mere external clothing to an essential core. They shape from within the way of thinking and the way of approaching the world of their members. A culture is imbibed; there is osmosis between any culture and its inhabitants. This means that the pluralist culture in which people live will influence their thinking, feeling and attitudes. It forms them. There will need to be a continuing dialogue between this cultural mind which people in our society bring to the liturgy and the word proclaimed and the symbols celebrated in that liturgy. The liturgy will need to speak to the pluralist culture of our time, just as the liturgy of the Middle Ages sought to speak in such a way as to affirm and develop the Christian culture and worldview of its participants, or the liturgy of the patristic age took into account the religious culture which was part of the overall culture of the peoples of those early centuries.

Karl Rahner, in at least one of his writings, suggested that in proclaiming the word, the Church needs to speak to the unbeliever in the believer. We might put that slightly differently and say that we

1. See *Liturgie es mission de l'Eglise La Maison-Dieu* 265 (2011). Note especially H-J Gagey, 'La liturgie, milieu de l'annonce de l'Evangile', 93–109.

need to speak to the member of the pluralist society in the believer. It is this that an evangelising liturgy would seek to do: to keep weaving together the experience of human beings and the discovery of Jesus Christ, a part of which discovery is finding a response to the questions which human life poses to us.

In his Apostolic Exhortation on Evangelisation of 1975, Paul VI suggests that the Church needs to evangelise the various 'strata' of our humanity.[2] This image of 'the strata' of our humanity is, I think, taken from the use of the word 'strata' in speaking of the levels of human occupation in an archeological site or from its use by geologists in speaking of the strata or levels of the crust of the earth. The image implies that there are various strata or levels of humanity embedded in or 'under-laying' human beings. These strata would also be the dimensions of humanity investigated by the various human sciences and by philosophy. In accord with circumstances and different histories of human experience, the presentation of the gospel needs to speak to human beings taking into account these various strata which make it up. Evangelisation has therefore to include but go beyond the presentation of doctrine to address such issues. This is of course part of the overall theological task of the Church in our day. It is part of the task of faith's seeking understanding in this new age, in which so much of the 'strata' of our humanity is revealing itself to research and thought.

Apart from an awareness of evangelisation in the actual celebration of the liturgy, thinking about the liturgy and the explanation of it needs to take evangelisation into account. The signs which are constitutive of the liturgy come out of the woof and weave of human existence and we need to appreciate them in their human setting if in turn we are to appreciate them in their liturgical usage. Take 'bread' and eating as an example. Food and the activity of eating are taken up into the eucharistic liturgy, the sacrament at which the Church becomes the Church. Every time human beings eat, they acknowledge by that very act that they are incapable of maintaining their own existence, of giving life to themselves. They must eat food which is commonly represented by bread.

2. Paul VI *Evangelii Nuntiandi* Apostolic Exhortation, 1975, #1. <http://www.vatican.va/holy_father/paul_vi/apost_exhortations/documents/hf_p-vi_exh_19751208_evangelii-nuntiandi_en.htm l9>. Accessed 20 March 2013.

The very act of eating is testimony to the fact that human beings are utterly dependent on 'something' beyond themselves. They do not so much possess their lives as receive their lives. Just as they have received life from their parents, so do they day-by-day receive life from the food they eat. Bread (food) stands between human beings and death, or if you like between human beings and life.

The Eucharist receives meaning from the fact that it uses this human sign which is constitutive of it as a sacrament. This human sign and the memorial of the Lord are put together in the action of the Eucharist in which believers stand at the very heart of the Christian life. *SC* expresses this in the following text: 'In the liturgy the sanctification of the man (sic) is signified by signs perceptible to the senses, and is effected in a way which corresponds with each of these signs'.[3] This sanctification is effected in a way proper to each of these signs! As a consequence due attention must be given to these signs.

This is but one strand of the meaning of bread and it has this meaning whether people are believers or unbelievers. Bread and eating have this same significance for all human beings. This approach is very important in presenting the sacraments today because it enables us to speak to the unbeliever in the believer and to find common ground on which to dialogue in an evangelical manner with those who do not believe. It is important that in presenting the Eucharist we do so in a way that also reaches into our human depths which I suggest the approach outlined above does. John also does this in his gospel by describing Christ as the bread of life.

Today the sacraments need to be presented as signs coming from the human context in which they originate. The sacraments come to life when grounded in human experience. Before anyone can know what the writer of John's Gospel means when he describes Jesus as the bread of life, they need to know what bread is; before anyone can know what the Eucharist celebrated in bread and wine is, they need to know—among other things—what bread and wine are.

This is true of all the gestures and signs used in the liturgy: immersion in water, anointing with oil, the joining of hands in marriage, the laying on of hands. These all have corollaries in human life and become windows into the mystery of Christ, helping us to see what we

3. *Sacrosanctum Concilium*, Constitution on the Sacred Liturgy #7. <http://www.vatican.va/archive/hist_councils/ii_vatican_council/documents/vat-ii_const_19631204_sacrosanctum-concilium_en.html> Accessed 20 March 2013.

cannot see. They are human things which, to use ancient theological terminology, are figures or types of Jesus the Christ.

The Sunday Eucharist

In pluralist societies the place where Christians will meet other Christians in an explicit faith context is fundamentally the Sunday Eucharist.

Living in a culture like our own where the strong persuasion of the socialisation process is no longer at work leading people to faith, there needs to be an alternative means of communication of faith and communion in faith. I suggest that frequent participation at the Sunday Eucharist is the major continuing means for this to happen. As Tertullian stated so many centuries ago Christians are 'made not born' and it is the Sunday assembly for Eucharist which will play the major role in this 'making' of Christians in the future.[4]

It is common experience for believers today that they live among people of many different persuasions and views of the world. This is the case in workplaces, neighbourhoods, friendship groups and, indeed, families. Being a believer can be a lonely experience in such pluralist societies and believers need to know in a concrete way that they are not the only ones on the journey of faith. More than ever each believer in this age needs the solidarity of the Christian community to reassure them and form them in the faith. The communion of the body of Christ which is the Church is needed and it is needed in concrete form. It is found in that concrete form in the Sunday gathering of the Church for Eucharist. This situation is not unlike that of the Abitanian martyrs who summed up their position before those threatening their lives in the words '*Sine Domenico non possumus*'. This is hard to translate precisely because '*Domenico*' or '*the Dominicum*' meant for them the gathering of the Lord's people on the Lord's day for the Lord's supper, but it could be translated as, 'without the Sunday Eucharist we will not be able to manage as believing members of the Church.'[5]

4. 'Apology 18' in *Anti-Nicene Fathers*, edited by Alexander Roberts and James Donaldson (Grand Rapids, MI: Eerdmans Publishing Company, 1976) Vol 3: 32.
5. Frank O'Loughlin, *Christ Present in the Eucharist* (Strathfield NSW: St Paul's Publications, 2000), 133-134.

Jesus gathered his disciples into a group around him and that group continued on after his death and eventually named themselves with his name. Christianity is a communal faith in principle. It is the initial gathering of human beings around Jesus as the sign of the future gathering of all human beings at the table of the Father. Our eucharistic tables are signs of that table in the Father's kingdom.

The Sunday Eucharist, for all its possible faults and undoubted difficulties, is the gathering point of believers. It is that celebration at which the Lord's people (his body) gather to celebrate the Lord's Supper on the Lord's day—the day of his resurrection. Our belonging to the body of Christ is personal, concrete, corporeal and communal; it is of the whole person; it is not merely individual and spiritual; it is the sign of God's gathering to himself all of humankind and its history, in its strength and weakness, in its goodness and capacity for evil.[6]

Christians gather around those things which Christ has left them as the means of his communication and communion with them—especially his word and the supper which we celebrate in his memory. They gather with those he has given to them to be his body with them and from them they receive ministry in its many forms, especially the ordained ministry, the symbol of the unity and universality of the Church.

We can see our present situation paralleled in the earliest centuries of the Church before Christendom came into being. Then the Sunday Eucharist was more than paramount, it was *the* activity of the Church. It was indeed a time when the Church made the Eucharist and the Eucharist made the Church. This parallel is that both then and now the Church was living in a pluralist situation in which it had no formal recognition or status in its surrounding society. It had to create strong internal bonds which gave it its integrity and identity. The creation of new members (catechumenate) and the reconciliation of failed members (penance) both happened within the ambit of the Sunday Eucharist precisely because there the Church became the Church.

---

6. The work of Louis-Marie Chauvet on the sacraments makes this point thoroughly. See *Symbol and Sacrament* (Collegeville, MD: Liturgical Press,1995), see esp. 355-365, 372-376 and *The Sacraments. The Word of God at the Mercy of the Body* (Collegeville, MD:Liturgical Press, 2001), 19-38.

I would like to draw out four points in consequence of the above. Firstly, there is a theological difference between the Sunday Eucharist and the Eucharist celebrated at other times.[7] The law concerning attendance at Sunday Mass is based on an important principle: all those belonging to the Church are called to the Sunday Eucharist. Going to Mass on weekdays or other occasions—as good a practice as it may be—is an option. It does not entail the question of one's belonging to the Church in the way that Sunday Mass does. The Sunday Eucharist calls into play in a way that other celebrations of the Eucharist do not that theological dimension of the Eucharist expressed in the patristic dictum 'The Church makes the Eucharist and the Eucharist makes the Church' (*Ecclesia facit Eucharistiam et Eucharistia facit Ecclesiam).*[8]

Secondly, in an explicitly Christian society with its strong social structure by which its members are socialised into the Christian faith, secondary ways of expressing the faith can be effective precisely because of the exclusive hold which Christianity has on the society and its members. This is different in a pluralist society in which one's socialisation itself raises questions about the meaning and validity of faith in Christ. In such a society we need to ground ourselves explicitly in the heart of the faith. A document of the French Episcopal Conference on the principles of catechesis/evangelisation in the current situation of the French church is entitled *'Aller au coeur de la foi'* (Going to the Heart of the Faith). The document then uses the Paschal Vigil as its means of seeing into the heart of the faith. Going to the heart of things is a principle of importance in our presentation of the faith today. For those living in a pluralist and highly secularised society, secondary practices such as devotions along the lines of past devotions will no longer be adequate. They will need to be grounded in the heart of the faith—in Christ and in his Paschal Mystery and so in the Mass.

Thirdly, this all means that Christians have to be able to give an account of the hope that is in them as the first letter of Peter suggests

---

7. 'The ecclesial dimension intrinsic to the Eucharist is realised in every eucharistic celebration. But it is expressed most especially on the day when the whole community comes together to commemorate the Lord's Resurrection.' John Paul II Apostolic Letter, *Dies Domini, On keeping the Lord's Day Holy*, 1998, # 32. <http://www.vatican.va/holy_father/john_paul_ii/apost_letters/documents/hf_jp-ii_apl_05071998_dies-domini_en.html>. Accessed 20 March 2013.
8. Henri de Lubac, *The Splendour of the Church* (San Francisco: Ignatius Press, 1986), 134.

(I Peter 3.15). It does not mean that we all need to be theologians but, both for our own sake and because we live in a pluralist and secular society, we need to be able to say at least what it means for us to believe and trust in Christ. This is part of going to 'the heart of the faith'. The efforts towards formation and education in faith that have been so prominent in recent decades are based on genuine pastoral insight into the present situation of the Church.

Fourthly, in such an age as ours there could be a temptation for the Church to concentrate on being elite or even becoming a sect, which closes itself off from the surrounding society. This of course would be a contradiction of the nature of the Church as the sign or figure of the future gathering of all humankind at the table of the heavenly Father.[9] This was also a temptation for the Church in the time before Christendom. We can see it in the disputes over the Sacrament of Penance where the purists wanted to exclude permanently from the Church people who had sinned after baptism. This involved an elitist understanding of the Church which virtually saw it as a sect. The official decision of the leaders of the Church was that these sinners should be re-admitted to the Church after doing penance. This was really a decision about ecclesiology, about the nature of the Church as open to all.[10] The Church in those early centuries could seem like a sect from a sociological point of view but the decision concerning the penitents made it clear that, theologically, the Church was open to all. This theological point is crucial for us in our day.

In writing about the importance of the Sunday Eucharist, I can hear the echo of voices crying out their frustration regarding their experience of Sunday Mass. Many Catholics—at least in Australia—find that they cannot get the nourishment that they need from the Sunday Eucharist as they experience it. This problem can only be addressed through a thorough and officially supported effort to improve the celebration of Sunday Masses involving an increased understanding and improved practice of the Mass on the part of priests and people; through developing the roles of all the faithful in the Mass, as well as developing a deeper understanding of the nature of the Church.

---

9. Second Vatican Ecumenical Council, *Lumen Gentium* (Constitution on the Church), 1, 48; *Gaudium et Spes* (Constitution on the Church in the Contemporary World), 1, 4, 45; *Ad Gentes* (Decree on the Church's Missionary Activity) 1, (London/Dublin: Geoffrey Chapmen,1966).
10. For a historical account of this development see: Frank O'Loughlin, *The Future of the Sacrament of Penance* (Strathfield, NSW: St Paul's Publications, 2007).

There is another critical point to be made here and that is that the liturgy cannot be entertainment. The liturgy requires conversion of its participants. It cannot simply play on the basic emotions and loyalties that other symbolic activities like football matches or national occasions evoke or that a human drama raises up in us. It is asking worshippers to 'passover' into the mind of Christ and therefore for a change in the alignments of our attitudes and choices.

The word conversion comes from the Greek *metanoia* which is a compound word of two elements: 'beyond' and 'mind' or 'mentality'. Conversion is the call of the Lord to go beyond present attitudes and mentalities under the guidance of his word which is 'a lamp to my feet and a light to my path' (Psalm 119:105). So liturgy cannot just be entertainment, leaving people where they are and giving them an outlet for their current attitudes and way of seeing things. It requires the capacity to listen and to allow oneself to be taken elsewhere by the word heard. It can demand much. This does not of course mean that liturgies should be without attraction and beauty in their presentation of the word and of the sacramental signs.

Understanding the Medium

One of the crucial factors involved in any continuing renewal of the liturgy is the need to take into account the medium with which we are engaged. The medium is that of symbol or sign.

There is a hangover from the past on the present celebration of Mass which we may call 'the Mass obligation mentality'. Despite all that has been achieved in the last few decades, there is still a strong mindset among Catholics that going to Mass is primarily about fulfilling the obligation to attend. This is understandable given the long term insistence on Church law concerning Sunday Mass. Obviously some people have emerged from this mentality, some are reacting to it, some go to Mass and see it as much more than an obligation, but there is still something of the obligation mentality motivating them. This mindset does not stand up well to questions about the meaning of Eucharist in Christian life. It can act as a straightjacket to the celebration of the liturgy, making its innate significance of secondary importance.

Along with this there is also a 'rubrical' mentality. By this is meant that the directions for the proper celebration of the sacraments determine the way the liturgy is celebrated without regard for the actual nature of the sacramental celebrations as sacramental or symbolic. There is no real conflict between the directions (the rubrics) and the nature of the signs or symbols that are an essential part of the liturgy, for the former are grounded in the latter. They are indicators concerning a celebration which is of its nature sacramental.

Everything about the liturgy is symbolic; all of it and each part of it bear the nature of signs.[11] They point beyond themselves to things that cannot be heard, touched or seen. And the interplay between those signs and the mystery of which they are symbols ought to be brought out in the actual celebration of the sacrament. These signs are signs indeed, they are not veils. Their purpose is to reveal not to conceal. So there is a certain 'transparency' between the sign and the mystery. The celebration of the sign suggests the mystery to which it is referring. This requires a symbolic or sacramental mentality in those engaged in the liturgy and this is especially so of course for the priest into whose ministry and care so much of the celebration falls. But to have this mentality is also crucial for the whole community which is the primary subject of the celebration. The whole liturgy is symbolic or sacramental in nature and very importantly includes that crucial part of the liturgy which is the celebration of the word.

The celebration of the word is symbolic or sacramental. The liturgy of the word can be reduced in our thinking to a catechetical activity. It is more than teaching; it seeks to bring about more than knowledge. The readings we listen to in the liturgy have as their purpose the evoking of our present relationship with God by means of these particular readings.[12] That is, the passages of the scriptures that we read are there to act as symbols of the relationship with God we now live. By the merging of that scripture passage and our own selves, a play of similarity and dissimilarity emerges to critique, develop and deepen our present relationship with the God whose words and activity are expressed in the scripture passage. Insight into the sacramental nature of the liturgy of the word is a critical element of the Church's future; it enables the proper understanding of the role of the scriptures in the context of the present life of the Church.

11. *SC* #7.

12. See Congregation for Divine Worship and the Discipline of the Sacraments, *Lectionary for Mass: Introduction*, 1998.

Shifting the Imagination

Given the new era of history that the Church is entering, we all need to be ready for and look towards the influence of a new imagination at work in a new era. This shift in imagination has occurred several times in the history of the Church, often unconsciously. We can see this in the transition from the biblical imagination at work in the Church's earliest times to the more philosophically inclined imagination at work in the patristic age and we can see it again in the later first millennium when the evangelisation of the European peoples was taking place. It is at work again in the age of Rationalism. This is not to suggest that one or other of these ages was particularly imaginative but that in all of them there was a presumed imagining of the world at work within peoples' minds. There is another such transition at work in this present time and it will bring with it other imaginings of the world.

To illustrate this I want to refer to the architecture of church buildings. There is a correlation between Church as the communion of faith in Christ and the church buildings in which that community gathers. There is a true sense that the Church at Eucharist makes the church building in its own image and that the church building in turn shapes the community celebrating in it. This type of correlation can be discerned between the Church gatherings of the earliest centuries and the house churches in which they gathered. Similarly it is possible to see the reflection of the larger church gatherings in the fourth and fifth centuries in the basilicas which they inherited from the Roman cityscape. In the Medieval Gothic cathedrals an image of the Medieval Church itself is visible in its highly structured and hierarchical character with bishop, choir and people firmly separated into their own areas of the building. More recent Church architecture and the contemporary renovations of Church buildings attempt to gather the people of God in unity around the place of the word and the table of the Eucharist.[13] In this there is another attempt to align the community of the Church and its 'house'.

As in the past, so today, the imagination at work in Church architecture and art ought to seek to make the Church of today present in the society of today. Such architecture and art needs to provide a

13. See the description of the Mass given in *The General Instruction of the Roman Missal* (Strathfield, NSW: St Pauls Publications, 2012) #27.

teasing of the imagination of all those living in a pluralist and predominantly secular society. This architectural and liturgical venture is of course a long-term process in which there will be a good deal of trial and error as well as success.

Jerome Alexandre, a French theologian and writer on art, suggests a very telling parallel between the Christian faith today and contemporary art. He suggests that just as art over the last century or so has been freed from certain art-establishment and socially-imposed canons whose requirements had to be met for something to be considered art, so the Christian faith has been freed from social and cultural requirements placed upon it by its former established place in society. Alexandre suggests that in this process art has been freed to search into reality to seek meaning in new ways, and that pluralism has freed the Christian faith from parallel restraints thus enabling it to plumb anew the mystery of life in the light of the gospel.[14]

There are examples of a shift in the religious imagination in contemporary Church architecture. It can be seen in some of the Cathedrals in Australia which have recently been rebuilt or renovated, for example, St Stephen's Brisbane, Queensland; St Patrick's Parramatta, New South Wales; St Mary's Perth and St Patrick's, Bunbury, Western Australia.

Another interesting shift in imagination is apparent in the arrangement of the place for the Eucharist in recent church architecture in Paris. With the deliberate intent of creating a presence of the Church in the public space of contemporary society, seven new churches have been built in that city since the late 1990s. In all of these—and of course in some more than others—can be discerned a shift in the imagining of the space for the Church, a space where there occurs that which makes the Church the Church, and a space which deliberately places the Church in the contemporary context.[15]

There has also been some new and imaginative Church architecture in Rome, built in response to the need for new church buildings in

14. Jérôme Alexandre, *L'art Contemporain. Un vis-à-vis Essential pour la Foi* (Paris: Editions Parole et Silence, 2010), 11–17.

15. The deliberate intention behind the building of these churches is evident in the introduction by Cardinal Andre Vingt-Trois to a DVD entitled: '*Sept nouvelles eglises pour aujourd'hui*'. The titles of these churches are: Notre Dame de l'Espérance, Notre Dame de l'Arche de l'Alliance, Chapelle de l'Agneau de Dieu, Saint Luc, Notre Dame de la Sagesse, Notre Dame de Pentecôte, et Saint François de Molitor.

the outskirts of the city. Notable among these is the commonly called Millennium church of *Dives Misericordia in Tor Tre Teste.* Other churches to note include *Santa Maria Madre del Redentore, via Duilio Cambellotti in Tor Bella Monaca* and *Santo Volto di Gesu* on the corner of *via della Magliana* and *via Caprese* in the *Portuense* quarter.

Architecture has an advantage among the arts because when people set about building a church, they are necessarily involved in a long term and very costly project which seems to enable people to project themselves more easily into the future and call on designs which draw on contemporary ways of seeing and imagining things.

In the whole area of liturgy, there is a need to be attuned to tradition and its history, and an aspect of that history is the history of the Christian imagination, a history enshrined in art, architecture, music, literature—in fact in each aspect of human culture. This same diversity of imagination can be seen at work in the great liturgical families of the liturgical tradition itself. With the radical change which is at work in our present cultural transition, we cannot afford to neglect the shifts in imagination that are at work in our contemporary time.

There is a limit to the pre-planning that we can put into this shifting of the imagination. It is a matter of attentiveness to the time in which we live and reading the signs of those times which appear in the imaginative works that find expression around us.

The changing imagination needs to be at work within the actual celebration of our liturgy as well. This of course applies to the new cultures in which the gospel is being planted. It also applies to Western cultures in the radical shift they are undergoing in these present times. This is an area of great delicacy but there is considerable history behind it. We can see examples of such changes in the adoption of so much of the Gallican Rites into the Roman liturgy, a particular example of which is the inclusion of the service of light of the Paschal Vigil into the liturgy of Rome. Similarly we can see attentiveness to changing times in the adoption of the Nicene Creed into the Eucharist, the use of the Kyrie and the change in the Introductory Rites of the Mass where what were previously private prayers of the priest became prayers of the whole assembly. In recent times we have also seen the re-imagining and re-shaping of the liturgy as a result of its rediscovery as an act of the whole Christian people, becoming one of the glories of Vatican Council II and its aftermath. This opens up questions that can only be dealt with in a spirit of communion and with true liturgical understanding.

Language and imagination are of a piece. Liturgical language needs to be imaginative enough to convey the fact that in and through this liturgical language we are celebrating things beyond language. This requires a balance and a beauty that is not always easy to achieve. Words need to come from the language of the assembly and we need to have some understanding of the imaginative power that lies behind them. This is not an easy task but a task which needs to take language itself quite seriously.

Translation is a crucial skill in this matter of liturgical language. Anyone accustomed to using a language other than their own soon discovers that translation is not only a long way from transliteration but that one often has to re-think—maybe we could even say re-imagine—the ways things are said in one language in order to translate it adequately into another. An imaginative underlay to language that is not in tune with the language of the assembly will act as an obstacle rather than an aid to communication and prayer. The old adage that translation is betrayal is not only true of a translation too far from the original but one too close to the original. In this sense I believe we have to consider the translation of the Roman Missal (2010) as creating another obstacle to the active participation of the people. In fact in terms of the above, it would have to be considered an unprofessional attempt at translation.

Participation

In the phrase of Yves Congar, it is the Church or the Christian community as a body which is the subject of the liturgical action.[16] This is a principle to which we need to have constant recourse. It is fundamental to *SC* that the liturgy is conceived as the action of Christ who associates his Body the Church with him in that action.[17]

16. Yves Congar, '"Ecclésia" ou communauté chrétienne, sujet intégral de l'action liturgique', in *La Liturgie après Vatican II*, edited by J-P Jossua and Yves Congar (Paris: Cerf, 1967), 241–282. and 'The Ecclesia or Christian Community as a Whole celebrates the Liturgy' in *At the Heart of Christian Worship. Liturgical Essays of Yves Congar*, edited by P Philibert (Collegeville, MN: Liturgical Press 2010), 15–68.

17. *SC* #7.

It is easy to give assent to this principle without it having due impact on the actual celebration of the liturgy. For so many centuries the actual celebration of the liturgy was treated as the business of the priest which the rest of the Christian community attended. That way of celebrating was so taken for granted that it went beyond practice and became practically-speaking the mentality of the Catholic Church. And this occurred to such an extent that the Catholic faithful by and large did not pray the liturgy at all, even though the liturgy belonged to them by right of their baptism. They did other things while they were at Mass: they prayed the Rosary or prayed from various prayer books available to them or they simply spent their own quiet time in prayer. Eventually for some of them the 'something else' they did was to read the prayers which the priest was praying in Latin from a People's Missal in their own language. But this was not direct participation in the liturgy which is 'their right and duty by reason of their baptism'.[18] I think that Catholics had grown so accustomed to this way of celebrating the liturgy that they failed—and often still fail—to be sufficiently scandalised by it.

All ministry—especially the ordained ministries—have as their purpose the building up of the whole body of Christ in its participation in the Paschal Mystery of Jesus.[19]It is not a healthy state of the Church when there is an imbalance of roles as was the case in the centuries preceding the Second Vatican Council's reform of the liturgy.

'In the restoration and promotion of the sacred liturgy, this full and active participation by all the people is the aim to be considered before all else; for it is *the primary and indispensable source from which the faithful are to derive the true Christian spirit*'.[20] If we are to take this statement of the Council seriously, participation in the liturgy cannot but be of paramount importance in the continuing reform and renewal of the Church.

Participation in the liturgy is described as the primary and indispensable source of the true Christian spirit. This is a very strong statement. And it is by engaging in the fundamental activities into

---

18. *SC* #7, #14.
19. Lumen Gentium #18.
20. *SC* #14 (Italics added).

which the liturgy invites us, and by tapping into the spiritual resources they embody for us that the true Christian spirit is formed within the People of God.

The pluralist age in which the Church now lives will ask of us a fundamental grasp of our identity. This has been referred to earlier in this essay as 'going to the heart of the faith' borrowing that phrase from the Conference of the Bishops of France. The phrase 'the true Christian spirit' used in the above quotation from *SC* speaks in somewhat different terms of this same reality of our lived Christian identity.

Conclusion

We turn to the original question: if *SC* were to be published in 2013, what issues ought it address? In the twenty-first century—fifty years after the Second Vatican Council—Western Christendom has disappeared and we live in societies which are, in principle, pluralist. Christianity through socialisation is, therefore, no longer an option. An evangelising liturgy is required, one that would seek to weave together the experience of human beings and the discovery of Jesus Christ. The Sunday Eucharist continues to be the gathering point for all believers and provides communion in the body of Christ: the concrete form of the Church. To understand the mystery of the liturgy requires a symbolic or sacramental mentality of those engaged in the liturgy—the presider and the whole community—the primary subject of the celebration. It also requires a new imagination for a new era—attentiveness to the time in which we live and reading the signs of those times which appear in the imaginative works that find expression around us. Fifty years ago *SC* changed the Church and declared that liturgy is an act of the whole Christian people. That prophetic voice of the Council Fathers echoes again in this age and urges the followers of Christ to dare to envision that things could be other than they currently are.

Afterword

Robert Gribben

An Afterword is not another chapter. It is not so long, for a start. Mine is a few reflections from a colleague outside the Roman Catholic fold, who has however travelled these fifty years with the majority of this book's authors, with the deepest appreciation for both them and their Church. There is one chapter by another 'outsider', an Anglican, Stephen Burns, and some of my responses will be parallel, but not greatly repetitive, of his. Join me for a few minutes as I remind you of some of the splendid phrases or challenging arguments you have read and marked in the margins.

The book has a context, of course an important anniversary in the world of liturgy. I remember Jake Empereur, whom I invited to lecture to some of my students in England thirty years ago, beginning by reminding them that they were going to consider matters of liturgy at a time when the rest of the world was worrying about the arms race and the threat of nuclear annihilation. And having delivered that sobering thought, he did indeed speak of the Church's liturgy, embodying the life-giving spirit of *Sacrosanctum Concilium* (I think by now you know its acronym).

The world has not changed since, and it has probably not got worse. We all know for how long doom has been predicted. The new factors, at least for the churches of the west, include the decline in numbers and influence, our position *vis à vis* our societies. The weight of this book has been on reclaiming the genius of *SC* for today; some essays have also considered the future. There is now also a need for writing on liturgy for the Christian communities which are not only growing in numbers but surely in influence on governments and others in power. *SC* actually has great wisdom for 'evangelicals', charismatics and Pentecostals, and for those who now find themselves trying to discover faith between the historic churches and the 'new' ones. Several authors rightly asked if a return to a Latinist form of English helps anyone in the face of these challenges to Church and society.

There is now, regrettably, an internal challenge—to our own integrity. I mean the churches' own moral failure, now placarded before all through the media, and fuelled by the anger of so many alienated ex-Christians. It will be some time before sober and balanced judgements about the kind of institutions in which trusted leaders went wrong can be calmly assessed. This is a time for saying sorry, and until that word is heard and truly accepted, changes in the liturgy will look pretty irrelevant. This is therefore a time, however, when the teaching and practice of reconciliation comes to the fore, and when the churches—all at different points on the journey, but all equally lacking courage—must recommit themselves to serious listening and incorporation of the voices of the laity and women at every level of our existence. Churches are not alone in this need, of course (I think of political parties). Bad theology underlies historic divisions in the celebration of reconciliation, particularly the meaning of the absolution and its relation to baptism (and the greeting of peace). It also underlies the profound discomfort in relation to the doctrine and actuality of the Church; 'the horror of the absence of God in the symbol of the Church'[1] alongside the pertinent affirmation that if the Church is 'sacrament', it is always in the process of becoming, a less-than-perfect creation on its way to becoming what the Spirit is calling it to be.

We were subtly reminded that it is the whole *laos* of the Church which is formed, by Baptism, Confirmation and the Eucharist, into a holy and royal priesthood, and that the vocation of all Christians is realised when the Church offers its thanksgiving of praise in the blessed sacrament. The implications of the Australian Bishops' document *Woman and Man: One in Christ Jesus* (1999) for full participation in the liturgy, at all levels, were spelled out. It has been interesting to see how many of the theological and liturgical arguments in this volume have subtly or directly called for a re-orientation of the ordained priesthood itself, a conversion indeed to the vision of the Second Vatican Council.

---

1. I will not identify the various *bon – or mal – mots* I cite. They are there in the chapters!

These are large agendas. They are, however, exactly what that Council addressed in 1963. *SC* is the only Council document which began with a foreword. It situated this first document within the stated hopes of the whole Council: 'to intensify the daily growth of Catholics in Christian living; to make more responsive to the requirements of our times those Church observances which are open to adaptation; to nurture whatever can contribute to the unity of all who believe in Christ; and to strengthen those aspects of the Church which can help to summon all mankind (sic) into her embrace'. It may be somewhat plodding language to a modern Australian ear, but its sentiments express the hopes of many Christians (I could say 'Catholics' beyond the Roman tradition): a call for renewal, appropriate adaptation, ecumenism and evangelisation, all in one sentence.

Vatican II 'changed the Church', turning it upside down, placing the life of the local Church at the top, with the apostolic hierarchy as its foundation and support. The distinguished historian Jaroslav Pelikan, who wrote an afterword to *SC* in Walter Abbott's early and much-studied edition of *The Documents of Vatican II*,[2] boldly claimed that the hopes of the sixteenth century reformers were fulfilled in its pages, though Pelikan later decided that his own Lutheran tradition had fallen short of realising its early dreams, and he joined the Orthodox Church. No, *SC* did more than acknowledge a need for reform already accepted in Europe nearly five centuries earlier; it opened the door to all Christians to understand the contemporary challenge to their life and health, and it started with the reform of the liturgy.[3] Paul VI is quoted: the liturgy is the 'first source of life communicated to us, the first school of our spiritual life, the first gift we can give to Christian people by our believing and praying, and the first invitation to the world . . .' That is surely true for all of us.

Much of what we have read has been a reminder of this starting point. For instance, the fundamental principle of 'full, conscious and active participation' was explored in several chapters, opening up the full impact of each of those words, and how that might be incarnat-

2. *The Documents of Vatican II* (London: Geoffrey Chapman, 1967) edited by Walter Abbott.
3. It built on it with decrees on the Church (*Lumen Gentium* and *Gaudium et spes*), Ecumenism (*Unitatis Redintegratio*) and Missions (*Ad Gentes*), to name only the principal ones.

ed in liturgical celebrations. In the process, we learnt that liturgy is 'about drawing people into the experience of doing, an experience which has both internal and external dimensions' or, as the best list of words in the book has it, understanding 'liturgical intelligibility' not only as linguistic, but 'semiotic, kinaesthetic, artistic, musical, proxemic, hierarchic, communicative, emotional, mimetic, anamnetic, temporal, theological and cultural forms of intelligibility also'.

Chapters which seemed at first straightforwardly to promote one or another practical way of renewing the liturgy in terms of music, architecture, language, actions, and the observance of sacred time all take us to core theological ideas in *SC* which illuminate and free us to 'make more responsive to the requirements of our times those Church observances which are open to adaptation'. Against the spirit of the age—its individualism, its secularity, and its fascination with relevance defined by the latest fashion—we need to invoke the Lord's criterion: that the keepers of the Father's household who have their eye on the coming kingdom take from the storehouse of treasures things *both old and new* (with apologies to Matthew 13:52).

The subject of 'sacrifice' discussed in several chapters has been such a central part of all ecumenical dialogues that it no longer has the impact it once had. It summons up the ghosts of old disputes wherein we have misunderstood what the other was saying, and thereafter defined ourselves over against them. This is the wonderful contrast of the moods of Trent and Vatican II. That there is now a 'clear measure of agreement' is evident in reports of theological dialogue.[4] In this we gladly honour the contribution of Bishop Michel Putney to such dialogue both in Australia and internationally. What is said in this book about sacrifice is at every point instructive for all Christians; to lose such a word out of old prejudice is to weaken both meaning and practice. There are many words in this book which the children of the Reformation need to reintroduce to their vocabulary—because they belong to us all.

The mysterious gift of *SC* in the field of liturgy is that it changed all of us who claim the name of Christian. It was, perhaps unintention-

4. Walter Kasper, *Harvesting the Fruits, Basic Aspects of Christian Faith in Ecumenical Dialogue* (London: Continuum, 2009)—summarising the Roman Catholic dialogue with Anglicans, Methodists, Lutherans and Reformed at the international level; see the individual dialogue reports.

ally, 'permission giving'. It was the voice of a *catholic* Council, so we all, by the Spirit, *heard* it. Its documents and its spirit gave permission to the *oikoumene* to consider its own need for *aggiornamento*. The Council's fundamental commitment to the unity of Christians gave courage for this enterprise, but above all, the Council's provision for the 'scientific' study of the liturgy in all its facets opened opportunities for other Christians to benefit from Catholic universities and seminaries (often in ecumenical faculties) and to examine their own distinctive traditions. Without *SC*, other churches would not have encouraged liturgical study in their teachers, or founded curriculae which required liturgy as a subject for their ordinands. Renewed Catholic scholarship has borne fruit in ecumenical discussions such as those in the Australian Consultation on Liturgy (ACOL) and the international English Language Liturgical Consultation (ELLC), as well as other learned bodies such as *Societas Liturgica* and the Australian Academy of Liturgy.

Protestants were, for example, amazed by what *SC* said of the role of Sacred Scripture. After four hundred years, they said, Rome has finally seen the light. Then we discovered the breadth, depth and freshness of Roman Catholic biblical scholarship, and the common lectionary, and the libraries of resources which were brought to the promotion of 'that warm and living love for scripture to which the venerable tradition of both east and western rites gives testimony' (*SC* 24). And we began to rethink and to revivify a venerable tradition of our own which we had allowed to become fixed and too familiar. One author here drew our attention to the important issue of *how* the words of scripture are used in liturgy: some new liturgies still have signs of the old 'proof-text' method—that the mere sprinkling of biblical words somehow adds the odour of sanctity when something more focussed is required! But at the same time that Catholics were challenged to embrace the scriptures, others also heard the balancing claim of the place of sacrament in our worship.

The conversation about the Divine Office also, and of its music and of liturgical music in general, could be elaborated by reference to what is happening in the whole Church, for the principles underlying its definition and choice are true for all. Here we could also draw on the chapter on architecture which asks whether 'noble simplicity' joined with 'beauty' does not require us to think more deeply about both.

As I say, more than Catholics will have read this book with great benefit. This book will have heartened them and bonded them again with Catholic brothers and sisters pursuing common goals. But there has been considerable dismay at the directions in which Catholic ongoing 'reform' has moved in recent times, marked perhaps particularly by the publication of *Liturgiam authenticam* (2001), which, in my personal experience as chair at the time, seemed to cast aside all the fruitfulness of the English Language Liturgical Consultation and its predecessors. It seemed that Rome was abandoning the ecumenical liturgical movement. There are plenty of signs that this was *not* its intention, but those outside are left in some confusion. I do not want this to be read simply as a negative critical comment; rather I am expressing my strong hope that cooperation might be resumed, perhaps, I pray, under Pope Francis whose inauguration was notable for the unprecedented involvement of ecumenical guests. For fifty years, the 'separated brethren' have increasingly been regarded as partners with the Catholic Church and with each other in a large enterprise, which at no point involves compromise or unjustified change, but rather moves by the 'exchange of gifts' (Pope John Paul II).[5] We are grateful for that partnership and have benefitted from it, and believe that this is part of the prayer of our Lord that his disciples might be one. Let this book encourage and cheer us on to further liturgical labour—together.

For together in the body of Christ, we need to receive and create a liturgy which, to complete the earlier quote from Paul VI, 'dissolves the tongue-tied into blessed and true prayer, and engages the ineffable, regenerative power of singing with us the divine praise and human hopes, through Christ the Lord, and in the Spirit.'

5. The phrase is in *Ut Unum Sint*, # 28 , and amply demonstrated, if I may say so, by recent dialogue reports, all of which bear the clear hand of Michael Putney—*The Grace Given You In Christ, Catholics and Methodists reflect further on the Church*, Report of the International Commission for Dialogue between the Roman Catholic Church and the World Methodist Council, 2006 (Seoul, Korea), *Encountering Christ the Saviour: Church and Sacraments*, Report of the same body (Durban, South Africa, 2011) and *Synthesis*, a mutual reassessment of forty years of the dialogue, (Durban 2011). At <http://www.vatican.va/roman_curia/pontifical_councils/chrstuni/sub-index/index_methodist-council.htm>. Accessed 2 July 2013.

Contributors

Rhodora E Beaton is an Assistant Professor of Theology at St Catherine University in St Paul, MN. She is the author of 'Realizing Unity: The One Table of the Prophetic Word and Body of Christ' published in *Worship* in 2012. Her dissertation, *The Sacramentality of the Word: Contributions of Karl Rahner and Louis-Marie Chauvet to a Roman Catholic Theology of the Word*, is forthcoming from Fortress Press.

Stephen Burns is Associate Professor of Liturgical Theology and the Study of Anglicanism at Episcopal Divinity School, Cambridge, MA (USA). He studied theology at Durham (BA, MA and PhD) and Cambridge (MLitt) and taught in Durham, Birmingham (UK) and Sydney (Australia). He is a priest of the Church of England. His publications include *Christian Worship in Australia* (co-editor with Anita Monro, St Pauls, 2009) and *Worship and Ministry: Shaped Towards God* (Melbourne: Mosaic Press, 2012). He is book reviews editor for the *Australian Journal of Liturgy*.

Tom Elich parish priest at Bulimba in the Archdiocese of Brisbane, studied at the Institut Catholique de Paris where he earned his Doctorate in medieval liturgy and sacramental theology. He is director of Liturgy Brisbane and an honorary fellow of Australian Catholic University. In addition to serving as editor of the quarterly bulletin, *Liturgy News*, Tom oversees the editorship of numerous liturgical publications including the *Ordo* for Australia and New Zealand. He has worked on liturgical commissions at diocesan, national and international levels, including ICEL's central advisory committee and its subcommittee on the presentation of liturgical texts.

John Francis Fitz-Herbert is a presbyter of the Roman Catholic Archdiocese of Brisbane and was ordained in 1992. He has served in parishes as associate pastor and parish priest and is a candidate for the DMin (CTU, Chicago). Since 1992 he has presented workshops and seminars on liturgy in Australia, North America and South Sudan. His articles are published in *Liturgy News* where he also served on the editorial board. John is a consultant to the National Liturgical Council and holds memberships of *Societas Liturgica*, the American Academy of Religion and the Australian Academy of Liturgy.

Robert Gribben studied liturgy and ecumenics at Cambridge before ordination in 1970 as a Methodist Minister, and is now a retired Uniting Church minister and Professor Emeritus of Worship and Mission at the Uniting Church and United Faculties of Theology, Melbourne. He has been twice President of the Australian Academy of Liturgy and presently edits the *Australian Journal of Liturgy*. He was the third Australian to be elected to Societas Liturgica, on whose Council he later served. He worked with Chris Willcock SJ to prepare the liturgies for the 22nd *Societas Liturgica* Congress in Sydney and preached at the Eucharist in St Patrick's Catholic Cathedral, Parramatta, New South Wales. His most recent book is *Uniting in Thanksgiving*, a commentary on the Eucharistic Prayers of the Uniting Church.

Stephen Hackett MSC is a priest of the Missionaries of the Sacred Heart. He has ministered in parishes, diocesan governance, secondary education, university chaplaincy, and the vocations apostolate. He chairs the National Liturgical Architecture and Art Board and serves on the National Liturgical Council, both of which are advisory bodies to the Australian Catholic Bishops Conference. He is a member of the Australian Academy of Liturgy and consults on liturgical design for church projects. He edited the proceedings of a national colloquium, The Cathedral: A Living Church at the Heart of the Diocese, and has authored and co-authored papers for the *New Catholic Encyclopedia, Chiesa Oggi, Australian Journal of Liturgy, Compass, Liturgy News* and *The Summit.*

Elizabeth Harrington has been the Education Officer at Liturgy Brisbane since 1995. This role involves conducting workshops in liturgy at diocesan, deanery and parish level, writing articles (including just over 700 'Liturgy Lines' columns for Brisbane's *The Catholic Leader* to date) and responding to requests for liturgical advice, information and resources. Elizabeth is a consultor to the National Liturgical Council, chairs the Archdiocesan Catechumenate Committee which has oversight of the RCIA in Brisbane and is secretary of the Archdiocesan Commission on the Liturgy.

Guy Hartcher CM was ordained a Vincentian priest in 1970. He studied liturgy and history at the Catholic University of America, and later education at the University of Tasmania. He taught Church History and Liturgy at Holy Cross College Mosgiel, the national seminary for the Catholic Church in New Zealand at the time, and at Otago University in Dunedin, including a term as Dean of the Faculty of Theology. He taught Church History and was Rector at St Francis Xavier Seminary Rostrevor, then the Regional Seminary for South Australia and Western Australia. He was Senior Lecturer in the Faculty of Theology at Flinders University, Adelaide, at the same time. He is now in administration.

Carol Hogan SSS is a Blessed Sacrament Sister who lived an enclosed monastic life for fifteen years. Since Vatican II, Carol has worked as a Chaplain at the University of Melbourne, while at the same time studying Feminist Theology. In 2008, she was awarded her Doctorate of Ministry degree by the Melbourne College of Divinity. She is currently active in the Australian Catholic anti-trafficking of humans movement and facilitates a Feminist Theology Group in her parish. Some of Carol's most recent research appears in *Reinterpreting Eucharist: Explorations in Feminist Theology and Ethics* (Equinox, 2013).

Clare V Johnson is Senior Lecturer in Liturgical Studies and Sacramental Theology at Australian Catholic University (Strathfield, NSW). Her research is published in Studia Liturgica, Worship, Liturgy, Australian Journal of Liturgy, Pastoral Liturgy, and other journals. She is editor of Ars Liturgiae: Worship, Aesthetics and Praxis (Chicago: LTP, 2003) and contributing co-editor of Vatican II: Reception and Implementation in the Australian Church (Mulgrave: Garrett, 2012). She serves as assistant editor of *Studia Liturgica* and is a member of the National Liturgical Council advising the Australian Bishops' Commission on the Liturgy.

William A Jordan is a Priest of the Archdiocese of Melbourne in Victoria. Ordained in 1960, he earned a Licentiate in Sacred Theology (Urban, Rome) and Doctorate in Sacred Music at the Pontifical Institute of Sacred Music (Rome). He worked on Liturgical and Musical Commissions at diocesan, national and international levels, including ICEL's music sub-committee, and combined his editorial work with pastoral responsibilities, primarily at St Brendan's, Flemington (1985–2010), and some seasonal lecturing in Gregorian paleography at Australian Catholic University in Melbourne. He edited the *Catholic Worship Book* (1985), and is currently a member of the National Liturgical Music Board producing a revised worship book/hymnal for Australia.

Anthony Kain is a priest of the Archdiocese of Adelaide in South Australia and has worked in rural and urban parishes. He is currently pastor of the parishes of Glenelg and Plympton. He holds an MA in Liturgical and Sacramental Theology from the Catholic University of America in Washington, DC and a DMin from Catholic Theological Union, Chicago. He teaches liturgy and sacramental theology at the Adelaide College of Divinity and he is also a facilitator of the Office for Worship within the Archdiocese. His interest is in the dynamic of communication in liturgical action.

Piero Marini is an Italian-born Archbishop and liturgist and current President of the Pontifical Council for Eucharistic Congresses within the Holy See. Ordained in 1965, Archbishop Marini has worked for the Congregation for Divine Worship in the Vatican and his work included a term as secretary to Archbishop Annibale Bugnini CM who was the principal architect of the post-conciliar liturgical reform. From 1987 until 2007, Marini served as the Pontifical Master of Ceremonies, and oversaw the inculturation of the papal liturgy during many pastoral and state visits of John Paul II and Benedict XVI. Marini's doctoral research at Sant'Anselmo Pontifical Institute of Liturgy focussed on the Roman Pontifical.

Gerard Moore is Head of School and a lecturer in Worship and Systematic Theology at Charles Sturt University, and a member of the CSU Public and Contextual Theology Research Centre. He holds a Doctorate in Sacred Theology from the Catholic University of America, Washington DC, and has published extensively. He has been a consultant to the International Commission on English in the Liturgy (ICEL) and contributed to national liturgical bodies including the ecumenical Australian Consultation on Liturgy (ACOL) and National Liturgical Council of the ACBC. He has contributed to *Uncovering Theology* (Charles Sherlock, 2009) and *Transforming Theology* (Les Ball, 2012).

Frank O'Loughlin is parish priest of Sandringham in the Archdiocese of Melbourne. Ordained in 1969, he completed a Doctorate in Sacred Theology at the Urban University in Rome (1972-75) and pursued Liturgical Studies at the Irish Institute of Pastoral Liturgy, Carlow (1975-6). He taught Fundamental Theology and Sacramental Theology over many years at Catholic Theological College, Clayton, and was director of the Diocesan Liturgy Centre, East Melbourne, from 1977-1991. He has written extensively and continues to write and lecture in a variety of pastoral contexts. Author of numerous books on liturgy, his latest work is entitled *This Time of the Church* (St Pauls, 2012).

David Orr OSB is a monk of the Benedictine Community at Arcadia, NSW. He has completed a Doctorate in Sacred Liturgy from the Pontifical Liturgical Institute at Sant'Anselmo, Rome, writing on the Priesthood of the Faithful. He has taught in this field at the Catholic Institute of Sydney and the Broken Bay Institute, New South Wales. Besides working as Pastor in the Catholic Parish of Arcadia, he regularly has offered formation days on liturgy in many Parish communities. He has served on both the National and Diocesan Liturgical Commissions. He is a member of the Australian Academy of Liturgy and *Societas Liturgica.* He continues to write liturgical commentaries for magazines, including *Worship* and *The Summit.*

Carmel Pilcher RSJ is a liturgical consultant and educator based in Sydney. Her PhD from Flinders University, South Australia, is entitled *The Prophetic Character of Eucharist.* Carmel has taught and worked across Australia, including the dioceses of Adelaide, Sydney where she was Director of Liturgy from 1997–2007, and Maitland-Newcastle. Her writings have appeared in *Worship, Liturgy News, The Summit* and other scholarly publications and she helped coordinate the writing of *Powerful Points for Liturgical Ministers* (The Liturgical Commission, 2007). Carmel is currently a member of the Council of *Societas Liturgica* and helped organise its Australian Congress in 2009. She is a member and past president of the Australian Academy of Liturgy.

Michael Putney is the Catholic Bishop of Townsville, Queensland. Ordained in 1969, he served in parish ministry in the Archdiocese of Brisbane before completing a Doctorate in Sacred Theology at the Gregorian University, Rome, in 1985 with a dissertation entitled *The Presence and Activity of the Holy Spirit in the Church, in the Studies of the Commission on Faith and Order (1927–1983).* After many years lecturing at the Pius XII Provincial Seminary in Banyo, Queensland, he was appointed Auxiliary Bishop of Brisbane in 1996 and Bishop of Townsville in 2001. A member of numerous episcopal commissions in Australia and overseas, Bishop Putney was recognised in the 2013 Queen's Birthday Honours with the Order of the Australia medal (AM) for his services to ecumenism. His contribution to the ecumenical movement has included chairing the National Council of Churches in Australia (2009–2013) and service as Catholic co-Chair of the International Methodist/Roman Catholic Dialogue.

Bernardus Boli Ujan SVD was ordained in 1982 and earned a Doctorate in Sacred Liturgy in 2001 at the Pontifical Liturgical Institute at Sant'Anselmo in Rome. Since 1987 he has been engaged in liturgical formation in Indonesia and Malaysia. From 2002 until 2008, he was Secretary of the Liturgy Commission of the Indonesian Bishops Conference in Jakarta, and between 2009 and 2012 he was head of the Liturgy Commission for the Archdiocese of Merauke. He is currently working in Ledalero-Maumere Flores as formator and lecturer on liturgy. His publications include *Dying and Rising Again: The Inculturation of the Celebration of Reconciliation for the Faithful in Lembata* (2012).

Julia Upton RSM is a member of the Institute of the Sisters of Mercy of the Americas. She holds a PhD in Theology from Fordham University and is Professor in the Department of Theology and Religious Studies at St John's University, New York, where she has taught since 1979. Dr Upton's most recent book, *Worship in Spirit and Truth: The Life and Legacy of HA Reinhold*, was published by The Liturgical Press in 2009. She is currently writing a biography of Adé Bethune, a liturgical artist, consultant and social activist whose work is most closely associated with the *Catholic Worker*.

Catherine Vincie RSHM is Professor of Sacramental and Liturgical Theology at the Aquinas Institute of Theology in St Louis, Missouri (USA), and she is the past president of the North American Academy of Liturgy. She has published extensively on a wide variety of topics regarding the liturgical reforms of Vatican II, including such issues as the liturgical assembly, the RCIA, liturgy and justice, liturgy and preaching, and eucharist, among others. Her most recent work has been on the implications of the new cosmology for liturgy.

Index

A

Adaptation, cultural, xv–xviii, 43n, 82, 85, 187, 218.
Adaptation of the liturgy, 4, 28, 67, 68, 69, 81, 94, 97, 84, 129, 183, 201, 202, 212n, 236, 240, 247, 248, 250, 289, 290.
Aggiornomento, 240, 250, 291.
Altar, 7, 21n, 22, 39, 42, 66, 76, 93, 117, 118, 124, 126, 131, 167, 176, 122, 219, 234, 240, 247, 248, 245, 250.
Ambo, 42, 240, 247.
Anointing, 163, 164, 169, 255, 273.
Apostolic See, 68.
Architecture, church, 140, 236, 233, 234, 238, 241, 242, 244, 247n, 248, 250, 280, 282, 290.
Art, liturgical, 70, 52, 94n, 218, 224, 232, 234, 242n, 244, 281, 282,
Assembly of the Church, xxvi, 4, 7, 9, 18, 26, 33, 39, 40, 42, 46, 54, 55, 57, 58, 65, 67, 72, 77, 95, 96, 98, 99, 104, 106, 110, 112, 119, 121, 122, 125, 126, 164, 169, 171, 177, 181, 218, 223, 224, 239, 240, 245, 247, 248, 250, 256, 258, 263, 267, 274, 283.
Australia, vii, x, xx, xxv, xxvi, 61, 62, 64, 66, 68, 70, 73, 74n, 77, 78, 97, 147, 148, 156, 179, 182, 203, 210, 212, 221, 228, 254, 256, 264, 267, 270, 276, 281, 288, 290–292, 294, 296, 298.

B

Baptism, Sacrament of, 7, 13, 19, 20, 25, 26, 31, 32, 34, 36, 39, 96, 111, 117n, 127, 133, 134, 135, 137, 157, 161, 162, 164–166, 168, 170, 175, 176, 183, 185, 188, 240, 254, 256, 259, 261, 277, 284, 288.
Baptismal Priesthood, 135.
Baptismal water, 34.
Bishop, xv, xvi, xxvi, xxvii, 3, 21, 23, 28, 37, 38, 67, 68, 70, 73n, 75, 84n, 90, 93, 130, 135, 139n, 147, 149n, 162, 165, 168n, 170, 174, 176,

178, 187, 190, 194, 214n, 218n, 220, 230, 225, 227, 233, 234, 255, 263, 280, 285, 288, 290, 296, 295, 298.
Blessing, xii, 66, 73, 74, 78, 93, 118, 133, 134, 138, 140, 144, 260.
Book of the Gospels, 75.
Book, liturgical, 1, 28, 31, 32, 68, 71, 84, 94n, 132, 194, 253, 256, 264, 266, 284.
Bread, 22, 35, 70n, 76, 103, 104, 112, 117, 124, 135n, 139, 140, 143, 144, 146, 150n, 157, 161n, 164, 240, 242, 257, 259, 260, 272.

C

Calendar, Church/liturgical, 68, 93, 98n, 196, 201, 209n, 234, 262.
Candles, 197.
Catechesis, 4, 58, 82n, 91, 93, 96n, 126, 166, 170, 180, 214, 216, 276.
Catechumenate, 170, 176, 185, 271, 275, 294.
Chair, 66, 89, 133n, 240, 247.
Chalice, 76, 112n, 142, 267.
Chant, 53n, 131, 133n, 190, 192, 194, 200, 219, 223, 224, 226, 229n.
Christology, 12, 14, 15, 16, 18, 36, 134n.
Christmas, 92, 94, 136, 209, 211.
Collect, xxvi, 86, 129, 130, 136, 138, 144, 260, 267.
Collection, 124, 140, 258.
Communion, xv, xvi, xx, 21n, 28, 31, 34, 72, 76, 110n, 112n, 118, 123, 124, 126, 133, 135, 140, 146, 161, 162, 165n, 166, 168, 170, 176, 180, 205n, 226, 242, 257, 260, 274, 283, 285.
Communion Extraordinary Ministers of Holy,
Communion Under Both Kinds, 111.
Communion of saints, 259.
Community, xii, xiv, xvi, xxvi, 19, 21, 28, 36, 39, 41, 46, 63, 67, 69, 71, 82, 88, 97, 99, 86, 87, 91, 95, 100, 102, 103, 105, 117, 120, 121, 133, 138, 139, 141, 144, 148, 156, 163, 174, 175, 176, 180–184, 188, 193, 196, 197, 200, 201, 203, 205–208, 214, 215, 222, 230–232, 239, 240, 242, 251, 258, 279, 280, 284, 285,
Concelebration, 28.
Confirmation, Sacrament of, xxvii, 161f, 166, 168, 288.
Congregation for Divine Wor ship, 51n, 63n, 122n, 146n, 194, 225, 279n, 296.
Congregation for Rites, 217, 228.
Congregation, the, 7, 26n, 67n, 74, 146, 218, 221, 226, 230, 239, 240, 256, 261, 263, 264,
Cross, 7, 12, 41, 45, 67, 85, 100–102, 104–106, 112, 114, 119, 120, 133, 134, 142, 146, 183, 265.

D

Deacon, 65, 117, 139n, 267.
Diaspora, 39.
Diakonia, 40, 100, 101, 106.

E

Easter, 21, 22n, 30, 66, 94, 164n, 179, 209, 211.
Eastern Churches, 2, 64, 129.
Ecclesiology, 12–15, 17, 20, 23, 35, 37, 40, 244, 262n, 277.
Ecumenism, xixn, xxviii, 2, 253, 289n, 296.
Episcopal Conference, 70, 71, 73n, 67, 68, 93, 130, 147, 194, 218, 220, 230, 276, 285, 298.
Eucharist, the, xvi, the, 76f, 110, 111, 120–122, 123–126, 142, 143, 146, 148, 149, 150, 151, 156–159, 161, 168, 169, 170, 240, 241, 276, 277, 280, 281.
Eucharistic, ecclesiology, 40
Eucharistic hospitality, 105,
Eucharistic liturgy, 51, 126, 136, 198, 258, 272.
Eucharistic prayer, xxvi, 20, 42, 35, 120, 124–126, 138, 142, 206, 294,
Eucharistic sacrifice, 38, 126.
Eucharistic theology, 148, 150, 152, 153, 158.

F

Faithful, Lay, viii, xv, xviii, ix, xx, 2, 7, 8, 13, 16, 17, 19, 26, 28, 29, 30, 34, 38, 40, 44, 46, 50, 52, 55, 56, 60, 82, 83, 90, 92, 94–96, 103, 110–112, 117, 120, 125, 136, 138, 141, 146, 162, 163, 165, 168, 171, 172, 177, 194, 198, 218, 234, 238, 243, 247, 248, 250, 259, 251, 254–256, 263, 277, 284.
Font, Baptismal, 241.
Funeral, 85, 208, 241, 255.

G

Grace, vii, viii, xiv, xxii, 11, 30, 32, 35, 44, 46, 53, 55, 59, 60, 72, 112n, 120, 130n, 136, 156, 165, 176, 177, 178, 184, 206, 207, 210, 240, 257, 260, 292n,
Gesture, Liturgical, 25, 32, 41, 42, 69, 77, 78, 122, 273.
God, viii, xii, xiv, xvii, xx, 8, 14, 16, 20, 21, 30, 35, 38, 44, 48, 50, 53, 54, 61, 62, 64, 72, 114, 117, 118, 124, 135–137, 150, 152, 156, 158, 163, 167, 174, 176, 180, 181, 182, 184, 195, 199, 200, 222, 242, 251, 256, 259, 260, 275, 279, 288
God's action, 26, 42, 120
God's future, x
God's grace, 46, 260
God's name, 206,
God's mercy, 184, 186
God's perspective, 188
God's presence, xxvi, 19, 23
God's purposes, 103

God's reign, 13, 101, 102, 214, 215
God's will, 112, 164
God's Spirit, 70n, 116
People of God, xxviii, 3, 4, 37, 58, 126, 172, 204, 208, 210, 212, 214, 216, 230n, 280, 284

H

Holiness, xii, xvi, 6, 23, 208, 215, 222, 256.
Holy Orders, Sacrament of, 7.
Holy Spirit, viii, xxii, 18, 22, 23, 30, 35, 42, 47, 70n, 76n, 92, 114, 116, 120, 124, 138, 164, 161n, 162n, 163, 166, 167, 171, 168, 169, 180, 184, 206, 207, 259, 288, 296.
Holy Thursday, 176.
Homily, 21, 44, 49, 93, 75, 121n, 129, 130, 159.

I

Incense, 197.
Inculturation, xxvi, 61f, 81f, 96n, 212n, 218, 224, 296, 298,
Indigenous, xxvi, 61f, 70, 72, 78, 211.
Individualism, 204, 290.
Indonesia, xxv, xxvi, 81f, 298,
Initiation, Christian, xxvii, 34n, 161, 162, 165, 166, 168, 170, 175, 185, 255.

J

Jesus Christ, xi, xii, xiv–xvii, xx, 6, 7, 12–14, 16, 32, 36, 37, 61, 62, 64, 72, 77, 92, 98, 99, 100–104, 107, 112, 114–117, 120, 121, 133, 134–137, 139, 140–143, 146, 147, 152, 153, 157, 158, 163, 175, 182, 183, 206, 207, 242, 251, 260, 264, 265–267, 272–274, 275, 284, 285, 289.

L

Laity, 14, 19, 20, 28, 30, 32, 109, 111, 167, 174, 190, 192, 195, 197, 198, 201, 202, 220, 225, 226, 288.
Language, xxv, 4, 17, 25, 45, 46, 51, 52, 56, 61–64, 67n, 83, 84, 93, 94n, 98n, 107, 124, 133, 135, 138, 141, 146, 151, 154, 193, 196, 201, 203, 217, 218, 227, 238, 255n, 266, 267, 283, 284, 289, 290, 292,
Latin, 25n, 26n, 27, 45n, 46, 52, 98, 111n, 130, 132, 134, 137, 138, 142, 146, 157, 170n, 177, 190, 192, 193, 196, 219, 246, 284, 288.
Lay Minister, 31, 111.
Leadership, Liturgical, 95f, 198, 206.
Lectionary, the, 75, 110, 155, 262, 264, 279n, 291.
Lent, xviii, 91, 92, 176, 178, 180n, 198.

Liturgical Music, xxvii, 30, 36, 39, 42, 50, 52, 77, 78, 94, 111, 189, 192, 194, 195, 202, 218, 220f, 230f, 290, 291.

Liturgical Year, 35, 183, 187,
Liturgy, *passim.*
Liturgy Committees, 31, 227.
Liturgy of the Eucharist, 3, 51, 49, 68, 73, 77, 85, 110, 112, 114, 117, 120, 123, 126, 136, 139, 140, 146, 148, 150, 153, 157, 169, 171, 176, 209, 241, 242, 267, 272, 276, 280, 288.
Liturgy of the Hours, 196f
Liturgy of the Word, 75f, 110, 126, 178, 257, 258, 260.
Lord's Day, 208f.

M

Marriage, Sacrament of, 85.
Mary, Blessed Virgin Mary, xi, 167, 242,
Masses with Children, 69, 166, 180, 230.
Music, Church, xxvii, 29, 30, 36, 39, 42, 49, 50, 77, 85, 189, 193, 194, 196, 197, 201, 217f, 234, 282, 290.
Musicians, liturgical, xxvii, 111, 217–222, 226–231.
Mystagogy, 4, 33, 174, 188, 185f,

O

Oil, 79, 101, 164, 165, 213, 272.
Ordinary Time, 70, 75, 136, 137, 154.

P

Papal Liturgy, xxv, 77, 78n, 296.
Parishes, xviii, xxi, 39, 65, 68, 69, 70, 75, 78, 109, 126, 187, 197, 201, 219, 225, 227–230, 296.
Participation, xxii, xxvi, xxvii, 3, 6, 7, 25f, 42, 44, 45, 46, 56, 58, 59, 69, 88, 90, 92, 95f, 98, 110, 111, 112n, 119, 120, 123, 142, 153, 159, 124–127, 138, 141, 145, 147, 148, 162n, 164n, 168, 171, 190, 210, 214, 218, 220, 226, 228, 231, 232, 234, 239, 240, 241, 243, 250, 254, 255, 274, 283, 284, 289.
Paschal Mystery, 7, 16, 17, 19, 20, 23, 68, 77, 92, 95, 98, 99, 105, 106, 107, 146, 163, 190n, 204, 241, 276, 284.
Peace, Sign of, 164, 180, 181.
Penance, Sacrament of, xxvii, 173, 174, 175, 177, 178, 181, 182, 183, 186, 277.
Polyphony, 219, 223, 224, 226n,
Postures, liturgical, 126, 202.
Prayer of the Faithful, 75, 135.
Preparation of Gifts, 259.
Presider, 46, 48, 50, 57, 59, 85, 87, 89, 112, 121, 124, 125, 126, 146, 158, 162, 165, 167, 198, 227, 229, 256, 258, 285.
Priest, Ministerial, xi, xii, xvii, 3, 6, 7, 8, 12, 19, 28, 36, 38, 39, 40n, 41, 42, 44, 46, 56, 73, 97n, 110–112, 118, 120, 122, 125, 127, 133, 135, 142, 143, 146, 156, 158, 163, 165, 167, 168, 169, 171, 172, 177, 181, 187, 184, 198, 219, 226, 227, 229, 240, 265, 277, 279, 284.

Priesthood of the Faithful, 7, 8, 38, 120n, 135, 162, 168, 170, 172, 256, 297.
Procession, 66, 69, 74, 76, 84, 89, 93, 94n, 124, 245, 248.
Protestant, xxvii, 131, 194, 253f, 291.

R

Reader, 41, 72, 99, 110, 111, 219.
Reconciliation, Rite of, 173f, 179, 181, 182, 183, 188.
Reform, liturgical, passim.
Resourcement, 4.
Rite of Christian Initiation of Adults/RCIA, 162n, 294, 299.
Rite, liturgical, 2, 3, 4, 6, 8, 26, 31, 43, 50, 56, 58, 66, 67f, 74f, 78, 81f, 83, 84, 85, 87, 110, 144, 160, 178, 180, 181, 184, 188, 192, 217n, 218, 222, 226, 234, 239, 241, 242, 250, 267, 291,
Roman Missal, 6, 8n, 34n, 43n, 44n, 49, 50, 52, 96n, 111, 112n, 125, 126, 129, 130, 131n, 136n, 139, 142, 181, 206n, 226, 235, 240, 283.

S

Sacrament, xxvi, xxvii, 8, 11f, 14–16, 18–23, 34, 44, 53, 55, 94n, 122, 138, 148n, 150, 162f, 168, 170, 172f, 180, 181, 184, 186, 188, 241, 242, 256, 257, 258, 265, 272, 273, 279.
Sacrifice, xxvi, 7, 22, 38, 39, 42, 49, 52, 73, 88, 106, 109f, 118–120, 122, 124, 126, 146, 148, 159, 160, 164, 165, 170, 206, 207, 210, 215, 290, 256.
Saint, xi, xii, 22n, 29n, 117n, 118n, 143, 163n, 164n, 167n, 178, 182,196, 201, 242, 258, 281n,
Sanctuary, 237, 240, 246, 248, 250.
Scripture, xv–xvii, xxvi, 4, 5, 109, 110, 129f, 144–146, 154, 156, 184, 197, 200, 219, 238, 240, 258, 260, 263–265, 267n, 280, 279, 291,
Second Vatican Council, viif, xiii, 1f, 5, 11, 21, 37, 43, 119, 134, 145f, 171, 192, 207n, 215n, 233, 253, 255, 257, 269, 277n.
Semiotics, 96, 98.
Sign, liturgical, ix, 4, 6, 11, 14, 18, 19, 21, 23, 30, 34, 35, 39, 41, 45, 48, 50, 55, 67, 87, 98n, 101, 112n, 119, 126, 127, 129f, 141, 142, 144, 145, 157, 164, 165, 175n, 180, 181, 183, 186, 196, 223, 226, 237, 257, 259, 242, 272, 273, 275, 277–279, 292.
Silence, 32, 35, 42, 103, 141, 142, 181, 226, 230.
Song, liturgical, 7, 32, 85, 129f, 144, 156, 193, 222, 226, 230, 231.
Sunday, 68–70, 71, 73–79, 110–112, 114, 121, 122, 124–126,

136, 137, 140, 164, 181, 197, 198, 201, 209, 210, 213, 214, 216, 219, 255, 258, 267, 274, 275–278, 285.
Symbols, 31, 45, 48, 50, 53, 56, 58– 60, 62, 77, 78, 83, 85, 94, 106, 132, 151, 153, 156–158, 211, 235, 271, 279.

T

Tabernacles, 111, 143, 235,
Text, liturgical, xii, 3–5, 26, 28, 43, 50, 52, 53, 56, 57, 60, 72f, 117n, 122, 126, 131–133 138, 156, 185, 193, 195, 218, 219, 224, 227, 230, 261, 266, 267.
Thurible, 66.
Time, liturgical, xxvii, 30, 92, 185, 203f, 290.
Translation, 1n, 22n, 25, 31, 45, 46, 49, 51, 52, 57, 62n, 81n, 95, 98, 109, 111, 117n, 122, 125, 126, 129–131, 132n, 136–138, 141, 146n, 155, 164n, 173, 193, 194, 196, 201, 217, 233, 266, 267, 283.
Triduum, 16, 66.

U

United State of America, xxv, 173, 177, 178, 221, 258.

V

Vatican, the, ixn, 15n, 25n, 49, 51n, 65, 95n, 109n, 123n, 129n, 143n, 145n, 203n, 225n, 273n,
Vatican II, xxv, 1f, 6, 12, 21, 23, 52, 54, 82, 84, 94, 145f, 149, 168, 171, 173, 177, 186, 193, 197, 203, 219, 220, 224, 236, 238, 240, 243–247, 265, 271, 283, 285, 289, 299.
Vernacular, 28, 30, 36, 45, 46, 51, 52, 56, 111, 121, 134, 141, 146, 177, 180, 191, 193, 218, 232, 219, 201.
Vessel, liturgical, 67n, 76, 78, 81, 189, 190, 217, 235.
Vestment, liturgical, 85, 235.

W

Women, xxvii, 67, 70, 87, 102, 106, 112, 145f, 153, 154, 155, 159, 160, 180, 196, 203, 208, 288,
Word of God, xi, xii, 8, 23, 138, 184, 186, 259.
Worship, *passim*.

Y

Year, liturgical, xxvii, 70, 75, 83, 84, 85, 90–93, 94, 145, 189, 203f, 209, 212, 214.

www.ingramcontent.com/pod-product-compliance
Lightning Source LLC
Chambersburg PA
CBHW031147150826
49772CB00003B/96